1,000,000 Books

are available to read at

www.ForgottenBooks.com

Read online
Download PDF
Purchase in print

ISBN 978-1-331-26120-9
PIBN 10165860

This book is a reproduction of an important historical work. Forgotten Books uses state-of-the-art technology to digitally reconstruct the work, preserving the original format whilst repairing imperfections present in the aged copy. In rare cases, an imperfection in the original, such as a blemish or missing page, may be replicated in our edition. We do, however, repair the vast majority of imperfections successfully; any imperfections that remain are intentionally left to preserve the state of such historical works.

Forgotten Books is a registered trademark of FB &c Ltd.
Copyright © 2018 FB &c Ltd.
FB &c Ltd, Dalton House, 60 Windsor Avenue, London, SW19 2RR.
Company number 08720141. Registered in England and Wales.

For support please visit www.forgottenbooks.com

1 MONTH OF FREE READING

at
www.ForgottenBooks.com

By purchasing this book you are eligible for one month membership to ForgottenBooks.com, giving you unlimited access to our entire collection of over 1,000,000 titles via our web site and mobile apps.

To claim your free month visit:
www.forgottenbooks.com/free165860

* Offer is valid for 45 days from date of purchase. Terms and conditions apply.

English
Français
Deutsche
Italiano
Español
Português

www.forgottenbooks.com

Mythology Photography **Fiction**
Fishing Christianity **Art** Cooking
Essays Buddhism Freemasonry
Medicine **Biology** Music **Ancient Egypt** Evolution Carpentry Physics
Dance Geology **Mathematics** Fitness
Shakespeare **Folklore** Yoga Marketing
Confidence Immortality Biographies
Poetry **Psychology** Witchcraft
Electronics Chemistry History **Law**
Accounting **Philosophy** Anthropology
Alchemy Drama Quantum Mechanics
Atheism Sexual Health **Ancient History**
Entrepreneurship Languages Sport
Paleontology Needlework Islam
Metaphysics Investment Archaeology
Parenting Statistics Criminology
Motivational

BY
C. E. WADE, M.A. Oxon.
OF THE INNER TEMPLE, BARRISTER-AT-LAW

LONDON: SIR ISAAC PITMAN & SONS, LTD.
No. 1 AMEN CORNER, E.C. . . . 1912

Printed by Sir Isaac Pitman
& Sons, Ltd., London, Bath
and New York . 1912

PREFACE

THE object of this book is to set before the general reader a clear account of a great man who has been too much forgotten.

No more vivid period of English history could be selected than that of which for several years John Pym was one of the central figures : it would be equally impossible to select a hero less romantic. He was not a man of action, and in speech he was inordinately prolix. His theological views lack the bite of those Genevan and Scottish Fathers from whom he derived them, but are at the same time unrelieved by any gleam of the toleration which gilds our own less robust convictions. His political philosophy is arid, he was no lawyer, and his history is mainly a mass of precedents hastily acquired for special purposes. "Barren as brick clay" writes Carlyle of his speeches, and the sentence, though severe, is just.

Nevertheless this man laid low men mighty in administration and intellect ; he destroyed the fabric of English polity ; he brought his country to civil war. Though he did not live to see it he sent his king to the block, and left the assembly which had witnessed his triumphs defenceless before the sword of a military adventurer.

He was able to do this because he was endowed with the very genius of organisation, of scheming and of controlling ramifications of intrigue. Equally at home in Court circles, in the Commons, in the City, and in the Country, he was everywhere in the centre of information and everywhere spinning new webs. In happier days his financial ability and his unwearied grasp of detail would have gained him a reputation as "old Parliamentary hand" unparalleled in the history of representative institutions.

Why a man thus endowed destroyed and built not is a question which may be answered in many ways; one is suggested in the pages that follow. It is at least due to him that he should be to the general reader something more than a name in a text-book. Yet no popular life of Pym has been written since John Forster published his in 1837.

The biographical notices of Pym by S. R. Gardiner, in the *Encyclopaedia Britannica* and in the *Dictionary of National Biography*, still more in the pages of his incomparable history, have rendered Forster obsolete, in any case an inevitable result of the passage of time, which Forster's own peculiarities of style and view have, perhaps, accelerated.

The works on which this book is mainly based, besides those of the historians named above, are indicated on another page.

To my friend and former Tutor, the Ven. W. H. Hutton, Fellow of St. John's College, Oxford, and now Archdeacon of Northampton, my debt is great, alike for his teaching in the past and for his unfailing help and counsel at all times, and more especially during the preparation of this work. To him and to my authorities I attribute anything that in this book is worthy of its subject.

C. E. WADE.

LONDON, 1912.

CONTENTS

CHAP.		PAGE
	PREFACE	V
I.	THE BEGINNING	1
II.	THE THIRD PARLIAMENT OF JAMES I	20
III.	THE THIRD PARLIAMENT OF JAMES I (CONTINUED)	50
IV.	THE LAST PARLIAMENT OF JAMES I	81
V.	THE FIRST AND SECOND PARLIAMENTS OF CHARLES I	99
VI.	THE THIRD PARLIAMENT OF CHARLES I	129
VII.	THE ADVENTURERS	150
VIII.	THE ELEVEN YEARS	165
IX.	STRAFFORD	184
X.	ROOT AND BRANCH AND THE TEN PROPOSITIONS	222
XI.	THE GRAND REMONSTRANCE	247
XII.	THE FIVE MEMBERS	268
XIII.	"KING PYM"	286
XIV.	THE END	308
	APPENDICES I–X	316–341
	INDEX	343

ILLUSTRATIONS

JOHN PYM	*Frontispiece*
STRAFFORD	*facing* 195

JOHN PYM

CHAPTER I

THE BEGINNING

As the year 1618 drew to its close, there passed over England a blazing star. What the comet might portend was differently interpreted. "The common people, great admirers of Princes,"[1] as Rushworth slyly says, saw in it the prognostication of the death of Anne, Queen Consort, which befel on the seventeenth day of November. He himself, more conversant with the values of events, preferred to read therein a warning of that appalling strife in Germany, of which this year saw the beginning and of which for thirty years there was to be no end.

If ever indeed comet bore message, none bore it in a year more fateful. Three weeks before the passing away of James' amiable Queen, a death had occurred significant to thinking men. On October 29th the head of Walter Raleigh fell on Tower Hill.

To attribute far-reaching consequences to one single apparition however brilliant, in the sphere terrestrial, is probably little less superstitious, and immeasurably more misleading, than to question the blazing stars of the celestial. None the less, the extinction of that superb Elizabethan seemed to his contemporaries, as it has seemed to their posterity, to have a significance more than normal.

To them it meant the triumph of Diego Sarmiento

[1] R. I. p. 10.

de Acuña, Count of Gondomar, Ambassador to the King of England and his personal friend. It meant that he was to report to the violated majesty of Spain, a worthy sin-offering for her ravished treasure ships, her harbours in flames, her intolerable calamity upon the Northern seas in 1588.

Felix opportunitate, Drake had been dead these twenty years, Frobisher still longer, Hawkins no more was praying amid the wailings of his tortured slaves. But Raleigh remained, lingering too long on that neglected stage, playing a part then sadly out of fashion. As adventurer, as politician, as courtier, he represented, even more than Drake, that aspect of the later days of the great Queen which had most profoundly impressed the imagination of her subjects. With his death vanished from the plain Englishman all hope of easy wealth from Spanish galleons and Spanish colonies ; he must give ear no more to tales of martyred Englishmen pulling out their hearts beneath the whip in Spanish galleys, screaming themselves into eternal silence under the unspeakable torments of the Inquisition.

Heart and conscience and pocket alike were pricked, and an implacable and unintelligent hatred of Spain and of that Roman Church, of which Spain was the foremost champion, prevailed amongst Englishmen, and seemed to them to be both patriotism and religion.

It is easy to criticise this animosity now, it reads unpleasantly enough in the Commons' Journals, Perrot organising his detective Communion, Pym harrying wretched recusants, crowds of obscurer men haling priests to dungeon and torture and gallows.

If this, indeed, were the *via media* of Parker and his Virgin Mistress, it were little better than the broad Roman road that led to Mary's bonfires in Smithfield, or the narrow Genevan path that led to the stake whereat Calvin burnt Servetus.

Such a judgment is as erroneous as it is easy. Toleration must in each instance justify itself as fully as must Intolerance. Both have been criminal in rulers who have indulged them at the expense of national safety. To erect an abstract principle of this kind into a maxim of government, is to indulge that *intellectus sibi permissus* which Bacon frequently denounced. It is to disregard the historic causes which have induced political complexities, and to administer to the national organism a specific which may prove fatal. Those who demand toleration irrespective of circumstances, are precisely those whom few States can tolerate with safety. Elizabeth, pre-eminently a Politique, recognised that first principles, if stimulating to youthful constitutionalists, are perilous to elderly constitutions; moreover, she had not allowed herself to be embarrassed by any serious prepossessions in matters of religion.

How far did her successor attain to her political detachment? James' love of peace was partly the result of a personal timidity, which some did not hesitate to call cowardice; partly of the series of events which had, on the death of Elizabeth, given to him the three crowns without a blow struck. The conclusion of the war with Spain immediately after his succession, was the more agreeable to him, in that it had been an Elizabethan War. That great Queen he was not especially desirous of commemorating, except by contrast. She had been assailed in Legitimacy, in Succession, in Religion. She had waged a desperate European conflict, sparing none, not even James' mother, and had triumphed over all her enemies. James' rôle, as imagined by himself, was to be altogether different. Hereditary right had placed him where he was. He was unhampered by Elizabethan straits and shifts. He would reign placidly, peacefully, as God's Anointed, alike over Scotland and England, and alike over Catholic and Protestant. The same Almighty hand which had guided him peacefully from the insults of an Andrew Melville, and the sordid penury of a Scottish Court, to the Crown of a Nation Episcopal and well-to-do, would guide him peacefully to the end. To that Power alone had he to make his last account.

It was a complete and a logical view, and was not without a dignity of its own, but the current of events was to upset it altogether. Of these events the more notable are the Gunpowder Plot, his daughter's Marriage, and the outbreak of the Thirty Years' War.

Of all criminal blunders few exceed Gunpowder Plot. This foolish attempt at Revolution made by some desperate men, alienated from the worthier Roman Catholics of England that tolerance which their admirable conduct in the days of the Great Armada had begun to gain for them. It let loose upon them, upon good and evil alike, that bitter rancour of English Puritanism, which runs like a poison in the blood through the history of this period, and which no account of the work of John Pym can leave out of sight for a moment. Worse still, it makes plausible this rancour of the extreme Puritan and of his spokesman Pym, even if it cannot justify it. He could maintain, not without some show of reason, that the seed of the Roman Church was watered with the blood of the Protestant martyr. He could point conclusively to Paris in 1572, to Delft in 1584, to Westminster in 1605. To such men James' policy of conciliation must have seemed full of danger.

True to the Hapsburg tradition of dynastic alliances, Spain and the Empire had resolved to attract the two

THE PALATINE MARRIAGE 5

hostile Western Kingdoms by marriage. The project was successful with regard to France; with England the difficulties were greater. Prince Henry, James' elder son, was a young man of energy and determination who had already shown strong Protestant convictions, and who was believed to cherish plans of aggression on the Continent in the Protestant interest, which, had he lived, might have changed the public History of Europe.[1] His premature death, in 1612, cut short the prospects of another Henry VIII, and the eyes of the country were turned on his brother Charles—cultured, studious and reserved—of whom Henry himself had carelessly said that he would make a good Archbishop of Canterbury.

Before the young Prince died, he had the satisfaction of witnessing the betrothal of his sister Elizabeth to a convinced Protestant, Frederick V, Prince Palatine, in 1612. The Catholic Powers had done their best to obtain the hand of this beautiful and fascinating Princess, who, in the darkest days of her chequered life, never failed to attract to herself the devoted adherence of those who came within her sphere of influence. The Duke of Savoy went so far as to seek a double marriage between his two children and the Princess and her brother Henry; but Elizabeth also had strong Protestant convictions, which the paternal affection of James was unwilling to oppose, even though his desire for a good understanding with the Catholic Powers was thereby thwarted. This momentous marriage was the last work of Robert Cecil. He died in the year of the betrothal, and with him passed away the Elizabethan tradition. A union which might have meant much, was doomed in the feeble hands of James and Charles, and by the evil influence of Buckingham, to bring to the Princess, to England

[1] Ranke I. IV. 4.

and to Europe, only disappointment, misery and bloodshed.

Since this unfortunate marriage brought England into the full current of Continental politics, and thereby introduced a new and disturbing element into the English constitutional struggle, it is necessary here to glance briefly at the condition of Germany at this moment.

In 1356, the famous Golden Bull of Charles IV became a fundamental law of the Empire. It recognised the independence of those great feudatories whom the Emperor was no longer able to control. Two centuries later, Germany, far from being an Empire, was scarcely a Confederation of the loosest kind. The Prince who bore the Imperial title gained little more thereby than the titular pre-eminence ; his real strength lay in his own possessions as a German King. When, as in the case of Charles V, he was also King of Spain, Lord of the New World, and ruler of a considerable part of Italy, he was formidable indeed. There were no institutions in Germany capable of enforcing peace upon sovereigns really co-ordinate with, though nominally subordinate to, the Empire if some great question should arise to divide Germany into two camps.[1] Such a question did arise when the Reformation, before fifty years were past, had converted ninety per cent. of the Germans to Protestantism. Were those Princes who adopted the new belief to be allowed to secularise the ecclesiastical property within their dominions to any extent ; further, were those Ecclesiastics who became Protestant to be allowed to carry with them their possessions ? The Peace of Augsburg in 1555, had made a compromise, whereby the *status quo* of 1552 was to be observed. Such lands as had been secularised at that date were to remain secular ;

[1] G. England and Germany, 1618-19 (Camden, 1865).

should a Bishop or Abbot thereafter turn Protestant he must vacate his post. *Cuius Regio eius Religio* was the principle adopted, and the population of the territories had no voice in the decision. Such a compromise had in it no elements of permanence, and secularisations went on as before. As the bitterness of the two parties increased, two associations were formed, the Protestant Union under the Elector Palatine, and the Catholic League under the Duke of Bavaria. Their purpose was defensive, but there was a grave danger that unless some compromise could be agreed upon, they would before long fly at each others' throats.

The real, but not the nominal Leader of the Protestant Union to which Calvinists as well as Lutherans were admitted, was a very remarkable man, Christian of Anhalt, the trusted counsellor of Frederick IV, the Elector Palatine, who was himself a drunken nonentity. Christian was willing, and even anxious, to destroy the last remnant of Imperial authority. Calvinists had no share in the benefits of the Peace of Augsburg, and therefore had nothing to lose by upsetting it. In Christian, they had a leader familiar with European politics and politicians, and an expert in diplomatic intrigue, but with no clear idea of an alternative to the institutions which he proposed to destroy. On the other hand, the leader of the Catholic League, Maximilian of Bavaria, was, perhaps, the most capable of all the German Rulers, well equipped with arms and troops and money: a man who knew what he wanted and was willing to bide his time.

The reigning Emperor Matthias had attained to that title on the death of his brother Rudolph II, in 1612, being already King of Hungary and of Bohemia.

Bohemia was the storm centre which was destined to convulse Germany. This famous land, the Hercynian

Forest of the Ancient World, is separated by lofty mountains from the rest of Germany, and has a population partly Slavonic or Czech and partly Celtic, from that famous Gallic tribe, the Boii, from whom the country derives its name, the rest mainly Teutonic. Throughout its history it has furnished difficult problems for its rulers. There John Hus and Jerome of Prague were burnt for heresy; there arose the Young Czech movement of our own day. Their sturdy independence had gained their wish for the Utraquists, and outside their churches was still to be seen the huge cup which indicated the privilege granted to their party by the Council of Basel of receiving the Eucharist in both kinds.

In such congenial soil Protestantism took root even more deeply than it had done in other parts of the dominions of the House of Austria. Therefore in Bohemia its suppression proved more difficult. Matthias, like his brother and predecessor on the Bohemian and Imperial Thrones, the astronomer Rudolph II, had tried severe methods of repression in vain. The stubborn nobility of Bohemia, who had embraced the principles of the Reformation, awaited with what patience they might the death of Matthias, who, though only fifty-five, was prematurely aged by the hardships of his exalted position. They promised themselves a Protestant successor, for the Throne of Bohemia was elective by the Constitution of the Golden Bull, as had been exemplified in the election of Matthias himself in 1611. Great was their consternation when the Bohemian Diet was suddenly summoned, in June, 1617, to appoint a King Designate, and to recognise hereditary right by choosing the Archduke Ferdinand of Styria.

Ferdinand was the most able and most determined of the Austrian Archdukes. He was by hereditary right

Sovereign of Styria, Carinthia, and Carniola. Matthias and his brothers were childless, and it was their unanimous wish that all the dominions of the House of Austria and the Imperial Crown as well, should fall to their cousin Ferdinand. He was a man of firm resolution, a pupil of the Jesuits and a devout Catholic. Within his own dominions he had been eminently successful in suppressing Protestantism.

Taken by surprise the Bohemian Diet accepted Ferdinand, contenting themselves with a guarantee from him that he would respect that Letter of Majesty, a compact between the Crown and the States of Bohemia, which had been granted by Matthias in 1612, and which legalised the position of the Protestants within his kingdom.

Not only the Bohemians were disappointed. In September, 1610, the drunken nonentity Frederick IV, Elector Palatine, had died, and was succeeded by his son Frederick V, who three years later married James' daughter. The Prince was in every respect unlike his father; he was an austere and convinced Calvinist, with ambitions which far transcended the limitations imposed upon him by a mind narrow and unilluminated. He assumed the active control of his dominions in 1614, and fell at once under the fascination of the involved diplomacy of Christian of Anhalt. It was part of Anhalt's plans that Frederick should be the next King of Bohemia, and this hope had been openly avowed when Frederick came to England to fetch his bride. Disappointed in this aim, it remained for Christian to endeavour to frustrate the election of Ferdinand as Emperor, and to attain this he employed all his arts. But before this great question came to be decided the inevitable had occurred.

The milder rule of Matthias in Bohemia had, after the election of Ferdinand as King-Designate, given place to a reactionary and anti-Protestant policy. The Letter of Majesty was flouted. Protestant worshippers on the Royal Estate were excluded from their Church at Braunau, and a new edifice which was being built at Klostergrab was pulled down by the Archbishop of Prague. The Defensores, appointed under the Letter of Majesty, protested in vain. They were led by Count Matthias Thurn, and demanded redress for their wrongs directly from the Emperor, after they had held a meeting of Protestant Deputies summoned to Prague from each Circle of the realm.

They were told that their meeting was rebellious, and their reply was prompt. Thurn and others went in deputation to the Chancery room in the Palace at Prague, where were sitting the Regents appointed by Matthias when he quitted Prague for Hungary at the end of 1617. Of these Regents two were especially obnoxious, Slawata and Martinitz; there was a violent altercation, and presently Thurn seized Slawata, one of his companions Martinitz, and both were hurled out of the window into the castle ditch. Their secretary Fabricius remonstrated, and at once shared their fate. The fall was some fifty to sixty feet, yet not one of the three was killed, a coincidence truly extraordinary. As Martinitz fell he cried " Jesus, Mary," whereupon, in derision, one of the Defensores retorted, " Let us see whether his Mary will help him ! " A second later he yelled, " By God, his Mary has helped him." It is not to be wondered that Catholics saw the direct intervention of God in the preservation not only of Martinitz but of his two fellow victims.

This calculated outrage, which was intended to make Revolution inevitable, was perpetrated on the 23rd day of May, 1618. The last, the longest, and the most hideous of the Wars of Religion had begun.

How do these incidents, and the still more terrible events which were to follow, concern the domestic conflict in England, and more especially how do they concern the subject of this volume ? The answer has been given by the great English historian of the period, when he says, " It is seldom that events which have taken place upon the Continent have affected the course of English history so deeply as the struggle between the two religious parties in Germany, which lit up the flames of the Thirty Years' War. The second growth of Puritanism and the anti-monarchical feeling which reached its culminating point in the reign of Charles I, may be distinctly traced to the dissatisfaction of the nation with the desertion by James of his Protestant Allies."[1]

James was, indeed, placed in a position of extreme difficulty. It had been his praiseworthy desire to reign as King of his Catholic as well as of his Protestant subjects ; to be able, as his great predecessor had not been able, to promote friendly relations with the Catholic as well as with the Protestant Powers of Europe, and abroad as at home, to act in the spirit of his favourite text, *Beati Pacifici*. He was now treating with Spain for a marriage between his son Charles and the Infanta Maria. Such a union was directly opposed to the Elizabethan tradition, but it is impossible to say that in 1618 it was wrong. To carry it into effect the King must needs encounter the fierce opposition of every country squire, to whom that Elizabethan tradition meant everything that was glorious, and who, untravelled and unlettered, knew nothing of the politics of other countries than his own. This is the argument which Sir Edward Coke thought good enough for his fellow Commoners, " Never any treachery against us by the Papists, but a

[1] G. England and Germany, 1618-19 (Camden 1865).

book preceded to take heed of Treaties of Peace, ... the first plague that ever came to our sheep came by a Spanish sheep , . . . if a sheep so dangerous, *Domine libera me a malo* . . . . . nothing can do us hurt as long as we are constant in our Religion."[1]

To reconcile such views with James' policy would, in any case, have been difficult. His son-in-law made it impossible. Events in Germany moved rapidly ; on March 20th, 1619, the Emperor Matthias died. This did not greatly alter the political situation, for Ferdinand was already King of Hungary, and was carrying on the Imperial Government in the name of Matthias.

The Imperial Election took place on August 18th, and Ferdinand was chosen unanimously. Anhalt's wild scheme for putting forward the Duke of Savoy as a rival candidate had come to nothing, and Frederick himself, with whatever of reluctance, was impelled to give his Electoral vote for the Hapsburg.

Two days before the Imperial Election, the Bohemian revolutionists had taken a decisive step. They deposed Ferdinand from the throne which they had allowed him to occupy two years before, and chose Frederick in his stead. We may well believe that the young Elector was distracted with anxiety.[2] He was urgently dissuaded by three of his fellow electors, Bavaria, Saxony and Mainz, by the King of France, and, not least, by his mother. But there was at his side not only his beautiful and ambitious English wife, to whom rightly or wrongly his decision has been attributed, but also Christian of Anhalt, who could, with his plausible tongue, conjure away those political disasters which even Frederick foresaw. On September 28th he cast the die, and by his acceptance

[1] C. J. I. 648, ii.
[2] M. A. E. Green, "Elizabeth, Queen of Bohemia," ed. Lomax, 1909.

THE BATTLE OF PRAGUE

threw down the gage to Catholic Europe. On October 31st Frederick and Elizabeth entered Prague, on November 4th he was crowned. " He is carrying the Palatinate into Bohemia," said his clear-eyed mother sorrowfully. Frederick's fatal decision was immensely popular in England, where church bells were rung and bonfires lighted. Archbishop Abbot had, indeed, in a letter to Elizabeth, taken it upon himself to urge immediate acceptance of the Bohemian Crown, with or without King James' sanction, and prayers for the Elector's success were offered in some of our churches.

James was far from sharing the enthusiasm of his subjects. Whatever hopes he may have entertained at the time of his daughter's marriage that she might be the next Queen of Bohemia, he had laid aside when the Bohemians themselves had acquiesced in the election of Ferdinand. Since then his attitude had been equally correct; he had held out no hope of support to his son-in-law, and he now refused to allow him the title of King. But it was impossible for him to maintain this attitude of neutrality.

On January 27th, 1620, Ferdinand declared the election of Frederick to be null and void, and called upon the Estates of Bohemia to return to their allegiance. On April 30th, he bade the Elector retire from Bohemia within a month on pain of being put to the ban of the Empire. The Catholic Electors, in conference at Mühlhausen, combined to urge this course upon their offending colleague. In vain. A few months later four armies were concentrating on Prague. On October 29th, a Sunday morning, Tilly and Bucquoi hurled themselves on Frederick's troops on the White Hill hard by the city. Anhalt, who commanded, showed in the field none of the astuteness which he had displayed in the Council

Chamber, and in a few hours the Winter King and his English Queen were in flight, to find at last a refuge at the Hague.

Heavy on the Bohemians fell the hands of Ferdinand and of Rome. The scaffold, confiscation and expulsion purged them effectually of their sluggish independence. And not on them only. On January 12th, 1621, Frederick was put to the ban of the Empire, and his lands and dignities declared forfeit.

James' perplexities might have drawn pity even from a Puritan. He had contented himself at first with efforts at negotiation. Neither the great ability of Digby, nor the social amenity of Doncaster could effect anything by expostulation, and James was in no position either to give or to threaten. From military operations he carefully abstained, both from poverty and from principle, except that in July, 1620, when it became known that the Lower Palatinate itself was threatened, he allowed Sir Horace Vere to take out English volunteers to garrison the strongholds of that region. In so doing he drew a distinction, correct enough in the main, between helping his son-in-law to keep that which was undeniably his, and assisting him to hold that which might fairly be held to be Ferdinand's. Under the guidance of Gondomar, moreover, he allowed himself to be drawn into the scheme for a Spanish marriage for Prince Charles, in the preposterous expectation that Spain would lay aside her family, political and religious destiny, in order, by persuasion or by force, to compel the Emperor to restore a bigoted Calvinist to the dominions which he had forfeited. The absurdity of such a hope goes far to show that James was at the end of his resources. The disaster at the White Hill, and the pathetic appeals of his daughter, for the moment stung him to action. He offered a military alliance to Christian IV, of Denmark, and in order to obtain those supplies, of which he stood so sorely in need, he also summoned a Parliament.

Such is the setting and such the stage on which appears for the first time in public life the illustrious subject of this sketch.

Elizabeth was Queen, Whitgift Archbishop of Canterbury, when in 1584, John Pym was born at Brymore, near Bridgwater, in the county of Somerset, the first son of his father Alexander. It was a notable birth in a notable year. On March 19th Ivan the Terrible, heroic, infamous, had passed to his own place, the Tartar power shattered, Russia half made. On July 10th William the Silent, founder of Dutch liberties, had fallen on the staircase at Delft to the bullet of an assassin. In this year Francis Bacon, of Gray's Inn, a young lawyer of twenty-four, first took his seat in the Commons as Member for Melcombe Regis.

The child was four when the great Armada fled shattered before the shrieking of the North Sea winds and the valour of Elizabethan buccaneers; he was ten when Henry of Navarre healed the wounds of France by an inexpensive sacrifice of conscience; twelve when Francis Drake set sail for his last voyage. He was barely nineteen when Drake's Virgin Mistress followed him upon the uncharted ocean.

On what manner of mind and with what significance fell these great events ? There is no answer ; the known facts of Pym's early life are of the scantiest. That he was of fair family ; that in 1599 he entered Broadgates Hall in the University of Oxford, a foundation which subsequently became Pembroke College ; that in due course he proceeded to the study of the law in the Middle Temple ; that he was befriended by the Earl of Bedford and obtained a post in the Exchequer; that he married; that some six years later his wife died, leaving him two sons and three daughters; that he did not marry again: such are the meagre results of the researches of his biographers.

It is for the imagination to paint the mind of a child as it may have developed in those spacious days. For Pym, no more than for his mighty contemporary Shakespere, did conscious nature heave a birthpang. In a kinder, if more Pagan dispensation, some ox would have spoken a word of congratulation, some priestess would have grown a premonitory beard. But the discriminating malice of Clarendon finds no more effective taunt for the patron of the Presbytery than a condescending allusion to his ancestry, " He was a man of a private quality and condition of life."[1] As Athene from the brain of Zeus, so Pym might seem to spring full panoplied at thirty-seven years into the Parliament of 1621.[2]

Few Englishmen who have played as great a part in our modern history have left such scanty memorials of themselves. Pym's premature death, the immediate overthrow of his policy under the rule of the Army and of the Restoration, the prudent and congenial self-effacement of his two sons, and the failure of male issue in the third generation, partly serve to explain this. No school has yet been able to claim the honour of his education, but it is certain that when fifteen years of age he entered Broadgates Hall in the University of Oxford, the date of his matriculation being 1599, May 18th. How long he remained there is unknown, but he became a student of the Middle Temple in 1602. He was not called to the Bar, and his study of the law was probably slight, for in 1629, on March 7th, Hakewill, who must have known, alluded to " Mr. Cooke and Mr. Pymme, who are no lawyers,"[3] and

[1] Cl. VII. 409. [2] Appendix I. a. [3] C. J. I. 543, ii (cf. Appendix II).

EXCHEQUER OFFICER

it is unlikely that he would pursue the study after that date. It is, nevertheless, notable that he was very frequently put on committees which were concerned with legal matters, as may be seen by reference to the appendices at the end of this volume. There are long stretches in the life of this eminent man when we pass from an almost daily intercourse with him in the Journals to absolute blankness. Parliament was indeed Pym's sun, and he its brightest constellation, but outside that orbit all is dark indeed. Of his life after 1602, Gardiner says,[1] "We know nothing of his career till he entered the House of Commons as Member for Calne in 1614."

In Appendix I reasons are given to show that Pym did not sit in the Parliament of 1614. Where then was he ? Clarendon gave the information incompletely when he wrote in his history of the Long Parliament of 1640, "Mr. Pym was looked upon as the man of greatest experience in Parliament, where he had served very long, and was always a man of business, being an officer in the Exchequer, and of a good reputation generally, though known to be inclined to the Puritan party : yet not of those furious resolutions against the Church as the other leading men were, and wholly devoted to the Earl of Bedford, who had nothing of that spirit."[2]

As "Mr. Hyde," a member of the Long Parliament very frequently called to the chair in the absence of the Speaker, and at a later date the astute author of Charles' countermoves to Pym's manœuvres, Clarendon had every reason to know the man, and all that there was to be known about him. But we are not left merely to this indication. The appointment of Pym is to be seen in the State Papers.

[1] D.N.B. Vol. 47, sub Pym.
[2] Cl. III. 30 and VII. 410.

In 1605, June 11th dated at Greenwich, an order[1] was issued by Lord Hume of Berwick, to Sir Thomas Windebank, that he should draw a grant to John Pymme in reversion after Henry Audley, of the Receivership of the Counties of Hampshire, Wiltshire and Gloucester.

That Pym duly received the appointment is proved by three documents. The first is a warrant to John Pymme, Receiver of Wiltshire, to pay yearly to George Hungerford, thirteen shillings and fourpence per load, for eight loads of hay for the King's deer in Braydon Forest.

The second,[2] dated 1614, July 9, at Westminster, is a grant to William Bowler, of the office of Bailiff of the Hundreds of Holford, Gretton and Kittesgate, in the County of Gloucester, with a certificate by John Pymme, Receiver General of the County, of his fitness for the place. The third[3] is a communication dated from Egham, 1618, September 28th, as to the impossibility of raising at once £2,000 by the sale of His Majesty's rent, iron, and fines on leases of the disforested grounds Blackmore and Pewsham. He can get no sale for the iron at the price required, twelve pounds ten shillings per ton, and has no offers save for part of one forest.

Here then was Pym during the eventful years preceding 1618, and here he had ample opportunity of developing and perfecting those remarkable aptitudes for business and for finance which were to make him the leader in Parliament of men of far greater genius than his own, and which shone equally, as will be seen, when he directed the destinies of the Company of Adventurers for Providence Island.

The date of Pym's marriage is not known, it must have been somewhere about 1614, for when his wife died in

[1] Cal. S. P. Dom, Vol. 8. [2] Cal. S. P. Dom, Vol. 9. [3] Ibid.

WIFE AND PATRON

1620, she left him two sons and three daughters, of whom all that need be said will be found in the Appendix.[1] Her baptismal name was Anne, her surname either Hooke or Hooker. Pym, handsome and urbane, was notoriously happy in, and welcome to, feminine society, but whether because of, or notwithstanding this, he did not marry again. In the same year his mother also died. After the death of Alexander Pym, she had espoused Sir Anthony Rous, and a turgid " Death's Sermon "[2] informs us that she lived with him for more than thirty years. Pym was now thirty-six.

In the passage from Clarendon's history quoted above, mention is made of the patronage extended to Pym by the Earl of Bedford. This was a cardinal factor in Pym's political life, and will be dealt with in due course. It is enough to say here that he owed his introduction to Parliamentary life to this nobleman, who was, until his untimely death, able to save Pym both from his enemies at Court, and from those extreme courses towards which his Puritan associates and sympathies were constantly urging him, and to which he ultimately succumbed.

[1] Appendix IX. [2] Wood. Ath. Oxon. Vol. II. sub. Fitzgeffry.

CHAPTER II

THE THIRD PARLIAMENT OF JAMES I

On the 30th of January, 1621, James I, wearing his imperial crown, set out from Whitehall to open his third Parliament. With him was his son Charles, and beside the Prince rode the Marquis of Buckingham.

If to James, as to his predecessor on the Scottish throne, there had been granted a glimpse of the future as he entered the Parliament House, he might have stood aghast on the threshold and have cried with Macbeth, "I'll see no more." His own course was nearly run. He was only fifty-five, yet in four more years he was carried to his grave. His favourite, Buckingham, was twenty-nine, and had still seven years in which to mislead his King and exasperate his fellow-subjects before a murderer rid the world of him at Portsmouth. Prince Charles was now twenty-one, and on him had been centred the hopes of England since the death of his elder brother Henry nine years before.

If it were well for his father it was still better for Charles that he had no such fatal gift of pre-vision and knew not that twenty-eight years later, on that very day of that very month, and in that very palace of Whitehall, he was to expiate the mistakes and the weakness of his father, of his friend, and of himself.

No gloomy forebodings troubled James. He listened in Westminster Abbey to a learned sermon preached at his command by Dr. Lancelot Andrewes, the admirable Bishop of Winchester, personal friend of his Lord Chancellor Francis Bacon, and familiar to-day to all who know his *Preces Privatæ*, a classic of the English Church.

PARLIAMENT MEETS

Then in the Palace of Westminster hard by he addressed his third Parliament.

Amongst the knights and burgesses assembled there with the Peers were many men who were to play great parts in the days to come. Sir Thomas Wentworth now, as in 1614, appeared as one of the Knights of the Shire of York, his colleague being a Secretary of State, Sir George Calvert, who, as Lord Baltimore, was founder of Maryland. John Hampden represented Grampound, a Cornish borough, which its own insignificance was to make famous in the struggle for the Great Reform Bill two hundred years later. Sir Ferdinand Fairfax sat for Boroughbridge, the little Yorkshire town which had sprung up near the ashes of the beautiful Roman Isurium. Hedon in the same county had elected his son Sir Thomas. Portsmouth sent a courtly supporter of Puritan beliefs in the person of Sir Benjamin Rudyerd, and from Liskeard came Sir Edward Coke.

Five years before, James had dismissed this great lawyer from his office of Lord Chief Justice. It was a notable victory for Ellesmere the Chancellor, for Bacon, his Vice-Chancellor and successor, for their Court of Chancery and for the Prerogative, but it was a Pyrrhic victory after all, for it set free for the service of the Commons a legal and constitutional erudition that is almost oppressive, and a mind whose vigour was the more irresistible because it ran in the narrowest of channels.

Amongst these famous men sat John Pym, now for the first time a Member of Parliament representing Calne, in company with his colleague John Duckett.

His Majesty began[1] as he was wont, with a quotation from the other Solomon, "*In multiloquio non deest peccatum*

[1] P. and D. I. 3.

saith the wisest man that ever was." Such had been his own experience. In many previous sessions of Parliament he had shown to the gentlemen of the Lower House a true mirror of his heart. Little had it profited him. "So it may be, it pleased God, seeing some vanity in me to send my words as spittle in my own face." Curiously prescient of his early death he alluded to the fewness of the days left to him, then, " not to instruct but to remind," he expounded the nature of a Parliament. It is an assembly composed of a Head and a Body, the especial function of the Commons is to make the King acquainted with the particular estate of their country, and the especial function of Parliament is to supply the King with sustenance for his necessities. Moreover let them, being legislators, remember that as the world grows older men grow more wise, more crafty, more sinful, and so the greater need of new laws to fit new crimes.

From these generals he descended to particulars, and first as to religion. For recusants there were laws enough were they but faithfully interpreted and put in force. Let no man say his king would be lax with such folk that he might the rather press on the Spanish match proposed for his son. Not so, if they did not believe him let them read his published writings.

Then he came to his chief point, why especially he had called them together. That they might supply his urgent necessities in urgent causes. For eighteen years he had been their King, and for those eighteen years he had kept the kingdom at peace. Did they blame him for that? Yet how sparse his supplies, far less than those of his predecessor Elizabeth of famous memory. Some said he had been extravagant. But he had made his economies, and Buckingham, his young Admiral now standing at his side, had much helped him in this. He would be more careful, and in his bounty would not make every day a Christmas.

Next for " the miserable and torn state of Christendom." What of his son-in-law, the hapless King of Bohemia, now in exile ? He had nothing to do with that design. He had sent Doncaster on an embassy to see what could be done, and a pretty penny that had cost him. His son-in-law meantime wrote to ask him whether or not he should accept the Bohemian Crown, but before he could answer Frederick had cast the die and taken it. It was not for him to undo that, deposing of kings he left to the Jesuits. Who was he that he should meddle ? Not but what he had gone so far as to let English volunteers go out to defend the Palatinate. Let them think what all this had cost him, ambassadors and troops and what not. He had had, indeed, to borrow of his brother of Denmark.

Lastly and very warily he touched on the highly distasteful subject of grievances, for which his hearers waited with what patience they might. Was there aught, he asked, they would desire of him by way of justice ? He had appointed Judges of the best learning and of the greatest integrity for this end, and if they should prove unjust he would not spare them.

James was followed by the Lord Chancellor. Francis Bacon had now attained the summit of his political and judicial career. He was Lord Chancellor of England, Viscount St. Alban, and enjoyed at last that Royal favour which had been so long denied him. His speech on this occasion was brief, but it had all his characteristics: it was sententious, sagacious and servile. He held it, he said, as great a commendation to be silent as to speak, when such a King was present, but he would fain urge on the two Houses the motto *Nosce teipsum*, that so they might show a modest carriage to so gracious a

Sovereign. He added a sentence memorable in the light of subsequent events, " As there is great expectation in the beginning of this Parliament, so I pray God it may be as good in the conclusion, that it may be generative begetting others hereafter." Some of his hearers would regard him grimly. Scarcely three months were to pass before those hearers would have him run to earth, stripped of his high offices, beggared, disgraced, yet in his fall the greatest of all their victims but one.

The Commons, at the outset of their deliberations, set before themselves four topics of the first importance. These were, " Liberty of Speech, Papists 'who swarm and grow insolent in this Town,' Supply for the King's wants, and the bleeding business of the Palatinate, Grievances of subjects and Commonwealth."

With regard to Liberty of Speech, the Commons had not forgotten that on the dissolution of the Addled Parliament in 1614, four of its members had been sent to the Tower, five forbidden to leave London without permission, and four others put out of the Commission of the Peace. It is true that the period of imprisonment was but short, and that they had used outrageous language which no fervour of patriotic zeal could justify, and which the Speaker, Ranulph Crew, should certainly have suppressed. None the less the Commons did no more than their duty in regarding such exercise of Royal supervision with the keenest jealousy. It was agreed that a petition *de iure* should be made to the King, claiming that the right of freedom of speech had always been theirs, and that he had infringed it after the dissolution of the Parliament of 1614. No issue could have been more plainly joined.

Three episodes will serve to show the attitude of this Parliament towards Religion. They are the Communion

PERROT'S PROPOSAL

at St. Margaret's, the episode of Sheppard, and the case of Floyd. All three are eminently symptomatic of the current of opinion in the Lower House, and speak eloquently of the difficulties in the way of those reformers who hoped to adjust the political system of the Tudors to the altered conditions of English society.

Those members of this Parliament who were inclined towards the doctrines, if not towards the Church system of John Calvin, were well aware that to the majority of Englishmen the indubitable clarity of that system had appealed as little as its dubious charity. There was, indeed, reason to fear that to complete their full picture of a Parliamentary Eden the Recusant Serpent was not wanting. To eliminate him they continued a device which it is as easy to defend on historical, as it is difficult to justify on moral grounds.

The Communion at St. Margaret's was the outcome of a proposal made by Sir James Perrot, Member for Haverfordwest, at the first meeting of the House for business, on Feb. 5, 1621.

Sir James had a family grudge against the clergy. His father, Sir John Perrot, had enjoyed great favour and suffered greater hardship at the hands of Elizabeth, to whom and to him, popular rumour assigned the same august Sire. Whether or not this was the origin of her favour towards him he was made Lord Deputy of Ireland, and in that capacity rendered valuable service to the country. But it was his fate, as it was of many Lords Deputy, to encounter that selfish hatred of officialdom which, in 1635, Wentworth determined to scotch in the person of the miscreant Mountnorris. The clergy, too, abhorred him, and his downfall was procured by means of forged documents. He died in the Tower, a broken man, some thirty years before this date.

Filial duty then, and possibly domestic unhappiness, for his own wife was a recusant,[1] may have led Sir James to move, as he had done before, in 1614, that the House should detect the presence of concealed Papists in their midst by partaking together of the Body and Blood of Christ in the Church of St. Margaret, in Westminster.

It was ordered accordingly that a small committee of four, of whom Sir James was one, should take the names of all members of the House, that it might be seen on examination whether or not all had received, "and those that receive not the Communion at the said time prefixed, are not to sit in the House until they have received it."

It may not here be out of place to observe the curious irony of time which has conferred upon the Royalist and the Tory the questionable distinction of making the central act of Christian worship to be the instrument of the agent provocateur. Here, indeed, is the seed of the famous and too long-lived Test Act of 1673, which itself was the offspring of that turbulent patriot Anthony Ashley Cooper, first Earl of Shaftesbury, whom the Whigs might well desire to concede, but the Tories would scarcely wish to adopt.

Some difficulties had still to be surmounted. The House desired that the sermon should be preached to them by James Usher, the youthful and learned Bishop of Meath, who four years later was to become Archbishop of Armagh, and whose hypothetical dates for the Creation and after, prefixed to the chapters of Genesis, still remain to make unnecessary demands on the faith of undirected readers.

But the House had reckoned without Dean Williams. That brilliant Welshman was now rapidly mounting the ladder of preferment, as well he might, who had both

[1] C. J. I. 776, ii.

James and Buckingham pushing him behind. He had now been Dean of Westminster for a year. Let the Commons come to the Abbey if they would, said Williams, they should have a Canon to preach to them. He would take care too, on this occasion, to banish the wafer bread. This had stuck in Protestant gullets in 1614.

The Commons were in no mood to argue with Williams. The Temple Church would suit them as well as St. Margaret's, they would go there instead and hear the preacher they preferred.

At this point James interfered. He bade Williams let the Commons have their way. The Dean at once obeyed, and the original proposal of Sir James Perrot was carried out. Fancy may picture the throng of country gentlemen in that beautiful church, half reverent, wholly curious, espying what gaps there might be in their number, whether this man or that whom gossip branded for Papist were present or away.

Thus they waited for the words: *Ye that do truly and earnestly repent you of your sins, and are in love and charity with your neighbours, draw near.* . . .

The second episode is that of Sheppard, against whom Pym made his first speech in Parliament.

Thomas Sheppard was a barrister, and had been chosen by the Electors of Shaftesbury to be their junior Member. On Thursday, Feb. 15th, a Bill was proposed "for the keeping of the Sabbath, otherwise called Sunday." It was obviously aimed at the "Book of Sports," that Declaration issued in 1618, which had made lawful on Sunday, dancing, maypoles, archery, leaping and Whitsunales, but only for those who had previously attended Divine Service. Such mitigation of the rigours of a Puritan Sabbath was eminently distasteful to the sterner professors.

Sheppard's speech was not conciliatory. The Bill he said was idle and indiscreet, in the first place because of its title, for as everyone knows *dies Sabbati* is Latin for Sabbath day, and *dies Sabbati* is Saturday, as it is taken in all writs and returns amongst lawyers. The Bill might as well be called, " An Act for the observing of Saturday otherwise called Sunday." Nor was the body of the Act any better than its head. The Act was made in the face and teeth of the King's Book, which allowed dancing on Sunday. King David had said, " Let us praise God in a dance." David they might leave to the Divines, but King James concurred with King David. So let them not make a statute against dancing. The proposer of the Bill must be a perturber of the peace and a Puritan.

This was too much. Sheppard was bidden to hold his tongue. His badinage had indeed struck home. Coke observed sententiously that, " Whosoever hindereth the Sanctification of the Sabbath is against the Scripture."[1] The senior Member for Ripon, Sir Thomas Posthumous Hobby, bore witness that Sheppard had said that no Puritan could be presented to the Ordinary for punishment, without some Justice of the Peace flying in the Ordinary's face.

A message from the Lords concerning public business interrupted Posthumous Hobby, but the House had by no means done with Sheppard, for on the following day Pym presented a formal report on his offence.[2] He had, it seems, offended the preferrer, or as we should now say, the introducer of the Bill. He had, moreover, offended the dignity of Justices of the Peace on the showing of Hobby—a misdeed that must needs ruffle the feelings of many of the little country magnates there present. He had been profane, and, worst of all, he had offended the

[1] C. J. I. 522, i. P. and D. I. 51-2. [2] C. J. I. 524, i.

dignity of the House and its rules. Pym was at pains to distinguish between David's exposition before the ark, and that dancing about maypoles in which the youth of England then took delight. In Pym's opinion, when Sheppard said that the Statute was directed against the King's Book, he was in effect setting up dissension between his Majesty and his Commons, and whoso did that must needs have an ill object.

Sheppard had too, it seemed, declared that the Commons " made gins, engines, and barricadoes against Papists, and not so much as a mousetrap against the Puritan."

Thus far Pym, following whom Sir Edward Coke pragmatically lectured the House. If a man, said he, in a matter of Religion go too much on the right hand he goes to superstition, if too much on the left to profaneness and atheism. Without reverence there is no obedience. *Maxima caritas facere iustitiam.* " Crush such birds in the shell."

It was left for Sir Jeremy Horsey, to whom the burgesses of Eastlow, in the county of Cornwall, had confided their franchises, to clinch the situation by a terrible warning, which he had culled from the history of the previous reign. In the thirty-fifth year of Elizabeth, a Bill was introduced to mulct such as came not to church of a Sunday twelve pence for each offence. A certain Member of the Commons was persuaded by a friend to refrain from voting for the measure. Now when the division was taken the numbers were equal. The Speaker's casting vote, it is true, made the matter right, yet not so could doom be dodged, " This gentleman that stayed behind so at his friend's persuasion, the next day, being to every man's thinking well and in good health, fell down in a swoon and was dead almost an hour."

This harrowing, if somewhat inconclusive, reminiscence was followed by stern action. Sheppard was called to the Bar of the House, and there on his knees he heard his sentence:—" That the House doth remove him from the service of this House as being unworthy to be a Member thereof."

Such was the exit of Sheppard, silenced but unquenched, we can easily believe. His seat for Shaftesbury was taken by the famous knight, Ralph Hopton, who was in days to come, at Stratton, Lansdown, and Roundway Down, to show to his Puritan colleagues a sword keener than his predecessor's wit.

The measure meted to Sheppard may appear harsh to those who regard the unhampered public expression of opinion as in itself desirable. It is but fair, on the other hand, to remember that it is an established principle of our constitution that each House has absolute control over its own procedure and its own members, a privilege not to be questioned even by the Courts. It is true that this principle was not established until 1840, when a grotesque series of events[1] had amply demonstrated its necessity, but at all periods the existence of the privilege has been the pre-requisite of the continued existence of the House. Therefore, though the Commons may have acted harshly in expelling this flippant barrister, they did not act illegally.

In the third episode, which is that of Floyd, the matter is altogether different. Like Sheppard, Floyd was a barrister; like him he was free with his tongue, but unlike him he was not a Member of the House of Commons. He could not be, for he was a Roman Catholic. He was an old man and poor, a prisoner in the Fleet for debt. Complaint[2] was made of him that while talking about the

[1] Stockdale v. Hansard, 1839.   [2] P. and D. I.

defeat at Prague with a fellow-prisoner, a Doctor of Physic named Pennington, " He did say in a scornful and malicious manner that Goodman and Goodwife Palsgrave were now turned out-of-doors." Worse still, he must needs continue that he, the said Floyd, had as much right to the Kingdom of Bohemia as the Palsgrave had." The Commons were informed of this on Monday, April 30th, and the following day they examined the Doctor of Physic and the Warden of the Fleet. The Doctor stated that he and Floyd had been good friends and used to visit each other. On the present occasion Floyd informed him that Goodman Palsgrave had taken to his heels and run, and that Goody Palsgrave was a prisoner. "Then," replied Pennington, "it is the duty of myself and of all other able men to go and rescue her." "You are a fool," said Floyd. He reported this to the Warden.

But the Warden who came next contradicted the Doctor. It was his niece, he said, who told him the story first, whereupon he sent for Pennington. Pennington persisted with some corroborative detail. He went to the Warden one day to borrow a chronicle, that he might settle a dispute with Floyd, "Whether Voltiger was a Saxon or a British King." It was while borrowing this book that he informed the Warden of Floyd's scandalous speech. Here Sir Edward Coke broke in. He had known this Floyd a long time, a pernicious Papist, a barrister it was true, but a wicked fellow. Witness followed witness: a motley crew, gossips, prisoners, bed-makers, a Bachelor of Divinity, testifying both to Floyd's words and to the fact that he had been very merry and drank many healths whenever there came ill news from Prague. The Committee appointed by the House to search Floyd's trunks and pockets, found there Popish books and beads and more Popish books hidden in his bed. The words spoken grew worse in many mouths. "What will the lad do now?" "Now Bess must come home to her father!" Floyd had said when he heard of the Battle of Prague.

By this time the House had worked itself into a very evil temper, and it proceeded to give an instructive display of what a popular body can do when it tries to exercise judicial powers.[1] Sir Robert Phelips would have Floyd ride from Westminster to the Tower, and there be lodged in Little Ease, "With as much pain as he shall be able to endure without loss or danger to his life." This was bad enough, for Little Ease is a horrible dungeon, still to be seen by favoured visitors to the Tower, so constructed that its inmates could not sit or stand or kneel. The terrible cramp produced even by a short incarceration may be better imagined than described. Ravenscroft raised a voice in Floyd's favour, perhaps to save a fellow barrister from punishment unbefitting a gentleman. Let him be fined a thousand pounds and be spared corporal chastisement. Sir Francis Seymour would none of this. Let Floyd go to the Tower at the cart's tail, his doublet off, his beads about his neck, and let him have a lash for every bead. Salter would give him both whipping and Little Ease. Sir Edward Giles would double the whippings, add the pillory, then remit him to the Fleet, for there could be no prison worse than that. Sir Francis Darcy would have a hole burnt through his tongue, since that was the offending member. Sir Jeremy Horsey preferred to slit it or cut it out altogether. Sir Edward Cecil would have him branded on the forehead, a hole burnt also in his tongue, then the whipping, and then Little Ease.

[1] C. J. I. 601, i and ii.

This might have been regarded as sufficient, but it did not satisfy Sir George Goring. He would have his nose, ears and tongue cut off, would whip him at as many stages as he had beads, make him ride to every stage with his face to the horse's tail, and hold the tail in his hand the while, compel him to swallow a bead at every stage, thus whip him to the Tower and there hang him. This last suggestion might almost be deemed to be an ironic parody of the preceding proposals, but the facts of Goring's life do not permit the suggestion.

Sir Edward Sandys calmed the House somewhat in a speech which did him honour. Let them not make a martyr of Floyd by directing their sentence against his religion, let them punish him for his scurrilous disloyalty. Nor let them whip him, for that was the punishment for a slave, and after all Floyd was a gentleman, and not they but only the Earl Marshall could degrade him. Otherwise let him be shamed as much as they liked by pillory and imprisonment.

The sentence was at last settled. Floyd must suffer the pillory three times, must ride from stage to stage on a barebacked horse facing and holding its tail, and must pay one thousand pounds "for false, malicious, and despiteful speeches against the King's daughter and her husband." Such was the punishment to be inflicted on a man who had committed no offence at all except against good taste.

"For the honour of Englishmen, and, indeed, of human nature, it were to be hoped these debates were not truly taken, there being so many motions contrary to the laws of the land, the laws of Parliament and common Justice." So in 1703 wrote Robert Harley of this affair, and so far as common justice goes nothing need be added.

It is scarcely more open to doubt that both the laws of the land and the laws of Parliament were also against the Commons. Such at least was the opinion of James, for on the following day his Chancellor of the Exchequer, on his behalf, thanked them for their loyal zeal, but also put to them these questions. Could they sentence one who was not a Member of their House, and had not offended against any Member of that House? Could they, moreover, sentence a party who denied his offence as Floyd had done, without substantiating his guilt by oath of witnesses? Thirdly, would it not be better if they were to leave Floyd to him, to be dealt with as should be most fitting? He referred to their consideration a precedent of the first year of the reign of Henry IV, wherein the Commons acknowledged that the punishment of evildoers was no part of their functions.[1]

Thus a question was raised to which the Commons did not find the answer easy. Were they to assert that they could exercise jurisdiction over anybody or everybody independently of the House of Lords? They had already in this same session, as will be seen presently, expressly repudiated such jurisdiction in the case of Mompesson.

Noy, Hakewill, and all the best lawyers of the House, knew that such a claim was entirely untenable, and that even if they were to ignore the precedent of 1399 on the ground that it was no Act of Parliament but merely an ordinance, they were none the less estopped, by their own action in Mompesson's case, from raising the issue afresh.

Better than any other, Coke, with his extraordinary knowledge of precedents, knew that the claim was untenable. He did what he could to save the dignity of the House. If they had not jurisdiction for all purposes,

[1] Hallam. C. H. ch. VI.

they had for some, he said, and certainly they were a Court of Record. Coke knew, of course, that neither of these propositions was in dispute, jurisdiction being a matter frequently exercised over Members of the House, and others who infringed their privileges, and the second contention having been recognised by James himself in 1604, on the occasion of the disputed return of Sir Francis Goodwin. Coke went on to admit that the Lords had such jurisdiction.

Answer was made by the Commons to his Majesty that they did not recognise the validity of the Lancastrian precedent, but that they besought him to carry out their sentence on Floyd himself. James remitted the matter to the Lords, who thereupon desired a conference with the Commons; the conference was held on May 5, and Pym was one of the representatives of the Commons. Coke made an unconvincing effort to prove that the insult to the Queen of Bohemia was an insult to the Commons, "For a daughter is part of her father and the King is ever intended to be resident in that House." Such hairsplitting could not be expected to carry conviction, and victory certainly lay with the Lords, though they courteously concealed it under a declaration of *status quo ante*.

They used their victory badly, for they raised poor Floyd's fine from £1,000 to £5,000, declared him for ever infamous and incapable of credence in any Court, ordered him to be whipped from London Bridge to Westminster Hall, and there imprisoned for life. The innocent, if foolish, old man was at least saved the whipping by Prince Charles, at whose instance his father remitted this disgrace. The rest he had to suffer.

The House of Commons had emerged from this affair with no dignity and with a distinct loss of position. It has been premised that the object of sound statesmanship at this time was to bring the autocracy of the Tudor system into harmony with new social aspirations. These were directed to greater political freedom and a more ample participation in the government of the country, and had been growing up under the protection, and in some degree under the direct encouragement of, that efficient Tudor dynasty. It is enough to cite the creation of Lords Lieutenants, the ampler powers entrusted to the Justices of the Peace, and the perpetual tendency of that House to enhance the country gentry at the expense of the great magnates. This favoured gentry now formed the backbone of the House of Commons, and, rightly led, they would have endeavoured to substitute by small changes, pacific and, as far as possible, imperceptible, a legalised and almost mechanical Regal Power for the arbitrary gusts of Henry VIII, or the petulant vacillation of Elizabeth.

To what extent had they done so in the episode now closed? They had alleged for themselves a right of jurisdiction which they had repudiated only two months before. Challenged by the King to substantiate this right, they had, rather than seek the co-operation of the Lords, in whom this right of jurisdiction did actually reside, preferred to request the King to carry out their unjust sentence by a sheer exercise of prerogative. More humiliation was theirs when James, instead of doing so, carelessly threw the whole matter to the discretion of the Lords, and still more when the Lords invited them to a conference wherein even the legal sophistry of Coke was unable to save them from an undignified retreat, which was only prevented from being ludicrous by the courtesy of the Upper House.

Some at least of the Commons were not satisfied with

PYM AND FLOYD

the *impasse* into which they were being led. After the sentence of the House had been passed upon Floyd, Sir Thomas Wentworth, with a foresight worthy of his greatness, desired that a committee should be appointed to collect the reasons of their censure " (because there will be many malevolent eyes on the same) that it may remain clear to posterity." It is here especially incumbent to ask what part Pym took in the sorry business. Reference to the list of his activities in this Parliament, which has been exhaustively compiled from the Journals of the House of Commons, and is printed as Appendix II to this book, will show that he spoke in the case of Floyd. It is reported in the Journals for May 1st with the utmost brevity.[1] " Mr. Pymme—to whip him, except within some reasonable time he pay £1,000 fine." This was uttered immediately after the pacific speech of Sir Edward Sandys mentioned above.

The anonymous author of *"Proceedings and Debates"* of this Parliament, who was himself a member of the House of Commons, omits this altogether and proceeds to the remark of Sir Francis Goodwin,[2] which, according to the Clerk of the House should come next after Pym's. It is possible that Pym did not make a speech, but merely an interjection called forth by the leniency of Sir Edward Sandys, which can scarcely have been agreeable to so unwearied an enemy of the Romanists as he. Further reference to the Appendix will show that he was, with others Committee to meet the Lords in Floyd's case on May 7th, that he spoke on May 16th as seconder to a motion of Mr. Solicitor to the effect " that they had not transferred the matter of Floyd only to the Lords."[3] This is too ambiguous to afford ground for safe conjecture, but on May 18th he spoke against granting the request

[1] C. J. I. 602, i.   [2] P. and D. I. p. 373.   [3] C. J. I. 623, i.

of the Lords to see Floyd's trunk, which, after examination by the Committee, had been sealed up and was then in custody of the House. The message from the Lords originally was, " That since the House had been pleased to refer the judgment of Floyd to them, they desired that the House would be pleased to send up the trunk with power to open it." The Commons instantly protested against the first part of this message, and the Lords as promptly withdrew it, saying that it was a mistake, and all they desired was to have the trunk.

Pym's view is very clearly expressed. It was not fit, he said, that they should send up the trunk. The Commons had it before them when they gave judgment and yet never looked into it. He went on to assert that the Lords could not give judgment in any matter other than a matter of Privilege of their own House, unless the Commons previously asked for such judgment.[1]

Second only to the question of Religion, this third Parliament of James I had at heart certain grievances, of which Monopolies and Illegal Exactions by Law officers were the chief. "*Funditus expellant monopolos et nomopolos,*" exclaimed Coke in a characteristic outburst.[2] The Commons appointed two Committees to deal with them. The first topic presented much difficulty. To grant to a particular person, or group of persons, the exclusive right of manufacturing or of trading in a particular commodity, is in the majority of cases to cause a restraint of trade. This is especially obvious to those who are excluded. What is less obvious is that such a grant may be the best if not the only method of protecting and developing an industry newly invented or newly imported from abroad. We recognise this to-day by the grant of Letters Patent, which create a temporary

[1] C. J. I. 624, ii.   [2] C. J. I. 575, i.

monopoly rigidly limited in area and incidence. The privileges that had been granted by Elizabeth to Versellini, or by James to Zouch, for the making of glass, might be defended on economic grounds, since the Venetian had the secrets of the famous glass works of Murano, and the Englishman had a method whereby he could use in his furnaces coal instead of the wood of rapidly diminishing English forests. The addition of a few idle courtiers to such syndicates of business men merely insured favour in high places, and the smooth working of the concession. Certain of the courtier monopolists, moreover, could fairly claim to be the honey bees of capital. We are so accustomed to-day to the amplitude and the mobility of the capital which enables even dubious schemes to be launched at the expense of public credulity, that it needs an effort to imagine a commercial community to which limited liability companies were unknown. To secure the active participation of men of means in these enterprises was then the only way to make the attempt feasible, and then as now, the only way to secure such participation was the appeal to self-interest.

Here then, as always, to the few who dared and succeeded, came envy and obloquy from those who could not afford to be daring. Just as the magnificent achievements of English agriculture in the eighteenth century were built up by the Bakewells and the Bedfords on the ruin of the English yeomen, just as machinery crushed the deftness of hand of thousands, and just as the vast commercial companies of our own day are built on the bones of the little man, so the monopolist of the sixteenth century triumphed and was hated, yet none the less his triumph was the essential preliminary of progress,—as progress is estimated in a commercial community.

To urge this is not to lay a withered leaf on the

forgotten grave of Mompesson. There are two varieties of monopolists, and he was the wrong one.

It is in the practical application, rather than in the principle, that monopolies are chiefly objectionable. Exclusive trading can only be maintained if interlopers be coerced, and such coercion is often unreasonable and harsh. The monopolist too, unless strictly supervised, is apt to outstep his privileges. One case of those now quoted will suffice. In 1616, Bassano and Vaudrey announced a device by which they could bring salmon and lobsters alive from Ireland to London. Supported by the Fishmongers' Company they obtained a patent, which gave them the exclusive right of conveying such fish from every river and sea which had not hitherto contributed to the London market. Their patent obtained, they troubled Irish waters but little. They found it more profitable to pounce on the poor fisherman as he entered the mouth of the Thames, compel him to hand over his fish at such prices as they chose to give, and themselves to sell it in the City at monopolist charges.[1]

A patent for alehouses had recently come very near to English hearths and homes, and it is small wonder that the House of Commons was appealed to with indignant clamour by the jealous and the ill-used. Even the great Elizabeth had receded before the wrath which monopolies had aroused, and two years before her death she consented to an abolition, and most of them were suppressed, only to spring up afresh after the accession of James.

The Commons needed not to go beyond the walls of their own house to find monopolists. For the Wiltshire borough of Great Bedwin, there had been returned to this Parliament Sir Giles Mompesson, familiar to readers

[1] G. IV. 33, 8.

of Massinger's *New Way to Pay Old Debts*, as Sir Giles Overreach, the extortioner.

Pym represented Calne, another Wiltshire borough, he had also, as we have seen, been Receiver General for the County, and it is, therefore, to be supposed that he knew as much about Mompesson as did any member of the House. By a curious coincidence, Mompesson had for colleague in the representation of Great Bedwin, that Sir Francis Popham with whom Pym was to be brought into hostile relations with respect to the representation of Tavistock in the next Parliament of the reign, which met in 1624, and which proved to be James's last.

The Commons could not have found a more thorough rascal than their colleague Mompesson. He was by marriage a kinsman of Buckingham, and had employed the influence of the Villiers family to push on his knavish but ingenious projects. He held two patents, one for the making of gold and silver thread, the other for licensing inns and alehouses. His frauds in regard to the former were as nothing to his scandalous proceedings in the latter. Small alehouses especially were liable to become the haunt of evildoers, and in the absence of any efficient police system the Justices of the Peace had much difficulty in controlling them. A central Commission to make out licenses to be authorised by the Judges of Assize, which was the scheme suggested by Mompesson, might have been very useful in strengthening their hands. But as the scheme was actually worked it produced nothing but evil. The Commissioners themselves were uncontrolled, Mompesson was their guiding genius, there was no fixed rate of charges for licenses, and it soon became notorious that the most disorderly house could obtain a renewal if Mompesson's charges were paid, while the best possible management was not secure from oppression and confiscation unless sufficient bribes were forthcoming.

One of Mompesson's accomplices in extortion was a knight named Francis Michell. This man had abused his power as a Justice of the Peace in a manner truly disgraceful. "He hath been the moth of the Justices of Peace, who hath eaten into the reputation of them and scandalised the dignity of that worthy office," said Coke. His misdoings were frequently mentioned in the enquiry in which the Commons were now engaged, and their enormity worked the members into a frenzy only less frantic than that which has just been described in the case of Floyd. There was much wild talk, and degrading punishments were suggested. At last a motion of Coke's was carried, " That he be committed to the Tower and declared unfit to remain in the Commission of the Peace."

We pause for a moment in amazement at this sentence. It was moved in the first place by a man who had been Chief Justice, who had before, during and since his occupancy of that high office, been renowned as a meticulous champion of the Common Law, even in its nicest absurdities, as an inveterate opponent of Equity however equitable, because it smacked of the arbitrary and because its foundation was reason and necessity and not the authority of Bracton or the Year Books. On his motion it was carried by a House which did not possess, nor had ever possessed, any power of punishing others than its own members or strangers who had been guilty of contempt. The author of *Proceedings and Debates* writes, " And so Michell was called to the Bar to hear his sentence on his knee—after sentence passed he desired to be heard, but it was denied. Mr. Chancellor of the " Dutchy "—That he might be heard after judgment so as it be an humble suit or anything not concerning the sentence given by the House. Sir Edward Coke—That he ought not to be heard after judgment: and so it was agreed by the vote of the whole House."[1]

When James, in 1603, made his Royal Progress from Scotland to assume the English crown, he hanged at the town of Newark, without any form of trial, a pickpocket who had been caught in the act. Thereupon Sir John Harrington spoke shrewdly, "I hear our new King has hanged one man before he was tried: it is strangely done; now, if the wind bloweth thus, why not a man be tried before he has offended?" Michell's guilt was as unquestionable as the pickpocket's, and Coke and the House of Commons showed themselves as little sensitive to an Englishman's rights before the law as had their Scottish Sovereign eighteen years before. Grave is the judgment pronounced upon them by the great historian of this period when he says, "Never in its worst days was the Star Chamber guilty of a more contemptuous disregard of the barriers which have been thrown up for the preservation of innocence by the laws of England."[2]

The greater villain Mompesson escaped from the clutches of the House. He was committed to the charge of the Sergeant-at-Arms as a measure of precaution, but by a ruse eluded his vigilance and made for the coast. A conference with the Lords and Crown officers led to the issue of a writ for his apprehension and the closing of the ports. It was too late. Mompesson reached France, and the Commons declared his seat vacant.

Why had not the Commons prevented his escape by sending him to the Tower with Michell? He at any rate was a member of their House. If they claimed

[1] P. and D. I. 85.   [2] G. IV. 33, p. 42.

jurisdiction over Michell, who was not, why did they hesitate to exercise it over Mompesson, who was? The reason was that wiser counsels had by this time prevailed. The arbitrary imprisonment of Michell was seen to have been indefensible. Hakewill and Noy had vainly exerted their legal erudition to find a precedent to justify it. They could only report that, without the co-operation of the Lords the House of Commons had no power to punish offences against the State, but only such as were against their own House, such in fact as that for which they had expelled Sheppard.

"The opinion of the Committee is that we must join with the Lords for the punishing of Sir Giles Mompesson, it being no offence against our particular House or any member of it, but a general grievance." Such was the declaration of the Committee announced by Coke himself on Feb. 28th,[1] yet, no later than May 1st, the Commons had abandoned this correct attitude, and in the matter of Floyd laid themselves open to the rebuff from the King and the Lords, which has already been described, on the very ground from which they now receded.

It especially concerns us here to know whether Pym was as inconsistent as others, or whether in this question he already displayed that admirable coolness and judgment which enabled him to steer clear of many a fatal shoal in the terrible days to come. In his action in the case of Floyd there is nothing to which exception can be taken by the most rigid constitutionalist. The interjection, "To whip him, except within some reasonable time he pay £1,000 fine," rests on the authority of the Clerk's Journal only. It is probably correct, for Pym had every opportunity of having it altered had he wished. The very last act of this Parliament was to authorise a

[1] C. J. I. 531, ii.

weighty Committee of twelve, of whom Pym was one, Coke, Hakewill, and Wentworth being others, all together or any four of them " to view the Clerk's book."[1] This is the last entry in the Appendix of Pym's activities in this Parliament. Admitting the exclamation, for it was probably little more, it does not follow that Pym intended the Commons to whip Floyd on their own responsibility and without the concurrence of the Lords; in fact his advice with regard to Floyd's trunk would seem to point directly the other way. Let the Lords understand, he says, that until we ask them they can do nothing in the matter, with an implied aside, any more than we can without them.

If we may assume that in May, 1621, Pym took the correct constitutional view, it is a matter of the first interest to know whether, like Coke, he was taught the lesson by the events of February, or whether he brought to the consideration of the question of the monopolists more coolness, if less erudition, than the great lawyer. Unfortunately his speech gives no indication.

Reference to Appendix II will show that Pym spoke against Mompesson on February 27th, that he was made a Committee to report on him the same day, a sub-Committee on March 6th, with Hakewill and Coke, to consider a particular department of his rascality—concealments. On March 7th, Hakewill desired that some others learned in the law might be joined with him, " Mr. Coke and Mr. Pymme being now his assistants, who are no lawyers,"[2] whereupon seven others were appointed. This comprises the whole of Pym's activity in the matter. His speech is not reported in *Proceedings and Debates*, but takes some fifteen lines in the Journals. He advises the Commons to defer any censure on Mompesson, for as yet

[1] C. J. I. 669, ii. [2] C. J. I. 543, ii.

they have not looked into the uttermost of his faults, and enumerates in his usual methodical manner seven or eight classes of these. He evidently impressed the House, for Sir Nathaniel Rich moved for a select committee to examine into "the residue of his offences mentioned by Mr. Pym, which was ordered to be done by the former committee." The expression of Pym's opinion on this important question is not, then, to be found in the case of Mompesson. But it is found stated in the clearest and most emphatic manner in the speech he made in the matter of Sir John Bennett on April 20th.

It has been said that the second class of grievances which chiefly interested the Commons was that of illegal exactions by Law officers. The question became urgent, partly owing to the conduct of the Referees in the matter of the Monopolies; partly owing to the direct corruption which disfigured the administration of justice.

The Referees were those Judges or Law officers of the Crown to whom was referred the decision as to the legality or otherwise of any proposed patent. It is clear that to be such a Referee at this time was to stand in a slippery place. The patentee came to him, urged by greed or gain, and not infrequently with gifts in his hands; worst of all he was usually supported by the sinister influence of Buckingham, which at this moment meant the influence of the King and of Prince Charles. It must be remembered, too, that the judges were then the servants of the King in no merely conventional sense: they held their office during his pleasure, not as now during good behaviour. Their salaries were paid out of the King's purse and supplemented by the fees of their Court. The political evil of this system will appear only too clearly in the next reign; here it is sufficient to note its connection with the monopolistic system.

The Commons were not much of a mind to enquire thoroughly into their methods and motives. Mr. Speaker was rebuked for alleged intricating or deferring the question. Sir Robert Phelips hoped the unwillingness to name them to the Lords was not in respect of the greatness of their places, and Neville held that their souls made a wilful elopement from their bodies when they made their certificates for Law and Conveniency. He held that the more active Referees were " Criminal, yea Capital offenders."[1]

The moment was critical. If James did not save his Referees, responsibility of Ministers to Parliament and no longer to the Crown would have begun. To save them James, it is said, on the advice of Dean Williams,[2] abandoned Mompesson and Michell to the Commons, and revoked the most obnoxious of the Patents. This diverted the attack on the Referees, but left the Commons no less keen on the quest of corruption in the Courts. They began with certain Registrars of the Court of Chancery, who had entered, as Orders of Court, decisions which they themselves had forged. But they did not long content themselves with such small game. The Chancery had few friends among the Common Law men, who were influential in this assembly both by numbers and by learning. Before many days were over, began that series of accusations of bribery which brought about the downfall of the Chancellor himself. Of the great drama of Bacon's ruin Pym was a silent spectator. It was otherwise when the Commons turned upon Sir John Bennett, a member of their House, who was also a Judge of the Prerogative Court. This was an Ecclesiastical Court, which tried Testamentary cases where the deceased's personality was worth at least £5 in different

[1] C. J. I.   [2] Hacket, Scrinia Reserata, pp. 49-50.

dioceses. In such cases the Archbishop, by specal prerogative, claimed jurisdiction. It was abolished in 1857. Sir John Bennett had been one of the Commissioners in the infamous Essex divorce case, and had done himself the honour of being in the minority of five with Archbishop Abbott, when the majority, including the saintly Andrewes, gave a decision to please the Court. He is said also to have offered £30,000 for the Chancellorship in succession to Ellesmere when Bacon obtained it.

Shortly after the inquiry into Bacon's conduct began, Bennett presented a petition to the House from the Masters in Chancery, relative to their fees, and at the same time disclaimed "either power or will to defend the Chancery." A few weeks later he was hard put to it to defend himself, for he was reported to the House for extortion as well as bribery, for which in due course he was condemned in Star Chamber to a fine of £20,000, the dissolution of Parliament having saved him from impeachment.

The question arose on April 20th, whether the case against Bennett should be submitted at once to the Lords, or whether the Commons should first inquire into the matter themselves; then, if necessary, expel Bennett from their midst and send him to the Lords for judgment. Pym's view was this: The two Houses, he said, were originally one, when they were divided the power was divided also, the power of Enquiry was left to the Commons, that of pronouncing Judgment to the Lords, except in cases where the Commons were equally entitled. The power of execution rested with the King. He advised them to reserve the power of Enquiry wholly to themselves. Let them find out from their own members or anyone who would testify, the truth of the charges against Bennett, and meantime inform the Lords of what they had already established.[1]

Such was Pym's view of the mutual relations of the Crown and the two Houses as they appeared to him in 1621. It is necessary now to see how, by his support of the claim of the Commons to participate in the highest affairs of State, he thus early made himself a marked man at Court.

[1] C. J. I. 583, i.

CHAPTER III

THE THIRD PARLIAMENT OF JAMES I (*continued*)

JAMES had watched with growing dissatisfaction the vigorous proceedings of his third House of Commons. From his point of view they had been busy and to spare, but they had not delivered him from that entanglement into which his own Spanish policy and the ambition of his son-in-law had led him. Five days after his speech to them at the opening of Parliament, when the Commons met for the first time for the transaction of business, Mr. Secretary Calvert at once reminded them why they had been called together. The King, he said, expected a supply in these his urgent necessities, and especially to recover the patrimony of his children. This he had resolved to regain, if not by treaty then by the sword. Not a moment could be lost, for of that patrimony Spinola had already conquered everything but Heidelberg and a few other places. Bohemia was defeated, and all the confederate Princes and countries had fallen off and were reduced to the Emperor's obedience.[1]

Calvert's melancholy statement was not without effect. Said Sir John Davys, " All men run together to quench a fire. The Palatinate is on fire. . . . Religion is on fire, all other countries are on fire." He moved for giving that very day. Sir George Moore preferred to have something for his money. Supply and Grievances should go hand in hand together. Sir Robert Phelips noted that the Roman Catholics were gathering in great numbers in London. He hinted that possibly they were preparing another Gunpowder Plot. This alarming suggestion

[1] C. J. I. 508, ii.

must have made members shift in their seats and think uneasily of the cellars beneath them. Sir Edward Coke took up the congenial topic. "I and Popham were thirty days in examination of the Gunpowder Plot at the Tower. The root of it was out of all the countries belonging to the Pope, and Faux repented him that he had not done it. God then, and in 1588, delivered us for religion's sake." His advice was that they should review their grievances against "the enemies of God and us: Jesuits, Seminaries, and Popish Catholics." It was decided that the various questions which had been raised should be referred to a committee of the whole House.[1]

Ten days later the Commons took the question of Supply in hand. The Army Council had decided that to maintain 30,000 men for the defence of the Palatinate, the least force which would make effective the intervention of England, £250,000 would be needed at once, and in addition a yearly vote of £900,000 for their pay and expenses. No Parliament had yet made in any one year a larger grant than £140,000. James saw the impossibility of obtaining such a gigantic sum, and instructed Calvert to state that 30,000 men would be needed, and that at least £500,000 would be required for their support.[2]

Seldom had James' boasted Kingcraft showed to less advantage. Had he flung the terrific figures straight at the Commons and bade them give it or leave it he would have gained one of two things: either they would have given the money or they would have learnt to hold their tongues. They would at least have been made aware that the baiting at once of Emperor, Pope and King of Spain, was like to be a costlier game than the torture of old Floyd. James let his opportunity slip. He had not only thus grossly under-estimated the expense

[1] C. J. I. 510, i. [2] G. IV. 33, pp. 31-2 note.

of the contingent but he gave to the Commons no indication whatever of the use to which he meant to put that army if he had it.

Left thus to their own surmises the Commons gave him two subsidies which would amount to some £160,000. For what purpose ? For intervention in the Palatinate ? Scarce a man in the Commons but must have recognised its inadequacy for that. From Sir Edward Coke's Report as given in *Proceedings and Debates* it is clear that they deliberately let the question of the Palatinate alone and gave only for James's immediate needs. " That there was given free gift of two subsidies, which was given, none gainsaying, and freely, not on any consideration or condition for or concerning the Palatinate."[1]

The Subsidy Bill was carried unanimously in the Commons on March 18th, and was sent to the Lords. It was on March 12th, when it was ordered that the Bill should be engrossed, that Pym made his only speech on this business. A question had arisen whether the Subsidy Bill should go alone to his Majesty or whether some other Bills for the removal of grievances should accompany it. A brief entry in the Commons Journal reports: " Mr. Pymme : Not to hinder the Subsidy : but yet to prepare some Bills, to go with it."[2] Pym cared as little as did Wentworth for James's foreign entanglements and financial shifts. Both were a hindrance to domestic reforms, and the sooner they were rid of them the better, even if it cost two subsidies.

Would it have been possible at this time for James, by greater candour, to have enlisted the intelligence of the House for foreign affairs as for domestic ? It is doubtful. " Black and white were the only colours on their canvas. To them every Protestant was a model of saintly virtue :

[1] P. and D. I. 50.   [2] C. J. I 550, i.

every Catholic a dark conspirator against the peace and religion of the world. Of the weakness and rashness of Frederick, of the low intrigues by which the election had been preceded, of the anarchical character of the Bohemian aristocracy, they had simply no conception whatever. . . ." "They believed, too, that the power of the Imperialist Party in Germany could only be made available for evil by the support of Spain." As for the King of Spain, they saw him "not as he really was, anxious to avoid war, hesitating to spend his money, and shrinking from doing anything which would split up Europe into two hostile camps." No; they saw in him the old Elizabethan conception of his father Philip II, "The aspirant by force or fraud to universal Empire for his own bad purpose; the restless, ambitious, insatiable vicegerent of Satan upon Earth."[1] Thus does Gardiner sum up the political attitude of the Commons of 1621 in regard to foreign affairs. It was the penalty which James paid for his temperament, perhaps for his character, that he allowed a humdrum fribble like Buckingham to sway his counsels, and to forget that he had at his side the acute intellect and the experience acquired in the Courts of Europe, of John, Lord Digby, afterwards Earl of Bristol.

The good temper which the two subsidies had induced in his Majesty was only likely to last as long as did those supplies, and in the desperate state of James's finance that could only be a short time. On April 20th, his Majesty suggested to the Commons that the two subsidies were already spent, and that he hoped for more. The only information vouchsafed by him was that he was still negotiating for peace, but meantime wished to prepare for war by the purchase of arms. The Commons ignored the hint absolutely. They continued their work

[1] G. IV. 33, pp. 25-6.

in the manner already described, until, on May 28th, they received a message from the King bidding them wind up their affairs within a week, in view of the adjournment upon which he had resolved.

His reasons, as given by the Lord Treasurer, were that the season of the year and the continual concourse of people might cause infection. Moreover the country gentlemen were needed in their own counties as Lieutenants and Justices of the Peace. Adjournment, not Prorogation, was proposed. They could therefore resume their interrupted efforts when they reassembled.

This was disconcerting. Even Sir Edward Sandys lost his usual equable temper. He saw the House was full of grief and fear, himself he had never been so full of either. Dangerous, indeed, was the state of the country. Their religion was rooted out of Bohemia and Germany and would soon be rooted out of France, if God did not miraculously defend them. Trade had decayed, and compared with that all other grievances of the kingdom were but trifles. To this the Commons Journals add: " Sithence his Majesty's pleasure for this Recess, by an adjournment to rest in it. To set in order and conclude now as much as we can. The Eyes of all England, and the Cries of all England upon this Parliament."[1] At a conference with the Lords it was decided that appeal to the King should be made. All they obtained was the offer to pass such Bills as they had ready to be sent up. This would involve a Prorogation instead of a mere Adjournment.

The fiercer spirits of the House were aroused. Sir Benjamin Rudyerd, indeed, expressed the wish that they might so part out of this House like a sweet odour ; after all, they were much bound to the King for his grace and favour in giving them leave to touch businesses of a high

[1] C. J. I. 629, ii.

nature, and to meddle with great persons on whom they had passed judgment, " which judgment is better far than many good laws, for laws will fall asleep when the fright of those judgments will keep men awake to do their duties."[1] The impetuous Phelips would none of this philosophic resignation. "I know not whether I shall ever be of this House again or no, and therefore I will now speak freely my conscience." Papists were never more impudent and daring, soon they would equal the Protestants in number. This part of Christendom never received a greater blow than in the loss of Bohemia. Were they to accept such a blow? For the Commonwealth, Parliament was the only Physician to cure the desperateness of the disease. His Majesty had promised to remedy the grievances of their hearts. What was he doing now but retarding those remedies? What were they to do?

Plain speaking indeed; perhaps too plain for policy. So thought the greatest Englishman there present, so also thought John Pym.

Sir Thomas Wentworth spoke directly after the fiery Phelips, and he answered his question. He believed the King's resolve to be immovable. Let them make up their minds to do nothing, or to do all they could in the time allowed them. He rejected the former alternative. To do nothing would leave an ill understanding between the King and his people. Let them rather urge the Lords to pass the Bills they had in hand as soon as they could. So they would have something to show to the people "who have paid their money." Twelve Bills at least he thought could be rushed through. Pym spoke in the same strain in a speech not reported in *Proceedings and Debates*, but summarised in the Commons Journals.[2] He advised the House to make the best use of the time,

1 P. and D. II., p. 123.   2 C. J. I. 631-2.

whether on Bills or Judgments, or Grievances. Let them seek a conference with the Lords and urge them to review, by means of an Ordinance of Parliament, those Judgments or Decrees which have passed by Corruption.

Wentworth's colleague, the Secretary of State, Calvert, also soothed the House. After all it was the Prerogative of the Crown to appoint the end as also the beginning of a Parliament. True, the state of Religion was dangerous indeed, but would their disunion amend it? "This Parliament hath married the King and the people by a right understanding of each other, and cursed be such as seek to part it."

"At this wish of Mr. Secretary all the House cried Amen."[1] This was the morning of Wednesday, May 30th; in the afternoon Pym further advised that in the conference then to be held they should first consider what could be prepared; if that could not be, then how they might best satisfy the people and the honour and good of King and of Kingdom. Also they should consider whether their Recess would be preferably by Prorogation, as in the King's second offer, or by Adjournment as in his first. It would also be for them to consider whether the adjournment should be by commission or effected by themselves. The Commons decided upon an adjournment as originally proposed. A Prorogation would have been necessitated by the passing of Bills, and a Prorogation as then understood, would have necessitated the resumption of their work *de novo*. When they reassembled the Lords, indeed, suggested a way out of this difficulty by means of a Short Act, but the Commons, probably wisely, declared that the time allowed them would only admit of hurried work, and adhered to their choice of Adjournment.

Before they separated the Commons unanimously

[1] P. and D. II., p. 125.

resolved, on the motion of Sir James Perrott,[1] to make a declaration concerning the recovery of the Palatinate " that the drawing back in so good a cause should not be charged on their slackness." Sir Edward Cecil expressed the general enthusiasm when he said that he thought this declaration came from Heaven, and would work better effects with the enemy than would ten thousand troops on the march. The Declaration asserted that they, the Commons in Parliament, assembled with the unanimous consent of themselves and of the whole body of the Kingdom, whom they represented, declared to His most Excellent Majesty and to the whole world their hearty grief and sorrow for the present estate of the King's children abroad, and the general afflicted estate of the true professors of the same Christian religion, professed by the Church of England, in foreign parts. Should His Majesty's endeavours to procure their peace and safety by treaty be unavailing, they would, at His Majesty's invitation, be ready at the utmost of their lives and fortunes, and by the help of Almighty God, to assist him to effect it by the sword. " Then," writes an eye-witness, " Sir Charles Coke, one of the King's Privy Council, with tears in his eyes, standing up, said the prayer (which is in the Common Prayer Book) for the King and his issue ; adding only to it ' and defend them from their cruel enemies.' "[2]

Then the Speaker standing up adjourned the Parliament, saying, " This House doth adjourn itself till the 14th of November next, then to meet in this Place again in Parliament, at nine of the Clock."

Before the Commons met again certain appointments had been made which were notable in themselves, and had grave consequences.

[1] C. J. I. 639.   R. 1, 36.   [2] P. and D. II. 174.

The ambitious Welshman, Williams, received first the Bishopric of Lincoln, and then the Great Seal. He was the last ecclesiastic to hold that high office. It was an amazing appointment, and drew from Bacon the caustic comment, "I had thought that I should have known my successor." Williams retained also his Deanery of Westminster.

Shortly afterwards William Laud passed from the Deanery of Gloucester to the Bishopric of St. Davids. While the fortunes of these able men, soon to be bitter enemies, rose high, disaster befel John Abbot, Archbishop of Canterbury. After consecrating a Chapel on Lord Zouch's estate at Bramshill, he was taken out into the park and there shot at a deer. Unfortunately he missed the deer and killed a keeper, who was passing unseen along a sunken path. "No one but a fool or a knave would think the worse of him. It might be any man's case." So said James, but both Williams and Laud were content to place themselves in one or other of his Majesty's categories, for they declined to be consecrated by a man whose hands were stained in blood. Of Abbot, Clarendon wrote in his History, "He had been Head or Master of one of the poorest Colleges in Oxford, and had learning sufficient for that province. He was a man of very morose manners and a very sour aspect, which, in that time, was called gravity . . . . and considered Christian religion no otherwise than as it abhorred and reviled popery, and valued those men most who did that most furiously."[1] With this ungracious Master of University College, the learned and pushing President of "St. John's College, in Oxford, the worst endowed at that time of any in that famous University,"[2] could have nothing in common except the poverty of their respective

[1] Cl. I. 185 and 187. [2] Cl. I. 189.

foundations. This mutual animosity is to be noted here, for there is little doubt that Abbot, rapidly advanced to London and to Canterbury, did much to instil into James that distrust of Laud which he is known to have entertained.

Not only were the Churchmen promoted. In July the London Merchant, Lionel Cranfield, was raised to the peerage. He had been an edifying example of the industrious apprentice, and his honour had been fully earned by his strenuous efforts to bring order into the King's finances.

Unfortunately James's activity during the recess was not confined to honouring his supporters. On June 16th, he arrested Southampton, Sir Edwin Sandys and John Selden. Selden was not yet a member of Parliament, but the offence of all three was believed to be that they had spoken too freely in connection with the events of the last session. No act could be better calculated to throw cold water on the enthusiasm displayed in the Declaration of the Commons, which their grateful sovereign had just caused to be translated into the chief European tongues.

Parliament met again for business, not on the 14th but on the 20th of November, the King having thought it well to change the date. Williams, the Episcopal Lord Keeper, addressed them on behalf of His Majesty, who was absent through sickness, in a speech which he himself described as " the natural bird, as it came from the nest, without so much as a feather of my own invention." This natural bird declared its chief want to be hunger, and urged the postponement of all business except Supply. Digby followed, " The one man in England who could avert, if yet it were possible, the evil to come."[1]

[1] G. IV. 39, p. 232.

At close quarters, in Vienna and in Madrid, John Digby had been able to estimate the present power of that Hapsburg policy which seventy years ago had clutched England into its tentacles by its usual weapon of marriage, and from which it was Elizabeth's eternal glory to have extricated her. He was able to estimate, as the Commons could not estimate, the diminution of Hapsburg power when the Imperial Crown of Charles V passed, not to his son Philip but to his brother Ferdinand. He could calculate, as James could not, as Gondomar took care he should not, the precise weight of Spain in the counsels of the Empire. He knew, in short, exactly that which the Commons from their position could not, and James from his temperament would not know.

Digby told the Houses of his own Mission to Vienna, how he had obtained a provisional promise from the Emperor, that the Palsgrave should be restored; how the Duke of Bavaria had persuaded the Emperor to withdraw his promise; how the same Duke was holding the Palatinate, and that the Lower Palatinate was preserved only by the efforts of Sir Horace Vere and his English volunteers. In conclusion, to support Vere and the mercenary soldiers of Count Mansfeld, and the additional forces necessary, it was held " by some commissioners best experienced and known in martial affairs . . . that to maintain an army one year would require the sum of £900,000, which he leaveth to our consideration."[1]

The truth was out at last, but King James, who ought to have spoken it, remained at Newmarket waiting to see what he should see. It was not to be supposed that the imprisonment of Sandys during the recess could pass unnoticed, though he, with his fellow-prisoners, had

[1] P. and D. II. 189.

been set free in July on the advice of Williams to Buckingham. Illness prevented his attendance on November 22nd, but Digges raised the question, and the House was only partially mollified by Calvert's explanation that his imprisonment had not been inflicted for anything which he had said or done in the House. It was ordered that the Secretary's words should be entered upon the Clerk's book.

In the debate which followed, opinion was almost unanimous for war, and war on a large scale. On the first day Phelips alone was for refusing Supply. Him Calvert's reply struck heavily. "It is said our King's sword hath been too long sheathed, but they who shall speak to defer a supply seek to keep it longer in the scabbard."[1] On the following day he found a stalwart supporter in Sir Edward Coke, but neither of them could move the House, dissatisfied though it was, from the correct attitude, and it was resolved that Supply should be made.

It is during this debate that Pym for the first time stands out in debate as a new leader of men.

Three speeches were composed by him on this "Great Subject," as it was fitly called by the Commons. The first he delivered on November 27, and it is reported in the *Commons Journals*[2] and in *Proceedings and Debates*. The second was spoken in a committee of the whole House on the following day, and the third he wrote for the King's own inspection in circumstances now to be described. The second and the third are reported only in *Proceedings and Debates*.

In the first speech Pym argued that if the Commons were to give nothing, those hopes of the King which he had founded on their promise would be frustrated : the

[1] P. and D. II. 214.   [2] C. J. I. 647, ii.

loss of the Palatinate would be followed by discouragement of the King's allies and friends, and disherison of his son-in-law. On the other hand, if they were contented merely to give, they must look for discontent in the people, who were as yet unrelieved of their burdens and who were affrighted for their religion. Then, in his usual methodical manner, by means of three "branches," he propounded a middle course. First, as regarded the promise expressed in their declaration there were three reasons why they should not conclude upon Supply in the manner just urged. In these money matters the enemy was stronger than they; again, on the plan proposed they would be debarred from enriching themselves on the spoil of the enemy, which in every war is allowed to subjects. Moreover the people were in fear because the laws against the Papists had not been enforced. This brought him to his second branch. He would move that they should have a session devoted to Supply, wherein in one day they should declare what they would give, and in the second place that they should petition the King to leave it to the Parliament to provide some course of execution of laws against Papists.

Last branch of all. He would move for an association to be devised for the defence of the King's person and religion, and this oath of association all must take before they were admitted to any places of government in the Commonwealth. "Then to expedite the Bills of most necessity: and to have a short Bill to continue the rest both public and private *in statu quo nunc*, till the King call us again, which methinketh will not be long."

It is needless to comment on the practical sagacity of this speech. Every line of it testifies to the clearness of observation, the recognition of aims, and the adaptation of means to ends which characterise pre-eminent men of affairs. Well might the Court scent danger, not least in the last significant phrase.

In committee next day Pym spoke again.[1] He praised his Majesty's affections, but through malice the adverse party had made ill use of them. Four of these affections he noted especially. First, his Majesty's mercy, which made him loath to force men's consciences or have any man suffer for his religion. Hence the Papists had wrought their ill ends. He would have the Houses petition the King that he might understand that the execution of the laws against them does not force their consciences but prevents mischiefs. He would have the Papists used like madmen, and all dangerous weapons taken from them. Secondly, his Majesty's lenity. He would have his Majesty to make himself the object of this lenity, and not the Papists. Third, his Majesty's too great bounty, " whereby they have by importunity obtained many advantages against our religion and too large a liberty for the recusants here." He desired that the King should be urged not to admit Papists to come so near him to work on his affections.

Pym went on to " speak of some things to be offered to the King's Judgment and Reason." The Pope hath blown over the fire of his Romish religion into this Kingdom, and the Popish party here are as tinder ready to take fire. The Papists flock to the Spanish Ambassador's, which is a thing in foreign parts not permitted, and whereof all are very jealous. He would have them beseech the King that there might be a commission from his Majesty to some members of both Houses to see that the laws of England were executed against the Papists.

James might well regard these two speeches as a personal attack, and indeed they were little else. Behind

[1] P. and D. II. 228-30.

the customary expressions of a subject's loyal deference, Pym had aimed directly at his complaisance to Gondomar and his confidence in Buckingham, who had for the moment constituted himself the ally of the Spanish Ambassador, and the patron of the English Catholics. Still more, he had aimed a shaft at James's Spanish policy. He had proposed that a committee of both Houses should be allowed to do that which James had not done. He had indicated not obscurely that Supply should only accompany Bills and he had added, as if to drive all home, his conviction that the King would soon need their services again. The speeches might be put thus summarily: Want of confidence—committee of management—power of the purse.

James was not slow to take up the challenge. Pym was informed by the Lord Treasurer and the Chancellor of the Exchequer that his Majesty was displeased with him by occasion of some reports touching a speech in Parliament, and had commanded him to deliver a copy of it in writing. Pym replied that he could not do this absolutely and precisely because he had written no part of the speech beforehand and had no notes or memorials of it except such as remained in his mind. He desired that he might be allowed to repeat his speech from memory in presence of his Majesty.

The cool courage of this request is amazing. Dramatic and pregnant indeed would the moment have been had the Lord's Anointed condescended to allow the ex-Receiver of Wiltshire to expound to him the lines of religious and national policy which it behoved him to follow. Probably an explosion of royal temper, like to that which had shattered the Hampton Court Conference, would have cut short the eloquent prolixity of Pym, but it would scarcely have abated his complacency or his convictions one jot. "By which petition he did not seek to decline the fulfilling of your princely command but that . . . if any of his words should be ambiguous or subject to any misrepresentation he might be present to give an exposition of them according to his own meaning."

Pym's request was not granted. "But having received from your Majesty a second and more strict command, in dutiful obedience thereunto he humbly beseecheth your favourable acceptance of the declaration following : . . ."

This consists of a lengthy summary of the two speeches, and in it two passages are worthy of note :

"The aim of the laws, in the penalties and restraints of Papists, was not to punish them for believing and thinking : but that they may be disabled to do that which they think and believe they ought to do."[1] The argument for political intolerance of religious parties could scarcely be put more clearly, and Pym's biographer has but to show that his dealings with Papists conformed to it. Can this be done ?

The second passage is this : "If they (the Papists) should once obtain a connivance, they will press for a toleration, from thence to an equality, from an equality to a superiority, from a superiority to an extirpation of all contrary religions."

It has been well said of Pym that his strength lay chiefly in his faculty of appreciating the ideas and the prejudices of the ordinary man, and of transmuting them into such a logical and attractive presentment that each of his hearers could feel in them kinship if not paternity. In the House of Commons the justification of the leader is the exclamation of the follower, "Just what I have always said." Pym was among the greatest as he was

[1] P. and D. II. 234.

among the first of our Parliamentarians to show that not intellect but enlightened common sense is the quality which there carries furthest. What he had just said was that which those of his hearers who had been born and bred in the epoch of Philip II and of Pius V would naturally and properly believe. Of such men Pym became leader because he was primarily their interpreter. In his proposal that all loyal subjects should take an oath of association to defend his Majesty's person, and to execute the penal laws against Papists, Pym was again falling back on an Elizabethan precedent—that association to protect the Queen from assassination, which had received Parliamentary sanction in 1584, the year of Pym's own birth. It anticipated, too, the decisive moment of the civil war when the fruition of Pym's tortuous diplomacy was apparent, two months before his death, in the acceptance of the Solemn League and Covenant with the Scots. The organisation of public opinion, whether in nation, in army, or in mob, so that it became a power that could strike, and no longer a confused noise without, is the real explanation of his wonderful success and of his instantaneous eclipse.

The discussion on the proposed Petition went on; Weston, Chancellor of the Exchequer, uttered a warning. Had that House ever begun treaties of war, marriage, and religion which had ended well or pleased Kings? He would have them search warily for precedents, lest, instead of a remedy, they should provoke his Majesty's displeasure by dealing with things of so high a nature without any warrant from him. Phelips would have it go on. Mary's marriage with Philip had been debated in that House; there was precedent enough. Moreover his Majesty, in his speech at Whitehall, had invited them to speak freely of the grievances of the Kingdom. Sir

THE PETITION 67

Thomas Crew wondered at the spiritual madness of such as will fall in love with the Romish harlot now she is grown so old a hag. He was more illuminating when he maintained that it is one thing to assume authority or interest, another to show humbly, by petition, what may be prejudicial to the King and State. Mr. Solicitor Heath advised that a clause should be inserted in the Petition expressly declaring that the House did not seek to prejudice or blemish, in the least point, his Majesty's royal prerogative.[1]

The Petition was at last completed. Pym was of the committee which drew it up, and it is easy to see the hand of the author of the Grand Remonstrance in the document. It was divided into Causes, Effects, and Remedies. The Causes were, "The vigilancy and ambition of the Pope of Rome and his dearest son : the one aiming at as large a temporal monarchy as the other at a spiritual supremacy." Their aggressions by means of ambassador's chapels, education of children of Papists, and dispersal of Popish books ; the disasters to Protestantism and to the King's children abroad ; and the proposed Spanish marriage at home. The Effects, " It hath a restless spirit and will thrive by these gradations : if it once gets but a connivance, it will press for a toleration. If that should be obtained they must have an equality, from thence they will aspire to superiority, and will never rest till they get a subversion of the true religion." For Remedies : let his Majesty take his sword in hand, strike down his children's enemies abroad, and crush the Popish faction at home by vigorous exercise of the penal laws, and " that to frustrate their hopes for a future age our most noble prince may be married to one of our own religion."

[1] P. H. I. 1322.

The clause of Effects sufficiently indicates the mouth that inspired, if not the hand that drafted this memorable document. Not only James, but Gondomar also, was watching the Commons closely. He wrote to the Infanta Isabella that at this juncture he had written from London to James at Newmarket and also to Buckingham that had he not been assured that his Majesty would punish "*la sedicion y maldad* . . . *en este Parlamento*" he would have left the Kingdom already. "This it would have been my duty to do as you would have ceased to be a King here, and as I have no army here at present to punish these people myself."

For the credit of a King of England it would be pleasant to believe that Gondomar never wrote this last sentence, and that it is a mere braggadocio to please his correspondent, or at least that it occurred in the letter to Buckingham and not in that to the King. But the great historian who gives us our knowledge of the letter from his researches in the Simancas MSS. does not suggest so gratifying a solution.[1]

On December 3rd it was resolved, without one negative, " upon question that this Remonstrance or Petition . . . be presented to his Majesty " on the motion of Sir Nathaniel Rich, to whose intimate association with Pym's designs reference has been made before. It was also decided " To send to-morrow morning—twelve sufficient : Some of the Privy Council with some other Courtiers." Rich also moved significantly " to spare all those which drew the Petition."

Pym then proposed that the Speaker should attend early next morning in order that the Remonstrance and Petition with the Instruction fair written might be read in the House.[2]

[1] G. IV. 39, 249.   [2] C. J. I. 657, ii.

THE KING'S ANGER

This was done when the House met at eight o'clock next day, and then the Commons considered the less exciting question of wool fells, wool yarns, and fuller's clay.

At this moment occurred a startling interruption, recorded in the *Commons Journals* with a brevity that is almost dramatic. "Mr. Secretary delivereth to Mr. Speaker a Letter even now received from his Majesty, directed to Mr. Speaker: which Mr. Speaker desired liberty first to read privately to himself: and was yielded unto. And then he read it publickly, dated 30th December, from Newmarket. It was then secondly read by Mr. Speaker."[1]

"To our trusty and well-beloved Sir Thomas Richardson, Knight, Speaker of our Commons' House of Parliament."

"Mr. Speaker, We have heard by divers reports to our great grief, that the far distance of our person at this time from our high court of Parliament, caused by our want of health, hath emboldened some fiery and popular spirits in our House of Commons to debate and argue publicly on matters far beyond their reach or capacity: and so tending to our high dishonour and to the trenching upon our prerogative royal. You shall therefore acquaint that House with our pleasure, that none therein shall presume to meddle with anything concerning our government or mysteries of State, namely not to speak of our dearest son's match with the daughter of Spain nor to touch the honour of that king or any other our friends and confederates . . ."

He went on to speak of Sir Edward Sandys' imprisonment. "You shall resolve them in our name that it was not for any misdemeanour of his in Parliament. But to put them out of doubt of any question of that nature

[1] C. J. I. 658, i.

that may arise among them hereafter you shall resolve them in our name, that we think ourself very free and able to punish any man's misdemeanours in Parliament as well during their sitting as after, which we mean not to spare hereafter upon any occasion of any man's insolent behaviour there that shall be ministered unto us." [1]

As to the Petitions, if in any of them they had touched upon any of those points he had mentioned, " you shall tell them that except they reform it before it comes to our hands we will not deign the hearing or answering of it."

As for the rest of the session let them look to it. " If good laws be not made at this time for the weal of the people the blame shall only, and most justly, lie upon such turbulent spirits, as shall prefer their particular ends to the weal of this Kingdom and Commonwealth. And so we bid you farewell."

When this royal onslaught had been digested by a second reading, the spirits of the House, turbulent or otherwise, may well have been depressed. Pym may have stared at Rich and Rich at Pym, but neither had anything to say. But it needed more than a scolding from James to subdue Sir Robert Phelips. He was the first to break the silence, and this time very sensibly. Let them recall their messengers to the King and rise at once and meditate till morning, " that then we may discharge our duty to his Majesty, and as true Englishmen." This was ordered to be done, and " upon the point of eleven of the clock " the House arose.

James's open attack on the immunity of speakers of Parliament had, no doubt, been the result of a sparkle of temper fanned by Gondomar and Buckingham which burst into expression when he saw, in advance, the advice

[1] P. and D. II. 277. R. I. 43-4.

the Commons were about to present to him, which ran directly counter to his Spanish policy. None the less he had raised an issue which the Commons could not allow to pass by default.

Delbridge began the debate next day "after a long silence in the House."[1] He would as willingly hang under the gallows as fry over a faggot. "So let us go to the King again and again with our Petition as we do to God, and no doubt but his Majesty will hear us at length." Phelips followed him. They had given his Majesty one subsidy more contrary to the provision of the last Act. What, then, was the cause of this soul-killing letter? He professed he had no other desire but God's glory, and the assurance of his Majesty and his posterity: they must search for precedents and endeavour to stand right in his Majesty's opinion. Sir Thomas Wentworth was for a committee of the whole House. Sir Francis Seymour held that the King was misled by some about him, "yea, by some members of our own House."

Mr. Speaker himself took the unusual step of moving for a committee, first to set the House right with his Majesty, secondly to justify their proceedings, third to maintain their privileges. It was so ordered, and the debate closed for the day with a phrase or two by Pym "to cast balm, to heal the wound, and not to make it wider." This phrase is all that the Commons' Journals ascribe to Pym,[2] but he spoke again in a committee of the whole House on the same day, of which Noy, much against his will, had been compelled to be Chairman. *Proceedings and Debates* reports him thus: "Mr. Pymme saith that the words of fiery, popular and turbulent are laid by his Majesty on the whole House; for, since we have not punished or questioned any such, but (as the

[1] P. and D. II. 279-80. [2] C. J. 659, i.

letter saith) been led by their Propositions, it is the act of the whole House. He desireth a petition may be from us to the King to know who his Majesty hath been informed, those fiery turbulent spirits are, that we may justify ourselves and clear the House of the taint of those words." [1]

Three days later the Explanatory Petition was ready. There had been a long discussion the previous day whether Mr. Speaker should go to the King or whether the Petition should be sent by the messengers appointed already. Noy suggested the Speaker, Phelips assented because this was the matter of greatest importance that ever was in that House.

Sir Nathaniel Rich cried that if he had a thousand voices they all should be for Mr. Speaker to go. Mr. Secretary Calvert, on the other hand, said if he had a thousand voices Mr. Speaker should have none, for his absence would hinder the end of the session and the passing of Bills. This common-sense view appealed to Pym. For once against Rich he said that there would be danger in discontinuing Parliament; they did not know when the King would give audience to Mr. Speaker—it was better not to let him go. Others followed till Sir Thomas Wentworth, always impatient of fruitless talk, urged that the question be put: should he go or not? Mr. Speaker himself desired, in respect of the honour of the House, they should not put that upon him which was never put upon any Speaker before. So it was resolved that the former messengers should go. Forster says that Pym was one of them. [2] He was not. In the *Commons* [2] *Journals* for December 3rd the names of all twelve are given. [3] None of the protagonists of the debate are there, they were officials and courtiers, among them

[1] P. and D. II. 284. [2] F. P. 20. [3] C. J. I. 657, ii.

being Buckingham's own brother, Sir Edward Villiers, who was ordered to go in place of Sir Francis Fane.[1] In his attempt to drag Pym into dramatic prominence Forster has belittled the diplomacy both of the man and of the House.

Though he was not present when the King received it, Pym had a considerable share in drawing up the Explanatory Declaration, for on December 8th, " the last petition agreed upon yesterday being found, by the Clerk, to be defective in the latter part and therefore left uningrossed: Mr. Pymme and some others, having perused it, and reformed it in a paper, the old and new were read over by Mr. Pymme. But the House not allowing it, divers Gentlemen were appointed to retire to the Committee chamber to perfect the same, which accordingly was done: and being brought back and twice read by the Clerk was ordered to be engrossed with the residue."[2]

Probably much to their relief, the Commissioners found James in a jovial mood when they appeared before him at Newmarket. "Stools for the Ambassadors," he cried ironically when they were introduced. He refused to look at the original petition, for to do that would be to give the lie to himself. The Explanatory Petition he answered at length. Indeed there was little in it to which he could take exception. It besought him that he would not give credit to private reports against all or any members of their House. He had himself commended the Palatinate to their consideration: in that consideration they had believed the penal laws and the Spanish marriage to be involved. They acknowledged without reserve that it was for him and not for them to determine peace or war, and to select a bride for his son.

[1] C. J. I. 661, i. [2] Ibid.

They looked for no answer to their petition except as to Recusants and the passing of Bills. Then they approached the dangerous topic. " Your Majesty by the general words of your letter seemeth to restrain us from intermeddling with matters of Government or particulars which have their motion in Courts of Justice . . . whereas your Majesty's letter doth seem to abridge us of the ancient liberty of Parliament for freedom of speech, jurisdiction and just censure of the House . . . wherein we trust in God we shall never transgress the bounds of loyal and dutiful subjects : a liberty which we assure ourselves so wise and so just a King will not infringe, the same being our undoubted right and inheritance received from our ancestors and without which we cannot freely debate nor clearly discern of things in question before us . . . we . . . beseech Your Majesty to renew and allow the same, and thereby take away the doubts and scruples your Majesty's late letter to our Speaker hath brought upon us." [1]

The King's answer was reported to the House by the Chancellor of the Exchequer on December 14th. Their complaints of the danger of religion within the kingdom, tacitly implied ill government by him in that respect. He was an old and experienced King, needing no cautions against false reports. Divers of their own members could tell them so if they did not prefer to listen to " some tribunitial orators amongst you." As to their protestation that they had not usurped upon his prerogative it was as if a robber should take a man's purse and then profess he meant not to rob him. Again they said their advice about the Spanish match and the war was involved in the question of Supply for that war. That was as if the merchant who lent the money for a war should

[1] P. and D. II. 292-3.

thereby be made Commander-in-chief. "The beginning of this miserable war which hath set all Christendom on fire, was not for Religion but only caused by our son-in-law's hasty and rash decision, following evil counsel, to take to himself the Crown of Bohemia . . . to conclude this point, this unjust usurpation of the Crowns of Bohemia and Hungary from the Emperor hath given the Pope and all that party too fair a ground and opened too wide a gate for curbing and oppressing of many thousands of our religion in divers parts of Christendom." [1]

He was engaged so far in that match with Spain that he could not in honour go back unless the King of Spain did not perform what was expected from him. Let him marry his son, they said, to a Protestant—he could not say Princess, for he knew none of these fit for him. No foreign Prince would treat with him at all if they learnt that he must needs submit his negotiations to his Parliament. As to Religion he would see to that, but not by undertaking a public war of religion through all the world at once, "which how hard and dangerous task it may prove you may judge."

Then he came to their Privileges. "And although we cannot allow of the style, calling it your ancient and undoubted right and inheritance; but would rather have wished that ye had said that your Privileges were derived from the grace and permission of our ancestors and us, for most of them grow from precedents, which shows rather a toleration than inheritance, yet we are pleased to give our royal assurance that so long as you shall continue to contain yourselves within the limits of your duty and respect to us, as we assure ourselves you will do, we will be as careful to preserve your lawful liberties and privileges as ever any our predecessors were, nay as

[1] P. and D. II. 322.

to preserve our own royal Prerogative. So as your House shall only need to beware to trench upon the prerogative of the Crown: which would enforce us or any just King, to retrench them of their privileges that would pare his prerogative and flowers of the crown: but of this we hope there shall never be cause given." [1]

Such are the chief points in the long and able, if disconnected, letter to which the Commons now listened. The soundness of James's views on foreign policy would naturally fix their attention less than the concluding portion which dealt with their privileges.

The general impression was at first good. Phelips believed that the answer would appeal to the affection and soul of every member present. He would defer the debate till the morrow. Sir Henry Poole deprecated an incessant harping on their privileges. Sir Dudley Digges was much comforted by the plain dealing of his Majesty, and, like Poole, would fain get back to their Bills, for he did not think that their privileges were touched. But next day, December 15th, Sir George Moore reminded the Commons that their liberties were their freehold and the fairest flower that grew in their garden: once nipped such would never grow again. Sir Francis Seymour was for some course which should settle their privileges, that they might not leave them worse than they had found them at their coming there. The Chancellor of the Exchequer reminded the House of the King's friendly attitude to the deputation, of which he had been one, but not so was he able to stem the growing dissatisfaction. Sir James Perrot moved for a committee on Religion and on Privileges.

Brooke suggested the course ultimately adopted, a

[1] P. and D. II. 327.

Protestation entered in the Journals of the House, wherein its Privileges should be claimed as of inheritance and not of royal grant. In this he was supported by Phelips, Sir Thomas Wentworth, and Digges, also by Thomas Crew, who, as it fell out, was to be Speaker of the next Parliament. Coke of course took the same view, and so did another notable lawyer, Noy. Mr. Secretary Calvert agreed that the committee should consider Privileges which indeed ought to be dear to them, but he reminded the House that it was not in the King's mind to question them and what he had written was only a slip of the pen at the end of a long letter. He wisely deprecated a suggestion made by Sir William Spencer that they should challenge again the assertion, made by James in his first moment of anger, that he was free and able to punish any member as well in or out of Parliament. Accordingly a committee of the whole House was appointed.

James heard of this and wrote another letter. "The plain truth is," he said, "that we cannot, with patience, endure our subjects to use such anti-monarchical words to us concerning their liberties, except they had subjoined that they were granted unto them by the grace and favour of our predecessors." He went on to protest strongly that he had no intention at all of infringing any of those privileges, rather he would preserve them in their entirety; he had no particular point whatever in his mind wherein he meant to disallow of such liberties. He advised them, then, to go on cheerfully in their business, "rejecting the curious wrangling of lawyers upon words and syllables." [1]

It might seem that James had by this sufficiently purged the effect of his unfortunate temper; but his

[1] P. and D. II. 340.

phrase about punishment still stuck, and the House was not to be cajoled from its committee. Sir Edward Cecil said, "The King is like a Father: he gives sharp words but good deeds." Sir Edward Coke was more discriminating. The King's letter, he said, drily, was gracious *in genere* for their privileges but what they were *in specie* was the question before them. Still another letter came from James next day. He was willing to postpone the passing of the Subsidy Bill till the next session if the Commons cared to go to business at once, and finish the session before Christmas. The Commons thanked the King for his letter, but preferred a simple adjournment. They also decided to go on with their committee without delay. Said Sir W. Earle, "Let us give thanks to his Majesty and then proceed with the committee formerly appointed." "Yes," added Pym, "Let us first satisfy the King and then look to our privileges."

At four o'clock on that wintry afternoon of December 18, 1621, Mr. Speaker again took the chair. Candles were lighted and the Protestation was read several times. Upon question it was allowed and order made that it should at once be entered of Record in the Journal of the House. The text of this famous Protestation will be found in Appendix VIII. Here it may be summarised. It reiterated the assertion that the Liberties, Franchises, Privileges and Jurisdictions of Parliament are the ancient and undoubted birthright and inheritance of the subjects of England. It asserted that the arduous and urgent affairs of King and State, the defence of realm and of church, together with redress of grievances, are for Parliament proper subjects of counsel and debate. It declared that Freedom of Debate was essential for the

[1] C. J. I. 668, i.

proper consideration of these great matters. It asseverated the right of each member to impunity from impeachment, imprisonment, or any punishment other than the censure of the House itself for his sayings and doings in Parliament. Finally it demanded that any such delinquent must be presented to the King by the advice and assent of the Commons themselves and not on the gossip of any private informer.[1]

This done the House wound up its ordinary business and adjourned until the 8th of February. It never met again, for on January 6th James dissolved Parliament.

The dissolution was expected after the King's action on December 30th.

On that day he had come to Whitehall, had sent for the Journals of the House and while Council and Judges looked on had torn the Protestation from the book with his own hands.

Gondomar and Buckingham were delighted. The Spaniard was sure that James would never summon another Parliament. "It is the best thing that has happened in the interests of Spain and the Catholic religion since Luther began to preach heresy a hundred years ago. The King will no longer be able to succour his son-in-law, or to hinder the advance of the Catholics."[2]

Such was the end of this most significant Parliament of 1621. Bacon's words when it began may well be quoted again: "As there is great expectation in the beginning of this Parliament so I pray God it may be as good in the conclusion: that it may be generative, begetting others hereafter." He, its most illustrious victim, from his learned retreat at Gorhambury would see in the mutilation of the Journals the abandonment

[1] P. and D. II. 359-60. R. I. 53.   [2] G. IV. 39, 266.

of all that practical wisdom which he had vainly expounded to James.

* * * * *

" Now the King sat in the winter house in the ninth month . . . and it came to pass that when Jehudi had read three or four leaves he cut it with the penknife and cast it in the fire on the hearth . . . Yet they were not afraid nor rent their garments, neither the King nor any of his servants. . . ."

CHAPTER IV

THE LAST PARLIAMENT OF JAMES I

PYM had desired to know who were those " fiery and popular spirits " to whom his Majesty had referred. He had not to wait long for the information. In January, 1622, he was ordered to consider himself a prisoner in his own house in London. Here he remained for three months, when a plea of ill health restored him to Brymore. He fared better than Coke and Phelips, who were sent to the Tower, and may have been envied by his friend Rich, who had to accompany Digges, Crew, and Perrot upon a journey to Ireland in the King's service—a mark of his Majesty's disfavour which they would accept in the spirit in which it was offered.

Freed from the criticism of the Commons, James had now the task of carrying into effect his admirable, but entirely impossible, policy of procuring the restitution of the dominions of his son-in-law by Spanish intervention, and of obtaining this intervention by the marriage of his son to the Infanta. It was indeed time for him to do something, for of the Lower Palatinate only three fortresses—Heidelberg, Mannheim, and Frankenthal— held out for Frederick. In March James sent Digby back to Madrid. He was now Earl of Bristol, and what ability could do, that he did ; but Gondomar well knew that when James tore up the Protestation he also tore up his own policy. In September Heidelberg surrendered ; in November, Mannheim ; and not long after, the Spaniards received Frankenthal. On February 13th the Electorate of Frederick was formally transferred to Maximilian of Bavaria for his lifetime. How did Spain act? Her Ambassador entered a formal protest, and that was the sole fruit of James's diplomacy.

There is no reason to believe that even now he was inclined to abandon his policy, but had he been so disposed, the decision had passed from him. Fired probably by Gondomar, first Buckingham, and then Prince Charles, who was now as completely swayed by the favourite as was his father, decided to demand in person what they had so long failed to obtain by diplomacy. They would pursue the courtship of the Infanta in Madrid itself. Clarendon states explicitly that James was opposed to the plan. " For it is not to be doubted that the King was never well pleased with the Duke after the Prince's going into Spain, which was infinitely against his will, and contrived wholly by the Duke, out of envy that the Earl of Bristol should have the sole management of so great an affair . . . " [1] They chose to accompany them Sir Francis Cottington, a shrewd worldling, who had spent a large part of his life in the King's service in Spain, and Endymion Porter, a first-rate intriguer, who had passed from the services of Olivares in Spain to that of Buckingham in England, and who had already been employed as an intermediary between the two. When James broke the news to the former : " Cottington, here is Baby Charles and Stenny, who have a great mind to go by post into Spain to fetch home the Infanta . . . and have chosen you for one. What think you of the journey ? He often protested that when he heard the King he fell into such a trembling that he could hardly speak." Recovering himself he advised strongly against it, whereupon the King " threw himself upon his bed and said, " I told you this before," and fell into new passion and lamentation that he was undone and should lose

[1] Cl. I. 20.

JOURNEY TO SPAIN

Baby Charles."[1] Cottington's objections were overruled, but they had laid him open to the fiercest animosity of Buckingham.

On February 18, 1623, they set out, wearing false beards, and styling themselves Tom and John Smith. Charles was not yet twenty-three, Buckingham eight years older, and no doubt both of them enjoyed the escapade hugely. They were chased by the Lieutenant of Dover Castle, who mistook them for foreign suspects, and the Lord Admiral of the Fleet was obliged to pull off his beard to establish his identity. At Dover the party of five boarded the ship which Cottington and Porter had in readiness, and arrived in Paris on February 21st. After a pleasant day or two there *incognito*, they rode hard for Bayonne, and at eight o'clock in the morning of March 7th were in Madrid.

Of their six months' residence in Spain, of the propositions, counter-propositions and intrigues of the diplomatists, of the insolence of Buckingham, and of the duplicity of Olivares, there is here no need to speak. In England feeling rose high against Buckingham. It was believed, not without reason, that the main object of Spain was to entrap the Prince into a change of religion. James himself was only desirous of seeing again " his sweet boys and dear venturous knights worthy to be put in a new romanso."[2] He was daily becoming more senile, and Buckingham's reasons for their protracted absence satisfied him less and less. He was ready to grant almost any concession the Spaniard chose to ask. " I care for match, nor nothing, so I may once more have you in my arms again. God grant it, God grant it, God grant it. Amen, Amen, Amen. . . . God bless you both my only sweet son and my only best sweet servant."[3]

[1] Cl. I. 29. [2] Hardwicke S. P. I. 399. [3] Ibid. I. 421.

When Charles set sail from Santander on September 18th, he gratified equally his father and the greater number of his fellow subjects, and when he set foot again in England he found himself the most popular of princes, and his friend the most successful of statesmen, not for what they had done but for what they had failed to do.

Buckingham's political levity was seldom shown so shamelessly as now. His quarrel with Olivares, and his hatred of Bristol had turned his affection for Spain into animosity equally violent. His wishes were soon made effective, the marriage was first postponed, then finally shelved. The demand for Spanish intervention in Germany, if not by peace then by war, was promptly rejected by Spain. The Spanish treaties were dissolved before his hatred like hoar frost in the sunshine, and much against his royal will, James, on December 28th, ordered writs to be issued for a new Parliament. Two days later Bristol was recalled with a reproof and bidden to explain his behaviour in agreeing to the betrothal on which three months before Buckingham and Charles had set their hearts. James's reign was over and that of Buckingham had begun.[1]

This, the last Parliament of James I, met him on February 19, 1624. Very different was the language of the disillusioned and suffering King, now within fifteen months of his grave, from that with which he had dismissed the Commons two years before. He spoke freely, confidingly.[2] He had sent his son to Spain, and with him the man he most trusted, Buckingham. He was as far disappointed of his ends as if he had waked out of a dream. Buckingham should explain that to them. He asked their advice. Never King gave more trust to his subjects than to desire their advice in things

[1] G. V. 46, 160.   [2] R. I. 115.

of this weight. " For I assure you, ye may freely advise me seeing of my princely fidelity ye are intreated thereto . . . and for matter of Privileges, Liberties and Customs, be not over curious, I am your own kindly King. . . . God judge me I speak as a Christian Prince. Never man in a dry and sandy desert where no water is, did thirst more in hot weather for drink than I do for a happy conclusion of this Parliament. I now hope after the miscarriage of the last that this may prove happy." [1]

These words may well serve as James's dying speech and confession. Not very good, not very great, not very wise, he had nevertheless sought peace and ensued it. From his relaxing fingers the reins had slipped to Buckingham, a violent charioteer willing to drive whither the seven devils of his undisciplined lusts should urge him.

The Commons chose for Speaker Sir Thomas Crew, who had now returned from that penal journey into Ireland which his opposition to the Spanish Treaty had drawn upon him: he was brother of Ranulf Crew, who had been Speaker of the Addled Parliament of 1614. Lord Keeper Williams replied to Crew's first speech, " It is impossible," he said, " by amicable means to recover the Palatinate, therefore ye do well to sort Cato's *Carthago evertenda* with *Palatinatus deglutinanda*—it ought to be unglued again." A conference of the two Houses showed them to be of one mind as to the need for abandoning the Treaties. James was informed of their opinion by a joint committee which attended him at Theobalds. He thanked them, likened himself to Moses on Pisgah, with the prayer that God might so far prolong his life that he might see the restitution of his children's inheritance. As for the war his navy was good, and " for Ireland

[1] P. H. I. 1390.

I leave it to you whether that be not a back door to be secured." But his debts were grievous and he sought their aid, making two remarkable offers.

"I will deal frankly with you; show me the means how I may do what you would have me, and if I take a resolution by your advice to enter into a war, then yourselves by your own deputies, shall have the disposing of the money. I will not meddle with it, but you shall appoint your own treasurers. . . . I protest none of the monies which you shall give for those wars shall be issued but for those ends and by men elected by yourselves."

These offers were probably suggested to James by Buckingham, who may well have been content at this juncture to diminish James's prerogative for the moment, if so he might bring about that war with Spain upon which he had bent the full intensity of his bitter resentment. But although James and the Houses agreed that the Treaties should be abandoned, and although the King was reluctantly coming to consent to war, there was no unanimity as to the enemy to be attacked. James's chief concern was the Palatinate. A war with the Emperor and his allies carried on by England and a new Continental union of Protestant Powers, and with the help of France, if possible, was his alternative to the discarded Spanish Treaties.

He was under no misapprehension as to the costliness of this alternative policy. On March 1st, at another conference, he asked for five subsidies with two-fifteenths additional to each subsidy. This for the war, "for mine own necessities, my crying debts, one subsidy and two-fifteenths yearly" until those debts should be paid. This would amount to £780,000, which six more subsidies, which might be expected from Convocation, would bring to £900,000, a grant unheard of in those days. The views of the Commons were much more moderate. Spain now, as always, was their enemy. A war with Spain would be not only cheaper but positively remunerative. Of Germany or German politics they knew little or nothing: for the misfortunes of the Palatinate family they were genuinely sorry, but their sorrow stopped considerably short of £900,000. Rudyerd summarised their desires in four points—repair of fortifications, fitting out of fleet, Ireland reinforced, Dutch succoured.

Finally, a middle course was adopted, three subsidies and three-fifteenths were granted, a sum amounting to about £300,000. James's offer, moreover, was accepted. Parliament appointed treasurers to whom the money should be paid, and it was arranged that one year after James had declared the negotiations with Spain to be abandoned, the whole grant should be in the Exchequer.

In the debates on these great matters it was not Coke or Phelips who took the lead, still less was it Pym; it was John Eliot. This patriot has attained a celebrity as well deserved by his melancholy death as by his agitated life. It is possible from his speeches, from his autobiographical "Negotium Posterorum," and from that curious treatise, the "Monarchy of Man," which he wrote while the shadow of death gathered round him in the Tower, to obtain some conception of the capacity of the man who now took upon himself the task of leading the Commons against the Government. It is more difficult, in the reek of party hatred which his name so long evoked, to obtain a clear view of his personal characteristics.

One point, nevertheless, is plain, and it is startling, that he was capable of inspiring in many a sentiment of profound aversion.

That Charles I was a cruel man his sternest critics

would hesitate to assert ; when the Cromwellians called him the man of blood they were merely using the technical vocabulary of their own Religion wherewith to indicate a political opponent. Yet the conduct of Charles in regard to the last moments of Eliot stands in blackness next only to his betrayal of Strafford. Thomas May, historian of the Long Parliament, a writer whose judgment has been diversely appraised, has for Eliot the curt sentence of Tacitus on a garrulous Roman, *sibi periculum nec aliis libertatem,* inasmuch as his rhetoric " was by the people in general applauded," and yet at the same time " censured by some of a more politic reserve . . ." as " a needless and therefore a foolish thing." [1]

His youth was apparently irregular ; a regrettable circumstance attributed by his apologists to the slackness of his father. On one occasion Mr. Moyle, a neighbour and friend of the family, sought an interview with this good easy man wherein he laid before him certain facts concerning his son's courses. On hearing this young Eliot went to Moyle's house and stabbed him in the side. Such is the bald story, which is, apparently, undeniable. Eliot's staunch supporter, John Forster, extenuates this " wild justice " of the future patriot on the ground that the stab was only a little one, that the stabber was only young—some eighteen years—that he wrote a note of apology to Moyle, and that stabber and stabbed lived as neighbours thereafter in amity. [2]

The temporary inconvenience to Mr. Moyle was, no doubt, amply compensated to him by the remarkable change in the deportment of his young assailant. Eliot would seem to have regarded the incident as one of those calls to grace familiar and acceptable to his religious

[1] May I. 1. [2] F. Eliot I. 5.

associates. Henceforth he became a model of decorum, and in 1607 proceeded to Exeter College, Oxford, but here, for some reason not handed down, he did not take a degree. John Forster believes that it was here that he acquired the facility in the use of classical similes and tropes which so strongly spiced his rhetoric in future years, and which on one too famous occasion earned for him the undying animosity of Charles. This may of course have been so.

On leaving the University he made some study of the law, and then went for a tour on the Continent. There he met George Villiers, like himself young and unknown, and like himself enlarging his experience by foreign travel. The friendship which sprang up between them led Villiers to make Eliot Vice-Admiral of Devonshire when his own bright star had guided him to the favour of the Court, and the office of Lord High Admiral. Whether this post were less remunerative than Eliot had expected, or its duties more onerous, a coolness arose between him and his patron which must have made more opposition to him in three Parliaments less painful to his sensitive nature. He was some eight years younger than Pym, having been born in 1592, of good family. Unlike Pym, he sat in the Addled Parliament of 1614, for St. Germans, being then only twenty, but made no mark there. He was not a member of the famous Parliament of 1621, but now rushed to the front as Member for Newport, in Cornwall, with all the vigour which a theatrical envisaging of political enemies, and a rare command of vituperative rhetoric afforded him. He had already, on February 27th, made a creditable, if inopportune, demand for entire freedom of speech, " for the King's sake more than for ours." He now threw himself into a shrill demand for war with Spain. " War only will secure and repair us.

To secure ourselves by setting out our own fleet and to do this by those penalties the Papists have already incurred," [1] of which John Forster characteristically remarks that it was "a means which would have been especially odious to the Court," but which Gardiner gravely condemns as "a proposal which, if it had been translated into figures, would have created a tyranny too monstrous to be contemplated with equanimity." [2]

Pym followed Eliot, and deeply it is to be regretted that we have only the two scrappy records of the *Commons Journals* as reports of this Parliament.

The first runs thus: "Mr. Pymme—against Continuance of any Treaty for Match of Palatinate. To pray a Conference with the Lords about a message to the King about it." [3] The second reports: "Mr. Pymme—Debate a Preparation to Judgment. To bring this to a conclusion. To give our advice for both negatively: and to desire a Conference with the Lords." [4] From these meagre scraps it is impossible to ascertain Pym's view of Continental politics. Probably the key sentence is, "To bring this to a conclusion." What Pym certainly wanted was to get to business and business to him did not mean Ferdinand or Frederick or Philip. What it did mean will be seen presently.

Pym spoke again on this topic on March 2nd, in support of a proposal of Digges concerning that committee of the House to meet the Lords of which Pym himself was chosen to be a member. [5] He also spoke on March 19th, on the question of the subsidies asked for by the King. Eliot had just declared, "Our common interests are at hazard, our friends at pawn, Religion at stake. We

[1] C. J. I. 675, i.   [2] G. V. 47 191.   [3] C. J. I. 675, i.
[4] C. J. I. 722, ii.   [5] C. J. I. 725, i.

must strain ourselves at once to be made safe once for all. Are we poor ? Spain is rich. That is our Indies. Breaking with them we shall break our necessities together." Mr. Treasurer followed him with some severity. Nothing, he said, was more needless than to use arguments here to stir up our affections, for every man plainly saw that nothing ever concerned them more greatly. The report of a large contribution from the House would prevail much with their allies abroad. And what would be a competent sum to enable the King to support the charge of the fleet, Ireland, and the Low Countries ? He suggested three subsidies and then a further consideration for future needs. Several speakers followed, and then Pym reminded the House that they were straying some degrees from the question of their danger. He feared such a relapse. Let them get back to the propositions of the Chancellor of the Exchequer, and for the ease of the King's subjects let there be a liberal allowance of time for payment. But, above all, first let them settle the general question that if necessity required they would yield to the demand made upon them.[1]

Such were Pym's small contributions to these great debates. His interests, as has been said, lay rather with domestic grievances, and especially with those that affected religion.

Of the domestic achievements of this last Parliament of James two are especially prominent—the impeachment of Lionel Cranfield, Earl of Middlesex, and the final declaration of the illegality of monopolies.

Cranfield had been brought to James's notice by his Treasurer Northampton. He was another Dick Whittington, for he began his career as an apprentice in the

[1] C. J. I. 741, ii.

City of London, won by his handsome face the love of his master's daughter, and with her portion started a business of his own. He was a member of the Mercers' Company, and, as their representative, had to appear before the Privy Council. Here it was that his remarkable business gifts had first attracted the notice of Northampton. He soon made his capacity felt and effected great economies in every department. His progress was rapid. As Surveyor General of the Customs, Master of the Wardrobe, Master of the Wards, Lord Treasurer, wherever he went he made his reforms. Successively the plain city merchant became Knight, Privy Counsellor, Baron, Earl. On the downfall of Bacon, with whom he was on bad terms, he had even raised his eyes to the Chancellorship. Such a man is always liable to two dangers: he must by his reforms make many enemies whose vested interests or perquisites he invades, and he will be hard put to it to hold his own in a society for which neither birth nor education has qualified him; and the second difficulty was, of course, greater in the seventeenth century than now. Both these difficulties befel Cranfield. So long as he had the favour of James, whose path he made easier, and still more the support of Buckingham, he could afford to disregard his detractors. Now when he had reached the summit of his career, at a time when James had become little more than a cypher, he incurred the animosity of Charles and of Buckingham alike. In the first place, he threw cold water on their scheme of a Spanish war. In such a scheme he foresaw the toil of his long years blown away in gunpowder; his hard-won surplus again a beggarly deficit. He poured scorn on their fond belief that predatory attacks on Spanish colonies and galleons could refill with dubloons those coffers which he had laboriously filled with English gold. This was bad enough, but Middlesex went further. He told Charles to his face after his return from Spain that he ought to marry the Infanta whether he wished it or not, " for reasons of State and the good that would thence redound to all Christendom." Charles's retort was obvious if unbecoming. " Let Middlesex," he said, go judge of his merchandises if he would, for he was no arbiter in points of honour."

This meant that Cranfield was condemned already, for, as in the case of Bacon, it was easy enough to let the Commons loose upon him, and to prove against him carelessness and lack of due formalities. He had, too, not neglected to pile up a fortune for himself while faithfully serving his master ; and it is likely that the methods by which he had done this would not stand the scrutiny of censorious eyes. But when this has been said, the condemnation and heavy sentence pronounced against him on May 13, 1624, were entirely unjust, for he was punished, not for his offences, small or great, but for his opposition to Charles and Buckingham. James was highly displeased with the impeachment, and ought to have saved Middlesex, for he knew well enough that it was to separate him from his faithful servant that Buckingham had engineered the precious scheme. He did nothing of the kind, but merely contented himself with two masterpieces of sagacity which Clarendon has made immortal : " And when he found the Duke unmoved by all the considerations and arguments and commands he had offered, he said in great choler, ' By God, Stenny, you are a fool, and will shortly repent this folly and will find that in this fit of popularity you are making a rod with which you will be scourged yourself.' And, turning in some anger to the prince, told him that he would live to have his bellyful of parliaments, and that when he should be dead he would have too much cause to remember how much he had contributed to the weakening of the Crown by this precedent he was now so fond of." [1]

What share, if any, did Pym take in this despicable affair? The question is of real interest if it be not fanciful to detect a similarity between him and Cranfield. Both were above all things men of practical sagacity, and both had been trained in business principles. In education Pym had the advantage, but this was more than compensated to Cranfield by the rapidity of his advancement. Of Pym's real greatness in finance and administration it would be idle to dispute; enough evidence of it will be given later. In this he was undoubtedly the equal of Cranfield. What Cranfield had not was statesmanship, far-reaching views, wide political principles. For Bacon he had only the contempt of the plain common-sense man. Had Pym these higher gifts? Were they likely to be gained or developed better on the floor of the House of Commons, in the conflict of debate and committee, than in those high circles of officialdom which Cranfield had attained at a bound? In the answer to this question lies the main interest of Pym's life.

It is a notable fact that no single speech of Pym's is recorded upon the articles of accusation against Cranfield. Just as he was silent when Bacon was being driven to his ruin so was he silent now, and dangerous as it always is to build upon the argument from silence, it is especially tempting to see here an appreciation of the quiet benefits which Cranfield had rendered to his country, and a detection of the mean reasons which had encompassed his fall.

The second achievement which makes this Parliament memorable is the abolition of monopolies. The strenuous

[1] Cl. I. 44.

DEATH OF JAMES I

action of the Parliament of 1621 against this grievance has already been described. The excellent beginning made when Mompesson, Michell and their fellows were put to flight remained unfinished because of the quarrel between the King and the Commons. In the unusual circumstances which now existed when Buckingham had snatched the royal prerogative from the supine hands of James, and had placed it blindly at the service of Parliament, the course was open and easy. In 1624 was passed the Act against monopolies, which with certain modifications is still law and which makes monopolies illegal with the important exception that letters patent may be granted, the familiar " patents" of our own day —for fourteen years " for new manufactures within the realm to the true and first inventor thereof."

On this " Act concerning monopolies, and Dispensation with Penal Laws and the forfeitures thereof," Pym spoke on February 26th. His speech is thus reported in the Journals:[1] Mr. Pym " to have it committed." Committed it was and Mr. Pym was one of the Committees. This was, according to the Journals, his sole contribution to the vexed question.

What other high matters, foreign or domestic, might have engaged the attention of this Parliament it is useless to conjecture. It had sat for a year and a week when, on March 27, 1625, King James died in the fifty-seventh year of his age and the twenty-third of his reign. Fate was hard upon him to the end; he had desired that Andrewes should give him his viaticum. But Andrewes was unwell and Williams came instead.

His death necessarily caused a dissolution of Parliament.

In dramatic interest the Parliament of 1624 may fall

[1] C. J. 719, ii.

behind the Parliament of 1621, but it has at least one aspect of profound significance. By a curious caprice of fortune the prime favourite of the King was able to throw all his weight on the side of the Commons against the policy of the King himself. *Suarumque legum auctor idem ac subversor* might indeed be the epitaph of James in regard to his pro-Spanish schemes. Buckingham, says Ranke, "may perhaps be set down as the first English minister who, supported by Parliament and by public opinion, induced or compelled the King to adopt a policy on which of his own accord he would not have resolved." [1]

What of John Pym in this Parliament, short and sharp, of 1624? It has been shown that the chief topics which engaged the attention of this assembly were, in foreign affairs, the Spanish negotiations, the subsidies and the war, and if war then war with whom? In domestic affairs, the impeachment of a Minister who still enjoyed the confidence of the Crown, and the almost final abolition of the monopolistic system. In these great questions we have looked to Pym, and the oracle is dumb, or nearly so. Was he then sleeping while Eliot was screaming and Coke was snarling? Those who have taken their view of this great man from the commonplaces of the text-books may well believe it. But those who have neither the leisure nor the desire to explore the untracked desert of the *Commons Journals*, or to read the enormous speeches of Pym in the Parliamentary History may well spare a moment to glance over Appendix III of this little book. There they will see in a few seconds what Pym was doing in the Parliament of 1624.

He was enabling Vincent Lowe to sell certain lands; he was helping the creditors of Cope; he was arranging the

[1] Ranke I. 530.

matter of the jointure of Dame Mary Scudamore; he was passing from the consideration of Bonnington's Estate, glancing meanwhile at Lady Jermy's Bill; the lands of Aucher, of James, and of Wroth occupied some of his leisure. A presentation to an advowson appendant to a manor detained him. His survey extended from Little Munden in Hertfordshire to Erith and the Plumstead Marshes, and included the lands of Magdalen College, Cambridge. He spoke of Sea Coals, Gold and Silver Thread, Tithes of Lead Ore, Felt makers, Legal Concealments, and Fees of the Exchequer; he cast a friendly eye on the naturalisation of James, Lord Marquis of Hamilton, and did not disdain to apply his patriotic zeal to the further description of a bankrupt.

But he had his relaxations. There were rare hunts for Romanists, fine baitings of Bishops. He was "discovering and repressing" Popish recusants "real as well as legal, especially such as live in any place near to the coast in dangerous places to let in the enemy"; he was eliminating simony from Colleges and Halls, he was pursuing a blackguard who had crept into the Presidency of an Oxford College, he was investigating the orthodoxy of another President at Cambridge and of an obscure Welsh schoolmaster, he was levying a penalty of twelve pence a Sunday from married women for not repairing to the church to hear Divine Service, he was objecting to settle Josse Glover, Clerk, because in so doing he would give Institution, Admission, and Induction, three Episcopal points of Jurisdiction which the Bishops above would oppose; with Ravenscroft he was examining a catalogue of seven or eight score Popish books printed within these two years. He was collecting charges against the Bishop of Norwich and before and above all he was considering for the committee for the Corruption in

Religion and Learning the book of Richard Montague, full fraught with dangerous opinions of Arminius, which will be fully dealt with in the next reign and the next Parliament when the matter came to decision.

In the Parliament of 1624 John Pym was doing yeoman service. Stone upon stone, course upon course, he was laying for himself, by knowledge, by influence and by incessant work, a foundation from which in a few more years, not Court nor King could sweep him away.

CHAPTER V

THE FIRST AND SECOND PARLIAMENTS OF CHARLES I

ON the day following his father's death, King Charles I, now duly proclaimed, set out from Theobalds to meet his Privy Council in London. In his carriage rode Buckingham, more firmly fixed, if that were possible, in the confidence of the son to-day than of the father yesterday.

A mind narrow, exclusive and suspicious, retains more easily than it admits friendship, and the favourite might well see in his stiff and self-conscious companion a bulwark even more impregnable against the assault of Eliot and of Pym than had been the garrulous wiseacre whom he had so long hailed as " Dear Dad and Gossip."

No change of note was made at the first Council, but to one of James's adherents the demise of the Crown boded no good. Bishop Williams, the Lord Keeper, had administered to the dying King his last Communion, and he was now bidden to preach his funeral sermon. But this was his *congé*. He was summoned no more to the Council board.

His fall was not unexpected, and least of all by his enemy Laud. For the night of Sunday, December 14, 1623, that prelate had noted in his diary one of those dreams which have, unfairly enough, made him ridiculous in the eyes of posterity. In his vision it seemed the Lord Keeper was dead, and he met his man in search of a monument for him, which " did trouble me." Next day in a conversation with Buckingham " I found that the Lord Keeper had strangely forgotten himself to him and I think was dead in his affections."[1] It was true,

[1] Laud, Diary, 7-8.

and by the evidence of his own diary, Laud had largely contributed to this result. For the moment he had triumphed in the long-standing feud, and bitterly did Williams make him rue it.

The disgrace of Williams marks the nature of Buckingham's influence. His grudge against the Lord Keeper had not been unearned. Williams had warned Prince Charles against the journey to Madrid, and he had given his voice against the war with Spain when the Prince returned. On July 10th he must needs advise the new King against the adjournment of his first Parliament to Oxford. These were reasons enough, but a stronger may be found in the advice which he was indiscreet enough to offer to the Duke early in March: that he should retire from the Admiralty and become Steward of the Household. This to a Carpet Knight, who was at that very time devising an expedition to Cadiz, which should rank with the exploits of Drake and of Essex!

On October 25th, he ceased to be Lord Keeper. Plausible, and of no great strictness of principle, he had always been on the side of peace, and in driving him from the Council of Charles, Buckingham was doing himself an ill turn.

But this is to anticipate the course of events. Parliament had not yet met its new Monarch. In his eagerness for supplies wherewith to prosecute a brilliant campaign against Spain, Buckingham could scarcely brook delay. The suggestion was indeed made that the dissolution effected by a demise of the Crown, should on this occasion be waived, and the fourth Parliament of King James continue its session. This curious anticipation of a usage not legalised until the reign of Queen Victoria,[1] was abandoned, and writs were issued in the usual course.

[1] Representation of the People Act, 1867.

CHARLES'S MARRIAGE

Whatever his eagerness for Supply, Charles might be pardoned if the forthcoming assembly did not occupy the first place in his thoughts. King James's funeral and his own marriage might well take precedence. The mournful duty of following his father's body to the Abbey at Westminster he fulfilled on the seventh of May : he was then a bridegroom, for he had been married by proxy to his fifteen-year-old bride in front of Notre-Dame in Paris six days before. Two exquisites of his court, the Earl of Carlisle and the Earl of Holland, were chosen by Charles to represent him, and both " clad in beaten silver," vied in splendour with the Court of France under the eyes of Louis XIII, of his beautiful Queen, Anne of Austria, and of that Cardinal who was at once their servant and their master, Richelieu.[1]

On May 14th, Buckingham arrived in Paris to conduct the Queen into England ; a period of festivity followed, and rumour credited the favourite with an effrontery and audacity of licentiousness far surpassing that which had scandalised the Court of Madrid.

On June 12th, Henrietta Maria, accompanied by her mother, arrived at Dover, and there Charles met her and conveyed her to Canterbury. Well for the innocent child, too soon a Queen and too soon a wife, that she could not foresee the ills which her marriage was to bring upon herself, her husband, and the country of her adoption.

Parliament met on June 18th, and eagerness was shown by members to be in attendance. Their curiosity involved some personal risk, for the plague had appeared in London and the number of deaths was daily increasing. Charles's first speech was short. He did not fail to remind his hearers that the Spanish war was one of their choosing. " It is true I came into this business willingly and freely

[1] R. I. 169.

like a young man, and consequently rashly, but it was by your interest, your engagement." [1] This warfare, then, they must expedite. He assured them of his adherence to " true religion," and made way for the Lord Keeper Williams, who said nothing worth hearing. Sir Thomas Crew was again chosen Speaker, and he did not fail to exhort Charles " really to execute the laws against the wicked generation of Jesuits, seminary priests and incendiaries, ever lying wait to blow the coals of contention."

In the debates which followed, one opinion was general. Supply should not be granted until the Government had informed the Houses as to the allocation of the previous subsidies and as to the use proposed for those which were now demanded. Two Yorkshire members, Mallory, burgess of Ripon, and Sir Thomas Wentworth, Knight of the Shire, were for asking the King to postpone the Session until Michaelmas in view of the plague then ravaging the metropolis. This would have had the additional advantage of compelling Charles and Buckingham to show their hands, and of postponing the collection of burdensome subsidies. But, as usual, it was " Religion " and not policy which was to carry the day.

On June 22nd, a speech was delivered in the House of Commons which Forster attributes to Pym, but which better authority assigns to Sir Francis Seymour. [2] Their duty to God must not be forgotten, therefore let them ask the King to put in execution the laws against priests and Jesuits. The words indeed may not have been Pym's, but it might well have served him for a confession of faith. Eliot followed with a sentiment worthy of William Laud, " Where there is division in religion as it does wrong divinity, so it makes distractions among men. . . . For the unity I wish posterity might say we

[1] R. I. 171. [2] G. V. 52 342.

had preserved for them that which was left to us." "I laboured nothing more," protested Laud in his last moments, " than the external public worship of God . . . might be preserved . . . being still of opinion that unity cannot long continue in the Church when uniformity is shut out at the Church door." So spoke two martyrs.

"When they do agree," said Mr. Puff on another occasion, "their unanimity is wonderful."

But if Pym did not sound this particular tocsin, he had been by no means idle during the first few days of the Session. On the day before Seymour's speech—June 21st—he had supported Strode's motion for a fast,[1] and had desired to have it made general, and not only for the Houses as had been suggested. This altruistic impulse was not shared by a majority of his colleagues, and it was decided to confine their abstinence to themselves. He was thereupon made a Committee to draw a petition to this effect to his Majesty. On the same day, with many others, he was also made a Committee on privileges, and on the 22nd he had a similar appointment to consider an act for the punishment of divers abuses, committed on the Lord's day called Sunday. He also drew up a petition asking the King to press the penal laws with the utmost rigour and to take other measures against the Romanists.[2] On such small but congenial game was he engaged, when on July 4th he was called to pursue a nobler quarry, no less a personage than Dr. Montague.

Richard Montague was a country clergyman, Rector of Stanford Rivers, in Essex, and also Dean of Hereford and a Fellow of Eton. In his parish he found the pamphlet of a Romanising writer, who had followed a favourite device of his church by identifying Anglican

[1] C. J. I. 799, i.
[2] G. V. 52, 343. Note. W. H. H. "Laud" also article by same writer in D.N.B.

doctrines with the principles of Calvin's *Institutions*. This pamphlet he called *A Gag for the New Gospel*, and in it he produced forty-seven propositions which he ascribed to the Church of England. Montague was a man of very considerable learning; moreover, he had the gift of the pen, and in 1622, stung by the unprincipled attack of the Roman controversialist, he gave him something better than he brought in a counter pamphlet which he called *A New Gag for an Old Goose*. He denied that more than eight of the Romanist's propositions were truly the doctrines of the Church; of the rest, some were undecided, some had been condemned, and others were "raked together out of the laystalls of the deepest Puritanism." The phrase is characteristic. Like Milton, Montague did not disdain flippancy, or abuse, or vulgarity, so long as his blow was felt. The matter of his book was better than its manner. In effect it adopted that view of the Anglican Communion which Pusey indicated in his letter to Keble in 1865, "The Church of England a Portion of Christ's one holy Catholic Church." Montague was, indeed, a bustling man-at-arms in the host inspired by Andrewes, organised by Hooker and led faithfully but unskilfully by Laud, which, submerged in successive waves of Calvinism, of latitudinarianism and of scepticism, emerged triumphantly as orthodoxy in the years following the Oxford Movement. For this reason *The New Gag for an Old Goose* would deserve remembrance.

It now became the battle ground between the Puritans and their opponents in the Church. It had occupied the attention of the previous Parliament, for on May 13, 1624, Pym reported from the Committee for Corruption in Religion and Learning a Petition and Articles against a book printed and published by Richard Montague "full fraught with dangerous opinions of Arminius quite contrary to the Articles established in five several points." It was thereupon resolved that Pym, with four others, should as from the House acquaint the Lord Archbishop of Canterbury with the petition against the book and with the book itself. Abbot had no sympathy with Montague, but much with his Puritan opponents. He asked James's advice and was told to send for Montague. This he did, and at the interview advised him to tone down the sharpness of his argument. Far from doing this, Montague went himself to James and triumphed. "If that is to be a Papist," said the King, "so am I a Papist." Further, Montague obtained his Majesty's permission to prepare a second book, which he called *Appello Cæsarem*. This maintained still more fiercely the doctrines asserted in *The New Gag for an Old Goose*, and was referred by James to Dr. White, Dean of Carlisle, who approved it, and it was licensed for the press. James having died meantime Montague issued it with a dedication to Charles.

Abbot told a deputation from the Commons what had occurred, and also that he had not even been informed of the proposed publication of the second book till it was actually in the press. The Commons thereupon referred the whole matter to a Committee of which Pym was one. On July 4th he moved for authority to send for the Party or Witnesses concerning Montague's book. On July 7th the Committee made their report, of which Forster says Pym was the author. As regarded his books they concluded that there were many things in them directly contrary to the Articles established by Parliament, and on these points of doctrine they were of opinion that a conference should be prayed for with the Lords. As regarded the second book they held it factious, seditious, against the honour and dignity of the House of Commons, tending manifestly to the dishonour of the late King and to the disturbance of Church and State. Montague had, it seemed, shown respect to Bellarmine, but spoken slightingly of Calvin, Beza, and Reynolds; he had belittled lectures—even preaching itself; and had used the objectionable phrase "Puritan" frequently. He had, moreover, therein attacked the two clergymen—Yates and Ward—who had originally complained of him, and who were therefore under the protection of the House.

The suggestion that a book which James had himself approved was manifestly to his dishonour was too preposterous even for a Puritan House. Many members, moreover, were by no means satisfied that they should thus set themselves up as a theological tribunal. On the other hand, they did not wish Montague to escape altogether; they therefore committed him to the custody of the Sergeant-at-arms, but he was allowed his liberty on giving a bond to the Sergeant for his reappearance.

Hereupon Charles made Montague one of his Chaplains in ordinary.

This significant appointment was announced to the House on July 9th, by Mr. Solicitor Heath. He added that the King said he had taken the cause into his own hand and desired that the House would set Montague free,[1] upon which he would take care to give the House satisfaction. Answer was made to his Majesty that the House had proceeded against Montague only for his contempt and that the Sergeant had already set him at liberty upon bail. On August 2nd, after the adjournment to Oxford, motion was made that Montague might now appear according to the former order. The Sergeant being called said Montague was ill. He was ordered to

[1] C. J. I. 807 ii.

bring him to the House, and it was resolved that Montague was to stand committed until he should be discharged by the House. On August 8th the Sergeant informed the House that Montague was sick in bed, and Mr. Speaker produced a letter which the invalid had written him. Some desired that it should be read, but it was resolved that, being a prisoner, he should not have written, but have petitioned.[1] Further action on the part of the House was prevented by the dissolution which took place four days later. The sequel of the affair and Pym's further connection therewith comes in the account of the second Parliament of Charles I. Here it is enough to point to the vital issues that had been raised.

The House of Commons had claimed to be a tribunal with power to decide upon theological dogma and controversy. In the debate on August 2nd Coke had pointed to the danger that would ensue if every private man may put out books of Divinity. He would have them all referred to Convocation, but this was not a view which would appeal to the extreme Puritans of the House unless they were sure of a predominant Puritan element in Convocation.

Charles had taken Montague under his protection and requested the Commons to desist from their attack on him. The House was not slow to recognise the meaning of this. In the same debate on August 2nd, Alford " put the House in mind of the danger to exempt the King's servants from questioning in Parliament." [2]

So began to take clear shape the two chief causes of our civil strife.

Meantime matters were not going well with regard to Supply. The Commons resented the lack of confidence shown in them. If they had known the truth they

[1] C. J. I. 812 ii. [2] C. J. I. 809 ii.

would scarcely have been better pleased. Charles's Government was pledged to find £30,000 a month for Christian IV, King of Denmark, to enable him to attack the Emperor in Germany; £20,000 a month for the German adventurer Count Mansfeld, who had a roving commission in the Palatinate; whatever might be needed to equip the fleet to attack the Spanish ports, and large sums for the Dutch Republic to use against Spain. This monstrous entanglement was the first fruits of Buckingham's administration. It is true that some three-fourths of Mansfeld's men, unfed and unpaid, were dead or dying by the frost-bound Rhine before they had set eyes on the enemy, but this news could scarcely have consoled the Commons. Moreover King James's funeral expenses had to be met, and a sum set aside for the Coronation. Phelips brought the matter to an issue on June 30th. He said, which was true enough, that they had been told of no war and shown no enemy; he spoke of the disaster to Mansfeld's forces: such reverses had not been usual in the days of Elizabeth. He hoped that they would press upon the King the need " to proceed in his government by a grave and wise counsel." He suggested two subsidies, *i.e.* about £140,000. His advice was followed, and the two subsidies voted. It is unnecessary here to follow the discussion in the House over the disputed election of Sir Thomas Wentworth, of which the facts were in question and the principles misunderstood. In it Pym took no part, but it gave Eliot an opportunity of exhibiting his rhetorical powers. Sir Thomas Wentworth was a Catiline, he declared, who had come into the Senate in order to ruin it. This for a trifling breach of rules, which, if we follow another authority, the House itself permitted. " To start aside for such panick fears, phantastic apparitions as a Prynn or an Eliot shall set up were the merest folly in the whole world," Wentworth wrote to Laud in 1633, and there was no more to be said.

The House was now reduced to some sixty members by fear of the plague, and on July 11th Charles adjourned the Parliament to Oxford, where the Houses were to meet on August 1st. There the King would give them an answer to their petition on Religion; meanwhile he would put the penal laws into full execution. Buckingham might hope that there, with a full House free from the fear of the plague, the Commons might look more favourably on those vast schemes on which he had embarked.

When Parliament met again at Oxford in the Hall of Christ Church on August 1st, two difficult matters had to be explained away, both arising from the French Marriage treaty, and both likely to irritate the Commons. In December, 1624, Buckingham had agreed to lend twenty English ships to the French Government; the Dutch had already agreed to do the same. They were to take part in an attack on Genoa, which had practically merged her independent interests in those of Spain. The ships were merely to be hired for pay, and in no sense involved the national relations of the lenders. Unfortunately before this attack took place the Duke of Soubise persuaded his fellow Huguenots to have recourse once more to arms. He succeeded in surprising six French men-of-war and carried them to Rochelle. Richelieu now proposed to use the Dutch and English contingents against the rebels; the Dutch raised no objection, for they could not afford to lose the protection of France, nor did either James or Buckingham protest. The ships had not yet been handed over, but just before James's death contracts had been made to send over to France the *Vanguard*, a man-of-war, and seven hired merchant vessels, under the command of Pennington.

It was eminently undesirable that such a transaction should come before a puritanically-minded House of Commons, and by a series of orders and counter orders, which bewildered Pennington and exasperated some of his men to mutiny, the ships were held over till the French King gave terms of peace to the Huguenots.

The second difficulty was not met so successfully. During the preliminaries to the French marriage contract Buckingham had promised concessions to the English Catholics, and three thousand letters were ready to be sent to Bishops, Judges, and other officials, ordering the present disuse of the penal laws.

In face of the impending Parliament it was held desirable to withold these, a view which was strengthened after Seymour's motion of June 22nd, and the King's promise to answer the petition on Religion, and meantime to execute the penal laws fully.

When Parliament reassembled at Oxford such concessions were seen to be highly embarrassing. Charles had, moreover, in accordance with his father's usage, allowed pardons to be sealed for priests imprisoned at the moment when the French ambassadors were about to return, in order that they might accompany their train, on the condition that they should not come back to England. It was a proceeding harmless enough, but it occurred at a critical moment. The order was given on the 10th of July, and the liberation of so many priests simultaneously with the adjournment might well seem to indicate a lack of good faith towards Parliament.

At Oxford matters moved swiftly. Charles met the Commons on August 4th in Christ Church Hall, urged that they should enable him to make use of his fleet, and promised a reply to the petition on Religion in two days. Sir John Coke afterwards addressed the House on behalf of the Government. He gave indications of the widespread schemes of war which were in progress, but he asked for no definite sum. The House was puzzled. Then Seymour boldly attacked the whole policy of Buckingham: he had, he said, no confidence in the advisers of the Crown. Phelips, too, saw no reason for giving: "In the Government," he said, "there hath wanted good advice . . . Let us look into the Estate and Government and finding that which is amiss make the Parliament the reformer of the Commonwealth." [1]

Heath, the Solicitor-General, made what defence he could. He urged that they were bound by their undertaking of 1624, when the Spanish Treaties were broken. Alford answered him promptly. Not the Palatinate, he said, but Spain was in their minds when they made that undertaking: the war in Germany they had especially struck out. Presently Sir Nathaniel Rich made five propositions. He desired to ask his Majesty (*i*) to answer their petition on religion; (*ii*) to declare the enemy against whom he meant to fight; (*iii*) that any war which his Majesty may desire to undertake be debated by "his grave council"; (*iv*) to ask his Majesty's revenue should be examined with a view to its increase; (*v*) that the question of the impositions should be settled once for all.

Buckingham accepted the challenge implied in these speeches, and on August 8th the Commons were summoned to hear him deliver a communication from Charles. The King granted freely and fully their Petition about religion. They should have their way in the matter of the penal laws. Buckingham then justified his foreign policy by pointing to the depression of France, the uprising of the German Princes of the Union, and the vigorous action of

[1] G. V. 54, 409-10.

Denmark, Sweden, and France. He denied that he had acted without the advice of the Council of War and the Privy Council. Let them put the sword into the King's hands and they should name the enemy themselves.

The Commons were not convinced. More and more the discussion was aimed at Buckingham. News poured in of a most inconvenient kind. Pennington's fleet was back and the whole tortuous tale of the eight ships was being spread far and wide. Sallee rovers, Dunkirk privateers, even the Rochellois Huguenots, had been making free with English merchandise. "Let us lay the fault where it is," cried Seymour. "The Duke of Buckingham is trusted, and it must needs be either in him or his agents." The indomitable Phelips did not fall behind. "It is not fit," he declared, "to repose the safety of the Kingdom upon those that have not parts answerable to their places."

"We are under the rod," said Sir Thomas Wentworth, "and we cannot with credit or safety yield. Since we sat here the subjects have lost a subsidy at sea."

On Wednesday, August 12th, Charles dissolved his first Parliament.

More than three centuries and a half before this day Oxford had witnessed the drafting of those famous Provisions which snatched from the feeble hands of Henry III control of counsel and of finance. Not one century had passed since another Henry had wrested Peers and Commons to his will for evil or for good. That noble hall in which Phelips had at last spoken the words of omen itself bore record of his fallen Minister.

Assuredly that night at least it was no festal light the Scholar Gypsy saw in Christ Church Hall. In the Loyal City the wheel again had come full cycle for the Monarchy of England.

Charles had saved Buckingham by the dissolution, but that was his only gain; the foreign entanglements remained, and the Exchequer was not refilled. It was clear that another Parliament must be faced before long. This might prove kinder if some profitable stroke of arms could be first achieved. The time, in fact, had arrived for Buckingham to play the part of Drake and Essex, to sack Cadiz and seize the Spanish treasure fleet.

He did not intend to perform this exploit in person. In September a Treaty for war and peace had been concluded between England and the Dutch; the Dutch were to patrol the Flemish harbours, the English those on the coast of Spain. Buckingham now resolved to go to the Hague, there to meet in conference the King of Denmark and the North German princes, and to form a new League, of which the Treaty of Southampton was the beginning. He also intended to raise money in Amsterdam on the royal plate and jewels.

He contented himself, therefore, with the title of Generalissimo of the fleet, and appointed as his deputy Sir Edward Cecil, son of the Earl of Exeter and grandson of Elizabeth's Burleigh. Cecil had seen service abroad, and was a member of the Council of War appointed in 1624, but he was unacquainted with naval affairs. The Earl of Essex, who was second in command, brought little more than a determination to repeat the exploit of his father in 1596, and Clarendon describes him as "a general very unequal to that great work."[1] Charles reviewed the fleet in person at Plymouth, and at the instigation of Buckingham created Cecil Viscount Wimbledon, as though he were already taking off his armour. It had been better if he had inspected the stores which were foul and the tackle which was rotten, and had

[1] Cl. I. 51.

then hanged at the nearest yard-arm Bagg and Apsley, who had victualled the ships.

The start was not auspicious, storm and consequent mutiny caused the fleet to put back for several days. On the arrival of the squadron in Spanish waters similar lack of discipline was shown, Essex himself setting an example of misbehaviour by dashing upon a small force of Spanish ships in defiance of the orders of Wimbledon, and so precipitating a premature general attack, whereupon the enemy fled into the inner harbour. An immediate onslaught upon Cadiz might have been successful, for it was slenderly garrisoned, but it was decided first to capture Fort Puntal, which commanded the harbour. This was taken after a sharp attack, in which the merchant crews behaved badly. But meantime Cadiz had been re-garrrisoned and re-victualled. The opportunity was lost. Wimbledon landed his troops and took them on a useless march inland. By an egregious blunder stores sent from the ships had been sent back again, and the weary soldiers, exhausted by the blazing sun, refreshed themselves from casks of Spanish wine. Soon almost the whole army was drunk, and might have been cut to pieces had Spanish troops come up.

On October 27th the men were re-embarked ; the captured fort was abandoned ; and on November 4th the English fleet set watch for the Spanish treasure ships. Here again they were foiled, for two days after they had left, the Plate fleet slipped into Cadiz behind their backs. Aware of their danger the Spanish captains had evaded it by adopting a circuitous course. Wimbledon found that his ships were fast becoming unseaworthy, and on the 16th he gave orders for the return voyage. The expedition had failed. Nor had Buckingham much success to report from the Hague. It is true that a triple alliance had been brought about by the adhesion of the King of Denmark, but France still stood outside. Worse still, war had blazed up again between Louis and the Huguenots, and Soubise had been routed off Rochelle. There could be no doubt that the English ships now in Richelieu's hands would be used against the defeated Huguenots. This would be rare fuel for Puritan firebrands in the new Parliament.

For a new Parliament there needs must be, Buckingham had obtained nothing on the security of the Crown jewels at Amsterdam, and the Spanish coup had resulted only in loss.

By an unworthy trick Buckingham had arranged that some, at any rate, of his personal opponents should not have the opportunity of attacking his measures in the forthcoming Parliament. They were to be pricked as Sheriffs; they would then be obliged to remain in their own counties and could not take their seats at Westminster. "The Judges proceeded in their old course, and so went it to the King: but when the names came to the King, the King declared himself that he had the names of seven that he would have Sheriffs."[1]

The old Irreconcilable, Coke, of course headed the list, and Seymour and Phelips had deserved the dubious honour at least as much as he. Alford, whose name and well-timed interpolations have been mentioned, and Palmer followed. The other was not the perfervid Eliot; it was Sir Thomas Wentworth, whom Ehot had thought fit to brand as Catiline. The seventh name was that of Fleetwood, who sat neither in the last nor the ensuing Parliament. Wentworth accepted the situation. He wrote to a friend: . . . " it being my part this year, *Laconicum agere,* as becomes best, to say truth a Man of

[1] Straff. L. and D. I. 29.

Affairs attendant upon Justices, Escheators, Juries, Bankrupts, Thieves, and such kind of cattle . . . yet I do lament sadly the miseries of these times." [1] His father-in-law, the Earl of Clare, wrote to him counselling submission, " for we live under a prerogative government where Book Law submits unto *Lex Loquens* . . . I may conclude it is not good to stand within the Distance of Absolute Power." [2]

Parliament met on February 6th, 1626. The King's opening speech was very short, and he was followed by the new Lord Keeper, Sir Thomas Coventry, who had taken the place of Bishop Williams. He spoke only generalities. The Commons chose for Speaker Sir Heneage Finch, Recorder of London, who made a long and complimentary speech especially urging the necessity for the war against Spain.

Pym again took his seat for Tavistock, and on February 10th privilege was granted to his servant to stay a suit—some trivial matter of which no more is heard. On the same day he moved for a wider reference to be given to the Committee on Religion, for which Rudyerd had just asked. Pym desired that " certain other articles set down last Parliament but not put into the Petition, and anything else concerning religion should be included within its scope. He was of course immediately placed upon this Committee. On the same day he was empowered, with five others—his friend Nathaniel Rich one, and Sir John Ehot another—to examine the Clerk's entries in the Journal of the House every Saturday.

Also on that same day Eliot, who in the absence of Charles's victimised Sheriffs found himself in a position of leadership, in his well-known emotional manner asked for an inquiry into the expenditure of the subsidies of

[1] Straff. L. and D.I. 32. [2] Ibid. I. 31.

1624, and into the disasters of the Cadiz Expedition; " Our honour is ruined, our ships are sunk, our men perished, not by the enemy, not by chance, but . . . by those we trust." A committee of Grievances was appointed and collected much evidence which was subsequently used as the basis of the charges against Buckingham; another was appointed for Religion, and to this was referred the case of Montague.[1]

The two books had already been submitted by Charles to Bishops Buckeridge, Howson and Laud, who had decided in their favour. They added an important consideration: " The Church of England . . . would not be too busy with every particular school point. The cause why she held this moderation was because she could not be able to preserve any unity among Christians if men were forced to subscribe to curious particulars disputed in Schools." In such disputed points they found that the books of Montague abounded. In this judgment there was a germ of toleration which would not please the Puritans of the Lower House.

On January 16, 1626, a conference of sixteen Bishops, amongst them Andrewes and Laud, reported that Montague's work was agreeable to the doctrine of the Church of England. Charles, however, left him to the Commons, and Pym reported on his books on behalf of the Committee for Religion, and the House resolved that Mr. Montague had endeavoured to reconcile England to Rome and to alienate the King's affections from his well-affected subjects. Pym's Report, as given in Rushworth, consisted of five articles.[2] The gist of the argument against Montague was that in the two works already cited, and in a third called, *A Treatise on the Invocation of the Saints*, he had treated the Church of Rome as

[1] R. I. 209. [2] R. I. 209-212.

a true Church, whereas the sixteenth of the Book of Homilies states that she is not ; that the Church of Rome is firm upon the foundation of the Sacraments, whereas the same Homily declares that five of her seven sacraments are no sacraments at all; that the points controverted between Rome and ourselves are of a lesser and inferior nature, though these include the essential Roman doctrine of Transubstantiation. Moreover, contrary to the second Homily, the " Gag " taught that images might be used for the instruction of the ignorant and the excitation of Devotion, and, lastly, whereas the Saints of certain countries are but *dii tutelares*, Montague had affirmed in his treatise on that topic that Saints have not only a memory but a more peculiar charge of their friends. He had said that a man might fall from Grace, he had cast the odious and scandalous name of Puritan upon certain of his Majesty's subjects, and the sum of it all was this : that Richard Montague had given encouragement to Popery, and induced many to scoff at Lecturing and Preaching, wherefore they prayed for his punishment. Here we may leave Montague. In July, 1628, Charles made him Bishop of Chichester, and in January, 1629, a special pardon was extended to him and *Appello Cæsarem* called in that it might trouble the Church no more.

Whatever Charles might think of Pym's theological efforts the House of Commons was delighted. He was now coming to be recognised as a safe man where any question of Religion was concerned, and his abilities were given a wider scope by his appointment as one of the managers of the impeachment of Buckingham.

For it had indeed come to this, those mutterings of the rising storm which had sounded in the words of Phelips, of Seymour, of Alford, and of Wentworth, had even under the leadership of such a man as Ehot become thunder.

THE COUNCIL OF WAR

Amongst the subjects which had come before the Committee for Grievances was the seizure of certain ships, each of the other country, by England and France respectively. The French alleged that they had done this merely by way of reprisals; the English justified themselves by the assertion that the French ships were conveying contraband of war to the Spanish ports in the Netherlands, and the dispute centred round a French vessel, the *St. Peter*, of Le Havre de Grace, which had been stayed and brought into Plymouth, and its goods seized and sold. The Committee proceeded to examine the whole Council of War who had been appointed to manage the affair of the Palatinate. Each was asked the question whether the advice was followed which he gave for the "four ends mentioned in the last Parliament of King James." There were seven of these councillors, and the examination was undertaken under the terms of the proposal which James himself had offered: that the subsidies should be spent entirely under the direction of treasurers appointed by the Commons themselves. These had taken oath that only under direction of this Council of War would they pay out the money, and in their turn the Council of War had sworn that only for those ends just mentioned would they make orders for payment, and further that they would be accountable to the Commons for their proceedings in that regard whenever called upon.

With regard to the *St. Peter*, Solicitor-General Heath was able to satisfy the House that the stay was in origin regular, but the results of the examination of the Council of War gave much dissatisfaction. On March 10th, the King sent a message by Weston asking for an immediate supply for the necessities of State. At this moment an incident occurred in the House of Commons which brought about a crisis. Clement Coke, son of the absent Sir Edward, who in a previous House of Commons had drawn his sword upon a fellow-member, made a senseless remark : " It is better to die by an enemy than to suffer at home." Another member of equally small account, Dr. Turner, plainly asserted that the Duke of Buckingham was the cause of all the evils, and enumerated six reasons for his statement.[1] Charles immediately demanded satisfaction for the seditious words of the two members.[2] The House ordered Coke and Turner to explain their words; they of course deprecated any seditious intent. This was not enough for Charles. The Commons were summoned to Whitehall on March 15th, and the King addressed them straight to the point. " Here is much time spent in inquiring after grievances. I would have that last . . . I thank you all for your kind offer of Supply in general, but I desire you to descend to particulars and consider of your time and measure. . . . Some there are, I will not say all, that do make inquiry into the proceedings not of any ordinary servant, but of one that is most dear to me." He went on with a warm justification of Buckingham. "In the former time when he was an instrument to break the treaties you held him worthy of all that was conferred upon him by my father. Since that time he hath done nothing but in prosecution of what was then resolved on . . . and yet you question him. . . . I would not have the House to question my servants, much less one that is so near to me."[3]

In spite of Charles's warning the Committees went on with their work. The King again urged the necessity of Supply, and the subject was debated on March 27th, after a remark from a daring member that the cause of all their greivances was that all the King's Council rode

[1] R. I. 217.　[2] C. J. I. 835, ii.　[3] G. IV. 57, 79.

upon one horse. Eliot made a fine debating speech : [1] "We have had a representation of great fear but I hope that shall not darken our understandings." He recalled the failure of the Cadiz expedition : "Can this great general think it sufficient to put in his deputy and stay at home?" He reminded the House of the disaster to Mansfeld's force : "We know well who then had the King's ear." He went on to speak of domestic affairs : "Are not honours now sold and do not they then sell justice again?" Here the undergraduate of Exeter burst into the Latin tongue, *vendere iure potest, emerat ille prius*. He recalled Tully, Verres, and the law *de pecuniis repetundis*.

Coming to earth again he cited the two cases of Hugh de Burgh and the Earl of Suffolk. While they were dominant there was no Supply, when they were removed by Henry III, and Richard II respectively, money flowed in. He concluded with a taunt at Buckingham's attempt to huckster the crown jewels in the market of Amsterdam : "I hear nothing said in this House of our jewels, nor will I speak of them, but I could wish they were within these walls." The House immediately decided that "common fame" was a good ground of accusation against Buckingham, the question having already been debated on the raising of Dr. Turner's resolutions, and sent notice to the Duke of the proceedings against him. At the same time they made a grant of three subsidies and three-fifteenths, but only if grievances had been first redressed. Charles saw clearly that this was the crisis : the time for warnings was past, he concluded that the time for threats had come. He bade the Commons meet him on the 29th. This was the day on which they had invited Buckingham to give them an account of his

[1] R. I. 220.

proceedings. Coventry addressed them. They must learn the difference between liberty of counsel and liberty of control. They had not censured Coke and Turner, they had followed Turner's lead in basing their attack on Buckingham on common fame. The Supply was not enough, and the manner of giving it dishonoured the King. Unless they gave a better answer within three days the session might not be allowed to continue. Charles then spoke shortly, as was his custom, but most concisely. "Mr. Coke told you it was better to be eaten up by a foreign enemy than to be destroyed at home. Indeed I think it more honour for a King to be invaded and almost destroyed by a foreign enemy than to be despised by his own subjects. Remember, that Parliaments are altogether in my calling, sitting, and dissolution: therefore as I find the fruits of them good or evil, they are to continue or not to be."

The Commons did not give way. At Eliot's advice they determined to draw up a remonstrance to explain their position to Charles. But before this was done they were summoned to a conference to hear Buckingham's statement. He told them the whole of the involved story about Pennington's ships, and assured them that they were coming home. He also told them of the immense labour with which he had endeavoured to carry out the warlike policy of Parliament since his return from Spain.

The Commons proceeded with their remonstrance and presented it to Charles. There was a short Easter recess, April 4th–13th, then the House voted a fourth Subsidy. Meantime Charles's relations with France had gone from bad to worse, the hope of the adherence of that Power to the triple alliance begun at Southampton and continued at the Hague was wrecked on the question

BUCKINGHAM IMPEACHED

of the seizures for contraband. Richelieu turned from England to Spain, the Rochellois appealed to the English Government; not only was the alliance broken but war was imminent. It was under these aggravated political, complications that the impeachment of Buckingham was undertaken.

On April 22nd the Commons had completed their charge against the Duke. They sent him the Heads of their Charges and asked him to reply within two days if he desired to do so. In courteous terms he informed them that the Lords did not think fit that he should.[1] On May 8th, the Commons desired a conference with the Lords concerning the impeachment and accusation of a great peer of that House. They appointed eight chief managers. These were Digges, Herbert, Selden, Glanville, Whitby, Pym, Wandesford, and Eliot. Each of these was allowed to choose two assistants, and Pym selected Sir Nathaniel Rich and Mr. Browne.[2]

There were twelve articles of impeachment, covering the whole field of recent maladministration. To Pym fell the ninth, tenth, and eleventh articles, which dealt with the sale of titles of honour, the sale of places of judicature, and the wholesale bestowal of titles of honour upon the Duke's own kindred.[3] Pym disclaimed all learning or ornament and promised as much convenient brevity as "one that knows that your Lordships' time is much more precious than my words." For all that his address occupies five full pages of Rushworth's folio. He drew a distinction, which is notable in view of his action in the impeachment of Strafford fourteen years later, between laws that are particular " according to the temper and occasion of several States," and " laws that be coessential and collateral with government ; and

[1] R. I. 247.   [2] C. J. I. 854, i.   [3] R. I. 334-340.

if those laws be broken, all things run to disorder and confusion. Such is that rule observed in all States of suppressing vice to encourage virtue by apt punishments and rewards."

If we may translate this into more modern terms the "particular laws" of Pym are the municipal laws of each country, his coessential and collateral laws are the Sovereignty or Imperium, in virtue of which each independent State makes, modifies, or alters its municipal laws. That this is the correct interpretation would seem to be proved by his next words : " And this is the fittest law to insist upon in a Court of Parliament, when the proceedings are not limited either by the Civil or Common Laws, but matters are adjudged according as they stand in opposition or conformity with that which is *Suprema Lex, salus Populi*." What Pym means is Sovereignty, not Law.

The rest of his speech is full of sound sense, and granted the existence of the venality complained of should carry conviction. Two characteristic passages show the man. He refers to Buckingham as " this Great Man whom they have taken notice of to be the principal patron and supporter of the Semi Pelagian and a Popish Faction set on foot to the danger of Church and State," and after quoting Aristotle's *caveat* to the Thebans that no merchant ought to have any place in the government until he was ten years distance from his commercial life and so purged of his habit of buying and selling, he continues: "Next to the Pagans the Popes, a generation full of corruption, yet they by their Bulls are full of declamation against such." " Religion " was still Pym's primary interest, though now he was to be found on the full tide of the civil strife as well.

Ehot had been appointed to make the Epilogue to the Impeachment, and he did it in his worst style. With the courtesy of the other managers, and notably of Pym, his shrill and venomous harangue struck discordantly.

He described [1] the inward character of the Duke's mind by comparing it to " the Beast, called by the Antients Stellionatus: a Beast so blurred, so spotted, so full of foul lines that they knew not what to make of it... In reference to the King, he must be styled the canker in his Treasure; in reference to the State the moth of all goodness."

The poor fanatic was now impelled to utter the fatal sentences which were to send him to his doom:

" I can hardly find him a match in parallel in all precedents none so like him as Sejanus who is thus described by Tacitus, *Audax, sui obtegens, in alios criminator, iuxta adulator et superbus.* To say nothing of his veneries if you please to compare them, you shall easily discern wherein they vary: such boldness of the one hath lately been presented before you, as very seldom or never hath been seen. For his secret intentions and calumniations I wish this Parliament had not felt them nor the other before. . . . Sejanus' pride was so excessive as Tacitus saith ' He neglected all counsel, mixed his business and service with the Prince, seeming to confound these actions and was often styled *Imperatoris laborum socius.*' " [2]

It is worth while to raise the question why, apart from the painful circumstances of his death, Ehot should be regarded as a type of a patriot. There may be times when a cause can be advanced by ribaldry, by invective: in the appeal to low natures low oratory best arouses low

[1] R. I. 353-355.
[2] This speech of Eliot's aroused John Forster to an ecstasy of delight. These are the epithets he uses in regard to it: " *impressive; nervous; daring; clear; gorgeous; eloquent; bitter; earnest; disdainful; terrible; serious; fearful; mournful; vivid; indignant; dreadful; tremendous.*" They will all be found on pages 42-45 of his earlier *Life of Sir John Eliot.* [Statesmen of the Commonwealth of England, Vol. I (1840).]

passions. It has been at times the painful duty of the patriot in the public interest to throw to the wolves those friends who have in the past been serviceable to himself in his private capacity, yet it has seldom been necessary to blacken them with infamy and to dwell upon their iniquities. Had Buckingham been all that Eliot says he was, and assuredly he was not, it was not for Eliot to say it ; had it been for Eliot to say it, it was not for him to say it as he did. Such men as John Eliot are the bane of the cause which they adopt. They are the playthings of subtle natures which exploit their sensibilities ; by incessant exaggeration they weaken the force of superlatives ; their brilliance destroys the infinite variations between black and white, and in the end they excite only the tedium and the ridicule even of their victims.

" If the Duke is Sejanus," said Charles, " I must be Tiberius." He addressed the Lords next day in Buckingham's favour. Sir Nathaniel Rich, representing the Commons, asked that the Duke might be put under restraint pending the conclusion of the impeachment, but this was refused on formal grounds. When he returned to the Lower House a surprise awaited him : Digges and Eliot had been seized and carried off to the Tower. There was much commotion, which Pym with his unshakable nerve and innate genius for leadership, attempted to check, but with slight success. The House broke up in confusion. Next day Carleton, the Vice-Chamberlain, addressed the House at once. He began by commending Pym's speech and advice of the previous day " to do things wisely and temperately, and not tumultuously." [1] He then told the House the cause of the imprisonment, viz., Eliot's violent language, and a phrase of Digges which had been misunderstood, and

[1] C. J. 859, ii.

which later he easily cleared to the satisfaction of the King. He went on to delicate ground when he warned them "Move not his Majesty by trenching upon his Prerogatives lest you bring him out of love with Parliaments." He warned them to beware of the example of those foreign countries where the turbulence of Parliaments had moved Kings to abolish them altogether.

Digges was released on May 16th, Eliot three days later; both justified their words in the eyes of the Commons, and, with the rest of the managers, were cleared of excess of duty.

On May 28th, Suffolk, the Chancellor of the University of Cambridge, died, and Charles decided that Buckingham should succeed him.[1] The royal pleasure was intimated to the University and the Duke was duly elected, but not without keen opposition. The election resolved itself into a contest between the Arminian and Calvinist parties in the Church, and the former carried the day by the small majority of five. The Commons were exceedingly annoyed that a person who had fallen so gravely under their displeasure should be advanced so highly. They resolved to draw up a general remonstrance on Grievances and give to their discussion thereof precedence of Supply. Herein they proposed to ask the King to remove the Duke from his counsels, "For we protest before your Majesty and the whole world, that until this great person be removed from intermeddling with the great affairs of State we are out of hope of any good success, and we do fear that any money we can and shall give will, through his misemployment, be turned rather to the hurt and prejudice of this your kingdom than otherwise, as by lamentable experience we have found in those large supplies formerly and lately given."

[1] R. I. 371.

position that he had already taken up,
liberty of counsel but not of control, a
he dissolved his second Parliament.

CHAPTER VI

THE THIRD PARLIAMENT OF CHARLES I

BETWEEN the dissolution of the second Parliament of Charles I and the assembling of the third, lay a period of two years. Abroad and at home they were momentous.1 Lower and lower in Germany sank the fortunes of the hapless Palatine and of the cause which he had wrecked. Before the Parliament had ceased to meet, the adventurer Wallenstein had routed Mansfeld at the Bridge of Dessau. A few months later Tilly put the Danes to flight at Lutter, and before the year was out Mansfeld was dead. In 1627, Wallenstein, his conqueror, had driven the Danes from Silesia, and had occupied Holstein, Schleswig and Jutland.

Less even than Germany did France offer consolation to the English Puritan. There his co-religionists were hard pressed by the great Cardinal. In 1626, Richelieu had come to grips with his enemies. The flower of the French aristocracy, led by the King's own brother, had shattered themselves in vain. Richelieu was pre-eminently a statesman and would have conceded much to avert another civil war. But Louis XIII was in no mood to endure longer the anti-national heresies of the Huguenot faction, and when in 1627 they again rebelled, he besieged them straitly in La Rochelle. The activity of the Huguenots coincided with the growth of hostile feeling towards the French amongst Englishmen. The Queen's French attendants were a perpetual source of irritation to Charles; they constantly reminded her of those concessions which her arrival was to bring to the English Catholics, but which they had never received. The reproaches of the high-spirited girl marred the happiness of the King's wedded life. In July, 1626, Charles sent them all away, a proceeding which Louis might well regard as both discourteous and a breach of the nuptial Treaty.

War with France began in March, 1627, and this time Buckingham resolved to lead in person. But first of all the sinews of war had to be secured.

On the dissolution of his second Parliament, Charles had, by Letters of Privy Seal, required certain sums of money from those whom the Lords-Lieutenant of each shire deemed to be best able to pay; the request specified the sum and promised repayment within eighteen months. The names of those who should refuse to pay were to be returned to the Council. Later this was extended to a general loan from every Subject in accordance with the rate at which he was assessed in the subsidy granted by the defunct Parliament.

Such was the famous Forced Loan of 1626, and its importance cannot be overestimated, insomuch as illegal taxation led immediately to illegal imprisonment.

It was not indeed likely that opposition would be slight or easily repressed. The lower class of those who refused payment had short shrift; they were pressed, by a delightful if unconscious irony, for the Navy, there to make a closer acquaintance with the Lord High Admiral. Gentlemen had to appear before the Council table, and if their determination survived browbeating, they were committed to imprisonment.

Amongst these was Sir Thomas Wentworth. He had found himself compelled to abandon that judicious

THE FORCED LOAN

attitude which he had announced to his friend Wandesford in 1625, when he had been so scurvily pricked for Sheriff, "For my rule, which I will not transgress, is never to contend with the Prerogative out of a Parliament, nor yet to contest with a King but when I am constrained thereunto." He added significantly, ". . . expecting that happy night that the King shall cause his Chronicles to be read, wherein he shall find the faithfulness of Mardocheus, the treason of his eunuchs, and then let Haman look to himself." [1]

For the present, Lord High Admiral Haman was stronger than the Yorkshire Mardocheus, but Mardocheus had set his back against the wall and would not pay the £40 demanded. In vain his correspondents urged him to yield. ". . . the stream runs daily stronger and stronger against the refusers, and this day the gentlemen of Lincolnshire are all committed to the prisons in London," wrote Lord Clifford, ". . . and every man here that loves you wishes you may not run so great hazard, both of your life and fortune." [2]

Not only the gentry resisted, "Sir Harbottle Grimston, was laid up last week : his neighbours of Chelmsford, the six poor tradesmen, stand out stiffly, notwithstanding the many threats and promises made them, which made one say that honour that did use to reside in the head was now, like the gout, got into the foot. Some of the Judges stagger and incline to pressing them, but Hyde, the late Chief Justice, will rather quit his minivers than subscribe to it." [3]

Stout old Calvert, now Lord Baltimore, just about to start for Newfoundland, wrote : "Never put off the matter to your appearance here, for God's sake, but send your

[1] Straff. L. and D. I., p. 33.   [2] Ibid. I., p. 36.
[3] Straff. L. and D. I., p. 38.

money in to the collectors in the County without more ado . . ."[1]

Wentworth remained unmoved. He appeared before the Commissioners at York, then before the Privy Council in London. He showed himself respectful but determined, and was committed to the Marshalsea. After a short period he was kept in partial confinement at Dartford in Kent, until he left it to take his seat in Charles's Third Parliament as a Knight of the Shire of York.

The name of Pym does not occur amongst those of the refusers of the Forced Loan, a fact which Forster omits to mention. Instead, he asserts that after the dissolution of 1626, " Pym was thrown into prison, and only again released on his return to the third Parliament for Tavistock." This assertion is absolutely incorrect. Neither Pym nor any other member of the Commons suffered an hour's imprisonment.

Some Supply being scraped together, Buckingham sailed in July, 1627, to raise the siege of La Rochelle. He determined to occupy the small adjacent island of Rhé; this would give him a base against La Rochelle and enable him to disturb French commerce by means of privateers. But the French had recently fortified St. Martin, the chief town of the island, and this it was necessary to take at once. The attempt to achieve this is a tale of three months' disaster, until in the last days of October, what was left of the expedition returned. Some 4,000 men had been lost, Rhé had not been occupied, the Rochellois were unrelieved.

England was ablaze with indignation. Holles wrote a fiery letter to his brother-in-law, Wentworth : " Yet for all this the Duke would stay, and would not stay, doing things by halves, for had he done either and gone

[1] Straff. L. and D. I., p. 39.

through with it, possibly it could not have been so ill as it is. . . . This only, every man knows, that since England was England it received not so dishonourable a blow." [1]

Charles did what he could. Another fleet must be equipped somehow. Already he had not shrunk from severe measures. Chief Justice Crew had been dismissed because he refused to recognise the Forced Loan as legal. Five knights who had been imprisoned for refusing to pay were denied a Habeas Corpus, on the ground that they had been confined by the special command of his Majesty, and not on any special cause assigned.[2] The decision of the Judges to this effect created a grievance even more pressing than had the Forced Loan, for the person now was touched as well as the pocket.

Such were the untoward conditions under which Charles found himself reluctantly compelled to meet his third Parliament.

The Houses met on March 17th, 1628. Charles told them plainly that the common danger was the cause of that Parliament, and that Supply was its chief end. Should they not contribute heartily he must needs " in discharge of my conscience use those other means which God hath put into my hands, to save that which the follies of some particular men may otherwise hazard to lose." He added : " Take not this as a threatening (for I scorn to threaten any but my equals), but an admonition." [3] On March 19th, the Commons chose Sir John Finch to be their Speaker. One phrase will show his position : " *Eritis sicut dii* was the serpent's counsel and ruined mankind, nor is it fit for private men, much less for me, to search into the counsels or actions of Kings." In reply Lord Keeper Coventry assured him that " My

[1] Straff. L. and D. I. 42. [2] Darnel's Case, 1627. [3] R. I. 477.

Lord the King is like unto an angel of God, of a quick, of a noble and just apprehension; he strains not at gnats, but will easily distinguish between a vapour and a fog, between a mist of errors and a cloud of ill wills." [1] These fine phrases finished, the Commons got to business and proceeded to belie them as quickly as possible.

There were two sessions of this famous Third Parliament: the first extended from March 19th to June 26th, 1628, the second from January 20th to March 10th, 1629. The first period is that of the Petition of Right and of the renewed struggle over Tunnage and Poundage. The interval is marked by the murder of Buckingham. The second session is mainly occupied with Rolles' Case, which made the dispute concerning Tunnage and Poundage acute, and culminated in the wild scene in the House on March 2nd. The first session witnesses the failure of reason in the rejection of Wentworth's proposals, and the momentary success of compromise in the acceptance of the lawyers' Petition of Right. The second shows the inadequacy of that measure to restrain the determination of Charles to persist in the path of dead Buckingham, and stops short in the deadlock created by the religious animosities of Eliot and of Pym. Nothing could be more significant of the future, nothing more distressing to sound statesmanship.

Pym was appointed, as before, Committee on Privileges, he was also a Committee to frame a petition to the King about a general fast, to which his Majesty assented. In the debates on Grievances and Supply which followed, the lead was taken by Eliot and Wentworth. On March 27th the latter indicated clearly the lines afterwards adopted in the Petition of Right; he denounced illegal imprisonment, compulsory employment abroad, forced loans, and

[1] R. I. 485.

billetting of soldiers on unwilling householders. Eliot's speeches took the same position but with divagations on recusants.

On April 1st a Committee of the House resolved, without one dissentient voice, that no freeman might be committed without cause shown. If no such cause were shown, anyone, however committed, had a right to the Habeas Corpus, and to bail. Next day certain heads of expenditure submitted by the King were considered, and there was difference of opinion as to the wisdom of dissecting in debate past errors of policy, or future plans of campaign therein disclosed. On this question Pym spoke with his usual judiciousness and right judgment. He deprecated random talk: " In no case is it fit to examine the Propositions, especially of the arrearages of the merchant ships and for preparations for the foreign wars." [1]

He showed the same discrimination on the more important subject of the relation of Grievance and Supply. On April 4th Supply was under the consideration of the House, which had just received another of several conciliatory messages from the King, assuring to all the fullest enjoyment of their liberties. As much as five subsidies were suggested. Eliot was alarmed at such generosity, but Wentworth supported the proposal in the strongest manner. It fell in with the method of procedure which seemed to him shortest and surest. This was to secure for the future those personal and proprietary liberties, which Charles had recently invaded, by a Bill which the Royal assent should make law for ever. The superiority of this method over a humble Petition of Right was obvious and convincing. The House would be spared the antiquarian reminiscences of

[1] P. H. II. 254.

Coke, the plethoric case law of his fellow-lawyers. It would be spared the heroics of Eliot, perpetually on the pounce to trip again his late patron Buckingham. By preventing these it would prevent the irritation produced in Charles's mind by the legal exposition of his subjects' rights, and that imputation of unworthy motives, of which Eliot was a past master.

On the other hand, assuming that the Lords would support such a Bill, Charles no doubt would be aggrieved, but with five subsidies in his left hand and the Bill in his right, Wentworth might well be confident of success. It was the policy of a statesman, but could scarcely be expected to approve itself to patriotic tonguesters. Pym supported it heartily in a speech delivered on April 4th.[1] " In business of weight," he said, " dispatch is better than discourse. We came not hither without all motives that can be towards his Majesty, had he never sent in this messsage. We know the danger of our enemies. We must give expedition to expedition, let us forbear particulars. A man in a journey is hindered by asking too many questions. I do believe our peril is as great as may be, every man complains of it, that doth encourage the enemy. Our way is to take that that took away our estates, that is, the enemy ; to give speedily is that that the King calls for. A word spoken in season is like an apple of silver, and actions are more precious than words. Let us hasten our resolutions to supply his Majesty." Well indeed would it have been for Charles and for his Kingdom had he been able now to give his confidence to Wentworth and to Pym. An instant jettison of Buckingham and of Eliot would have saved the ship of State a stormy tossing.

On April 7th, Mr. Secretary Coke reported to the House

[1] R. I. 525.

his Majesty's acceptance of the subsidies and his gratification therewith. He also informed them of a pacific speech made by the Duke of Buckingham at the Council Table, wherein he had expressed his joy at the devotion of the Parliament to his Majesty, his grief that he had himself so long been accounted " the man of separation, and that divided the King from his people. . . . Therefore this day I account more blessed to me than my birth to see myself able to serve them, to see you brought in love with Parliaments, to see a Parliament express such love to you." [1] The makebate Eliot saw his chance. What need, he would fain know, of any third person of whatsoever quality, to commend or add to their affections to his Majesty. Let no man take the boldness to introduce it within those walls—and so on, and so on, for ever darkening counsel, for ever exasperating latent animosities.

A sub-committee was appointed on April 28th to draw up a Bill on the liberty of the subject. It consisted of all the lawyers of the House and of eighteen others, of whom were Pym, Coke, Rich, Eliot, and Wentworth, and met in the Inner Temple Hall.[2] They did their work rapidly, for on the next day they presented their draft to the Grand Committee. There was no recital of grievances, Charles was not reminded of his breaches of the law, but he was to be invited to give his assent to an Act which would debar him in future from billetting soldiers without the householders' authority, from levying loans or taxes without consent of Parliament, and from committing a man to prison. If he did commit a man the Judges were to disregard the King's orders and bail him or set him free. Some hostile opinion being shown to such complete clipping of the King's

[1] R. I. 526. [2] C. J. I. 890, i.

power to commit, Wentworth suggested a modification. Let them strengthen Habeas Corpus, then "the too speedy commitments at Whitehall would be rectified by equally speedy bailments at Westminster."

At this point Charles intervened. He sent to ask the House " whether they would rest on his royal word and promise." In reply, the Commons prepared a Remonstrance, which should declare that the laws had been violated by his Majesty's Ministers, and that their desire to proceed by Bill was in conformity with ancient practice. Charles would have none of it. He was willing to confirm Magna Charta and six other statutes, but it must be " without additions, paraphrases, or explanations." Wentworth's hope of vindicating the liberties of the subject by Bill was vain, and his leadership of the House was over.

There was some plain speaking in Committee on May 6th, when Charles's answer was received. Sir Nathaniel Rich went so far as to compare his Majesty to a debtor who said, " I owe you nothing but pray trust me." Pym remarked that their assurance in the King's word would be sufficient if they knew what the King's sense and meaning was. " We have not his word only, but his oath also at his Coronation. We complain of unjust imprisonment upon loans, I hear not any say we shall be [troubled] no more, or that matter of State shall be no more pretended when there is none. . . . We all rest on the King's royal word. But let us agree in a rule to give us satisfaction."[1] Mr. Secretary Coke demurred to Pym's view. Did then, he asked, the King's word add nothing to the force of a law. His namesake, Sir Edward, came to Pym's rescue. They did not, he said, distrust

[1] G. VI. 273.

the King, but they must have his word "in a Parliamentary way," viz., by a Petition of Right.

Thus was originated that declaratory statement of law as it then existed on the points in dispute which his Majesty affirmed as a Petition of Right, and which took the place of Wentworth's rejected scheme of a Bill. The lawyers' appeal to custom was adopted rather than the legislators' appeal to sovereignty.

Pym and the leaders of the House at once accepted it, and the same sub-committee which had drawn up the previous Bill was now empowered to draw up the Petition. On May 8th Selden produced the result of their labours. After the usual conferences the Lords proposed the following addition: "We humbly present this Petition to your Majesty not only with a care of preserving our own liberties but with due regard to leave entire that sovereign power wherewith your Majesty is trusted for the protection, safety and happiness of your people."

This clause met with much disapproval in the Commons. Alford asked, "What is sovereign power?" and answered in the words of Bodin, "That it is free from any condition, by this we shall acknowledge a regal as well as a legal power. Let us give that to the King the law gives him and no more." Sir Thomas declared, "If we do admit of this addition we shall leave the subject worse than we found him. . . . Let us leave all power to his Majesty to punish malefactors but these laws are not acquainted with 'Sovereign Power.' We desire no new thing nor do we offer to trench on his Majesty's prerogative."

Pym spoke to the same effect: "I am not able to speak to this question, I know not what it is. All our Petition is for the laws of England, and this power seems to be another distinct power from the power of the law. I know how to add sovereign to his person but not to his power, and we cannot leave to him a 'sovereign power.' Also we never were possessed of it." [1]

In reply the Lords denied that in using the phrase "Sovereign Power" they meant to give the King anything new. As his Majesty was a King, he was a Sovereign and must have power. This futile explanation was supplemented by a phrase which was more illuminating. The words, they said, were easier than the word "Prerogative." In adding this the Lords put the matter in a nutshell, and did so none the less that they did it by chance. That "sovereign power" which Pym was unable to understand, and which they were unable to define, was yet the very real upshot of the whole constitutional struggle. In every State there must needs be a power above the law, in virtue of which the law is law or ceases to be law, which stands ready to smite down the invader and to punish the evildoer. In the days of the Tudors it was to be found in the Prerogative, to-day it is to be found in those who can make an Act of Parliament. Pym, who knew naught of this *imperium* or its whereabouts, was yet destined to be one of the main instruments of its transference from King to Commons.

After several conferences the Lords consented to withdraw the obnoxious phrase and join with the Commons in the Petition. On May 28th, it was presented to his Majesty, and on June 2nd he came to the House of Lords and told them and the Commons attending, that in formal things as in essential, he desired to give them as much content as in him lay. This answer did not please the Commons, and on June 3rd, Eliot, in a long and rambling speech enumerated every grievance and misgovernment as if they had not been heard before. He ended by proposing a remonstrance to the King.

[1] R. I. 562.

Rushworth reports[1] that many of the members thought it not suitable to the wisdom of the House in that conjuncture to begin to recapitulate those misfortunes which were now obvious to all; Sir Henry Martin indeed went so far as to attribute Eliot's oratory to disaffection to his Majesty. Nevertheless the House accepted his motion.

The effect on the King and on Buckingham of this tactless performance might have been foreseen. Two days later Charles sent a message to the Commons commanding them that in the short time remaining before the end of the session they should not " lay any scandal or aspersion upon the State—Government or Ministers thereof."

The guileless Eliot was amazed. It must be their sins, he conceived, that made God thus turn his Majesty's heart from them. " I am confident no Minister how dear soever can—" Here the Speaker started up from the chair, apprehending Sir John intended to fall upon the Duke . . . said, with tears in his eyes, " There is a command laid upon me, that I must command you not to proceed." Whereupon Sir John Eliot sat down.

" ' I am as much grieved as ever,' said Sir Dudley Digges, ' Must we not proceed? Let us sit in silence, we are miserable, we know not what to do.' "

" Hereupon there was a sad silence in the House for a while, which was broken by Sir Nathaniel Rich in these words :—

" We must now speak or for ever hold our peace, for us to be silent when King and Kingdom are in this calamity is not fit. The question is, whether we shall secure ourselves by silence—yea or no ? I know it is more for our security, but it is not for the security of those for whom we serve. Let us think on them.' "

[1] R. I. 592.

In the Committee into which the House presently resolved itself several members opined that the speech lately spoken by Sir John Eliot had given offence, as they feared, to his Majesty.

Finch, the Speaker, himself sought an interview with the King, and his well-known affections towards the Court may have reduced some of the inflammation caused by Eliot's folly. It was not till June 7th that Charles gave way. On that day the Commons were summoned to the bar of the Lords. The King was on the throne. "I am willing," he said, "to please you in words as well as in substance." The petition was read and then the Clerk pronounced the words "*Soit droict fait comme est désiré.*" The Petition of Right was now law of the land.

None the less the Commons proceeded with their Remonstrance. When it was completed it contained the inevitable demand for harsh treatment of the Roman Catholics, and the equally inevitable denunciation of Arminians within the Church of England. Then it turned upon Buckingham. Upon him it fixed the responsibility for everything that had gone wrong since Charles ascended the throne, and it requested the King to keep him no longer "in his great offices, or in his place of nearness and counsel about your sacred person."

Charles received the Remonstrance on June 17th. He told the Commons shortly that he would consider of their grievances as they should deserve. The Commons then resumed their debates on Tunnage and Poundage and their attempt to fix the principle that without Act of Parliament no such duty could be imposed by the Crown. Charles announced that he would prorogue Parliament on June 26th. The Commons then began to draw up a second remonstrance, reiterating this principle, and also alleging that the imposition of Tunnage, Poundage, and other like charges was contrary to the Petition of Right. On the 26th, Charles prorogued Parliament. He declared roundly that " the profit of my Tunnage and Poundage, one of the chief maintenances of my Crown," did not lie within the four corners of the Petition of Right. " It is a thing I cannot want, and was never intended by you to ask, nor meant, by me I am sure, to grant." [1] The session was prorogued to October 20th.

It remains to notice Pym's activity in this first session in the matter of Religion, which indeed occupied him more than did civil grievances. He was especially concerned with the attack on Dr. Roger Manwaring.

The fiercer of the Puritan preachers had their counterparts on the royal side, and already Parliament had taken notice of one of them, Dr. Robert Sibthorpe, who had laid it down in a sermon that subjects were bound to obey their King unless his commands were contrary to the laws of God or of nature, and that even then they were not to resist him. The refusal of Abbot to license this sermon brought about the Archbishop's disgrace at Court.

Dr. Roger Manwaring, Vicar of St. Giles' in the Fields, now transcended Sibthorpe's efforts in two sermons, which he preached before the King himself in the month of July, 1627. Those who disobeyed the King would, he asserted, be damned eternally. He proceeded to apply this preposterous assertion to those, who, like Sir Thomas Wentworth, had refused to pay their assessment of the Forced Loan.

The Commons might well have disdained to notice this absurdity had it not been for two considerations. The first was that Charles wished the sermons to be licensed

[1] R. I. 631.

and published, against the better judgment of Laud, and this was accordingly done. The second was that in them Manwaring had strengthened his eulogy of absolute monarchy by a proportionate depreciation of Parliamentary assemblies. They accordingly took up the gauntlet and, of course, chose Pym for their champion. Part of their Declaration ran as follows : " Whereas by the laws and statutes of this realm the free subjects of England do undoubtedly inherit this right and liberty not to be compelled to contribute any tax, tallage, aid, or to make any loans not set or imposed by common consent by Act of Parliament. . . . Nevertheless the said Roger Manwaring in contempt, contrary to the laws of this realm, hath lately preached in his Majesty's presence two several sermons, both which sermons he hath since published in print in a book intituled *Religion and Allegiance*, and with a wicked and malicious intention, to seduce and misguide the conscience of the King's most excellent Majesty touching the observation of the Laws and Customs of this Kingdom and of the rights and liberties of the subjects." [1] They therefore demanded that he should be punished.

Pym's speech before the Lords on this occasion covers ten pages of Rushworth's folio. [2] Here it may be summarised. He divided his discourse into three parts, the Preamble, the Body of the Charge, and the Conclusion or Prayer of the Commons. From these resulted three Positions, the first that the form of government in any State cannot be altered without apparent danger of ruin to that State. The second position was that the law of England, which exempted the subject from non-Parliamentary taxation, was " the ancient and fundamental law issuing from the first frame and constitution of the

[1] R. I. 594. [2] R. I. 595-604.

Kingdom.'" The third position was that the liberty of the subject is not only profitable for the people, but most necessary for the King. " The best [1] form of government is that which doth actuate and dispose every part and member of a State to the common good, and as those parts give strength and ornament to the whole so they receive from it again strength and protection in their several stations and degrees."

" If this mutual relation and intercourse be broken, the whole frame will quickly be dissolved and fall in pieces, and instead of this concord and interchange of support, whilst one part seeks to uphold the old form of government and the other part to introduce a new, they will miserably consume and devour one another. Histories are full of the calamities of whole States and nations in such cases. It is true that time must needs bring some alterations, and every alteration is a step and degree towards a dissolution; those things only are eternal which are constant and uniform. Therefore it is observed by the best writers upon this subject that those commonwealths have been most durable and perpetual which have often re-formed and re-composed themselves according to their first institution and ordinance; for by this means they repair the breaches and counterwork the ordinary and natural effects of time." Pym traced these laws back to the days of the Saxons; they had often been broken, it was true, but as often confirmed by Charters of Kings and by Acts of Parliament. " The Petitions of the Subjects upon which those Charters and Acts were founded were ever Petitions of Right demanding their ancient and due liberties, not suing for any new."

[1] " Best " not in R. adopted from P. H. II. 391, accepted by G. VI. 64, 313.

He proceeded to enumerate the different resources provided at different periods of English History " for the support of the Sovereignty " and to show how these had been dispersed, and concluded, " The hearts of the people and their bounty in Parliament is the only constant Treasure and Revenue of the Crown which cannot be exhausted, alienated, anticipated or otherwise charged and incumbered."

As regards Absolute Power " it is all one to leave the Power absolute, and to leave the Judgment arbitrary, when to execute that Power ; for though these limitations should be admitted, yet it is left to the King alone to determine what is an urgent and pressing necessity . . . and the subject is left without remedy. . . . All Kings that are not tyrants or perjured, will be glad to bound themselves within the limits of their laws and they that persuade them to the contrary are vipers and pests both against them and the Commonwealth."

So spoke Pym in what is perhaps his most important contribution to the political speculation of the period. Nothing could be more constitutional, nothing more safe. *Stare super antiquas vias. Via trita tuta.* Hyde might have fathered it. This is what Pym said. It has yet to be seen what he did, and comparing the word and the deed " . . . the comic Muse is grave . . . she compresses her lips." As for Manwaring he was sentenced by the Lords to imprisonment, fine, and temporary suspension. From these he was saved by Charles, who not only pardoned him, but bestowed on him the benefice of that very Stanford Rivers which the other stalwart, Montague, had just vacated on his appointment to be Bishop of Chichester. The new incumbent followed his predecessor still further, for he, too, was presently raised to the Episcopate as Bishop of St. David's.

THE RECESS

During the recess occurred three events of profound significance. Sir Thomas Wentworth was created a Peer on July 22nd; on August 23rd Buckingham was assassinated at Portsmouth; on October 18th Rochelle surrendered to the King of France. The fall of this city was a fitting epitaph on Buckingham. It marked the complete bankruptcy of that policy which had so long entangled Charles. On the other hand, the adherence of Wentworth to the Court opened the way to the new counsels which were to guide England till 1640.

Another prorogation postponed the meeting of Parliament from October 20th to January 20th, 1629. From this date, till March 2nd, the House was mainly concerned with the discussion of Church Ceremonies and Tunnage and Poundage. With regard to the former Pym spoke in Committee on January 27th. The King had requested the House by Mr. Secretary Coke to give precedence to the question of Tunnage and Poundage and so end that dispute. Instead, the Commons decided to proceed with grievances in religion. Pym said that there were two diseases, the one old which was Popery, the other new which was Arminianism. He alluded to superstitious ceremonies and instanced Angels, Crucifixes, Altars, and " Candles burnt on Candlemas Day after the Popish manner." He urged the House to inquire into these, and also into the conduct of those persons who had departed from the teaching of the Elizabethan reformers and the Articles agreed upon at Lambeth. He alluded not obscurely to the preferment of Montague and Manwaring when he said, "Let us inquire after the abettors : let us inquire also after the pardons granted of late to some of these and the presumption of some that dare preach the contrary to truth before his Majesty." His last sentence as reported in Rushworth[1] is notable as containing his conception of the relation of Church and State in England.

"It belongs to the duty of a Parliament to establish true Religion and to punish false, we must know what Parliaments have done formerly in Religion. Our Parliaments have confirmed General Councils. In the time of King Henry VIII the Earl of Essex was condemned for countenancing Books of Heresy. For the Convocation it is but a Provincial Synod of Canterbury, and cannot bind the whole Kingdom. As for York, that is distant, and cannot do anything to bind us or the Laws: for the High Commission it was derived from Parliament."

With regard to Tunnage and Poundage, the goods of a member of the House named John Rolle had been seized on his refusal to pay the Customs duties, and so to the original question of the legality of non-parliamentary customs, was added the additional question whether privilege of Parliament freed the property as well as the person of a Member from execution of process of law. It need only be mentioned here, as providing an instructive contrast between the sagacity of Pym and the wrong-headed impetuosity of Eliot, who since the departure of Wentworth had constituted himself the leader of the House.

Eliot was for keeping the House to the narrow question whether privilege of a member had been broken. Pym took a wider view. "The liberties of this House are inferior to the liberties of this Kingdom," he declared. "To determine the privilege of this House is but a mean matter, and the main end is to establish possession of the subjects, and to take off the commission and records

[1] R. I. 647.

and orders that are against us. This is the main business; and the way to sweeten the business with the King and to certify ourselves, is, first to settle these things, and then we may in good time proceed to vindicate our own privileges." [1] Eliot, and not Pym, had his way, and the unprofitable session came to an end on March 2nd with a scene of violence.

The Speaker, Sir John Finch, declared the King's pleasure that there should be an adjournment until the 10th. He was interrupted by Eliot and others, and then declared that his Majesty had bade him leave the chair if any one attempted to speak. Holles and Valentine fell upon him at once and held him down by force. A long and unseemly wrangle ensued. Eliot endeavoured to make the Speaker read a protestation; Finch refused, and Eliot, enraged, threw his protestation on the fire. The doors were ordered to be locked, and the Serjeant sent by the King for the mace was dismissed without it. Black Rod next came to say that the King had sent for his guard to break in. Thereupon Holles recited from memory the contents of Eliot's protestation, which in three clauses denounced as capital enemies of the Kingdom, all who should introduce innovations in religion, or Popery, or Arminianism, or opinions disagreeing from the true and orthodox Church, all who should advise the levying of Tunnage and Poundage not passed by Parliament, and all merchants who should voluntarily pay such levy. Then the House adjourned and Parliament was at once dissolved by Charles. For eleven years it was to meet no more in England.

[1] G. VII. 67, 62.

CHAPTER VII

THE ADVENTURERS

In the disorderly scenes which marked the end of Charles's third Parliament Pym took no part. The reason for this is not far to seek. His main interest lay in the pursuit of those " Papists and Arminians " who were never far from his thoughts. Reference to Appendix VI will show him much occupied in committee with these topics. After the rejection of his advice to place English liberties above Parliamentary privileges, he may well have been content to permit Eliot to blunder along to his doom in the struggle concerning the Customs. In consequence he escaped the wrath of Charles, which now fell heavily upon the leaders of the Opposition.

They could not be punished directly because of the recent statute against arbitrary imprisonment, so Charles brought pressure upon the judges, and Eliot, Holles, and Valentine were tried for conspiracies in Parliament, in that they had resisted the King's orders and incited others to do likewise. They were sentenced to fine and imprisonment until submission. Holles yielded at once and was set free; of the rest, Eliot died in prison in 1631, and Strode and Valentine remained in confinement until the Election for the Short Parliament in 1640.

From 1628, March 2nd, until 1640, April 13th, John Pym is seen no more in politics. He watches the efforts of Charles, of Wentworth, and of Laud, of Weston, Noy, and Windebank to govern without a Parliament to advise, and more especially without a Parliament to subsidise. He sees the administration, though increased in efficiency, unable to maintain itself against the calls made upon its empty exchequer. He sees, with what satisfaction may well be imagined, the unadvised energy of Laud raise against himself the hostility of a great party in England, and the hatred of a majority of the Scottish nation. All this he sees as a business man going daily about his work in the City of London. It will be needful to sketch an outline of the political events of these eleven years, but first it is well to see John Pym at his business week by week as he is depicted in the Colonial State Papers.[1]

The first voyage of adventure to Providence and Henrietta, islands of the Bahama group in the West Indies, was undertaken in 1629, by the Earl of Warwick, Sir Nathaniel Rich and others, "which stood them in 2,000 and odd pounds, to be discharged out of the first proceeds from those islands." On November 19th, 1630, a meeting of the Adventurers was held at Brooke House, and the Earl of Holland was chosen Governor of the Company for the first year. John Dike, a London merchant residing in Billiter Street, was Deputy Governor, John Pym Treasurer, and William Jessop Secretary ; the following day Oliver St. John was admitted a member. On the 22nd Lord Wallace and Lord Brooke undertook the charge of providing arms and ammunition for the use of the Company, and each Adventurer was empowered to obtain as many men and boys as were willing to be employed in their service. On November 23rd, a provisional and a permanent Governor were appointed for the Colony, and arrangements made for the payment and maintenance of such ministers of religion as should be sent over. One of the officers is William Rudyerd,

[1] Cal. S. P. Col. I. 1574-1660, to which refer under dates given in text.

another is Rous. It will be remembered that Pym's stepfather was Sir Anthony Rous. On December 2nd, a meeting, held this time at Warwick House, engaged to hold harmless for two bonds of £300 apiece for the Company's use, Sir Nathaniel Rich, John Pym, and John Dike.

On December 4th, a Patent of Incorporation was granted by the King to Robert, Earl of Warwick; Henry, Earl of Holland; William, Lord Saye and Sele; Robert, Lord Brooke; John Roberts, Sir Benjamin Rudyerd, Sir Gilbert Gerrard, Sir Edward Harwood, Sir Nathaniel Rich, Sir Edmond Mountford, John Pym, Richard Knightly, Christopher Sherland, Oliver St. John, John Gourden, Gregory Cawsell, John Dike, John Grant, and others hereafter to be joined with them.

The title of the Company was to be "The Governors and Company of Adventurers for the Plantation of the Islands of Providence, Henrietta, and the adjacent Islands between 10 and 20 degrees of North Latitude and 290 and 310 degrees of Longitude." The Earl of Holland was to be the first Governor of the Company, and John Dike, Merchant of London, Deputy Governor; to the Company was given power to hold a Court on the last Thursday of each term for ever, to be styled "The General Court of the Company," and therein to ordain forms of government and elect Officers of the Company and Colony. They had full jurisdiction of life and death, and might transport men, women, and children unless expressly forbidden by the King in the case of any particular person; they might also repel all invaders by force of arms, execute martial law, monopolise trade, and coin money. His Majesty promised his assent to these letters patent in case they should be confirmed by Parliament.

On January 21st, 1631, a meeting of the Court of Providence Island was held in Mr. Dike's house in Billiter Lane, when Sir Thomas Barrington was admitted and instructed to pay his adventure of £200 to John Pym, Treasurer. On February 2nd they issued a commission appointing Captain William Rudyerd, Chief Commander of all passengers in the *Seaflower* bound for that Plantation; on the 7th they instructed the Governor and Council of Providence Island to proceed by way of jury in capital offences as well as in civil and criminal causes of great importance. They sent out a minister, Lewis Morgan, " a very sufficient scholar for his time and a studious and sober man." They ordered the erection of a Church and a Parsonage house, and gave special instructions for setting up God's ordinances; they also prohibited the cultivation of that " scurvy weed tobacco " to the neglect of staple commodities. On February 10th, at Warwick House, John Pym was settled in the place of Treasurer till next Election day, and a dinner " not exceeding the value of forty shillings " was ordered to be provided for the Company at every General Court. William Hird was allowed to take his wife with him to the Island, "No other woman goes in the same ship, and as yet there is no woman at all in the island." On November 21st, at Brooke House, Pym, as Treasurer, made his report on the state of the accounts. On December 3rd, Deputy Governor Dike's request for more money on account of the *Seaflower* was referred to Treasurer Pym. On February 14th, 1632, the minutes were read in Mr. Treasurer's chambers, but the locality where Pym resided is not named. On April 11th, at a meeting at Brooke House, there was read a letter from that " very sufficient scholar " Mr. Morgan to Sir Nathaniel Rich, " stuffed with bitter expressions and avowing of a spirit inclined to sedition and mutiny." It was resolved that he should be brought home by the next ship, he being the author, or at least the fomenter, of the Planters' seeming discontent, which might cause a revolt in the island from the Company's government. On April 13th, the Company saw to the spiritual interests of the Colonists by electing Arthur Rous as one of their ministers for the island, " he being contented to transport himself and family thither," and on the same day considered their own temporal welfare by instructing the Governor and Council to measure and set out 20 parcels of ground of 25 acres each in the most fertile places in the island, to be assigned to the first 20 Adventurers of the Company. On May 3rd, instructions were sent to the Governor and Council for the trial of Captain William Rudyerd, accused of drunkenness, swearing, ill-carriage towards the Governor and other misdemeanours since he had been in the island. Two days later more merciful counsels prevailed, and they advised concerning Captain Rudyerd that if he were a reformed man and not likely to breed division, to oppose government, or hinder the progress of religion, the trial might be forborne. On May 7th, Mr. Pym was desired to write a letter to the Customs for discharge of the charity and satisfaction of the goods now ordered. A letter was received from the Earl of Holland, who mediated for a friendly accord of the differences with Captain Rudyerd. Sir Nathaniel Rich was requested to consider this letter before the next meeting. At the next meeting Mr. Pym was desired to draw out a general instruction to the Governor and Council of the island, how to proceed against any factious person or any hinderer of religion, and the former order for the trial of Captain Rudyerd was revoked.

On May 10th, at Brooke House, the Earl of Holland was

re-elected Governor, Sir Thomas Barrington took Dike's place as deputy, Pym was re-elected Treasurer, and William Jessop Secretary. On May 10th, the Company informed the Governor and Council that, whereas they had formerly entertained a favourable opinion of Mr. Morgan's diligence as a minister, they had now evidence of his seditious and malignant spirit in two letters sent by the late Mr. Essex in the *Seaflower*. They directed that he should be suspended forthwith from his ministry and sent home by the next ship.

On May 10th, a long admonition was sent to the colonists, in which the hand of Pym is clearly visible. They were informed that the missing *Seaflower* arrived in April last, her demurrage was due to an attack by a Spanish man-of-war, wherein four Englishmen were slain. Then followed severe rebuke; the Company had read the petitions from the Planters, and marvelled how men could so much forget their duty to God and respect to the Company as to complain that half profits were too small an allowance, when the Company who had done so much got only the other half. The Planters are compared with the Israelites for their murmurings. The Company encourages those who are godly and discreet, admonishes those that are guilty, and threatens them when they return home with shame and dishonour. They express regret at the " illness " of former commodities sent out by them to the Planters, this being due to the neglect of the late Deputy Governor Dike, and they commend Ralph Walcott, nephew to Lord Brooke, to the care of Mr. Rous the minister. The Company specially approves the desire to procure Indian children, and recommends that a small number of free men should be persuaded to accompany them, but no Indian woman. They hope that by wise carriage and religious conversation these poor creatures may be won to the love of religion; they promise a midwife by next ship, also they have sent three more ministers. They direct the Governor and Council by their behaviour and carriage to set a powerful example of piety, virtue, and peace. In a letter of the same date to Governor Bell, they reiterate their Christian motives, desiring him to use with all respect and tenderness the Indians who come from the main, the spreading of the gospel being " the greatest work both in itself and in our aim."

On May 14th, at Brooke House, a request of John Pym to be relieved from his place of Treasurer was referred to the next meeting. On the following day they informed Governor Bell that they had heard that some in the island had sent for cards, dice, and tables; they pray that if any arrive they will have them burnt, or at least sent back, and that he will strictly prohibit their use under severe penalties. They add that they " mislike not lawful recreations such as chess and shooting." The Court held on June 12th referred for consideration the Treasurer's desire that every Adventurer bring in £100 to defray necessary engagements. On June 19th, at Brooke House, it was stated that Sir Nathaniel Rich and Mr. Barber had agreed to accept the composition proposed for their expenses in the first voyage of discovery, but that the late Deputy Governor, Mr. John Dike, was obdurate and held out. On November 26th Mr. Treasurer's accounts were audited at his lodging. The first meeting in the year 1633 was also held " in Mr. Treasurer's house," on February 2nd, when it was announced that Mrs. Sherland would pay no more money into the Company's stock, and on February 4th, at Brooke House, it was proposed that each member should make up his adventure to £1,000, when he might refuse to go further. This would bring the island to perfection and prevent the hazard of a total loss; this was agreed to on February 12th, when Mr. Upton was admitted and Mrs. Sherland advised to join the Company in that engagement. Sir Nathaniel Rich was to draw up rules for the future proceedings of the Company. Next day the Company considered a petition of the Earl of Holland, then Governor, to the Crown, for an exemption from the customs on their exports and imports. A resolution was come to that if no answer were received within three days they would present a petition for a grant for themselves, and two of their number were desired " to treat with the Lord Treasurer for his assistance in the effecting thereof." There were meetings on March 4th and 5th at Mr. Treasurer's lodging, and on March 15th Mr. Morgan submitted, acknowledging his two calumnious letters from Providence Island, and his wrong to the Company. On March 26th five pounds were bestowed upon him, and Mr. Treasurer Pym was desired to make the payment agreed upon for his books. On April 10th supplies were promised by the next ship, particularly necessaries for the surgeon, a good quantity of wine for the Communion, and a convenient supply of strong waters to be " used for health and not for disorder." On April 15th instructions for Richard Lane's proposed trading excursion to the Bay of Darien were drawn up ; he was to go thither with goods to trade; to provide against fear of discovery by the Spaniards and foul weather. He must ingratiate himself and his company with the Indians, concealing the object of his coming but expressing his desire to renew friendship with them as they are " favourers of the English nation," and especially of Don Francisco Draco, " whose name they seem to honour." While making what advantages he can from them he must labour to possess them with the natural goodness of the English nation, and restrain any boisterous carriage to the women, and particularly " mocking, pointing, or laughing at their nakedness." On June 1st the eldest son of Lord Saye and Sele, and John Michell, were admitted Adventurers. On December 2nd, Mr. Treasurer Pym being sued by the Attorney-General for remaining in town, it was ordered that the Company do petition the King for the Treasurer's stay in London, as their affairs would be greatly prejudiced should he be forced to remove to the country.

In 1633 Treasurer Pym's accounts were audited at Brooke House on February 19th. At the same house on May 15th, the Earl of Holland was again elected Governor, Sir Gilbert Gerrard became Deputy Governor, Pym remained Treasurer, and Jessop Secretary. On May 17th Pym gave his opinion on raising funds for further supply to the island. On June 9th the Company accepted £500 from Lord Brooke for this purpose. On the 19th painful details were to hand about Minister Rous, Mr. Ditloff saying that he was informed Mr. Rous was insufficient, not able to pray extemporary, and would, soldierlike, beat his men : that he wrote if those things were true Mr. Rous was fitter for a buff coat than a cassock, but afterwards found it otherwise. Mr. Rous taught him songs called catches, " the meaning of which word he understood not," the matter of which was the motion of creatures as the nightingale and the like, and Messrs. Rous and Sherland sang with him, but never on the Sabbath day. Ditloff denies that he had ever been reproved for singing such songs in Providence on the Lord's Day. Mr. Rous was since deceased.

On June 30th an entire share was made up to Sir Nathaniel Rich, on July 5th the Company taking into consideration the many noble favours of the Earl of Holland their Governor, although he has not paid any money unto their stock, conclude to repute him, in all dividends, an Adventurer of one entire share. Another Rous, a lieutenant who had fallen under their displeasure, was, at the request of Pym, pardoned with a caution as narrated on August 6th: "Remission by the Company for Providence Island of the public acknowledgment of Lieutenant Rous. Although the Restitution of Lieutenant Rous by the Governor to the Council table had been declared void, his offence of striking Forman is freely remitted at the entreaty of John Pym, Treasurer of the Company, without any public acknowledgment." On December 2nd Mr. Treasurer made his statement of accounts and was fully discharged.

In 1633, on February 4th, at a meeting at Warwick House, it was resolved to petition the King for incorporation under a new name, with a new patent to trade on the mainland. The Earl of Holland promised to move the King for a grant and to procure the assistance of the Lord Treasurer. On February 22nd a proposition for Mr. Lane to be of the Council of Providence was debated, and several considerations submitted by the Treasurer, John Pym, were answered, but the Treasurer refused to give his opinion, conceiving that the committee was not fully enabled to determine the question. On March 2nd a patent for the trade at Cape Gratia de Dios was read, and Mr. St. John was desired to show it to the Attorney-General. On March 9th Mr. Treasurer Pym stated his objections to the appointment of Mr. Lane to the Council in Providence, Mr. Lane was, nevertheless, elected by a majority of the committee, and Mr. Treasurer then gave his reasons for consenting to the election.

On April 20th the Company condemned Mr. Rishworth's behaviour concerning the negroes who ran away as indiscreet ("arising, as it seems, from a groundless opinion that Christians may not lawfully keep such persons in a state of servitude during their strangeness from Christianity") and injurious to themselves. They expressed also an opinion : "For the word absolute power we do utterly dislike the language and therefore would not have it once named." All respect of persons was to be avoided. On May 4th, at Brooke House, was considered Mr. Treasurer Pym's proposition that he be discharged with credit and without loss from the office he had held from the first incorporation of the Company, as also were proposals for clearing off debts owing by the Company.

Mr. Treasurer's reluctance was apparently overcome, for on May 7th, he was re-elected, with Holland again Governor and Sir Nathaniel Rich Deputy Governor, and on May 11th it was decided to pay debts of the Company out of the proceeds before making any dividend. On June 8th the Treasurer's accounts were audited and allowed, and he submitted certain financial business.

On Sunday, December 27th, the Earl of Holland presented to the King in Council a declaration on behalf of the Company for Providence Island, of which he was Governor. This declaration stated that letters from the Governor, Council, and other inhabitants of the islands informed them that on the 24th of July last, a Spanish fleet attacked the island but was beaten off by the ordnance of the forts. The island was of extraordinary importance from its position in the West Indian Seas and its interest in the trade of the richest part of America. It had a large harbour which could accommodate 100 ships of good burden. Already £30,000 had been spent upon the plantation, which yielded the King in customs £1,000 a year. The Spaniards had asserted that the

THREATS FROM SPAIN

King of Spain would send gerater forces to destroy the plantation, and the Planters were so alarmed that, unless relieved by May next, they threatened to desert the island. On December 27th an order was made thereupon, in which further consideration of the declaration was referred to the Privy Council until the treaty with Spain should be duly weighed, the King giving licence to his subjects to defend themselves from assaults, and to act on the offensive against any who attempted to injure their trade.

In 1636, on January 29th, several propositions were made whether the Company should carry on the Plantation by themselves, deliver it over to the State, or otherwise; on February 5th, Mr. Treasurer was requested to set down some propositions for carrying on the plantation, and it was unanimously declared that the work ought not to be deserted; this he did three days later. On May 21st Lord Mandeville was admitted to half of Sir Nathaniel Rich's share of adventure; on the 26th the Earl of Holland was again elected Governor, and Henry Darley chosen Deputy in the room of Sir Nathaniel Rich. Then debate arose whether it were necessary to have a Treasurer, and Pym reminded the Company of his great charges and of a previous entry in his favour. He was desired not to relinquish the office of Treasurer and the choice of a new one was respited. Sir William Waller was admitted to a quarter part of John Pym's entire share of adventure. On June 3rd it was resolved that by reason of the great charges and pains of John Pym some way should be resolved upon to recompense him. On June 14th, Sir William Waller was admitted to join John Pym's adventure in the voyage of Captain Rudyerd, and on the 23rd Pym announced that Sir B. Rudyerd bears £100 part of his adventure in Association.

In 1637, on February 9th, Lord Mandeville was admitted

to the share of the adventure formerly belonging to Sir Nathaniel Rich, deceased. On Monday, March 19th, the Company informed the Governor of Providence Island that the King took special notice of the island, and had very much enlarged the Company's privileges. A good account would be therefore expected, particularly as " it may be very serviceable to some designs that are now thought on in this Kingdom." He was very likely to see some members of the Company or those of a very good quality, shortly.

On May 18th, after Pym's report of the proceedings of the Committee last term, Holland was again elected Governor, but the election of Treasurer was suspended.

On December 9th it was resolved to move Lord Holland to obtain leave from the King for the Deputy Governor and for John Pym to stay in town at Christmas to attend to the Company's affairs.

In 1638 John Pym, on January 29th, related to the Company what had been done on behalf of Captain Rous, who had been captured and was now a prisoner in Spain; two days later Lord Saye engaged to go himself to the Plantation with others of the Company; a refusal by Pym, to whom the matter had been referred, to accept the demands of Captain Bell was referred to arbitration, the Company choosing for the arbitrator John Hampden. On February 15th, the Earl of Warwick, Lord Brooke and Mr. Darley declared their resolution to go to the Plantation. On March 3rd it was resolved that the King should be petitioned to " countenance any of the Company or other persons of quality that shall go to the island in their own person to settle things there."

On March 20th, at a Court of the Company held at Brooke House, £6,000 new adventure was underwritten in confidence of some members of the Company going over; the Earl of Warwick, Lord Mandeville, Lord Saye, and John Pym each subscribed £1,000, and Lord Brooke £2,000.

On May 8th, again at Brooke House, Pym was chosen Deputy Governor of the Company and the oath administered to him. On July 3th, the Governor of the Island was assured by the Company of their hope of sending by the next ship "a certain and full supply of ministers, knowing them to be of great importance for the contentment of the island." In 1639, at a meeting on February 16th at Warwick House, the financial situation of the Company was considered. The debts of the Adventurers were in round numbers as follows: The Earl of Warwick, £2,000, Lord Saye, £2,660, Lord Mandeville, £2,280, Lord Brooke, £4,150, and John Pym, £3,185. Hopes were held out of profits from "a silver mine found in an island within the Company's grant." On May 8th, Samuel Border proposed that a ship be sent forth by the Company for the lading of silver ore in the Bay of Darien, the mine being twelve miles long and two miles broad. On May 23rd the Earl of Holland was elected Governor of the Company and John Pym Deputy Governor, and an agreement was made with Samuel Border about his wages "if the ore prove right . . . and if it prove not right." On June 7th, they direct the Governor of the Island to keep the negroes harder at work, regret to hear of inconvenience "for want of administration of the Sacrament," but assure him that "God makes no difference between them that do faithfully and heartily seek Him, though there be in the appearance of man some difference between them in opinion and practice concerning outward things." They also say in regard to Samuel Border's undertaking that they will not subject themselves to men's scorn and derision as others have done when their ships brought home nothing but dirt. On November 19th, Pym informed the Company that Captain Rous had returned from Spain, leaving his friends at St. Lucas engaged to pay several sums of money for his maintenance which the Company must discharge.

In 1640, on March 16th, Pym, as Deputy Governor, signed a commission for the employment of Edward Thompson, commander of the *Hopewell*.

On May 12th, a news letter from Edmund Rossingham stated that last Wednesday the Earl of Warwick, Lord Saye, Lord Brooke, Sir Walter Earl, John Pym, and John Hampden, all Parliament men, had all their papers taken from them.

Here, then, the flood of political life again sweeps away John Pym into its fullest stream. As in 1621, the plain Receiver of Wiltshire, so now in 1640, the Deputy Governor and late Treasurer of the Company of Providence Island advances to his high destiny.

Not unconscious, not unprepared, not destitute of friends; he was now the centre of a circle knit together by kinship: Saye and Fiennes, Hampden and Cromwell, Holland and Rich, Warwick and Mandeville, Pym and Rous, by common interests and by common hatreds, accustomed to act together, and with agents and friends at the Court, in the City, and in Scotland.

Well equipped were the Adventurers of Providence Island to embark on their new and greater Adventure, and in nothing more fortunate than in the ability of their leader, Pym.

CHAPTER VIII

THE ELEVEN YEARS

IF government without Parliament were to be successful in England peace was urgently necessary, for war would involve expenditure, and increased taxation would raise at once all the old difficulties. Charles was fortunate in being able to make peace with France in 1629, and with Spain in 1630. He then endeavoured, without much success, to arouse by diplomatic negotiations a body of Continental opinion in favour of the restoration of the Palatinate. The cause of his exiled sister was always close to his heart, and when in June, 1630, Gustavus Adolphus of Sweden landed in Pomerania and began a brilliant series of operations, the prospects of Frederick were bright. But the gleam was transient. On November 6th, 1632, the battle of Lützen was fought and the great Wallenstein was at last defeated, but in the moment of victory the only brain that could have used that victory aright was no more, for Gustavus was killed. Frederick V survived this last blow but a fortnight. On November 19th he died, leaving his wife and family to the tender mercies of a world where, with the best intentions, he had done nothing but harm. His claims and titular dignity were at once assumed by his eldest surviving son, Charles Lewis. In the period covered by this book the foreign politics of England are from this year of little account.

Parliamentary subsidies being no longer available, the

ingenuity of Charles's advisers was directed to other methods of obtaining money. In 1630 all freeholders of £40 a year or upwards were compelled to assume the dignity of knighthood or to pay fines by way of composition. Next, large areas of land were resumed as Royal Forest which had gradually been encroached upon by neighbouring landowners. Thus Rockingham Forest was enlarged from six miles to sixty. But the gain to the Crown was only small and in no way compensated for the uneasiness and instability produced in the minds of the great landholders by the upsetting of boundaries which had been recognised by law for some three centuries.

Perhaps the most objectionable of the minor imposts to which the Government had recourse was the revival of monopolies in a new form. It was impossible in face of the Act of 1624 to grant them to private persons. But there was in that Act nothing to prevent the granting of such privileges to corporations. A beginning was made in December, 1631, with soap; it was soon extended to other articles, such as salt, starch, and bricks, as well as to the products of brewers and vintners. Excise was always unpopular in England, and the domestic nature of the articles selected made the grievance the more widespread, so much so that Culpepper was able to say of the Monopolists in the Long Parliament of 1640: "These men, like the frogs in Egypt, have gotten possession of our dwellings, and we have scarce a room free from them. They sup in our cup, they dip in our dish, they sit by our fire; we find them in the dye-vat, washbowl and powdering tub; they share with the butler in his box, they have marked and sealed us from head to foot. . . . They have a vizard to hide the brand made by that good law in the last Parliament of King James: they shelter themselves under the name of a corporation, they make by-laws which serve their turns to squeeze us and fill their purses." [1]

Burdensome as were these, their fame is eclipsed by the next demand. In 1634, Noy, then Attorney-General, suggested the revival of Ship Money. This famous tax had been demanded already in 1628. But the country was then at war, now it was at peace with all the world. A pretext was found in the pirates, who were a real scourge, and the sum of £100,000 was the result of the first imposition on the seaports and coast towns. This was collected without any great opposition. It was different when in 1635, a second levy of Ship Money was made, this time on inland towns also, on the plea that the defence of trade was the concern of the whole nation. Richard Chambers, who had in 1628 resisted Tunnage and Poundage, appealed against this levy, but received no hearing, ten of twelve Judges having already given a decision in favour of the Crown on the ground that his Majesty was the only judge as to when the Kingdom was in danger.

In October, 1636, a third writ of Ship Money opened the eyes of all to the fact that a new permanent tax was designed. It was true that the money collected by the two previous levies had really been spent on the navy, and that naval expeditions, under Lindsey and Northumberland respectively, had actually done some useful work against the pirates. But the question naturally rose whether it would always be thus used and what limit there would be to amount and incidence. The fear was general that it would become in Clarendon's phrase, "a spring and magazine that should have no bottom and for an everlasting supply of all occasions."

One of Wentworth's correspondents wrote to him : " I

[1] Cl. I. 148.

tell my Lord Cottington that I had rather pay ten subsidies in Parliament than ten shillings this new old way of dead Noy's." The tax was thoroughly unpopular and many began to call for a Parliament. Charles again laid a case before the Judges, and this time all twelve gave the same reply in his favour, two merely for conformity.

A test case was at last provided. Lord Saye and John Hampden, both Adventurers, refused to pay. Hampden's was the case selected for argument. Holborne and St. John, the latter an Adventurer, were his counsel. St. John pointed out that if the King were free to levy taxes at his pleasure no man could call anything his own. Two of the twelve Judges decided in favour of Hampden on technical grounds, three on the merits, and the other seven were for the Crown. Ship Money, therefore, was collected as before. The position of the Judges was at this time not to be envied: they had to be "lions under the throne" or to share the fate of Chief Baron Walter, who was suspended in 1629 either as insufficiently leonine or insufficiently under the throne. There were obvious disadvantages in making the Judges arbiters of the Constitution with liberty to decide in one way only.

The Common Law, as Coke knew well, always stood in the way at once of the efficiency and of the mischief of personal government. Wentworth stated the case with his usual acumen when he wrote, "I confess I disdain to see the Gownsmen in this sort hang their noses over the Flowers of the Crown, blow and snuffle upon them till they take both Scent and Beauty off them: or to have them put such a prejudice upon all other sorts of men as if none were able or worthy to be entrusted with Honour and Administration of Justice but themselves." [1]

[1] Straff. L. and D. I. 130.

There spoke the President of the Council of the North. It was indeed not the Courts of Law but the Extraordinary Courts of Star Chamber, of High Commission, of the North, and of Wales, which assisted personal government. Of these Courts all were of Tudor origin except Star Chamber; this was a Court in which was exercised the criminal jurisdiction of the Privy Council. Its origin is uncertain, but is at least as remote as the third Edward. Henry VII in 1487 had made it statutory and to a very small extent increased the judicial element in its composition, but even this subtle course, characteristic of the monarch, could not purge it altogether of its abnormal character.

Under the Tudors it had been a most effective instrument for crushing out the remnants of baronial independence which had survived the Wars of the Roses. It was by its very nature a dangerous weapon in autocratic hands, for it could fine, imprison and mutilate. Clarendon, as a Common Lawyer, was no friend to such Courts and he thus expresses his view: "For the better support of these extraordinary ways, and to protect the agents and instruments who must be employed in them, and to discountenance and suppress all bold inquirers and opposers, the Council-table and Star-chamber enlarge their jurisdictions to a vast extent 'holding' (as Thucydides said of the Athenians) 'for honourable that which pleased, and for just that which profited,' and being the same persons in several rooms, grew both courts to determine rights and courts of revenue to bring money into the treasury: the Council-table by proclamations enjoining this to the people that was not enjoined by the law, and prohibiting that which was not prohibited; and the Star-chamber censuring the breach and disobedience to those proclamations by very great fines and imprisonment." [1]

In these fateful eleven years it was the Ecclesiastical even more than the Civil policy of Charles that roused the fiercest animosity of his Puritan subjects and ultimately led to rebellion and civil war. He was badly advised at this juncture in placing Churchmen in the highest civil posts. By doing so he turned upon the Church a large part of the odium necessarily incurred by any autocratic government. He excited, moreover, jealousy between the churchmen thus favoured and the lay politicians who regarded the high offices of state as their own. It was well enough that he should in August, 1633, elevate Laud to the Primacy vacant by the death of the Puritan Abbot, it was quite a different thing that he should permit him first place at the Council Table. Again, when the great post of Treasurer fell vacant on the death of the corrupt and ill-natured Weston, after a brief interval he bestowed it, in 1636, on Laud's friend, William Juxon, who had succeeded the Archbishop as President of St. John's College, Oxford, and as Bishop of London, and was one day to sit on his throne at Canterbury.

The Court of High Commission, the creation of Elizabeth and of Whitgift, did for the Ecclesiastical what Star Chamber and the kindred Courts did for the lay side of Charles's government. The punishment in one or other of these Courts of Leighton, for writing "Sion's plea against Prelacy," Prynne for his "Histriomastix," Burton for a diatribe against ceremonies "For God and the King," Bastwick for "The Litany of John Bastwick," and Lilburn for having printed Puritan books in Holland, roused the Puritans to fury, none the

[1] Cl. I. 149.

ACTIVITY OF LAUD

less that in at least two of these cases the victims were as worthless as their books.

Ill-feeling was augmented by the metropolitical visitation which Laud made of all southern England between 1634 and 1637. Everywhere, in the interest of that uniformity which he believed to be essential to unity, he removed the Holy Table to the East End of the Church, suppressed Nonconformist meeting houses, abated the number of " lecturers " who were Clerks in Holy Orders without any cure of souls and the chief disseminators of Puritan beliefs. He also discouraged the Puritan veneration of the Sabbath by reviving King James's " Declaration of Sports." Nor was his activity confined to England. He became aware that many Puritans were fleeing across the seas to avoid him. He therefore procured a command that the English Prayer Book should be used in all our plantations abroad, and even in the English regiments employed and paid by the Dutch. Further, in April, 1634, he got himself appointed the head of a commission to control all the English Colonies, with the widest powers over constitutional laws, governors and clergy, authorised to inflict punishment, to set up ecclesiastical courts, and to call Charters into question. A little later the Privy Council forbade any man who had means sufficient to pay subsidy contribution to go to New England without a special licence from themselves, and any poorer person without a certificate of conformity from the minister of the parish in which he lived. There is a significant minute of the Somers Island Company for 1639, November 27th, " Concerning Richard Caswell, who confessed to having given information to the Archbishop of Canterbury as to the discipline used in the churches in those islands, and the non-conformity of the Deputy Governor and most of the ministers and Council there : he is to be suspended from his place in Court until the business is fully determined." [1] The regulations of the government with regard to this emigration of Puritans to the New World are reflected in the State Papers. Two instances will suffice : "May 2nd, 1638, Insula Vectis, Sir John Oglander to Archbishop Laud. In obedience to his letter of 17th April sends certificates of provisions which were found after a diligent search, prepared to be transported to New England and of which he has made stay." [2] Again, under date of May 25th, same year : "Examination of Nicholas Trevyse of Wapping, mariner, before Attorney-General Bankes. Was to go Master of the *Planter* to New Island with about 180 passengers, Maurice Thompson, Mr. Foote and others being partners with him. Received about £493 in gold from one Hybbins or Libbins, to supply the wants of the passengers, but gave neither bond nor bill, nor paid duty for shipping it, knows not where to find Hybbins or Libbins." [3]

Amongst those who expatriated themselves about this time was Henry Vane, the son of the Comptroller of the Household of the same name, who was later to become a Secretary of State. The younger Vane was an able, cranky lad of twenty-three. He believed himself to be a Republican and had been unable to matriculate at Oxford because he refused to take the oaths of allegiance and supremacy. He was destined to weaken every party which adopted him and to perish on a well-earned scaffold. Garrard wrote to Wentworth in 1635, September 17th: " . . . also Mr. Comptroller Sir Henry Vane's eldest son hath left his Father, his Mother, his country and that fortune which his Father would have left him here, and is for conscience' sake gone into New England, there to lead the rest of his days, being about twenty years of age.

[1] Cal. S. P. Col. I. 304.   [2] Ibid. 273.   [3] Ibid. 274-5.

He had abstained two years from taking the Sacrament in England, because he could get nobody to administer it to him standing. He was bred up at Leyden and I hear that Sir Nathaniel Rich and Mr. Pymme have done him much hurt in their persuasions this way. God forgive them for it if they be guilty." [1]

To this period also, if the story be true, must be assigned the decision of Hampden, Pym, and Cromwell to sail for New England. A change in the political situation induced them to remain.

It was not in England, Old or New, that at last the storm burst. It was in Scotland.

In 1633 Charles went to his Northern Kingdom which he had not seen since childhood. He there received his Scottish Crown and held a Parliament. With him was Laud, then Bishop of London, and while there they conceived the idea of introducing the English Liturgy into Scotland. A few months later Laud was Primate. In 1636 the fatal step was taken, and by autumn the new service-book was ready. It had been preceded by a new Court of High Commission for Scotland and a new book of Canons, both highly unpopular.

On Sunday, June 23rd, the new liturgy was to be read in Edinburgh, and the chief officers of Church and State assembled in the Cathedral Church of St. Giles. The fishwives of Edinburgh, keen theologians, were well represented. The Dean of Edinburgh had begun to read, when a stool hurtled past his head. It was thrown, fortunately with a feminine aim, by one of these women, to whom tradition assigned the name of Jeanie Geddes. " Wilt say Mass in my lug ? " shrieked the virago. Knox was speedily justified of his daughters ; all Scotland was aflame, and every true Scot was signing a National

[1] Straff. L. and D. I. 463.

League and Covenant, after the habit of that nation when deeply moved. High and low, rich and poor were of one mind. Many, we read, wept as they signed.

They were ready to shed more than ink and tears. They brushed aside Charles's offer to retreat, to revoke High Commission, Canons, and Prayer Book too. They would fain be done with Bishops as well. A General Assembly in Glasgow swept them away root and branch, and with them Charles's sovereignty.

In a few weeks a Scottish army was in the field led by Alexander Leslie, a rare, little, crook-backed soldier of fortune whom the great Gustavus had honoured for valour in many a foreign fight. The royal fortresses in Scotland fell before him like houses of cards, and presently he was on the Border.

Charles did what he could. Straightened in means as he was he got some forces together and sent them North. He knew there was treachery abroad, and to test his English nobles he tendered them an oath to fight in his cause. Saye and Brooke, Adventurers both, refused. Holland and Essex, also Adventurers, agreed to take command under Arundel and Hamilton. They failed to fire a shot; the Scots were too sagacious to attack an enemy with no stomach to fight, under leaders who desired nothing better than to be beaten. Negotiations began: they were called the Treaty of Berwick. Both sides agreed to disband: all should be settled presently. No such settlement took place, for the Scots refused to admit the Bishops into the General Assembly held at Edinburgh in August, and Charles was equally determined to compel them.

He now summoned to his side Wentworth, who since the dissolution of Parliament, had been raised from the Presidency of the Council of the North to be Lord Deputy for Ireland. This was in January, 1632, and he arrived in Dublin in July of the following year. In the six years during which he ruled that distracted country he did wonders, for he possessed the very genius of government. With what little money he could obtain he paid his soldiers and gradually reduced them to good discipline. He swept St. George's Channel free of pirates, and by his introduction of flax began what is now the staple industry of the country. His own words, written to Sir William Boswell in October, 1635, were prophetic : " The bearer I send to buy some flax seed which I find by this last year's trial to take extremely well in this country, and very ambitious I am to set up a trade of linen clothing in these parts, which, if God bless so as it be effected, will, I dare say, be the greatest enriching to this Kingdom that ever befel it."[1] Hides, tallow, fishing, forestry, and cattle breeding concerned him, too.

He made his influence equally felt in the Church of Ireland, which was in a deplorable state of neglect and poverty. By his energy ruined churches were rebuilt, and desecration stopped. How needful this was a passage in his letters shows : " There being divers buildings erected upon the fabric of Christ Church, and the vaults underneath the Church itself turned all to alehouses and tobacco shops, where they are pouring either in or out their Drink-offerings and Incense, while we above are serving the High God. . . . I have taken orders for the removing of them."[2] Ecclesiastical revenues, too, which the laity had filched were restored ; for example, he compelled the Earl of Cork to restore the revenues of the Bishopric of Lismore which he had bought for an anuual payment of £20. The revenues were worth £1,000 a year. In July, 1634, an Irish Parliament met

[1] Straff. L. and D. I. 479. [2] Ibid. p. 173.

which he had induced Charles to permit him to summon. Charles was very doubtful. "As for that Hydra," he wrote, "take good heed, for you know, that here I have found it as well cunning as malicious,"[1] and again, "My Reasons are grounded upon my Experience of them here, that they are of the Nature of Cats, they ever grow curst with age, so that if ye will have good of them put them off handsomely when they come to any age for young ones are ever most tractable."[2] The Parliament did prove tractable, and voted six subsidies. Strafford desired also to continue in Connaught the plantation system begun in Ulster, whereby large bodies of English Colonists were to be settled among the native Irish. In carrying into effect this very desirable object it cannot be denied that he acted with absolute disregard of the claims of the native owners. The greedy and unpatriotic gang of nobles and officials who hindered him at every turn—Cork, Willis, Mountmorris, and their like—he made no attempt to propitiate. His arrogant vehemence cowed them and the state which he assumed in the hitherto squalid vice-regal Court did not allow them to forget that he was in reality, as in name, the representative of the Crown.

Such was the man whom Charles now called to his counsels at home. Wentworth advised the King to summon a Parliament, and meanwhile to collect a loan from his Privy Councillors, towards which he himself contributed £20,000 on the security of the recusants' fines in the North. On January 12th, 1640, he received the honour of the Earldom of Strafford. "He would needs," says Clarendon, "in that patent have a new creation of a barony and was made baron of Raby," a house belonging to Sir H. Vane, and an honour he made account should

[1] Straff L. and D. I. p. 233.   [2] Ibid. p. 365.

belong to him, too: "which was an act of the most unnecessary provocation (though he contemned the man with marvellous scorn) that I have known, and I believe was the loss of his head."[1] Almost immediately after he was made Lord-Lieutenant of Ireland. On March 18th he was again in that country and prevailed on the Parliament there to vote four subsidies. He also offered to bring over nine thousand men to fight against the Scots if money could be sent pending the collection of the subsidies.

On April 13th met what was to be known to history as the Short Parliament. "Whilst men gazed upon each other looking who should begin (much the greatest part having never before sat in Parliament), Mr. Pimm, a man of good reputation, but much better known afterwards, who had been as long in those assemblies as any man then living, brake the ice . . . in a set discourse of above two hours."[2] Clarendon is wrong in saying that Pym broke the ice. That was done by Harbottle Grimston on the 16th; Pym's great speech was delivered on the following day, and at once assured to him that leadership of the House which he never lost until his death. Of this speech May says: "Master Pym also, a grave and religious gentleman, in a long speech of almost two hours, recited a catalogue of all the grievances which at this time lay heavy on the Commonwealth, of which many abbreviated copies as extracting the heads only were with great greediness taken by gentlemen and others throughout the Kingdom, for it was not then the fashion to print speeches of Parliament."[3] The ground for this great speech had been carefully prepared. Bedford, Holland, Essex, Saye, Hampden, and Pym, every one of them Adventurers, had met in consultation with the

[1] Cl. II. 101.   [2] Cl. II. 68.   [3] May I. VI. 40.

Scottish Commissioners. The nature of these meetings is not known. Later Charles believed them to have been treasonable, nor can there be any reasonable doubt about it. It is at any rate certain that in Pym's lodgings in Gray's Inn Lane, the course to be adopted in the coming Parliament was decided. He had also with Hampden ridden through several counties urging that petitions should be sent to the House of Commons when it met.

Pym arranged his Grievances under three heads,[1] those against the Liberty and Privileges of Parliament, those in matters of Religion, those against the Property of Goods. In what he was about to say he would be very careful to maintain the great prerogative of the King, which is, " That the King can do no wrong. A parliament is to the commonwealth what a soul is to the body for it alone is able to understand the symptoms of disease."

He enumerated the ways in which the Liberty of Parliament had been assailed, of which the worst was the dissolution, for the breaking of a Parliament is death to a good subject. As to Religion he did not desire any new laws against the Papists nor even a strict execution of those already made, merely such restrictions that the Roman religion " which can brook no co-rival, may not be the destruction of ours by being too concurrent with it." He then mentioned one by one the methods, by which, in his opinion, that religion was attempting to win back England, and complained that the Ecclesiastical Courts had claimed a power to compel and to punish which had not been granted to them either by Crown or by Parliament. Under this third head of Grievances he complained of Tunnage and

[1] P. H. 546-551. R. II. 2, 1131-1163.

Poundage, Knighthood Fines, Monopolies, Ship Money, Enlargement of the Forest bounds, Sale of Public Nuisances, Military Charges and Impositions upon Counties, and Extra-Judicial Judgments and Opinions of the Judges. He then turned to the recent action of Star Chamber, " which was not of old wont to be a court of revenue." Next as to the Royal Prerogative. He did not dispute a transcendent power in the King whereby by proclamation he might guard against sudden accidents. " But yet I must go higher than this. It hath been in the pulpit applied and also published in books and disputations asserting a power unlimited in the King that he may do what he pleaseth. This Grievance was complained of in the last Parliament in the case of Dr. Manwaring who, for maintaining that opinion in a sermon " that a subject had no property in his goods but that all was at the King's pleasure " made his submission upon his knees in this place and was then brought so low that I thought he would not have leaped so soon into a Bishoprick."

Pym now came to the greatest of all his grievances. " I have by this time wearied you as well as myself : but I am come to the last grievance which is the fountain of all these, and that is the Intermission of Parliaments : whereas by two Statutes, not repealed or expired, a Parliament ought to be held once in a year. The breach of Parliaments is much prejudicial, for by this means the great union and love which should be kept and communicated between the King and his subjects is interrupted; they cannot make known their petitions, nor the King his wants. He then returned to his first metaphor, " Where the intercourse of the spirits, betwixt the head and the members is hindered the body prospers not."

Pym's speech was heard with favour by the House,

which proceeded to appoint a committee to consider grievances. On April 22nd, Convocation unanimously granted six subsidies from the clergy at Laud's request. This the Commons much resented. They were still more annoyed when they received a message from the Lords asking them to give Supply precedence over Grievances.[1] By the mouth of Pym they told the Lords plainly that this was a breach of privilege which they must not repeat. Hereafter " they desire your Lordships to take no notice of anything which shall be debated by the Commons until they shall themselves declare the same unto your Lordships." On his return he was thanked by the Commons for his service.

On May 4th Mr. Secretary Vane announced that Charles was willing to abandon Ship Money if twelve subsidies were granted him. A debate of two days' duration followed. Meantime Pym was in communication with the Scottish Commissioners, and some arrangement was come to with them by which they were to be called before the House to answer questions in connection with their printed Declaration. On this a petition to the King against the war was apparently to have been based.

Whatever Pym intended was prevented by the sudden action of Charles. On May 5th he dissolved Parliament, which had sat for three weeks and had done nothing except disclose the deep dissatisfaction of the Commons with the Government and with the war, the complete ascendency of Pym and his colleagues, and their collusion with the Scots. Next day Lord Brooke's house was searched upon suspicion of such collusion, but nothing was found. It is certain, however, that Pym and his friends were at this moment especially active. Clarendon says, " Mr. Pym continued after the unhappy dissolution

[1] C. J. II. 13 ii.

about London in conversation and great repute amongst those Lords who were most strangers to the Court and were believed most averse to it : in which he improved all imaginable jealousies and discontents towards the State." His plottings now with the Scots brought him within the law of treason, and explains much of his policy afterwards. His eulogist, Forster, writing of the eve of the Short Parliament, says, " Let the friends of Charles make what use of the admission they please, it is quite certain that at the London meetings of the Scotch commissioners from the Covenant, headed by Lords Loudon and Dumferling, not only Pym and Hampden took an active part, but also Lords Essex, Holland, Bedford and Saye." [1] It will be observed that all these were Adventurers of Providence Island. Again Forster writes of the period just before the Long Parliament : " There is no doubt that a close correspondence with the Scotch commissioners was now entered into, under the management of himself [Pym] and Hampden : and two places, Broughton Castle, in Oxfordshire, the seat of Lord Saye, and Fawsley, in Northamptonshire, the house of Sir Richard Knightley (whose son had married Hampden's daughter) were from their position with reference to the North Road and their easy distance from London, fixed upon for the purposes of frequent consultation. Pym, Hampden and St. John, with Lords Saye and Brooke, and somewhat later in the year the Earls of Bedford, Warwick, and Essex, Lord Holland, Nathaniel Fiennes and young Vane here held their meetings; and a private press, which Sir Richard Knightly's father had established at Fawsley, was brought into constant requisition. Whenever, on the other hand, necessity obliged the meetings to be held in London, they took place at Pym's house in Gray's Inn

[1] F. P. 84.

Lane, from whence various reports were instantly communicated to the chief places in the country."[1] It will be noticed that, with the exception of Nathaniel Fiennes, all the persons here named were Adventurers of Providence Island.

The war with the Scots was resumed. Charles's troops were mostly pressed men, disorderly and badly armed. But Strafford was now commander-in-chief, and, broken though he was with gout, stone, and sharp attacks of dysentery, he drove some sort of order into his ragged regiments. On the other hand, the Scots were full of confidence. Strong in the assurances of their English confederates they resolved to invade England. But they asserted that they did so merely to lay their grievances before the King. There should be no bloodshed unless they were attacked; they would pay for their supplies and would look for recompense to the next English Parliament. On August 20th Leslie crossed the Tweed at Coldstream. There was a faint show of resistance at Newburn on the 28th, but on the following day the Scots occupied Newcastle. Shortly after, all Durham was abandoned, as well as Northumberland, by the English, and the Scots being now short of money began to levy contributions from both counties.

Meanwhile twelve peers had presented to Charles a petition for a new Parliament to redress grievances and call his counsellors to account. Half of this number were Adventurers of Providence Island. Of them Clarendon writes: "At the same time some Lords from London (of known and since published affections to that invasion) attended his Majesty at York with a petition signed by others (eight or ten in the whole) who were craftily persuaded by the liegers there, Mr. Pym, Mr. Hampden,

[1] F. P. 125-6.

A NEW PARLIAMENT

and Mr. St. John, to concur in it. . . ."[1] Acting no doubt collusively with these Peers, the Scots also a few days later presented a petition for an English Parliament to help them to redress their grievances. Charles compromised by summoning a Great Council of Peers, a form of assembly which had not been seen in England since the fourteenth century. These peers could only repeat the advice of the twelve petitioners, who were reinforced by riots in London—a foretaste of what was to come. Negotiations were concluded at Ripon by which Charles left the two northern counties in the hands of the Scots and undertook to pay them £850 a day. Writs were then issued for a new Parliament, which was destined to be the most famous of them all, and to suffer the extremes of exaltation and of abasement.

[1] Cl. II. 93.

CHAPTER IX
STRAFFORD

"It must be worse before it can be better," said Oliver St. John to Mr. Hyde after the dissolution of the Short Parliament. Pym also had expressed himself in similar terms to Hyde, when they met by chance in Westminster Hall some days before the new Parliament assembled. "They must now be of another temper than they were the last Parliament: that they must not only sweep the house clean below, but must pull down all the cobwebs which hung in the top and corners, that they might not breed dust, and so make a foul house hereafter: that they had now an opportunity to make their country happy by removing all grievances, and pulling up the causes of them by the roots, if all men would do their duties." [1]

The immediate object of Pym and his friends was the maintenance of the Scots in the North of England. So long as they were there the King was in a desperate position.

But from this desperate position he might extricate himself by a desperate effort requiring an audacity lacking indeed in him but ready to his hand in Strafford. If the Lord Deputy should persuade Charles to unmask and punish the treason of Pym and his friends, he might yet turn the tables upon them.

Strafford then must at all costs be destroyed.

The next difficulty to be surmounted was the precarious life of Parliament itself; this the confederates determined to overcome by inducing the King to renounce, at any rate temporarily, his right of dissolution. This of course

[1] Cl. III. 3.

he would only do under pressure of his urgent poverty. Through his purse they must attack his prerogative.

These points gained, the abolition of abnormal taxation and the punishment of unpopular Ministers would be easy.

To what extent these measures involved a permanent diminution of the power of the Crown, or in what degree the possibility of such diminution had presented itself to Pym and his friends, it is impossible to say. Some of their number may have looked further ahead; the younger Vane was indeed an avowed republican, but it is unlikely that Pym at this time had in view anything beyond an amelioration of what he regarded as abuses in Church and State, and the establishment of machinery sufficient to prevent them in future. To those revolutionary steps, to which we shall find him committed a few months later, he was urged by the nature of the force on which he relied, and the agencies through which he exerted that force.

The force was Puritanism, or rather that negative aspect of Puritan belief which expressed itself in detestation of the Roman Catholic faith and its professors, and in hatred scarcely less bitter of the organisation and rites of the Church of England as they were conceived by Andrewes and enounced by Laud, and which were styled by the Puritan "Arminian." It was believed, honestly by many, that Laud did really desire an understanding which might amount to a reconciliation with the Roman Curia. Incredible as this must appear to all who have the slightest acquaintance with Laud's polemical work, this belief was a cardinal feature in the downfall of Charles's political system, of which, following the traditions of his house he had made Episcopacy a principal column.

The political side of Laud's work had, then, made Episcopacy odious to English Puritans and inclined them to a sympathetic consideration of the ecclesiastical system of the Scottish Calvinists, who were themselves roused to fury by the ill-considered and ill-timed introduction of the English Liturgy. The rancour of Puritanism was thus the motive force which lay behind Pym's measures, and which forced into cohesion, English and Scots, whose political interests were diverse enough. It was made effective through four agencies—petitions, lectureships, pamphleteers and mob violence—and through it all runs the secret and therefore more deadly combination in both Lords and Commons of the Adventurers of Providence Island.

The Houses met on November 3rd, and there were speeches from the King and the Lord Keeper of no moment. On the 5th William Lenthall, a Barrister of Lincoln's Inn, and a man of courage and resource, was conducted to the chair to begin the longest and most stormy tenure of office that had ever befallen a Speaker of the House of Commons.

Pym again sat for Tavistock,[1] all his political associates were around him, and at once he began to make good the promise he had made to Wentworth eleven years before, if indeed the story be true: "You are going to be undone, and remember also that, though you leave us now, I will never leave you while your head is upon your shoulders."[2] Probably the story was made after the event. In any case Wentworth would have cared nothing for such a threat. "I am not ignorant," he had written from Ireland to Laud in 1634, "that my stirring herein will be strangely reported and censured on that side, and how I shall be able to sustain myself

[1] Cf. Appendix I. [2] Cl. III. 263.

THE CONFEDERATES

against your Prynnes, Pims, and Bens, with the rest of that generation of odd names and natures, the Lord knows."[1] Of Pym and his group Clarendon wrote:—
". . . the fate of all things depended upon the two Houses, and therefore it will not be amiss to take a view of the persons by whose arts and interests the rest were disposed, the lesser wheels moving entirely by their virtue and impulsion. In the Lords' House the Earls of Essex, Bedford, Warwick, the Earls Saye and Kimbolton were the governing voices, attended by Brooke, Wharton, Pagett, and such like. In the House of Commons Mr. Pymm, Mr. Hampden, Mr. St. John, Mr. Hollis, and Mr. Fynes absolutely governed, being stoutly seconded upon all occasions by Mr. Strode, Sir John Hotham, Sir Walter Erle, young Sir Harry Vane, and many others of the same tempers and dispositions: but truly I am persuaded, whatever design either of alteration or reformation was yet formed, I mean in the beginning of the Parliament, was only communicated between the Earl of Bedford, the Lords Saye and Kimbolton, Mr. Pymm, Mr. Hambden, Mr. Fynes, and Mr. St. John, who, together with the Earl of Rothesse and the Lord Lowden [Rothes and Loudon] of the Scots' Commissioners managed and carried it on; and that neither the Earl of Essex, Warwick, nor Brooke himself, no, nor Mr. Hollis or Strode, or any of the rest, were otherwise trusted than upon occasion, and made use of according to their several gifts."

In a society which valued achievements more than words, performances more than professions, Strafford's work would have gained for him imperishable renown. He is the peer of Warren Hastings and of Lord Durham. But to every greatness is attached its appropriate penalty, and around administrative genius curl

[1] S. L. and D. I. 344.

perpetually the tarnishing fumes of envy and resentment. The circle of his enemies was now complete. In Ireland the cormorants had returned to their prey, the Scots saw in him the one will that could stand against them in the Council Chamber or on the battlefield. To the majority of the English House of Commons he was the embodiment of the system which they detested on its secular side, as Laud was on its ecclesiastical.

Charles had summoned Strafford to London immediately Parliament met. He gave him an assurance that he " should not suffer in his person, honour or fortune." The great Earl at once left Yorkshire for the last time, well knowing the magnitude of his danger and the weakness of the promised protection. Arrived in London, he gave the King advice which was accordant to his own courage and vigour. Let his Majesty accuse the leaders of the Commons of that High Treason of which they had indeed been guilty when they plotted with the Scots to throw their armies across the border and hold their King in thrall.[1]

It was bold counsel and needed more courage than Charles could muster. He had called upon Strafford too late. A few years before that great genius might have saved his King from the financial and political bankruptcy in which he now stood.

Pym was aware of the imminence of the danger. Hitherto, while Strafford was still in Yorkshire, he had been content to remind the House that offenders must be punished, and to ask for a Commission of Inquiry. To investigate Strafford's conduct in Ireland, a sub-committee had been appointed by the committee for Irish affairs, which had been considering Lord Mountnorris's petition against the Lord Deputy. It consisted

[1] R. Straff. 2.

of Pym, Strode, St. John, Digby, Clotworthy, and Hampden.[1] The missionary efforts of Pym and Hampden had not been in vain. Troops of horsemen came from several counties with petitions for redress of grievances and exorbitancies in Church and State. The Commons were by these means kept inflamed, and a prey to the most violent animosities.

Strafford arrived in London on November 10th. Pym's emissaries at the Court speedily informed him of the line of attack proposed by the great Minister. Pym acted at once with admirable promptitude. On the following day he moved that the doors should be locked, and this being ordered, he called on Sir John Clotworthy to tell what he knew. Clarendon thus describes the scene: "Sir John Clotworthy (a gentleman of Ireland and utterly unknown in England, who was by the contrivance and recommendation of some powerful persons returned to serve for a borough in Devon, that so he might be enabled to act this part against the Lord-Lieutenant), made a long and confused relation of his tyrannical carriage in that Kingdom and of the army he had raised there to invade Scotland.[2] The Commons eagerly gulped down this and much similar stuff; they had already been regaled with a story of a military movement to be directed against the City from the Tower, and of a great Popish Plot. Clarendon gives the substance of a speech by Pym about this time which he attributed, probably incorrectly, to the first day of the session: "We must inquire from what fountain these waters of bitterness flowed: what persons they were, who had so far insinuated themselves into his [Majesty's] royal affections, as to be able to pervert his excellent judgment, to abuse his name and wickedly

[1] C. J. II. 26, 2 R. Straff. 3 adds Earle. [2] Cl. III. 5.

apply his authority, to countenance and support their own corrupt designs . . . he believed there was one more signal in that administration than the rest, being a man of great parts and contrivance and of great industry, to bring what he designed to pass; a man who, in the memory of many present, had sat in that House an earnest vindicator of the laws and a most zealous assertor and champion for the liberties of the people : but that it was long since he turned apostate from these good affections, and, according to the custom and nature of apostates, was become the greatest enemy to the liberties of his country, and the greatest promoter of tyranny that any age had produced, and then named the Earl of Strafford, Lord-Lieutenant of Ireland and Lord President of the Council established in York for the northern parts of the Kingdom . . . if they took a short survey of his actions and behaviour they would find him the principal author and promoter of all those counsels which had exposed the Kingdom to so much ruin." He " concluded that they would well consider how to provide a remedy proportional to the disease, and to prevent the further mischiefs which they were to expect from the continuance of this man's power and credit with the King, and his influence upon his councils." [1]

This probably represents rather the gist of Pym's several utterances than a definite speech, for it was written by Clarendon many years after he had heard it. It is, nevertheless, noteworthy as illustrating the complete ignorance of, and contempt for, the value of Strafford's work in Ireland, and the growth of the absurd legend of " apostacy " which will be seen later in Digby's speech, and which has survived to this day, glorified by a poisonous tinsel unworthy of Macaulay's greatness. [2]

[1] Cl. III. 3. [2] Macaulay, "Essay on Hallam's Constitutional History."

Clarendon adds that " Lord Falkland (who was very well known to be far from having any kindness to him) when the proposition was made for the present accusing him of high treason, asked whether it would not suit better with the gravity of their proceedings first to digest many of those particulars which had been mentioned by a committee ? "

Pym's answer was conclusive. If they did so, he said, they would undo themselves, for such was Lord Strafford's favour with the King that he would " procure the Parliament to be dissolved rather than undergo the justice of it, or take some other desperate course to preserve himself, though with the hazard of the Kingdom's ruin," and, he added with characteristic subtlety, " whereas if they presently sent up to impeach him of high treason before the House of Peers, in the name and on the behalf of all the Commons of England who were represented by them, the Lords would be obliged in justice to commit him into safe custody, and so sequester him from resorting to council, or having access to his Majesty : and then they should proceed against him in the usual form with all necessary expedition."[1]

The House was convinced, and very properly chose Pym to be their messenger.

Strafford, suffering and infirm, entered the House of Lords about three o'clock in the afternoon of November 11th. He had been told that the Commons were demanding his impeachment, and hastened to meet them there.

It had become known that he intended to denounce several peers for treasonable dealings with the Scots, and the hearts of the Adventurers misgave them. Nor is it likely that Pym's friends, members of his commercial

[1] Cl. III. 8.

coterie, had been idle at this crisis of their lives. The lion was indeed enmeshed in the snares. He was refused leave to speak, sequestered from his place in the House, and committed to Maxwell, the Usher of the Black Rod, who took from him his sword and led him from the House, the first of the steps that should lead him to the martyrdom on Tower Hill. Pym was then called in and informed of what the House had done.

The mouth of his friend Ratcliff was then stopped by an order for him to return from Ireland to answer certain charges made by Pym's creature Clotworthy.[1] The Committee, urged on by Pym, lost no time in preparing the articles against Strafford. The compliant Lords, some driven on, as Holland, Warwick, and Saye, by their guilty fears, and all by these Adventurers, went so far, on November 26th, as to permit the examination of Privy Counsellors upon oath. Next day Pym carried nine charges to the Lords. These declared "that Thomas, Earl of Strafford, hath traitorously endeavoured to subvert the fundamental laws and government of the realms of England and Ireland, and instead thereof to introduce an arbitrary and tyrannical government against law, which he hath declared by traitorous words, counsels and actions, and by giving his Majesty advice by force of arms to compel his loyal subjects to submit thereunto."

He had moreover, they alleged, converted to his own use that which belonged to the King, and had encouraged Papists in order to procure their support. He had stirred up enmity between England and Scotland, and had betrayed Conway of set purpose at Newburn that he might embroil the two countries beyond repair. Then, to save himself, "he had laboured to subvert the rights of Parliaments and the ancient course of parliamentary

[1] R. Straff. 5. C. J. II. 28, ii.

proceedings."[1] Grotesque indeed seem the charges to all who know Strafford's Letters and have there been admitted to his projects. But the ground had been carefully prepared by Pym and the Adventurers; they had taught the many what they must expect, and now they proceeded to give it to them. Strafford in prison wrote to his wife with stedfast courage ". . . albeit all will be done against me that art and malice can devise . . . yet I am in great inward quietness and a strong belief God will deliver me out of all these troubles. The more I look into my case the more hope I have, and sure if there be any honour and justice left, my life will not be in danger; and for anything else, time, I trust, will salve any other hurt which can be done me. Therefore hold up your heart, look to the children and your house, let me have your prayers, and at last by God's good pleasure we shall have our deliverance when we may as little look for it as we did for this blow of misfortune, which I trust will make us better to God and Man."[2] Strafford had yet to learn what "honour and justice" meant to the hounds of Puritanism in full cry, and whipped in by John Pym.

On December 23rd, the Lord Keeper, Sir John Finch, was impeached for his statement that the power of levying Ship Money was a part of the prerogative of the Crown which Parliament could not touch, and for his personal solicitation of the judges to support the view. Sir Thomas Jermyn aptly asked whether this were a treason within the Statute, or by the construction of the House. Pym's answer must have given pause to many: "To endeavour the subversion of the laws of this Kingdom, is treason of the highest nature."[3]

What the laws of England meant to Pym had been

[1] R. Straff. 8-9.   [2] G. IX. 95, 241.   [3] Ibid. 218.

sufficiently shown on December 16th, when, on his motion, Archbishop Laud was impeached of high treason. The impeachment of Laud had been led up to by a grand demonstration on December 11th, when a petition, couched in violent language and purporting to be signed by 15,000 Londoners, demanded Church Reform and the abolition of Episcopacy. But not all the Commons were Puritan, and the petition, though read, was heard in ominous silence. The Adventurers were sufficiently strong to pass a resolution to consider the petition later.

Side by side with the manufacturing of a case against Strafford, went on the preparation of a Bill for ensuring the regular assembly of Parliament. The Bill as originally introduced by Strode, was to be for an annual Parliament, and was brought in on December 14th. On the 30th, at the motion of Oliver Cromwell, it was read a second time, and Pym was placed upon the committee to consider it. Charles had expressed his intention of refusing to pass the Bill, and in committee a new proposal was made, whereby, if a meeting of Parliament were not held for a period of three years, elections should be put in motion without the concurrence of the Crown. On February 5th, 1641, the Lords passed the Bill, and on the 15th it was presented to Charles. The dose was sweetened by an accompanying Bill for four subsidies especially granted for the relief of the two armies in the North, but the proportion allotted to the Scots would but the more firmly cement their understanding with Charles's Parliamentary enemies.

On February 16th, Charles gave his assent to the Triennial Bill, "I think never Bill passed here in this House of more favour to the subjects than this is . . . you have taken the government almost in pieces, and, I may say, it is almost off the hinges."

SIR THOMAS WENTWORTH, EARL OF STRAFFORD.

Sweet Harte. It is long since I writt unto you, for I am here in such a trouble as giues me little or noe respect. The chardge is now cum inn, and I am now able I prayse god to tell you, that I conceaue ther is nothing Capitall, and for the rest I know his Ma[jes]ty will par- at the worste don all without hurting my fortune, and then wee shall be happy by gods grace. Therfore comfort your self, for I trust thes cloudes will away, and that wee shall haue faire weather afterwardes. Farwell.

Tower of London.
4 Febr. 1640.

Your louing husbande
Strafforde

Thus two of the objects which had engrossed Pym and the Adventurers were achieved. Strafford was imprisoned, and a long period of unparliamentary government had been rendered impossible.

But Strafford's head was yet on his shoulders, and so long as it was there none of the Confederates felt his own secure. On January 28th, Pym presented the detailed charges against him from the committee. They had been drawn up by himself and his fellow Adventurer St. John. There were now twenty-eight, and they dealt with a period of fourteen years. Strafford asked for three months in which to answer them. Three weeks were given to him. Of the Articles Strafford wrote to his wife: "Sweet Harte,—It is long since I writt unto you, for I am here in such a trouble, as gives me little or no respitt. The charge is now come in, and I am now able, I praise God, to tell you that I conceive there is nothing capitall; and for the reste, I know at the worste his Majestie will pardon all, without hurting my fortune; and then we shall be happy, by God's grace. Therefore comfort yourself, for I trust these cloudes will away, and that wee shall have faire weather afterwardes. Farewell. Your loving husband, Strafforde." On February 24th, the Earl presented his answer to the articles at the bar of the House of Lords. "The answer held three hours' reading, being above 200 sheets of paper."[1] He was himself confident that there was nothing which he would not be able to answer. But the kind of justice likely to be meted to him was already indicated by a sinister, though fruitless, proposal made on March 16th, in the Commons, "That no further advancement of monies should be made for any purpose until justice were done upon the Earl of Strafford."

[1] R. Straff. 22.

On March 22nd the trial began in Westminster Hall, and lasted fifteen days. "The most glorious assembly the isle could afford," said Baillie the Covenanter and representative of that " whole Scottish nation, an enemy more terrible than all the others, and like to be more fatal." Westminster Hall was scaffolded from floor to roof, eleven stages being built on each side. Upon them were the Commissioners from Scotland and the Lords of Ireland. The Peers sat in the centre wearing their Parliamentary robes. The Lord Keeper was there and the Judges, all in their scarlet.

Two cabinets with trellis in front were erected. In one were the King, Queen and Court, in the other foreign nobles present in London. Noble ladies were seated on a scaffold at the foot of the State cloth. Two hundred trained bands guarded Strafford each day as he entered Westminster Hall. He was dressed in deep mourning and wore his George : tortured with excruciating physical pain, he was still more distracted by the hubbub and clamour of the throng around, which continually passed in and out. The Articles of Impeachment, originally nine, were now twenty-eight. On the first day the proceedings were merely formal, but on the 23rd Pym opened the case against the Lord Deputy.[1]

Strafford, said the orator, had put the vizard of goodness on his actions, thus to make them appear beneficent to the Commonwealth. It was for him to strip them off. The Lord Deputy was no better than the adulterous woman of Scripture, who wiped her mouth and said she had done no evil. Did he say he had made good laws for Ireland ? What was the best law if it set one man well above the law ? Did he point to the Irish Parliament which he had summoned ? " My Lords, Parliaments

[1] R. Straff. 102, *et seq.*

without parliamentary liberties are but a fair and plausible way into bondage." Did he urge that he had put down monopolists? Yes, that he might be himself the sole monopolist. Certain acts of harshness were alleged against Strafford; yes, but it was not these acts that he would urge, it was the habit of mind of which they were the product. "The habit of cruelty in himself is more perfect than any act of cruelty he hath committed." After this amazing piece of pleading he dealt with the claim that Churches had been built, and met it in the narrowest snuffle of Puritanism. If, indeed, the Lord Deputy had set up good preachers, that would have stirred up devotion in men . . . but he heard nothing of spiritual edification, nothing of the knowledge of God spread in Ireland by his means. God is not worshipped with walls, but with hearts. The accused Earl had bid them not charge him with errors of understanding or judgment, since he was not bred up in the law, or with weakness to which human nature is subject. No, said Pym, we will not do so, "We will charge him with nothing but what the law in every man's breast condemns—the light of nature, the light of common reason, the rules of society."

What is to be said of such a speech as this? This is what Forster said: "It appears to me that Pym, and of all the managers Pym alone, argued the accusation and conviction of the Earl as of the substance of eternal right in opposition to the technical forms which the defence assumed."[1] Such a view would justify every partisan murder since the beginning of the world.

Strafford protested his good intentions and showed his good results, even where he had strained the letter of the law. For those good intentions his life was now

[1] F. P. 163.

sought. Gardiner writes : " The time might soon arrive when treason would be as light a word in the mouth of a member of Parliament as damnation had been in the mouth of a mediæval ecclesiastic," and again, " It might be well that the law of treason should be altered so as to include some actions which had been done by Strafford : but it was hard upon him, and of the worst possible example to future times, to inflict the penalty of death under an interpretation of the law which was now heard of for the first time." [1]

Behind the bombastic phrases and the religious twang lay the conviction, bringing panic into the Adventurers, that if Strafford escaped from their snares they were but lost men. They determined that he should not escape. On April 5th the accusations against the Earl concerning his Irish administration were dropped, and those concerning England begun. He was charged with raising an army in Ireland composed of Papists, and of offering to serve the King " in any other way in case the Parliament would not support him." He had declared it to be his opinion that if Parliament failed to grant Supply, the King was free to use his prerogative as he pleased, to levy what he needed, and that he should be acquitted of God and man if he took some courses to supply himself, though it were against the will of his subjects."

Then came the Short Parliament, after the dissolution of which assembly he had advised his Majesty " that having tried the affections of his people, he was to do everything that power would admit : and that his Majesty had tried all ways and was refused, and should be acquitted towards God and man : and that he had an army in Ireland which he might employ to reduce this Kingdom."

[1] G. IX. 9, 307.

A question of moment arose from this. Did the words " this Kingdom " refer to England or to Scotland ? At the time they were spoken Charles was at war with Scotland, the natural interpretation would be, therefore, that " this kingdom " meant Scotland. But this was not what the Adventurers desired. If they could make it appear that England was intended, they would be able to count on a storm of indignation in the Commons, and ensure Strafford's death. They had to overcome the difficulty, urged with force by Lane, who argued the matter of law for the Earl, that " two lawful and sufficient witnesses " were by the Statute of the first year of King Edward VI necessary to convict a person of high treason.[1] They had recourse to a device which redounds more to their ingenuity than to their honour.

The agents of their scheme were the old Secretary of State, Sir Henry Vane, and his son, the notorious Sir Harry Vane of Cromwell's famous ejaculation, " The Lord deliver me from Sir Harry Vane ! "

Vane the younger, had produced to Pym a paper which purported to be a copy of certain notes taken by his father at a meeting of the Committee of Eight after the dissolution of the Short Parliament. These notes Vane had stolen from his father's cabinet. Herein certain disconnected words were attributed to speakers indicated by initials. " There were then written two *L Ls* and a *t* over, and an *I*, and an *r*, which was urged could signify nothing but 'Lord-Lieutenant of Ireland,'" and the words written and applied to that name were, "Absolved from rules of government—Prosecute the war vigorously—An army in Ireland to subdue this Kingdom."[2] Besides Strafford and Vane, six Councillors had been present on the occasion, of whom four, one of

[1] Cl. III. 123-127. [2] Cl. III. 133.

them Juxon, denied any remembrance of such a proposal, the other two, Laud and Windebank, were under impeachment, and therefore could not give evidence. The whole affair has an ugly look. Alone Strafford fought the enormous forces against him. For nine hours on April 5th he faced Whitelock, Maynard, and Glyn. The Lords began to be impressed by his rugged honesty and unmistakable conviction. All the ladies present had long been converted to his side, and the Lords even granted him a day's rest, of which he stood sorely in need. The extreme party in the Commons were alarmed; it seemed likely that, after all, their prey would escape from them. On April 10th Pym disclosed to the House his possession of the copy of Vane's alleged notes. The elder Vane, apparently much troubled, arose, and with many upbraidings of "An unhappy son of his" who "had brought all this trouble upon him" asserted that the original notes had been destroyed by the King's command. It was not only the original note that was destroyed, the copy also disappeared strangely. "The House being informed that a paper of consequence, being the minutes of the Council discovered by Sir Henry Vane aforesaid, was taken out of the chamber where the secret Committee do usually meet, which did relate to the Earl of Strafford's business, it was referred to a Committee to examine the matter, who agreed upon a Protestation to be made by every one of the Secret Committee, which being reported by Mr. Martin was as followeth :—

"' I do solemnly affirm and protest in the Presence of God and this Assembly, that I did not directly or indirectly take, carry or convey away the paper in question supposed to be lost or taken away from the

[1] Cl. III. 128.

House where Mr. Pym lodges ; nor know who did take, carry or convey away the same. Nor have seen the same since it was lost or taken away. And this Protestation I make sincerely and truly without any mental reservation or equivocation.' "

"Sir Walter Erle, Sir John Clotworthy, the Lord Digby, Mr. Pym and Mr. Grimston, did, all in their places, solemnly take this Protestation."[1] Did the materials exist, the whole matter would deserve the minute dissection accorded by Sir James Fitz-James Stephen to the evidence regarding Warren Hastings and Nand Kumar. It may be permissible to imagine that under cross-examination the younger Vane would have come out badly, possibly his father, possibly another.

The same day Sir Arthur Haselrig, Pym's " dove from the ark," brought in a Bill of Attainder. Strafford was to be knocked on the head like a wild beast. Clarendon thus describes him : " Sir Arthur Haselrig, brother-in-law to the lord Brooke, and an absurd bold man, brought up by Mr. Pym and so employed by that party to make any attempt."

Was Pym really responsible for the introduction of the Bill of Attainder ? Those who maintain that he was not, rest their belief on his expressed desire that the impeachment should proceed. In wishing this he was undoubtedly sagacious. The proposed attainder would be likely to, and as a matter of fact did, irritate the Lords and strengthen them in their resolve to proceed by way of impeachment. Moreover, he had not yet sent to Westminster Hall the alleged notes of Vane which he believed would suffice as the second witness required by the Statute. A Bill of Attainder may well have appeared to him to be premature. On April 13th Strafford

[1] R. III. i. 229. C. J. II. 127, i.

made his defence. He asked with justice how that could be treason as a whole which in each separate part was no treason. If this were to be the reward of the Ministers of State, what man would take upon himself so hard an office. "That I am charged with treason by the honourable Commons is my greatest grief: it pierces my heart, though not with guilt, yet with sorrow, that in my grey hairs I should be so misunderstood by the companions of my youth, with whom I have formerly spent so much time." Glyn, answering him, said he had these many years past been an Evil Spirit moving amongst them that had persuaded the King that he was absolved from all rules of government. Pym followed. He asserted that it had been proved that the Earl of Strafford had endeavoured by his words, actions and counsels, to subvert the fundamental laws of England and Ireland and to introduce an arbitrary and tyrannical government. His treason was not, as he had complained, held to be cumulative, it was there in form and in essence. He would appeal to that *Salus Populi* to which Strafford himself had appealed, and by that would convict him. The law is the boundary between the King's prerogative and the people's liberty, each working in its own orbit, otherwise prerogative will become tyranny, and liberty anarchy. The history of those Eastern Countries where Princes ordered the government on the principles of Strafford, "loose and absolved from all rules of government," was "frequent in combustions, full of massacres, and of tragical ends of princes."

Nearly fifteen years had gone by since the King received supplies from his people in a regular way, his needs being supplied meanwhile by illegal ways, which brought in less, he affirmed, than the bounty and affection of her subjects gave to Queen Elizabeth in the last fifteen years of her life. Should it be held treason to embase the King's coin, though but a piece of twelve pence, or sixpence, and must it not needs be the effect of a greater treason to embase the spirits of his subjects, and to set up a stamp and character of servitude upon them, whereby they should be disabled to do anything for the service of the King and Commonwealth? Strafford's treason was no transient act, it was to be a constant and permanent treason, not determined within one time or age, but transmitted to posterity even from one generation to another, " Neither will this be a new way of blood. There are marks enough to trace this law to the very original of this Kingdom, and if it hath not been in execution as he allegeth these two hundred and forty years, it was not for want of law, but that all that time hath not bred a man bold enough to commit such crimes as these." [1]

Here a curious incident occurred. Pym lost his self-possession and broke down. The Covenanter Baillie gives a fatuous explanation. " Mr. Pym, who truelie to the confession of all, in half an hour made one of the most eloquent, wise, free speeches, that ever we heard or I think shall ever hear. . . . To humble the man, God let his memory fail him a little before the end. His papers he looked on, but they could not help him to a point or two." [2] Forster has a more dramatic explanation. " Through the whole of the speech Strafford is described to have been closely and earnestly watching Pym; when the latter, suddenly turning as the above words were spoken, met the fixed and faded eyes and haggard features of his early associate, and a rush of feelings from other days so fearfully contrasting the youth and friendship of the past, with the love-poisoned

[1] R. Straff. 661-670. [2] B. I. 348.

hate of the present, and the mortal agony impending in the future—for a moment deprived the patriot of self-possession."[1] Unfortunately Forster lacks corroboration.

Pym's speech was a fine, if laboured, forensic achievement, and if certain assumptions be granted it was convincing. These are first, that Strafford did use the famous phrase which was to destroy him: " Loose and absolved from all rules of government," second, that if he did so use it, he placed it before him as a maxim of government, and not merely as a make-shift policy for temporary mismanagement; third, that a Minister acting on such a principle as a matter of policy was, *ipso facto*, a traitor, because thereby he destroyed the fundamental laws of the land. What these fundamental laws were Pym does not say, and when Edmund Waller, the poet, asked that very pertinent question in the House of Commons, he got no better answer than a jibe from Maynard: if he did not know that he had no business to be in the House. It is, indeed, difficult to avoid the impression that the fundamental laws of England at that moment were what the Puritan majority in the House of Commons, led by the Adventurers, thought they ought to be. St. John, the sour and brutal Solicitor-General, whom Charles had feebly attempted to attach by office, speaking later on the legality of the Bill of Attainder, did not trouble himself overmuch about them. " It is true we give laws to hares and deers because they be beasts of chase: it was never accounted either cruelty or foul play to knock foxes and wolves on the head as they can be found, because they be beasts of prey. The warrener sets traps for Polcats and other Vermin for the preservation of the warren."[2] Essex, too, when Hyde approached

[1] F. P. 183. [2] R. Straff. 703.

DIGBY'S SPEECH

him with a proposal for more merciful treatment of Strafford, would none of it. "Stone dead hath no fellow," he growled.

Such speeches showed that the end was near, the time for argument past. The Earl was gaining ground even in the Commons.

In the debate on the question of procedure by Attainder no speech is more notable than that of Lord George Digby, son of the Earl of Bristol. As early as January 19th, when speaking on the Triennial Bill he had alluded thus to Noy and to Strafford: " And yet, Mr. Speaker, to whom now can all the inundations upon our Liberties under pretence of Law, and the late shipwreck at once of all our property be attributed more than to Noy? And can those and all other mistakes, whereby this Monarchy hath been brought almost to the brink of destruction, be attributed so much to any as to that Grand Apostate to the Commonwealth, the now Lieutenant of Ireland?

" The first I hope God hath forgiven in the other world; and the latter must not hope to be pardoned in this till he be dispatched to the other." [1]

He now referred to this denunciation in his speech on April 21st, which is in the highest degree illuminating. [2]

" Mr. Speaker, we are now upon the point of giving, as much as in us lies, the final sentence unto death or life on a great Minister of State and Peer of this Kingdom, Thomas Earl of Strafford, a name of hatred in the present age by his practices, and fit to be made a terror to future ages by his punishment. I have had the honour to be employed by the House in this great business from the first hour that it was taken into consideration . . . some (I thank them for their plain dealing) have been so free

[1] R. III. i. 148. [2] R. III. i. 225-228.

as to tell me that I suffered much by the backwardness I have shown in this Bill of Attainder of the Earl of Strafford, against whom I had been so keen, so active. . . . Truly, Sir, I am still the same in my opinions and affections as unto the Earl of Strafford. I confidently believe him to be the most dangerous Minister, the most insupportable to free subjects that can be charactered. I believe his practices in themselves as high, as tyrannical, as any subject ever ventured on, and the malignity of them hugely aggravated by those rare abilities of his, whereof God has given him the use, but the Devil the application. In a word, I believe him still that Grand Apostate to the Commonwealth, who must not expect to be pardoned in this world till he be dispatched to the other; and yet let me tell you Mr. Speaker, my hand must not be to that Dispatch. I protest as my conscience stands informed, I had rather it were off. Let me unfold to you the mystery, Mr. Speaker, I will not dwell much upon justifying unto you my seeming variance at this time from what I was formerly, by putting you in mind of the difference between Prosecutors and Judges. How misbecoming that fervour would be in a Judge, which perhaps was commendable in a Prosecutor. Judges we are now, and must put on another Personage. . . . In prosecution upon probable grounds we are accountable only for our industry or remissness, but in Judgment we are deeply responsible to God Almighty for its rectitude or obliquity. In cases of life, the Judge is God's Steward of the Parties' Blood and must give a strict account for every drop. . . . But truly, Sir, to deal plainly with you, that ground of our accusation, that spur to our Prosecution, and that which should be the basis of my Judgment of the Earl of Strafford as unto Treason, is to my understanding quite vanished away.

DIGBY'S SPEECH

"This it was Mr. Speaker, his advising the King to employ the Army in Ireland to reduce England. This I was assured would be proved before I gave my consent to his accusation. I was confirmed in the same belief, during the Prosecution, and fortified in it most of all since Sir Henry Vane's preparatory Examinations, by the Assurances which that worthy member Mr. Pym gave me, that his Testimony would be made convincing by some Notes of what passed at the Juncto concurrent with it, which I, ever understanding to be of some other Councillor, you see now prove but a copy of the same Secretary's Notes, discovered and produced in the manner you have heard; and those such dispointed [disjointed] fragments of the venomous part of Discourses; no results, no conclusions of Counsels, which are the only things that Secretaries should register, there being no use of the other, but to accuse and bring men into danger.

"But Sir, this is not that which overthrows the Evidence with me concerning the Army in Ireland; nor yet that all the rest of the Juncto upon their oath remember nothing of it. But this, Sir, which I shall tell you is that which works with me under Favour to an utter overthrow of his Evidence, as unto that of the Army of Ireland. Before, whilst I was a Prosecutor and under tie of Secrecy, I might not discover any weakness of the Cause which now as a Judge I must. Mr. Secretary was examined thrice upon Oath at the preparatory Committee. The first time he was questioned to all the Interrogatories, and to that part of the seventh which concerns the Army in Ireland, he said positively these words, 'I cannot charge him with that' but for the rest he desires time to recollect himself, which was granted him.

"Some days after he was examined a second time, and then deposes these words concerning the King being absolved from Rules of Government, and so forth very clearly, but being prest to that part concerning the Irish Army again can say nothing to that.

"Here we thought we had done with him, till divers weeks after My Lord of Northumberland and all others of the Juncto, denying to have heard anything concerning these Words of reducing England by the Irish Army, it was thought fit to examine the Secretary once more, and then he deposes these Words to have been said by the Earl of Strafford to his Majesty: 'You have an Army in Ireland which you may employ here to reduce (or some word to that sense) this Kingdom.'

"Mr. Speaker, these are the circumstances which I confess with my conscience, thrust quite out of doors that grand Article of our Charge concerning his desperate advice to the King of employing the Irish Army here. . . . I do not say but the rest may represent him a man as worthy to die, and perhaps worthier than many a Traitor. I do not say but they may justly direct us to enact that they shall be Treason for the future.

"But God keep me from giving Judgment of Death on any Man and of Ruin to his innocent Posterity upon a Law made *a posteriori*.

"Let the Mark be set on the Door where the Plague is, and then let him that will enter, die. . . .

"Let every Man lay his Hand upon his own Heart, and sadly consider what we are going to do with a Breath, either Justice or Murther, Justice on the one Side, or Murther heightened and aggravated to its supremest extent . . . doubtless he that commits Murther with the Sword of Justice heightens that Crime to the utmost.

"Let us take heed of a blood-shotten Eye of Judgment.

... Away with all Flatteries to the People in being the sharper against him because he is odious to them ; away with all fears lest by the sparing his Blood they may be incensed ... let not former vehemence of any against him, nor fear from thence that he cannot be safe while that man lives, be an ingredient in the Sentence of any one of us.

"Of these Corruptives of Judgment, Mr. Speaker, I do before God discharge myself to the uttermost of my power. And do with a clear Conscience wash my Hands of this Man's Blood, by this solemn Protestation that my Vote goes not to the taking of the Earl of Strafford's Life."

George Digby was fated to bring by his desperate counsel only disaster to the Royal cause which later he espoused. But to his eternal credit must be set this magnificent attempt to right a wrong he himself had helped to bring about. He had exposed himself to the bitterest hatred of Pym, Hampden and the Adventurers. Especially must they have been stung by that sentence, "Let not former vehemence of any against him, nor fear from thence that he cannot be safe while that man lives, be an ingredient in the sentence of any one of us." Exception was immediately taken to his speech, and he was called upon later to explain several passages. Later, on June 8th, a speech of his on the so-called Army Plot led to a wild scene of riot, when he was lucky to escape from the House without personal injury. D'Ewes says that the Speaker confessed that he had not expected to come away alive. Next morning Digby was sent for by the Commons, but the messenger returned with the news that he had been made a Peer, and was then putting on his robes. Thus Charles saved him from the Adventurers and their friends, who had to content themselves with declaring him a delinquent, with ordering copies of his speech to be burnt by the common hangman at Westminster, Cheapside and Smithfield, and with requesting the King not to employ him in any office of trust.

Pym and Hampden had with difficulty induced the Extremists thirsting for the attainder to proceed with the impeachment also. Both of them now supported the third reading of the Bill, and it was passed on April 21st by 204 votes to 59 in a thin House. The necessary panic was induced in the House by rumours of military plots and armed force in the City. The chief sources of danger were three: the undisbanded English army in the North, which had become disaffected by the favour shown to the adjacent Scottish army in the discharge of pay and arrears by Parliament—£10,000 voted for them had been transferred to the Scots—the Irish army, which Charles on April 14th had definitely refused to disband, and the troops in the Tower. It is certain that overtures had been made in all these cases with a view to save Strafford by force. The Queen certainly, and the King probably had lent ear to them.

Two days after the Bill of Attainder had passed the Commons Charles wrote to the prisoner in the Tower:—[2]

" Strafford, The misfortune that is fallen upon you by the strange mistaking and conjuncture of these times being such that I must lay by the thought of employing you hereafter in my affairs: yet I cannot satisfy myself in honour or conscience without assuring you now in the midst of all your troubles that upon the word of King you shall not suffer in life, honour or fortune. This is but justice, and therefore a very mean reward from a master to so able a servant as you have showed yourself

[1] R. Straff. 735. [2] Straff. L. and D. II. 416.

to be : yet it is as I conceive the present times will permit, though none shall hinder me from being your constant faithful friend.

Whitehall, April 23*rd*, 1641.

Not content with this, on April 30th, the King went to the Lords, and having summoned the Commons to appear, told the Houses that he did not consider Strafford to be guilty of High Treason, and denied that he or any other person had, at any time, advised him to bring the Irish army into England or to alter the laws of England. " I desire to be rightly understood. I told you on my conscience I cannot condemn him of high treason, yet I cannot say I can clear him of misdemeanour. Therefore I hope that you may find a way to satisfy justice and your own fears and not to press upon my conscience. My Lords, I hope you know what a tender thing conscience is. Yet I must declare unto you that to satisfy my people I would do great matters, but in this of conscience no fear, no respect whatever shall ever make me go against it. . . . I will not chalk out the way, yet let me tell you that I do think my Lord of Strafford is not fit hereafter to serve me or the Commonwealth in any place of trust, no not so much as to be a High-Constable. Thereupon I leave it to you, my Lords, to find some such way as to bring me out of this great strait."[1]

Charles's intervention was well meant, but Strafford saw the danger of it and advised against it. Indeed Clarendon asserts that Saye had advised it out of set malice against the prisoner. It gave Pym the opportunity he needed.

On April 24th a petition, said to be signed by 20,000 Londoners, called for the execution of Strafford. On

[1] R. Straff. 734.

Sunday morning, May 2nd, Captain Billingsley, at the head of a hundred men, appeared at the Tower, and presenting an order from the King to Sir William Balfour, Lieutenant, demanded entry. Balfour refused, and told the Parliamentary leaders what had occurred. Whether or not it was Charles's intention to attempt violence with so inadequate a force the incident destroyed Strafford. On the following day a mob gathered at Westminster, threatened the Peers, and yelled for Strafford's blood. The "Brief and perfect Relation" says that Bristol was especially attacked. "For you, my Lord of Bristol, we know you are an apostate for the cause of Christ and our mortal enemy. We do not therefore crave justice from you, but shall, God willing, crave justice upon you and your false son." Another cried, "If we have not the Lieutenant's head we shall have the King's." The crowd then posted up the names of the fifty-nine members of the House of Commons who had voted against the Bill of Attainder, under the title, "Straffordians, betrayers of their country."

It is known that this crowd did not consist of the usual rough apprentices, but of merchants and shopkeepers. By whom were they organised? How deep ran the ramifications of the Adventurers and their City agents? Balfour, again, was a Scot, and must have been sure of his ground when he refused to obey Charles's order. The events in the House of Commons that morning are significant. Pym's creature, Clotworthy, told the House of an armed gathering got together by Sir John Suckling in a tavern in Bread Street. This carpet knight, whose life was as elegant and as loose as the verses which still preserve his name from oblivion, had already proposed to Charles a plot for bringing up his army from the North to overawe Parliament. Charles had very properly

THE PROTESTATION

refused to have anything to do with him. Nevertheless Suckling was a favourite at Court, and gossip on "the Queen's side," as it was called, invariably percolated to Pym. Clarendon describes the incident contemptuously enough : " It is true there had been some idle discourses in a tavern between some officers about raising men for Portugal, which was immediately carried to Mr. Pym, as all tavern and ordinary discourses were."[1] In his own speech Pym contented himself with declaring again that Strafford was guilty of Treason "in the highest degree," and pointed out that it would be with the King to accept or refuse the Bill of Attainder as he saw fit after the Lords had passed it. " Truly I am persuaded that there was some great design in hand by the Papists to subvert and overthrow this Kingdom, and I do verily believe the King never had any intention to subvert the laws or bring in the Irish army : but yet he had counsel given him that he was loose from all rules of government : and though the King be of a tender conscience, yet we ought to be careful that we have good counsellors about him, and to let him understand that he is bound to maintain the laws, and that we take care for the maintenance of the word of God."

It was therefore decided to draw up a Protestation, which was in effect as Baillie described it. " All this time," he wrote, " the Lower House was inclosed from seven in the morning to eight at night. After much debate, at last, blessed be the name of the Lord, they all swore and subscribed the writ which here you have, I hope in substance our Scottish Covenant. God maketh our Enemies the instruments of all our good. We see now that it hath been in a happy time that so much time hath been losed about Strafford's head. But to-day,

[1] Cl. III. 329.

and hereafter, great things are expected, whereof you shall be advertised." Forasmuch as this Protestation was to be the shibboleth, whereby the malignant should be detected among the godly, it is given in full in Appendix VIII.

The Protestation was sent to the Lords with a request that they also should take it, a recommendation which had the support of a riotous mob without, howling "Justice, Justice against the Earl of Strafford!" "After that the Commons returned to their House, Doctor Burgess was desired to acquaint the multitude with the Protestation which both Houses had taken, which being read by him, and also made known unto them that the Parliament desired that they should return home to their houses, they forthwith departed."[1] So admirable had Pym's manipulation of his forces become. Rushworth continues: "The said Protestation was afterwards ordered to be tendered to the whole Kingdom with this intimation: that whosoever refused to take it should be noted as disaffected to the Parliament."

Meantime Strafford wrote to the King.

"May it please your sacred Majesty. It hath been my greatest grief in all these troubles, to be taken as a person which should endeavour to represent and set things amiss between your Majesty and your people, and to give counsels tending to the disquiet of the Three Kingdoms ... it is most mightily mistaken, for unto your Majesty it is well known my poor and humble advices concluded still in this, that your Majesty and your People could never be happy till there were a right understanding betwixt you and them, and that no other means were left to effect and settle this happiness

[1] R. III, i. 250.

but by the counsel and assent of your Parliament . . . yet such is my misfortune that this Truth findeth little credit, yea, the contrary seemeth generally to be believed, and myself reputed as one who endeavoured to make a separation between you and your People : under a heavier censure than this I am persuaded no Gentleman can suffer. . . . Here are before me the things most valued, most feared by mortal men, Life or Death. To say, Sir, that there hath not been a strife in me were to make me less man than, God knoweth, my infirmities make me. . . . But with much sadness I am come to a Resolution of that which I take to be best becoming me . . . and therefore in few words, as I put myself wholly upon the honour and justice of my Peers, so clearly, as to wish your Majesty might please to have spared that declaration of yours of Saturday last, and entirely to have left me to their Lordships : so now to set your Majesty's conscience at liberty, I do most humbly beseech your Majesty, for prevention of evils which may happen by your refusal to pass this Bill : and by this means to remove (praised be God) I cannot say this accursed (but I confess) this unfortunate thing, forth of the way towards that blessed agreement which God, I trust, shall ever establish between you and your subjects. Sir, my consent shall more acquit you herein to God than all the world can do besides. To a willing man there is no injury done, and as by God's grace I forgive all the world with a calmness and meekness of infinite contentment to my dislodging soul, so Sir, to you I can give the life of this world with all the cheerfulness imaginable, in the just acknowledgment of your exceeding favours, and only beg that in your goodness, you would vouchsafe to cast your gracious regard upon my poor son and his three sisters, less or more and no otherwise than as their (in present) unfortunate father may hereafter appear more or less guilty of this death. God long preserve your Majesty."[1]

The Adventurers were not idle meantime. Rumours of plots to save Strafford, some with grounds of truth, others with none, flew from mouth to mouth. Pym, in a speech probably of May 5th, brought to a focus all the scattered gossip. Rushworth has a vivid account of the state of nerves induced thereby. " Wednesday the 5th of May there happened to be a strange hubbub in the City, upon a false alarm that the Parliament House was beset and on fire, and all their lives in danger, which occasioned such running up and down in a confused manner, to come to protect them, that the like hath scarce been seen. This hubbub and alarm happened upon this occasion, Sir Walter Erle was making a report to the House of some plot and design to blow up the House of Commons ; Whereupon some members in the gallery stood up the better to hear the Report, and Mr. Moyle of Cornwall, and Mr. Middleton of Sussex, two persons of good bigness, weighed down a board in the Gallery, which gave so great a crack that some members thought it was a plot indeed ; And Sir John Wray speaking out he smelt Gunpowder, hastening back out of the Gallery ; some members in fear running out of the Hall crying out, The Parliament House was falling, and the members were slain, and the people running in a hurry through the Hall, Sir Robert Mansel drew his sword, bid them stand for shame. . . ."[2]

The Lords were not exempt from the general panic. On May 8th they passed the Bill. Charles was put to his fatal election.

His position was indeed terrible. On one side lay

[1] R. Straff. 743-4.   III. i, 251-2.   [2] R. Straff. 744-5.

THE BETRAYAL

gratitude, honour, the word of a King, conscience towards God : on the other riot, rebellion, probably death, not only for himself but for his wife and children. Armed resistance was impossible. If the King had dared to move a fragment of a regiment, Pym had denounced it for an army plot. Flight was impossible, the ports were closed, and to foil his last hope the fortifications of Portsmouth had been handed over to Parliamentary Commissioners by the twofold traitor Goring, with whom Pym seems to have had a perfect understanding.[1]

An armed mob accompanied the Houses when they brought the Bill of Attainder to his Majesty on Saturday, May 8th. He promised them his reply on Monday, and, ill-content they left him to spend the interval more miserably by far than his faithful servant in the Tower.

He sought his Council; " Consent," said they all. He sought his Bishops. " Refuse," cried Juxon, to his eternal honour. The knavish Williams bade him consent. Kings it seemed, were providentially endowed with two consciences, one for private use, the other for public needs like the present. The learned Ussher was called in. He was for righteousness and Juxon. It was time to decide. All day the mob faced Whitehall, wilder and fiercer every hour. Even Pym could scarcely have restrained them now. The lust of blood was upon them, and if they might not have Strafford's they would have the Queen's.

At nine o'clock on Sunday night, unnerved, unmanned, undone, Charles made his decision.

It is well to turn from this pitiful scene, to pass by the feeble effort of Charles subsequently to obtain a commutation, a reprieve, even a brief delay. Pym held in his grip

[1] G. IX. 97, 317 and 99, 386. Cl. V. 440 note, and VI, 32 note.

men paralysed with terror of the obscure and hideous dangers with which he had so long fed their imaginations. They had forgotten how to be merciful.[1]

"My Lord of Strafford's condition is more happy than mine," Charles had said, and it was true, for on Strafford lay no shadow of that shame or that remorse which were to be his master's portion till the day should come for him, too, to go through the dark valley.

Strafford was to die on the morning of the 12th; on the evening of the 11th he asked if he might see once more his old friend Laud, like him a prisoner in the Tower. He was told that he might not, unless by an order of Parliament. "Mr. Lieutenant," he replied with a flash of his old wit, "you shall hear what passeth between us. It is not a time for me to plot treason or for him to plot heresy." The Lieutenant bade him petition Parliament for the favour. "No," said Strafford, "I have gotten my despatch from them, and will trouble them no more." "But, my Lord," said he, turning to the Primate of Ireland, Ussher, then present, "what I should have spoken to my Lord's Grace of Canterbury is this, 'You shall desire the Archbishop to lend me his prayers this night, and to give me his blessing when I go abroad to-morrow, and to be in his window, that by my last farewell I may give him thanks for this and all other his former favours.'" The message was taken to Laud.

Rushworth, the Clerk of the Commons, to whom we owe so much, was present with him on the scaffold when he died, and his account of the last moments is here given :—

"This noble Earl was in person of a tall stature, something inclining to stooping in his shoulders, his hair

---

[1] Lord Newport, Constable of the Tower had undertaken to put Strafford to death even though Charles should refuse his assent to the Bill of Attainder.

black and thick, which he wore short, his countenance of a grave, well-composed symmetry, and good features, only in his forehead he exprest more severity than affability, yet a very courteous person.[1]

" The next morning, at his coming forth, he drew near to the Archbishop's lodgings, and said to the Lieutenant, ' Though I do not see the Archbishop, give me leave, I pray you, to do my last observance towards his rooms.' In the meantime, the Archbishop advertised of his approach, came out to the window. Then the Earl, bowing himself to the ground, 'My Lord,' said he, 'your prayers and your blessing.' The Archbishop lift up his hands and bestowed both, but overcome with grief fell to the ground *in animi diliquio;* the Earl proceeding a little further, bowed the second time, saying ' Farewell, my Lord, God protect your innocency.'[2]

" And as he went from the Tower to the scaffold his countenance was in a mild posture between dejection in contrition for sin, and a high courage, without perceiving the least affectation of disguise in him.[3]

" When he was marching to the scaffold, more like a general at the head of an army, as many of the spectators then said, to breathe victory, than like a condemned man to undergo the sentence of death, the Lieutenant desired him to take coach, for fear the people should rush in upon him and tear him in pieces, ' No,' said he, ' Master Lieutenant, I dare look death in the face, and I hope the people too. Have you a care that I do not escape, and I care not how I die, whether by the hand of the executioner, or the madness and fury of the people. If that may give them better content it is all one to me.'[4]

" Before he fitted himself to prostrate his body to execution, he desired patience of the people to hear him

[1] R. Straff. 772.   [2] Ibid. 762.   [3] Ibid. 773.   [4] Ibid. 762.

speak a few words, which the author took from his mouth, being then there on the scaffold with him.

"'. . . I come here, my Lords, to pay my last debt to Sin, which is Death, and through the mercies of God to rise again to Eternal Glory. . . . In all the honour I had to serve his Majesty, I had not any intention in my heart, but what did aim at the joint and individual prosperity of the King and his people. . . . One thing I desire to be heard in, and do hope that for Christian charities sake I shall be believed. I was so far from being against Parliaments that I did always think Parliaments in England to be the happy Constitution of the Kingdom and the nation, and the best means under God to make the King and his people happy. . . . I profess heartily my apprehension, and do humbly recommend it to you. . . . Whether the beginning of the people's happiness should be written in letters of blood, I fear they are in a wrong way, I desire Almighty God that no one drop of my blood rise up in judgment against them.

"'I have but one word more, and that is for my religion. . . . I do profess myself seriously, faithfully, and truly to be an obedient son of the Church of England. In that Church I was born and bred, in that religion I have lived, and now in that I die. Prosperity and happiness be ever to it.'

"He then took leave of those present, charged his brother, Sir George Wentworth, with messages for each of his children, and then said, 'I thank God I am no more afraid of death, nor daunted with any discouragements arising from any fears, but do as cheerfully put off my doublet at this time as ever I did when I went to bed.'

"Then he put off his doublet and wound up his hair with his hands and put on a white cap.

DEATH

"Then he called 'Where is this man that should do this last office? Call him to me.' When he came and asked him forgiveness, he told him he forgave him and all the world; then kneeling down by the block he went to prayer again himself, the bishop of Armagh kneeling on the one side, and the Minister on the other; to the which Minister after prayer he turned himself, and spoke some few words softly having his hands lifted up. The Minister closed his hands with his.

"Then, bowing himself to the earth to lay down his head on the block, he told the Executioner that he would first lay down his head to try the fitness of the block, and take it up again, before he laid it down for good and all. And so he did. And before he laid it down again he told the Executioner that he would give him warning when to strike by stretching forth his hands, and then laid down his neck on the Block, stretching out his hands.

"The Executioner struck off his head at one blow, then took the head up in his hands, and showed it to all the people and said

"'God save the King.'"

. . . .

So died Thomas Wentworth, Earl of Strafford, who living was misjudged, and dead was belied, greatest of all the statesmen whom an age fertile in greatness produced. So he, conscious of the right, faced calumny and infamy and death, and passed to the immortals.

. . . .

And round about his scaffold capered Pym's patriots. "His head is off! His head is off!" they screamed in glee.

CHAPTER X

ROOT AND BRANCH AND THE TEN PROPOSITIONS

HIS head was off, and with it fell his splendid scheme whereby the whole force of the Tudor monarchy was to be put at the back of enlightened reform in every department of administration.

Two months later that force was already diminished. Star Chamber was gone and the Privy Council with a couple of judges could no longer fine, imprison and pillory without a jury. Gone too was High Commission. Bishops and lawyers who practised in ecclesiastical cases could no longer deal with offenders against Church discipline at their own sour will. With Star Chamber and High Commission had gone the Council of the North at York, the scene of Wentworth's earlier ascendency, and the Council of Wales, themselves Star Chambers in miniature.

Equally was the King's extra-Parliamentary source of supply taken from him. Ship Money was declared illegal, so was the Limitation of the Forests, and it was no longer to be possible for his Majesty to exact knighthood fines.

The position of the judges was entirely altered; their office was henceforth no longer *durante beneplacito regis* but *quamdiu se bene gesserint*. Their own good behaviour and not the favour of the Crown was to ensure their independence. "Let them be lions," Bacon had said, and lions they might continue to be, but his significant addition was no longer to be possible: they were not to be "lions under the throne."

As to the minor agents of the unparliamentary system, they were of no more account now Strafford was stone dead and Laud was in the Tower, with the indefatigable malice of Prynne diligently building a scaffold for him, too. Windebank and Finch had fled over sea, and to point a moral to their tale, the Commons had dragged Judge Berkeley from his own Bench to their bar and clapped him into custody. It was a time for fallen Agags to step delicately. So far so good, but destruction is always easy. The institutions and agents lately in use might have been bad, it remained for Parliament to put something better in their place.

The soundest course would have been to act on that well-established principle of administration which makes of the poacher a gamekeeper. Pym, in the seat of Weston and of Juxon at the Treasury, would have presented from every point of view the gratifying spectacle of the critic compelled to create.

". . . If Mr. Pim, Mr. Hambden and Mr. Hollis had been then preferred, with Mr. St. John, before they were desperately embarked in their desperate designs and had innocence enough about them to trust the King and be trusted by him, having yet contracted no personal animosities against him, it is very possible that they might either have been made instruments to have done good service or at least been restrained from endeavouring to subvert the royal building, for supporting whereof they were placed as principal pillars."[1]

It had nearly come to pass. Clarendon asserts that immediately after Finch's flight, the Marquis of Hamilton had persuaded the King to admit several of his chief opponents to his counsels. Pym's patron, the Earl of Bedford, was to be Treasurer in place of Juxon ; Pym himself was to be Chancellor of the Exchequer in the room of Cottington, who would, it was assumed, be glad to get off so cheaply. Together Bedford and Pym

[1] Cl. IV. 76.

were to overhaul the revenue completely. Saye was to be Master of Wards, a post also to be taken from Cottington, and Holles was to have Windebank's position as Secretary of State. The post of Solicitor-General was to go to Oliver St. John, "a gentleman of an honourable extraction if he had been legitimate." This last was the only one of the proposed appointments which was actually made, and as already it has been seen, by this appointment Charles served Strafford an ill turn and did himself no good.

Bedford died shortly after this, and thus the plan became impossible, if indeed it had not already been abandoned. "He fell sick within a week after the Bill of Attainder was sent up to the Lords' House, and died shortly after, much afflicted with the passion and fury which he perceived his party inclined to, insomuch as he declared to some of near trust with him that he feared the rage and madness of this Parliament would bring more prejudice and mischief to the Kingdom than it had ever sustained by the long intermission of Parliaments.[1] Twice in one week, in the middle of April, Pym was received by the King in interview, and deeply significant must have been the unrecorded conversation of Charles bent on saving Strafford's life, with Pym equally determined to destroy him. Whether Pym's principles were too high or Charles's price too low, nothing came of this momentous meeting, except possibly that each may have taken his measure of the other's capacity.

Thus far there had been in the Commons a passable appearance of unanimity, if we may except the hostility shown by a large minority to the violence and chicanery with which Strafford's death had been encompassed. But there had already been signs that this unanimity

[1] Cl. III. 192.

would disappear as soon as the question of the Church was dealt with. It could not long be deferred, for not only were "the godly party" in the Commons anxious to begin, but all alike were spurred on by their allies and taskmasters, the Scottish army, who wished the purification of religion to go on side by side with the payment of large sums to themselves.

As early as December 11th, 1640, as already mentioned, a petition was presented to the House of Commons by Alderman Pennington, praying that the government of Archbishops and Lord Bishops, Deans and Archdeacons ". . . with all its dependencies, roots and branches may be abolished, and all laws in their behalf made void." [1] The Petitioners gave twenty-eight particulars in support of their request, enumerating amongst other things " the faint-heartedness of ministers to preach the truth of God, lest they should displease the prelates ; as, namely, the doctrines of Predestination, of Free-Grace, or Perseverance, of Original Sin remaining after Baptism, of the Sabbath, the Doctrine against Universal Grace, the Election for Faith foreseen, Free-Will against Anti-Christ, Non-residents, human inventions in God's worship, all which are generally witheld from the people's knowledge because not relishing to the Bishops."

Before the Commons could digest this morsel they were invited to lament " the suppressing of that godly design set on foot by certain saints, and sugared with many great gifts by sundry well-affected persons, for the buying of impropriations, and placing of able ministers in them, maintaining of lectures, and founding of Free Schools which the Prelates could not endure lest it should darken their glories."

They went on to attribute to the unfortunate prelates

[1] R. III. i, 93.

" the swarming of lascivious, idle and unprofitable books and pamphlets, play-books and ballads . . . the frequent vending of crucifixes and Popish pictures . . . the standing up at *Gloria Patri* and at the reading of the Gospel, praying towards the East, bowing at the name of Jesus, the bowing to the Altar towards the East, the cross in baptism, kneeling at the communion." They bewailed the fact that England had not, like other Reformed Churches, " upon their rejection of the Pope, cast the prelates out also as members of the Beast, nay the prelates had gone so far as to say that the Church of Rome was a true Church . . . and that salvation is attainable in that religion."

This document purported to be signed by 15,000 Londoners and a crowd of 1,500 accompanied it. But they had overshot their mark, this time there was no unanimity in the House, " There were many against and many for the same." Order was made that the Petition should be debated on the 17th, and that the rolls of names brought with it should be left in custody of the Speaker, sealed with his seal and those of the two aldermen of London who had brought it. Members of the House might have copies of the Petition, but no one else.[1] The debate did not take place till February 8, 1641, the Commons being much occupied till that date with Strafford and the Triennial Bill.

The Petition was no spontaneous effervescence of Puritanism, but the result of careful missionary effort. The Commons were now establishing a new High Commission of their own with the parts reversed. The procedure was simple : a petition was presented against a clergyman, one or two of the petitioners attended to swear to their particulars, the victim was sent for " as a delinquent,"

[1] C. J. II. 49, ii.

examined and re-examined in committee, and so kept cooling his heels at Westminster, or bailed indefinitely in large sums.[1] The *Commons Journals* show that this ingenious practice was begun within three weeks of the assembling of the Long Parliament. On November 25, 1640, they sent for Dr. Lafield, vicar of All Hallows Barking, and a member of Convocation, who amongst other monstrous deeds " hath caused I.H.S. to be set in Gold Letters upon the Table and forty places besides." On December 22nd they sent for Thomas Preston, Vicar of Rothersthorp, in the county of Northampton, as a delinquent on the petition of Richard Farmer " for very scandalous speeches spoken by him against this House."[2]

On January 1, 1641, David Bandinell, Dean of the Isle of Jersey, was summoned for " very heinous crimes "; on the 4th William Piers, Archdeacon of Bath, for " very malicious and wicked words by him spoken against the last Parliament "; on the 7th, Dr. Potter, Vice-Chancellor of the University of Oxford, was brought to the bar " for suspending Mr. H. Wilkinson for a good sermon preached by him "; on the 8th Dr. Samuel Utie, Vicar of Chigwell in Essex, and William Ward, Rector of St. Leonard's Parish, Foster Lane, London, were ordered to be fetched by the Serjeant-at-Arms as delinquents. On the 13th, the Committee for the Bishop of Ely received authority " to receive all complaints of Pressures and Enormities committed by or under the present Bishop of Norwich. On the 23rd, Thomas Jones, Clerk of Offweld, in the county of Devon, was sent for " scandalous words by him used against the Parliament, in a sermon preached by him at Tiverton, in the said county of Devon, the last day of July, 1640, attested by a member of this House." The name of the member is not given,

[1] C. J. II. 70, i. [2] C. J. II. 56, i-ii. R. III. I. 151-2.

but the gentleman who sat for Tavistock is perhaps open to suspicion.

Dr. Chaffin on the same day incurred the same penalty for the same offence in the Cathedral Church of Salisbury. This day was further notable for the presentation of a Petition presented by Sir Robert Harley, and signed by some thousand ministers, asking for a complete reform of the government of the Bishops, and also for an instruction given to " the Committee for Secretary Windebank . . . concerning commissions to be sent into all countries for the Defacing, Demolishing and quite taking away of all Images, Altars or Tables turned Altarwise, Crucifixes, Superstitious Pictures, Monuments and Relicts of Idolatry out of all Churches or Chapels." [1] On the 25th Thomas Gawler, Parson, of Chisleborough, was sent for as a delinquent on the petition of three of the inhabitants, " and the greatest part of it was likewise attested by a Member of this House," no doubt Pym again. On the first day of February, Sir Nathaniel Brent, Sir John Lamb and Dr. Roane, were summoned " by a warrant under Mr. Speaker's hand to appear here to show Reason why they laid the Tax upon the Town of Waddsden, in the County of Bucks, contrary to law, for the maintaining of a Pair of Organs and an Organist in the said Town of Waddsden." On February 5th Edward Bowen, Parson, of the Parish of Woodchurch in Kent was sent for, and on the 9th the Committee for Scandalous Ministers was empowered to consider a petition from Lancaster and all Petitions of a like nature.

On the previous day the adjourned debate on the Londoners' Root and Branch Petition had at last taken place. The point to be decided was whether this petition, which demanded the complete abolition of Episcopacy,

[1] C. J. II. 72, i.

should be sent to Committee as well as the Ministers' Petition of April 23, which was content to ask merely for definite rules by which Bishops must be guided. The Adventurer Rudyerd opened the debate by suggesting a council of clergy in each diocese, and the exclusion of the Bishop from all political concerns. Digby ridiculed the 15,000 petitioners. "Methought the comet had a terrible tail with it, Sir, and pointed to the north."[1] " I am confident there is no man of judgment that will think it fit for a Parliament under a monarchy to give countenance to irregular and tumultuous assemblies of people, be it for never so good an end." He was, nevertheless, all for clipping the Bishop's wings, for they had imposed on men of nice and tender consciences things which they knew to be but indifferent. If they were opposed they contented themselves not only with the spiritual sword of St. Peter but with his temporal one, and cut off their enemies' ears. He would himself be inclined to cry, "Down with them even unto the ground," but he believed triennial Parliaments would be "able to keep many a worse devil in order." Monarchy could not stand with Presbyterian government. Lord Saye's second son, Nathaniel Fiennes then attempted to disprove Digby and persuade the House that assemblies need not necessarily be opposed to monarchy. As the debate proceeded Hyde, Culpepper, Selden, Hopton and Waller followed Digby, while Pym, Hampden, St. John, and Holles were all in favour of sending the petition to Committee. Bagshaw, at this time member of Southwark, speaks in his book *A Just Vindication* of Pym as "a gentleman with whom I had familiar acquaintance and knew his mind in that point," and Pym is reported to have said "that he thought it was not the intention of the House to abolish either

[1] R. III. i, 171.

Episcopacy or the Book of Common Prayer, but to reform both wherein offence was given to the people." [1] Clarendon says of this momentous question, "In the House of Commons, though, of the chief leaders, Nathaniel Fynes [Fiennes] and young Sir H. Vane, and shortly after Mr. Hambden (who had not before owned it) were believed to be for "root and branch" (which grew shortly after a common expression, and discovery of the several tempers); yet Mr. Pimm was not of that mind, nor Mr. Hollis, nor any of the Northern men, or those lawyers who drove on most furiously with them: all who were pleased with the government itself of the Church," [2] and again "Mr. Pym was concerned and passionate in the jealousies of religion, and much troubled with the countenance which had been given to those opinions that had been imputed to Arminius, yet himself professed to be very entire to the doctrine and discipline of the Church of England."

It was inevitable that the rupture in the Commons should arise out of the question of the Church. Not only was it impossible to find a common standpoint for the authors of the Root and Branch Petition and a churchman like Montague, there was also the political antithesis. "No Bishop, No King," James had said, and Charles had followed his father's policy. On the other hand, the nearer the Puritan extremists could drag the Church towards the doctrines and organisation of Calvin, the more firmly would they bind the Scots to their alliance. Moreover, even men with little liking for Puritanism, and genuinely attached to the Church, had been alienated by the liberal grant made to Charles by the Convocation of Canterbury after the dissolution of the Short Parliament the year before, and by the new Canons which

[1] G. IX. 96, 281 and note. [2] Cl. III. 147.

expressly declared that " the most high and sacred order of Kings is of divine right," and that " for subjects to bear arms against their Kings was to resist the power ordained by God." The Church had indeed there flung down the gage. Finally it was resolved, without division, to refer to Committee the greater part of the Londoners' Petition, and also the Ministers' Petition, but to refer the question of Episcopacy to the whole House. Meanwhile on June 30th the Commons impeached thirteen Bishops for their share in passing the obnoxious Canons in 1640.

The Scots were turning the screw; they still occupied the northern counties, and it was a difficult task to find the money to satisfy them. In February a loan of £60,000 was due to fall in to be handed to Sir William Uvedale, the treasurer of the army. But the City held back, disgusted it was believed with the slow progress of Strafford's trial. Only £21,000 came in, and Pym suggested that, in respect of the great necessity of the public, they might compel the Londoners to lend. For this amazing proposal he was instantly called to order, and one member moved that he should be called upon to give satisfaction to the House. D'Ewes admonished him that arbitrary rule by a Parliament was very much the same as arbitrary rule by a King. He was surprised to hear from " that worthy member " a proposal which conduced to the violation of the liberties and properties of the subject, and he hoped that such words would not be whispered abroad lest men should hide their store and lend them nothing.[1] It was probably no chance impulse that prompted Pym's sentence, for as early as November 13th he had suggested that the two armies in the North should be paid out of the estates of those who had caused the mischief.[2]

[1] G. IX. 96, 295.   [2] Ibid. 95, 236.

The Scottish Commissioners in London, under the guidance of Henderson, at this moment thought fit to draw up a declaration that they desired the abolition of Episcopacy in England as well as at home. Copies of this declaration were sent to members of Parliament, and one fell into the hands of a bookseller who printed others for general circulation. Like their friends the Londoners, the Scots here over-reached themselves. The House of Commons was immensely indignant, and there was a stormy scene. Nevertheless the extreme party was still in the ascendant, and on March 1st Laud was committed to the Tower. The Articles of Impeachment against him had been carried to the Upper House by Pym, Hampden, and Maynard on February 26th. They were fourteen in number, and the object of them was to show "that he had traitorously endeavoured to subvert the Fundamental Laws of Government of this Kingdom of England." [1] The same policy was adopted as in the case of Strafford. The Fundamental Laws were not formulated. Assertions were treated as facts, and the flimsiness of the evidence was concealed by illogical deductions and strong denunciations. The tenth Article will illustrate as well as another at once the method and the candour of Laud's accusers. " He hath traitorously and wickedly endeavoured to reconcile the Church of England with the Church of Rome : and for the effecting thereof, hath consorted and confederated with divers Popish Priests and Jesuits, and hath kept secret intelligence with the Pope of Rome : and by himself, his agents and instruments, treated with such as have from thence received Authority and Instruction ; he hath permitted and countenanced a Popish Hierarchy or Ecclesiastical Government to be established in this Kingdom, by all

[1] Cf. W. H. H., p. 197.

which traitorous and malicious practices this Church and Kingdom hath been exceedingly endangered, and like to fall under the tyranny of the Roman See."

The Articles having been read Pym followed with a lengthy speech, beginning, " My Lords, there is an expression in the Scripture which I will not presume either to understand or to interpret, yet to a vulgar eye it seems to have an aspect of something suitable to the Person and Cause before you. It is a description of the Evil Spirits, wherein they are said to be Spiritual Wickednesses in High Places." He proceeded to examine such " crimes acted by the Spiritual Faculties of the Soul " from the point of view of Theology, of Morals, and of Law. As to this last he asserts, "If they be examined, my Lords, by legal rules in a civil way as they stand in opposition to the Public Good and to the Laws of the Land, he will be found to be a Traitor against his Majesty's Crown, an incendiary against the Peace of the State : he will be found to be the highest, the boldest and most impudent oppressor both of King and People." He then took the Articles one by one. " I shall now run through them with a light touch, only marking in every [one] of them some special point of Venom, Virulency and Malignity." This was an ambiguous sentence which describes more truly than Pym intended, the nature of the charges against Laud. " It is a miserable abuse of the Spiritual Keys to shut up the Doors of Heaven, and to open the Gates of Hell, to let in Profaneness, Ignorance, Superstition and Error. I shall need say no more, these things are evident, and abundantly known to all." He concluded with the usual sinister request : " The Commons desire your Lordships that they may have the same way of Examination that they had in the case of the Earl of Strafford, that is to examine Members of all kinds of your Lordships' House and their own, and others as they shall see cause, and those Examinations to be kept secret and private that they may with more advantage be made use of when the matter comes to trial."[1] "Nothing," wrote Forster, "is more striking in this speech than the utter absence of sectarian intolerance."[2]

Laud had already been ten weeks in the custody of Maxwell, usher of the Black Rod. On March 1st he was conveyed to the Tower, "and so they followed me with clamour and revilings even beyond barbarity itself, not giving over till the Coach was entered in at the Tower Gate. Mr. Maxwell out of his love and care was exceedingly troubled at it, but, I bless God for it, my patience was not moved." There he lay for three years, until on March 12, 1643, the trial began which sent him to the scaffold.

On the 10th, the Committee on the two petitions having made its report, the House resolved that the legislative and judicial functions of the Bishops were an impediment to their spiritual work, and next day they followed this by a resolve that the clergy should not have any judicial functions of any kind whatever. From March 23rd, when Pym began his case against Strafford, to May 12th, when the great Earl perished, all eyes were fixed on that tragedy. When the Lord Deputy was dead, Charles had to face the position created by his own weakness in abandoning his Minister, and his folly in assenting to the Bill for the Perpetuation of this Parliament.

On May 1st a Bill "to restrain Bishops and others in Holy Orders from intermeddling with secular affairs" was, "upon question, passed." On the 27th, the Lords decided that the Bishops should be retained in

[1] R. III. i, 199-202. [2] F. P. 194.

Parliament, but that the clergy should exercise no civil functions. The Lords indeed were not pleased with the Commons, who, "if they might send up a Bill this day, at once to take out one whole bench from the House, as this would do the Bishops, they might to-morrow send another to take away the barons or some other degree of the nobility."

The Commons were not to be put off. On May 27th the younger Vane and Oliver Cromwell brought to the House a Bill, said to have been drawn up by St. John, to extinguish Episcopacy entirely. This was the famous Root and Branch Bill. They did not propose the Bill themselves but induced Sir Edward Dering to do so, "a man very opposite to all their designs, but a man of levity and vanity, easily flattered by being commended." [1] Dering afterwards confessed, "This Bill was pressed into my hand by Sir Arthur Haselrig, being then brought unto him by Sir Henry Vane and Mr. Oliver Cromwell. He told me he was resolved that it should go in, but was earnestly urgent that I should present it. The Bill did hardly stay in my hand so long as to make a hasty perusal. Whilst I was overviewing it, Sir Edward Ayscough delivered a petition out of Lincolnshire, which was seconded by Mr. Strode in such a sort as that I had a fair invitement to issue forth the Bill then in my hand. Hereupon I stood up and said this, which immediately after I reduced into writing."[2] It was not until June 21st that the constructive part of the Bill was determined on. On the proposal of the younger Vane, it was resolved that in each diocese the place of the Bishop should be taken by Commissioners appointed in equal numbers for laity and clergy. The Bill was stoutly opposed by Falkland and by Selden, but had the support of Pym

[1] Cl. III. 155.   [2] P. H. II. 814-15.

and of Hampden, and was read a second time by a majority of 135 to 108.

It was evident that Henderson's demand for Presbyterianism in England had seriously alarmed many who had hitherto voted steadily with the majority in the Commons, and the voting showed their strength. The loss of Digby might easily be borne, but the defection of such men as Selden and Falkland was ominous indeed. This Bill never went further, nor did a plan proposed by Archbishop Williams in the House of Lords, whereby each Bishop was to have an advisory committee of twelve, of whom King, Lords, and Commons were respectively to choose four. This measure also received the honour of a second reading and then dropped. There was a complete deadlock on the question of Episcopal government, and it was suffered to remain as it was, till a greater storm swept it away altogether.

Thus a line of cleavage had begun in the House of Commons on the question of Church government which would ultimately give Charles a Royalist party within its walls. But there was little difference of opinion as to the necessity for clipping the wings of the Tudor monarchy. On June 8th, three Bills were brought in, which imposed grave limitations on the Prerogative, and it is notable that they were introduced by John Selden. This great lawyer had been the indefatigable supporter of the Petition of Right in 1628. His integrity revolted from the *privilegium* which had sent Strafford to his bloody grave, and he had been placarded in consequence by the London mob as a Straffordian, betrayer of his country: his hostility to the Root and Branch Bill has just been described. The Bills now introduced by him declared Ship Money to be illegal, limited the extent of the forests, and abolished knighthood fines.

On the same day a third reading was given to a Bill for the Abolition of Star Chamber, of the Councils of the North and of Wales, and of the Palatine Duchies of Lancaster and Chester, and to another for the destruction of the Court of High Commission.

The Lords passed them all. On July 5th, Charles gave his assent to the two latter, and on August 7th and 8th, to the three former measures.

He had already, on June 22nd, assented to the Tunnage and Poundage Bill, which declared illegal the collection of such taxes without Parliamentary sanction, but at the same time gave to him all such dues as had at any time been granted to himself or to his father. A limitation hitherto unknown had been added to this grant: it was to be for a short definite period only, from May 25th to July 15th. This limitation was dictated by the fear felt by the Commons of the result of Charles's proposed visit to Scotland, and by their desire to control his action to some extent by an instant stoppage of supplies.

Charles's resolve to go to Scotland was, he declared, made in pursuance of his intention to bring about the disbandment of both armies and a general settlement of disputes there. There is no doubt that he also hoped to strengthen his position towards Parliament by a visit to his northern Kingdom. He had won over his old opponent the Earl of Rothes. Still more he had now on his side the heroic Montrose, at last alienated from the Covenanters by the covert disloyalty of Argyll, who was believed to contemplate the deposition of the King. Moreover, Charles had come to some sort of understanding with the Scottish Commissioners in London, whose solicitude for their English brethren had been to some extent damped by the slow trickle of the promised Supply, by the lack of enthusiasm for the spread of

Presbyterianism in England, and by the open distrust shown by the Commons of any direct communication of Charles with Scotland. These were motives sufficient to account for the King's determination, without the attribution to him of any serious intention of using the English or the Scottish army against Parliament. But it was this intention which Pym and the Adventurers attributed to him, and it was easy enough for their satellites in the northern counties to collect or to manufacture idle gossip which would lend colour to the aspersions. There is no doubt that Pym and his friends were at this moment seriously alarmed. The irritation of the Lords shown in the matter of the Bishop's Votes and the growth of the party hostile to Puritanism in their own House disturbed them. If the King should remove himself from their clutches, he might, in the bracing air of Scotland, develop an independence he had long ceased to show in London. It was plainly time for Pym to do something.

On June 24th, he carried up to the Lords the Ten Propositions.[1] The first of these dealt with the disbanding of the English Army in the North, and also desired that " the Commissioners for Scotland be entreated to retire some part of their army." The second considered the proposed journey of the King to Scotland, and he was requested to postpone it until both armies should have been disbanded and certain business of importance settled in Parliament. The third besought his Majesty to remove from him " all such counsellors as I am commanded to describe," and in their place to receive such " as his people and Parliament may have just cause to confide in." The fourth proposition was concerned with " the Queen's Most Excellent Majesty,"

[1] R. III. i, 298-300.

and implored his Majesty to persuade her to accept some of the nobility and others of trust into such places as were then at her disposal, and not to receive into her service any Jesuit or any other priest, whether French, Italian, English, Scottish, or Irish; that all such should be restrained from coming to Court, and that the College of Capuchins at Somerset House should be dissolved and sent out of the Kingdom. Her Majesty's children were the care of the fifth proposition, which prayed " that some persons of public trust and well affected in religion " might be placed about the Prince of Wales and his brothers and sisters. The sixth desired that " such as shall come into the Kingdom with titles of being the Pope's *nuncio*, shall be declared guilty of high treason and be out of the King's protection, and out of the protection of the law." Count Rossetti, who was then the Papal agent at Court, was mentioned by name.

" The seventh head is concerning the security and peace of the Kingdom." It consists of one of Pym's favourite nostrums: " That a special oath may be prepared, by consent of both Houses, authorised by Law, and to be taken by the Lord-Lieutenants and Deputy Lieutenants, Captains and other officers. Such an oath as may be fit to secure us in these times of danger," and that Parliament should be especially informed as to the state of the Cinque Ports and others. The eighth Proposition was a measure of precaution, for it desired that his Majesty's learned Counsel might be directed to prepare a general pardon in such a large manner as may be for the relief of his Majesty's Subjects. The ninth requested that a permanent committee of both Houses should confer from time to time on some particular causes, as shall be more effectual for the common good. The tenth was directed against Papists, male and female, at Court and in the Country, and went so far as to desire the imprisonment " of the most active."

The Commons had for some time past been persecuting the Queen. She was made responsible for every wild ejaculation or rash expression which persistent oppression wrung from her co-religionists. A demand persisted in, and ultimately successful, was that her mother should be driven from the country. Her honour was not spared aspersion if she showed any mark of favour to Digby, Jermyn, or any other man about her Court who was obnoxious to the Adventurers. They had their spies amongst her household, led by the notorious Lady Carlisle. As if this were not enough, her life was threatened by their howling mobs from the London slums, as in the last terrible days of Strafford's life. She now desired to take the waters at Spa. A storm of indignation burst upon her. She was going to pawn the Crown jewels abroad, she was going to fetch in foreign troops. A message was sent privately to the guardians of the jewels, bidding them be ready to give an account of them, and stronger measures were threatened if the Queen attempted to leave the country. The unfortunate lady was compelled to submit. Five days later Pym was avenged upon her for the release of Goodman, an aged priest condemned to death, whom she had induced Charles to pardon, for on July 26th, William Ward was hanged and quartered at Tyburn. He was another old Roman priest, seventy-six years of age. The Spanish and Portuguese ambassadors were present and saw their fellow-believer make a good end, but whether Pym was present is not known.

The Lords accepted the Ten Propositions, but altered some particulars which lacked deference to the Queen. They were no doubt influenced by the vague and disturbing rumours of plots which the Adventurers were disseminating everywhere. When Charles received the Propositions he consented to the disbandment of the army and the immediate dismissal of Rossetti, but he repudiated the suggestion of evil counsellors, and refused point blank to abandon his journey to Scotland. On August 10th he departed thither. Thus foiled, the Commons on August 20th appointed a committee to attend the King, nominally to assist in the disbandment of the army, really to act as spies upon him, and to report at Westminster whatever they could pick up against him. They chose Fiennes, Armyn, Stapleton, and Hampden, and from the Lords the new Earl of Bedford, who did not go, and Lord Howard of Escrick.

But by what authority could they empower these Commissioners? The Lord Keeper Lyttelton refused to pass their commission under the Great Seal without express instructions from his Majesty. Some of the wilder spirits were for compelling him, but D'Ewes persuaded them to proceed by " ordinance." In the middle ages an ordinance had signified a declaration of the Crown without the concurrence of Parliament. It was now made to mean a declaration of the Houses without consent of the Crown. Already, on August 17th, the Houses had concurred in an order to Holland to secure Hull and the war materials there, and to Newport, Constable of the Tower, to take up his residence in that fortress and see to its defences. It is to be noted that this was done after a curious letter from Holland to Essex, hinting at danger to the Houses.[1] Holland, as we have seen, was chief of the Adventurers. The issue of the order and of the ordinance alike were new and revolutionary proceedings. It was no longer a question

[1] G. X. 100, 3.

of paring off Tudor accretions, Pym had now laid his hands upon the Prerogative.

On September 9th the Houses adjourned for six weeks, having accomplished a work on a scale unheard of since the Seven Years' Parliament registered Henry VIII's edicts on the Reformation.

Meantime Charles's visit to Scotland had sorely disappointed him. His reception, it is true, both on his way to Scotland and when he arrived, was cordial and loyal. He passed through both armies without attempting to raise those dogs of war with which Pym and the Adventurers had shaken the nerves of the weaker brethren. He received a royal reception in Edinburgh, and proceeded to throw the handle after the hatchet by assenting to all the Acts which he had so long refused. He even attended the Presbyterian service and listened to hot-gospelling sermons, " where the bishops were not spared, but such downright language as would a year ago have been at least a Star Chamber business." [1]

Such heroism was not rewarded. A confused plot, alleged to be directed by certain Catholic notables against the lives of Argyll and Hamilton, distracted the attention of the Scottish nobility, and indeed gave material to the Parliamentary spies around Charles to implicate him also in the " Incident," as it came to be called. Argyll had Montrose safely under lock and key; the Scottish army was now disbanded, the Scots had got from him all they wanted. There was nothing for Charles to do but to retire. He made Argyll a Marquis, Hamilton a Duke, and the " little, crook-backed general," Alexander Leslie, an Earl. He then returned to London, which he entered on November 25th. Much had happened in the interval.

[1] G. X. 100-18.

On October 3rd, the Houses had re-assembled. The cessation of their debates for six weeks and the absence of the King in Scotland had relaxed the political tension. Thoughtful men had reflected upon what had already been done. They saw the swollen prerogative of the Tudors reduced to becoming proportions; after the death of Strafford, the flight of the extreme Courtiers, and the overthrow of the extra-ordinary Courts, they believed reaction to be unlikely, if not impossible. Many of them had beheld with dismay the virulence of the attack on the Church, some even began to ask whether the grounds of Laud's impeachment were adequate. Indeed, amazing things were going on ; simple pietists, who called themselves Adamites, had felt themselves called upon to discard in public worship those vestments which had been habitual in Britain even before the arrival of Julius Cæsar. The village idiot and the village wastrel had joined hands in urging on church reform by smashing painted windows and mutilating the ancient sculpture of the Ages of Faith. The cobbler and the tailor, professions curiously prone to theological speculation, had occupied the village pulpits in the enforced absence of those Incumbents who were attending Pym's committee as " delinquents." In Fleet Street a godly man of the trade of Cleon, an authority on infant baptism, preached so loudly to a conventicle of Separatists in his house that he attracted the notice of some of the mob who were so servicable to Pym at Westminster. They proceeded to storm the house and to hang the preacher on his own sign. The constables only arrived in time to save the neck of the leatherseller, Praise God Barbone, and thus enable him to give his name to one of Cromwell's experiments in government.

Moreover the Parliamentary poll tax brought home to

every hearth a grievance that obliterated the bitterness of dead Noy's Ship Money. It was an anxious time for Pym and the Committee of Safety, of which he was the guiding spirit. But neither he nor his fellow Adventurers were idle. Hampden was, in his sly quiet way, weaving hypotheses in Edinburgh which might implicate Charles in the violence of the "Incident." Holland had listened not unfruitfully to the gossip of disaffected soldiers at the disbandment in the North. Lady Carlisle carried to the ears of Pym all the malicious gossip that centred round the entourage of the persecuted and lonely Queen, whose confidence she betrayed. On October 19th, Pym disclosed the reports of the "Incident" which he had received from Edinburgh, and asserted that for the last ten days he had been receiving warnings that a similar stroke might be looked for in England. By his adroit manipulation of the material so laboriously prepared by himself, by Hampden and by the other Adventurers, Pym might hope in the coming session to find himself in a stronger position than ever.

He had now reached the parting of the ways. It was for him to decide whether he would be leader of a truly national party, binding up the wounds of the country by associating the moderate men of both sides : whether he would accept that position of trust which Charles had twice offered to him, and would carry with him into the counsels of the King those gifts of intrigue and of leadership which had enabled him to bring his Monarch to his knees. True, such a choice would have involved the loss of many old associates, the brutal genius of Cromwell, the ready venom of the younger Vane ; it would have been the breaking of many ties. But other ties were already strained to snapping ; Hyde, Falkland, Culpepper, Selden, were drifting away. Holborne and

PYM'S OPPORTUNITY

others were ready to follow. It was a momentous decision for the man to make whom Clarendon describes as "the most able to do hurt that hath lived in any time."

We do not know that Pym ever hesitated, that he even recognised at all that the decisive hour of his life had come. No journals of his survive to indicate the motives which urged him now. The fact only remains that he continued on the road upon which he was treading, the road that led to bloody civil war, to judicial murder, to the crushing of all those Parliamentary privileges and institutions which he professed to hold so dear; to confiscation, to massacre, to the rule of the sword of Cromwell's saints. He may have thought that between himself and the King would rise up for ever the shade of Strafford, as the shade of murdered Buckingham had risen up between Charles and Eliot, and had hardened the King's heart against his wretched suppliant in the Tower. It is more likely that a guilty knowledge both of his share in the Scottish invasion of England and of the law of treason, which he had wrested to Strafford's destruction, impelled him to self-preservation. He had yet a great career before him in the two years of harassed life that were left to him. He was yet to be "King Pym," the idolised and the detested, to sway as he had never swayed before the tempestuous wills of violent men; his wishes were to be accounted for law and his long speeches for righteousness. But never for him was to be the crowning glory of politics—the glory that more and more adorns the memory of fallen Strafford. He would destroy and to spare, but he would never construct again; he would never do what Strafford had done in Ireland: bring order where chaos reigned, bring peace where there was strife, make the land which was barren rejoice. He had chosen to be leader of a party when he might have been leader of a nation.

"... the Long Parliament itself had said its last word in politics. Everything that it had done up to this point with the single exception of the compulsory clauses of the Triennial Act, was accepted at the Restoration and passed into the permanent constitution of the country. Everything that it attempted to do after this was rejected at the Restoration. The first was the work of the whole Parliament, the second was the work of a majority. Failure, and it must be confessed deserved failure, was the result of Pym's leadership." [1]

[1] Gardiner X. 100, p. 34.

CHAPTER XI

THE GRAND REMONSTRANCE

PARLIAMENT met again on October 20, 1641, and " Mr. Pym reports and gives an account of what the Committee appointed to sit during the Recess had done in pursuance of the Order of the House given to that Committee." [1] Hampden had sent certain letters from Scotland providing the requisite scares. To the House, the " Incident " appeared as terrifying as the Army Plot, and Essex and Holland hinted darkly to Hyde that " other men were in danger of the like assaults." Hyde and Falkland endeavoured to lessen the impression made by the alarmists, but with little success, for Pym thus reported the Heads for a Conference with the Lords concerning the safety of the Kingdom : " That when there was a design somewhat of the same nature in this Kingdom, to seduce the King's Army, to interrupt the Parliament here, that there was the like design at that time in Scotland. Next the principal Party named in that Design in Scotland, is a Person suspected to be Popishly affected, and therefore may have correspondency with the Party here. That it hath been published here lately, that some things were to be done there in Scotland before it broke out there. Therefore we may suspect some Correspondency here." [2] These obscure hypotheses led to a very practical conclusion : " So upon these Grounds, to propound that a strong Guard be kept in the City of Westminster and London, then secondly, that Care be Taken for the future for the Defence of the whole Kingdom."

The Lords concurred, and a Watch was appointed

[1] C. J. II, 289, i.   [2] C. J. II, 290, ii.

from the Westminster Trained Bands to guard them day and night in Palace yard. The command was given to Essex. This was one of the cleverest of Pym's moves, for the presence of the guard was, to the illogical mind of the London mob, an ocular proof of the reality of the dangers of which he warned them.

On the same day a new Bill was brought in to deprive the Bishops of their seats in the House of Lords and to exclude the Clergy from all secular authority. Two days later it was read a third time. Its object was mainly political, for it would remove at one stroke twenty-six stalwart opponents. But the measure was by no means unanimously approved. Hampden had now returned from his Scottish eavesdropping. To his dismay he found not only Sir Edward Dering but also Lord Falkland amongst the opponents of the measure. "I am sorry," said Hampden, "to find a noble lord has changed his opinion since the time the last Bill to this purpose passed the House: for he then thought it a good Bill, but now he thinketh this an evil one." Falkland's reply was severe. "Truly," he said, "I was persuaded at that time by the worthy gentleman who hath spoken to believe many things which I have since found to be untrue: and therefore I have changed my opinions in many particulars, as well as to things as persons." [1]

If any proof were needed of the pre-eminence of Pym at this moment, it is afforded by an incident which occurred on October 25th. A letter delivered to him in the House of Commons was found to contain a filthy rag that had covered a plague sore, together with an abusive screed denouncing him as a traitor and a taker of bribes, and promising him a dagger thrust should the plague-rag fail. The letter had been brought to the Serjeant

[1] F. G. R. 168.

THE PLAGUE RAG

of the House by a messenger, to whom it had been given by a gray-coated horseman that morning on Fish Street Hill together with a shilling for his pains. Pym opened the letter and something dropped out on the floor; not heeding this, Pym read a few words, then holding up the paper he cried out that it was a scandalous libel. The letter was carried to the Clerk's Assistant, John Rushworth, who read it aloud until he came to the explanation of its contents, " Whereupon the said Clerk's Assistant, having read so far, threw down the letter into the House, and so it was spurned away out of the door." [1] The affair is noted in the *Journals* for October 26th, when one George Mordant, suspected of being the author of the outrage, was acquitted and discharged. [2] Clarendon says that the House was kept in perpetual uneasiness by rumours of plots against Pym's life, but he does not refer to this incident, and it is of course possible that the whole thing was a device of some of the baser of Pym's following to enhance his popularity and give colour to the rumours to which Clarendon refers.

As it happened, fortune was to do more for Pym and his Puritan friends than all his own machinations. On October 23rd a terrible rebellion broke out in Ireland, and all over the country there were hideous massacres of Protestants. The wildest estimates of the number who perished were believed. May, a dispassionate writer, says, " The Innocent Protestants were upon a sudden, dismissed of their Estates and the persons of above two hundred thousand men, women, and children murthered, many of them with exquisite and unheard-of tortures, within the space of one month." [3] This estimate probably exceeds the total number of Protestants then in

[1] F. G. R. 184-5. [2] C. J. II. 295, ii. [3] May. II. 1, 81.

Ireland, but a more reasonable account places the loss at one-third of the total population.

The cause of the insurrection was opportunity. England had long been holding the wolf by the ears, and the House of Commons let go when it sent Strafford to the scaffold. Leicester, appointed to succeed him, remained loitering in England, and the incapable hands of the Lords Justices Parson and Borlase bungled the dangerous scheme of the Connaught Plantation. Strafford's great work was falling to pieces already.

Mention has already been made of Sir John Clotworthy, one of Pym's obscurer creatures. He was an Ulster settler, and had made himself very useful when Pym was devising the charges against Strafford in November of the previous year. He had since purveyed certain alarmists reports as to the doings of agents of the King in the Irish Army, and had been rewarded by a position as Committee on that mysterious commission on the Army Plot, which included Pym, Holles, Fiennes, Hampden, Strode, and Culpepper. This committee was placed under an obligation of secrecy, which obligation was reported in the *Journals*, although the appointment of the committee was not. The first intimation of danger came to the Lords Justices in Dublin from a servant of this Clotworthy, a fellow named Owen O'Conolly, who had been chosen by two Irish Lords to form one of a band of eighty men who were to seize Dublin Castle. O'Conolly escaped to Parsons and told him all he knew; he was rather deep in liquor at the time, but his information enabled the Lords Justices and the Council to save Dublin. Their report was read in both Houses at Westminster on November 1st, and action was promptly taken. £50,000 was to be borrowed for use against the rebels. Leicester was to go to Dublin at once and 8,000 men were to be raised as soon as possible. Three days later it was resolved that if the Scottish Parliament would send 1,000 men into Ulster, the English Parliament would pay them. This was done upon the King's suggestion.

Pym's action in this grave national crisis is most significant. On November 5th, on the occasion of instructions being drawn up for the Parliamentary committee in Scotland, he proposed an Additional Instruction that unless the King would remove the evil counsellors by whom he was surrounded, and take such as might be approved by Parliament, the Houses would not hold themselves bound to assist him in Ireland.[1]

This was a hard saying even for Puritans, for some of them still placed the welfare of the country and the maintenance of Protestantism above their personal antagonism to the King. One member present, Waller the poet, was stung to anger that did him credit. He denounced the proposal as being a declaration that the House was absolved from its duty as Strafford had declared the King to be absolved from all rules of government. The words do not occur in the *Journals*, where the incident is thus described : " Exceptions were taken at words spoken by Mr. Waller which reflected upon Mr. Pymme in a high way : For which he was commanded to withdraw. And he being withdrawn : the business was a while debated. And then he was commanded to return to his Place. And then Mr. Speaker told him that the House holds it fit, that, in his Place, he should acknowledge his Offence given by his Words, both to the House in general and Mr. Pymme in particular : Which he did ingenuously and expressed his Sorrow for it."[2]

[1] G. X. 101, 55 and note. [2] C. J. II. 306, i.

Waller might be crushed, but Pym could not carry his proposal. He was obliged to accept the adjournment of the debate, and on the following day the House " deliberately rejected his motion." Again it is to be noticed that neither the adjournment nor the rejection are mentioned in the *Commons Journals,* which nevertheless finds room to report that O'Conolly was rewarded with £500, " in part of Recompence," and that Dr. William Fuller, Dean of Ely, was ordered to be sent for as a delinquent for divers dangerous and scandalous Matters delivered by him in several Sermons."

Gardiner describes Pym's additional Instruction as " a startling proposal," and adds, " it is extremely difficult to realise Pym's position with respect to the Popish Plot. We do not know how much he knew, and we certainly do not ourselves know all."

The connection of Clotworthy in the matter does indeed suggest curious possibilities.

Pym was not to be denied. He introduced on November 8th another motion, reiterating the charge which referred the miseries of past years to the malice of persons admitted into very near places of council and authority about the King : it was feared that these persons would divert the aids now granted for the suppression of the Irish Insurrection " to the fomenting and cherishing of it there, and encouraging some such like attempts by the Papists and ill-affected subjects in England." His Majesty was therefore to be urged " to employ only such Counsellors and Ministers as should be approved by his Parliament." If he should refuse their request, they would be forced to take such steps to defend Ireland as they should think fit, and to commend such aids and contributions "to the custody and disposing of such persons of honour and fidelity as we have cause to confide in."

"Undoubtedly no proposal of so distinctly revolutionary a character had yet been adopted by the Commons. The Act taking away the King's right of dissolution had, after all, left Charles in possession of such powers as law and custom had confided to him. The Additional Instruction seized upon the executive power itself . . ."[1] Culpepper was of opinion that Ireland ought to be defended whatever the result, because it was a part of England, and the acrid Puritan, D'Ewes, ridiculed the idea that an inquiry into the moral character of the householder should be a preliminary to assisting him to put out the fire raging in his house.

Pym, nevertheless, carried his motion by a majority of 41 in a house of 261. How came this about? By what wave of emotion were members moved on November 8th from the position they had adopted on November 5th?

The fluctuation may be partly explained by the example afforded in the summary treatment of Waller, partly by an ingenious planning of public business which was well calculated to keep the House agitated. Thus, in the *Journals* for the day, above the brief entry describing the passing of this revolutionary measure, occurs the following: "Mr. Chamberleyne, who gave information of words spoken by one Carter, the Schoolmaster of Highgate, was called in to attest the said Words: That in his Presence and in the Presence of Mr. Greene and others, the said Mr. Carter said, "They were mad that would read the order of the House of Commons concerning Innovations": and for the Protestation " that none but Fools had taken it." Whereupon Mr. Greene said " He had taken it." He said " It was for want of Information: and, he would maintain, it was against

[1] G. X. 101, 57.

Reason, Justice and Law : and whereas (said he) it is to maintain the privilege of Parliament, no Justice of Peace, nor Constable, but has as much Privilege as they have." And said further " that it was against the King and State." I answered him, " Are you wiser than two Kingdoms ? for the Scots have taken it likewise." " What do you talk (said he) of a company of Rebels and Rascals ? The Parliament has dishonoured the King and Kingdom, by making a Peace with them." I wished him to declare a sorrow for these Speeches, otherwise I would complain of him. He answered me, " his name was Mr. Carter of Highgate, and he would justify what he said, if he were called to account for it." Resolved upon the Question that Mr. Carter, the Schoolmaster of Highgate, shall be forthwith sent for, as a Delinquent, by the Serjeant-at-Arms attending on this House, for divers scandalous and dangerous words spoken by him, against the State and the Honour of this House.[1]

It was by such management as this that the House was kept cowed and irritated. On November 25th, Charles was once more in London, and was sumptuously entertained in the City, where every mark of loyal respect was shown to him.[2] The King was naturally much gratified. In his speech to the Recorder he told him that he could not sufficiently express his contentment, " for now I see that all these tumults and disorders have only risen from the meaner sort of people . . . and likewise it comforts me to see that all those misreports that have been made of me in my absence have not the least power to do me prejudice in your opinions." He assured them that he would govern according to the laws of the Kingdom, and that he would maintain and protect the true

[1] C. J., II. 307, ii.   [2] R. III. i. 429-434.

Protestant Religion " according as it hath been established in my two famous predecessors' times, Queen Elizabeth and my Father : and this I will do, if needs be, to the hazard of my life and all that is dear to me."

It seemed then, that at last there was a reasonable chance that the wounds of the Commonwealth might be healed. The absolutism of the earlier part of Charles's reign had vanished for ever, it was clear that there would be no general rising of Englishmen to restore Star Chamber and High Commission. If the cautious legal intellects of Selden and Hyde were satisfied that enough had been done, as satisfied they were, it might well seem that the time for mere destruction was past, and that the day for rebuilding had dawned.

This was the moment deliberately chosen by Pym to drive the King to despair, to divide the House of Commons itself into two bitter warring sections, to reproduce in the country the animosity he had created in the House, to make civil war inevitable.

This he did by presenting to the King on December 1st, 1641, the Grand Remonstrance.

This bombshell was no haphazard contrivance hastily got together to undo the effect of Charles's recent welcome in the City. It had long been excogitated by Pym and his fellow Adventurers.

Some time before this, Pym had left his lodgings in Westminster and had taken others at Chelsea, that he might be near Lord Mandeville, also one of the Adventurers, who had recently been called to the barony of Kimbolton, and had a house at Chelsea. Hither came Lady Carlisle with the gossip which she had culled in the young Queen's bedchamber. That these lodgings were a hotbed of intrigue against his Crown and peace was not unknown to Charles. Nicholas had written to him : " I hear there are divers meetings at Chelsea at the lord Mandeville's House and elsewhere by Pym and others, to consult what is best to be done at their next meeting in Parliament."

What then was this Grand Remonstrance?

It consists [1] of a wordy exordium, which maintains that the Remonstrance has been made necessary by the existence of a corrupt and ill-affected party who have abused the royal authority and trust. This corrupt party has for its aim the advancement of Popery, and consists largely of Jesuits : it has corrupted many of the Bishops, and also others in positions of trust near the Royal family. It has caused the war with Scotland and the insurrection of Papists in Ireland, and is directly responsible for the " bloody massacre of your people."

His Majesty is besought to deprive the Bishops of their votes in Parliament and diminish their authority in the Church, to abolish " ceremonies by which weak consciences have been scrupled," and to remove all such persons from the Council as are not agreeable to Parliament, and to reject all mediation and solicitation to the contrary " how powerful and near soever."

The Remonstrance then, in no fewer than 206 clauses, proceeds to revive from the beginning of Charles's reign, every grievance that had been raised, even where such grievance had been since redressed. The root of them all was alleged to be " a malignant and pernicious design of subverting the fundamental laws and principles of government, upon which the religion and justice of this Kingdom are firmly established." Those who harbour the design are a mixed body of Papists, Arminians, and Libertines, of whom the Jesuits are the leaders. Fourteen sections enumerate the grievances incidental to the *régime*

[1] R. III, i. 438-451.

of Buckingham and the struggle for the Petition of Right, the imprisonment of Members of Parliament, "of whom one died by the cruelty and harshness of his imprisonment . . . and his blood still cries either for vengeance or repentance . . ."

An odd professional reminiscence of the Receiver of Wiltshire comes out in Clause 25, which complains of " the general destruction of the King's Timber, especially that in the Forest of Dean, sold to Papists, which was the best storehouse of this Kingdom for the Maintenance of our shipping." With Clause 51, begins the list of religious grievances. High Commission was asserted to have grown to such excess of sharpness and severity as was not much less than the Romish Inquisition, so that " great numbers, to avoid their miseries, departed out of the Kingdom, some into New England and other parts of America; others into Holland, where they have transported their manufactures of cloth."

Moreover, asserted Clause 63, " There must be a conjunction between Papists and Protestants in doctrine, discipline and ceremonies ; only it must not yet be called Popery " and, adds 64, " The Puritans, under which name they include all those that desire to preserve the laws and liberties of the Kingdom, and to maintain religion in the power of it, must be either rooted out of the Kingdom with force, or driven out with fear. In Clause 86 it was further objected against the Bishops that " they showed themselves very affectionate to the war with Scotland, which was by some of them styled *Bellum Episcopale*, and a prayer composed and enjoined to be read in all churches calling the Scots rebels."

Clause 111 showed that six subsidies had been granted, and a Bill of poll money, in all £600,000, "besides we have contracted a debt to the Scots of £220,000. Yet God hath so blessed the endeavours of this Parliament, that the Kingdom is a great gainer by all these charges," through the cessation of arbitrary taxation and of monopolies. Clauses 125 and 126 described the Triennial Act and the Act forbidding the adjournment or dissolution of that Parliament without its own consent, " which two laws well considered may be thought more advantageous than all the former, because they secure a full operation of the present remedy, and afford a perpetual spring of remedies for the future." Clause 143 asserted " the malignant party whom we have formerly described to be the actors and promotors of all our misery, they have taken heart again . . . they have endeavoured to work in His Majesty, ill impressions and opinions of our proceedings, as if we had altogether done our own work and not his."

The Remonstrance proceeded to enumerate the sums paid to the Scots for their " brotherly assistance." " So that His Majesty hath had out of the subjects' purse since the Parliament began £1,500,000, and yet these men can be so impudent as to tell His Majesty that we have done nothing for him."

Clause 172 asserted that by their instruments and agents they have attempted to disaffect and discontent His Majesty's army, and to engage it for the maintenance of their wicked and traitorous designs : the keeping up of Bishops in votes and functions . . . and when one mischievous design and attempt of theirs to bring on the army against the Parliament and the City of London hath been discovered and prevented : They undertook another of the same damnable nature with this addition to it: to endeavour to make the Scottish army neutral, while the English army, which they had laboured to corrupt and envenom against us by their false and slanderous suggestions, should execute their malice to the subversion of our religion and the dissolution of our government . . . only in Ireland which was farther off they have had time and opportunity to mould and prepare their work, and had brought it to that perfection that they had possessed themselves of that whole Kingdom, totally subverted the government of it, routed out religion, and destroyed all the Protestants whom the conscience of their duty to God, their King and country, would not have permitted to join with them, if by God's wonderful providence their main enterprise upon the City and Castle of Dublin had not been detected and prevented upon the very eve before it should have been executed. Notwithstanding, they have in other parts of that Kingdom broken out into open rebellion, surprising towns and castles, committed murders, rapes and other villainies, and shaken off all bonds of obedience to his Majesty and the laws of the realm."

The Remonstrance went on to describe Pym's intention with regard to Church discipline: "We do here declare that it is far from our purpose to let loose the golden reins of discipline and government in the Church, to leave private persons or particular congregations to take up what form of divine Service they please; for we hold it requisite that there should be throughout the whole realm a conformity to that order which the laws enjoin according to the word of God. And we desire to unburden the conscience of men of needless and superstitious ceremonies, suppress innovations, and take away the monuments of idolatry." The next Clause, 185, showed how this was to be done: "And the better to effect the intended reformation, we desire that there may be a general synod of the most grave, pious, learned and judicious divines of this island : assisted with some from foreign parts professing the same religion with us, who may consider of all things necessary for the peace and good government of the Church, and represent the results of their consultations into the Parliament, to be there allowed of, and confirmed and receive the stamp of authority, thereby to find passage and obedience throughout the Kingdom."

" They have maliciously charged us that we intend to destroy and discourage learning, whereas it is our chiefest care and desire to advance it, and to provide a competent maintenance for conscionable and preaching ministers throughout the Kingdom, which will be a great encouragement to Scholars and a certain means whereby the want, meanness and ignorance to which a great part of the clergy is now subject, will be prevented."

"And we intend likewise to reform and purge the fountains of learning, the two Universities, that the streams flowing from thence may be clear and pure, and an honour and comfort to the whole land."

Clause 197 contains a plain threat, " That his Majesty be humbly petitioned by both Houses to employ such counsellors, ambassadors and other ministers, in managing his business at home and abroad as the Parliament may have cause to confide in, without which we cannot give his Majesty such supplies for support of his own estate nor such assistance to the Protestant party beyond the sea, as is desired."

The wide extension given to such selection by Parliament is shown in the next clauses: " It may often fall out that the Commons may have just cause to take exception at some men for being counsellors and yet not charge those men with crimes, for there be grounds of diffidence which lie not in proof. There are others which, though they may be proved, yet are not legally criminal.

To be a known favourer of Papists, or to have been very forward in defending or countenancing some great offenders questioned in Parliament: or to speak contemptuously of either Houses of Parliament or Parliamentary proceedings, or such as are factors or agents for any foreign prince of another religion: such are justly suspected to get counsellors' places or any other of trust concerning public employment of money: for all these and divers others we may have great reason to be earnest with his Majesty, not to put his great affairs into such hands, though we may be unwilling to proceed against them in any legal way of charge or impeachment."

Such are the main features of the Grand Remonstrance of which Pym was the author. By this his claim to statesmanship must be judged. It proposed, in effect, to erect a new autocratic power in State and Church, directed by the predominant party in the House of Commons, over whom Pym's influence was now absolute. To the Church and the Universities were to be applied the purgatives of Geneva and Scotland, and rumour of malignancy was to be sufficient to drive the victim from the King's council or from the humblest cure of souls.

"Barren as brick clay," is Carlyle's verdict on Pym and his oratory, and of nothing is it more true than of the Grand Remonstrance. It is dead, and not even the adjectival exuberance of Forster was [1] able to revive it. It is dead because in it there is no line worthy to live. From end to end the Grand Remonstrance is a partisan diatribe. It is able, ingenious and dishonest. Those who would defend it have to justify these words: "To cherish the Arminian part in those points wherein they agree with the Papists, to multiply and enlarge the differences between the common Protestants and those

[1] F. The Grand Remonstrance, 1860.

whom they call Puritans, to introduce and countenance such opinions and ceremonies as are fittest for accommodation with Popery, to increase and maintain ignorance, looseness and profaneness in the people : that of those three parties, Papists, Arminians and Libertines, they might compose a body fit to act such counsels and resolutions as were most conducible to their own ends."

As was to be expected, this revolutionary document met with the fiercest opposition, even in the House of Commons. As soon as it was introduced in its first rough draft on November 8th, Secretary Nicholas wrote to the King in Scotland urging his immediate return. His concluding request throws a fierce light on the tyranny of the Adventurers. He implored the King to burn his letter, or he, Nicholas, would be lost. On November 11th, Strode, the most blatant performer in Pym's band, disclosed the ultimate object of the document, when Pym would, doubtless, have been silent. "Sir, I move against the order of the Committee that we should not admit of giving of money till the Remonstrance be passed this House and gone into the country to satisfy them." Pym had let Strode know too much, the object of the Remonstrance was to inflame the country against the monarchy, and Strode had let it out. The fight was fierce ; over one clause alone a whole day was spent. Candles were ordered, a very rare procedure. Things were going so badly that on November 17th, Pym decided that the time was come for the House to have a fresh dose of Army Plot. He carried the following resolution : " That upon the examinations now read, there is sufficient evidence for this House to believe that there was a second design to bring up the army against the Parliament, and an intention to make the Scotch army stand as neutral."[1]

[1] C. J. II. 318, i.

A FIERCE DEBATE

On Saturday, November 20th, the Grand Remonstrance now formally engrossed, was laid upon the table and a resolution was moved that it should be read and finished that night. The opposition was too strong, and Pym had to yield to an adjournment until Monday.

Clarendon gives an entertaining anecdote about this adjournment: "Oliver Cromwell (who at that time was little taken notice of) asked the Lord Falkland 'Why he would have it put off, for that day would quickly have determined it?' He answered, 'There would not have been time enough, for sure it would take some debate.' The other replied, 'A very sorry one,' they supposing, by the computation they had made, that very few would oppose it. But he quickly found he was mistaken: for the next morning the debate being entered upon about nine of the clock in the morning, it continued all that day, and candles being called for when it grew dark . . . the debate continued till after it was twelve of the clock with much passion."[1]

The notes of Sir Ralph Verney[2] contain a summary of the chief speeches in this momentous debate, Falkland protested that Arminians agreed no more with Papists than with Protestants, that *Bellum Episcopale* had been said by one Bishop only, whereas the Remonstrance imputed it to the whole Bench, similarly with the phrase "bringing an idolatry."

Sir Edward Dering followed in the same strain. Many Bishops had brought in superstition but not one idolatry. Sir Benjamin Rudyard agreed with the narrative part but not with the prophetical, "lest we fail of our performance." Culpepper said that the Remonstrance in going from that House only "goes out on one leg," for they had not

[1] Cl. IV. 51. [2] "Notes of proceedings in the Long Parliament," p. 120-125. (Camden 1845.)

desired the Lords to join. They should address their remonstrances to the King and not to the people, for their writ of summons did not warrant them to send any declarations to the people but to treat with the King and Lords. No such thing had been done by any Parliament before, and such a course was dangerous to the public peace.

Culpepper's speech showed plainly that he saw through the design of Pym's party, and recognised that the Remonstrance was not intended for a sedative but for an irritant. Pym, seeing the ground slipping from beneath his feet, was fain to make what answer he might to these grave objections. The honour of the King lies in the safety of the people, he declared. They were bound to tell the truth for the plots had been very near the King, and all driven home to the Court and the Popish party. Ministers had been driven out of England for not reading the Book of Sports, and they were now Separatists beyond the sea. The Popish lords and the Bishops had obstructed their work. It was no breach of privilege to name them, for the Commons had often complained of the absence and the mismanagement of the Peers. Nothing but a declaration of this sort could take away the accusations that were laid upon their own House. They had, moreover, suffered so much from counsellors of the King's choosing, that they desired him to take their advice about such counsellors. Why should Parliament not so advise, when the King's servants about his Court were able to do so? He reminded them that a peace had been made with Spain without consent of Parliament, contrary to the promise made by King James.

"Altar worship," cried Pym, "is idolatry, and that has been enjoined by the Bishops in all the Cathedrals." He assured them that the general interests of learning would be better provided for. The declaration made no prophecy, but only declared what was fit to be done and easy to be done. The English Courts had usurped an unjust and arbitrary jurisdiction. As to consulting the Lords, the matter was not for them, for the topics had been dealt with in their own House only, and moreover many of the Lords themselves were implicated in their charges.

Lastly remonstrances were not directed either to King or to people, but showed the Acts of the House. Such a declaration as this, would bind the hearts of the people to them when they saw how they had been used.[1]

Even in the disjointed jottings of Verney's Notes Pym stands out as the Revolutionist. The crisis which he and the Adventurers had created must end in their favour or their ruin. Their insults to the King, to the Court, and to all religious men except the straitest sect of the Puritans, were such as admitted of no other answer than war.

Hampden's contribution to the debate was apocalyptic. "The moon is not so useful to the Church as the stars. When the woman shall be clothed with the sun, the moon shall be under her feet." Holles was only less enigmatic. " The Kingdom consists of three sorts of men, the bad, the good and the indifferent, and these we hope to satisfy. They can turn the scales."

The debate waxed hotter. At last the division was taken. Ayes 159, noes 148. The Grand Remonstrance was carried by eleven votes.

" The verdict of a starved jury," Sir Benjamin Rudyard described it, and indeed the strain and stress of that terrible debate may have driven home many weaklings, besides Secretary Nicholas, who, tired and dispirited, had

[1] F. G. R. 301-5. Verney 122-3.

gone home to write his despatch to Charles before the vote was taken. At once a motion was made that the Remonstrance should be printed. It was moved by Peard, a barrister of the Middle Temple, " a bold lawyer of little note."

A wild outburst followed. Hyde and Culpepper at once offered to enter protests. They were told that the assent of the House was required for this. The proposal for printing was not pressed for the moment, but " about one of the clock of the morning ensuing . . . Mr. Geoffrey Palmer, a lawyer of the Middle Temple, stood up." He demanded that the Clerk should then and there enter the names of all those whose claim to protest would afterwards be determined. A fierce shout of approval, " ' All! All! ' burst from the minority, and some waved their hats over their heads, and others took their swords in their scabbards out of their belts and held them by the pummels in their hands, setting the lower part on the ground ; so, as if God had not prevented it, there was very great danger that mischief might have been done."[1]

" I thought," wrote Philip Warwick of this moment, " we had all sat in the Valley of the Shadow of Death ; for we, like Joab's and Abner's young men, had catched at each other's locks, and sheathed our swords in each other's bowels."

Hampden saved the situation by a timely interruption. The debate was adjourned till the next day, and at four o'clock in the morning the members poured forth. " Has there been a debate ? " Falkland asked Cromwell. " I will take your word for it another time," replied Oliver, " if the Remonstrance had been rejected I would have sold all I had the next morning, and never have seen

[1] F. G. R. 324-5.

d any more; and I know there are many other men of this same resolution." Clarendon adds n comment: "So near was the poor Kingdom at me to its deliverance."[1]

IV. 52.

CHAPTER XII

THE FIVE MEMBERS

THE Grand Remonstrance is a perfect example of that reminiscent recrimination, which, when employed by one man to another, makes friendship impossible for ever.

It proved to demonstration, that no concession which Charles might make could purge his original offence. In vain he had incurred the blood-guiltiness of Strafford's death; in vain he had exposed his wife to insult and bodily dangers from Pym's myrmidons of the pavement; in vain he had torn jewels from the English Crown at that leader's behest.

Now, at last, if not before, he saw clearly the nature of the men with whom he had to deal, and recognised in Pym, Hampden, and the younger Vane, not reformers but revolutionists. In the grave phrase of Clarendon, they had indeed " poisoned the heart of the people." Henceforward his plain policy should have been to put them in the wrong, and especially to outwit them with their own weapons. A direct attack had become impossible, since he had tacitly ratified Pym's treasonable dealings with the Scots in 1640, by his recent favour shown to them in Edinburgh.

But Pym was pervious through his allies; the motley crowd of sectaries,—Anabaptists, Antinomians, Adamites, Bedlamites, who supplied his petitions and his mobs, laid him open to judicious attack. To direct educated opinion against ignorance and fanaticism should have been a possible task, especially if undertaken by an intellect so shrewd and so free from illusions as that of " Mr. Hyde."

One thing was essential: there must be no appeal to force, no suggestion of anything violent. Nothing had done the King more harm than the disingenuous calumnies with which Pym and Hampden had sought to enmesh him in the so-called Army Plots and the "Incident," even in the bloody atrocities of the Irish Insurrection.

The return of Charles to London brought to an end the commission granted by Parliament to Essex. The King at once dismissed that guard,[1] and instead ordered the Earl of Dorset to appoint some of the trained bands to undertake the duty for a few days. Meantime the Houses were free to convince him that there was need of such protection. The challenge was promptly taken up. On November 29th, a mob of London apprentices, brandishing swords and clubs, rushed into Palace Yard howling, "No Bishops!" Dorset ordered his guard to fire, but fortunately the order was not obeyed, and shortly after the King withdrew Dorset's guard on a petition made by the Lords at the request of Pym, Hampden and Holles.

In the inquiry held concerning this tumult by the Commons, evidence was given as follows: "One said he was newly come from Westminster armed, and that a thousand more were ready there. He said the Parliament men sent for them. The reason of his going was, because the well-affected party were likely to be overvoted by the worser, but being they agreed well together, he and his followers came all away in peace."[2] "The well-affected party" was the cant name for Pym, Hampden, and their followers, and the phrase "the Parliament men sent for them," indicates clearly the nicety with which Pym could organise and control mob violence. Another deponent stated that he and others had been sent for by Mr. Venn, a member of the House. In the debate which

[1] R. III. 434-5. [2] Verney, 129.

ensued upon this Pym declared that such accusations as this against Mr. Venn were tantamount to a conspiracy by some members of the House to accuse other members of treason. It is significant that inquiry into the matter was postponed from day to day and finally dropped altogether. The incident had served Pym's purpose, for it gave him an opportunity of demanding a guard agreeable to the House. He did not fail to bring the usual charges of murder-conspiracies in Scotland and Ireland, and to hint at ramifications in England.[1] He moved that a watch should be set by the local authorities at Westminster, and this was done.

On December 1st the Grand Remonstrance was presented to Charles by a Committee which contained none of the anti-court leaders, unless Haselrig be counted as such. Pym had been nominated but had withdrawn.[2]

With it went a petition, embodying more concisely the request contained in the Remonstrance concerning the exclusion of the Bishops and the appointment of Counsellors, to be approved by Parliament. Charles received the deputation with good temper. He wished them to give him a promise that the Remonstrance should not be published, but they declared themselves not empowered to give any such understanding. He sent, therefore, a request by them that the House should not publish the Remonstrance until he had answered it. But to grant this reasonable request would have been to abandon the whole object of the Remonstrance, which was to irritate popular opinion against the Crown.

Pym now felt sufficiently strong to attack those of the Lords who had for some time shown distaste for his recent proceedings. Occasion was given him by their alleged supineness in the matter of Ireland. News had

[1] C. J. II. 327-8.　[2] C. J. II. 327, i.

come that the rebel, Sir Phelim O'Neil, had taken Armagh, and claimed to have done so by virtue of a commission under the Broad Seal of England, whereby the King had authorised him to restore the Roman Religion in Ireland. The document was a mere forgery, and the seal imitated was that of Scotland. But it was good enough for Pym. On November 25th, a committee was appointed to prepare for a conference with the Lords, concerning Bills passed by the Commons for the safety of the Kingdom, but thrown out by the Lords. It informed the Peers " that this House, being the representative body of the whole Kingdom, and their Lordships being but as particular persons, and coming to Parliament in a particular capacity, that if they should not be pleased to consent to the passing of those Acts and others necessary to the preservation and safety of the Kingdom, that then this House, together with such of the Lords that are more sensible of the safety of the Kingdom, may join together and represent the same to his Majesty."

Hereupon Godolphin, who was Waller's colleague for St. Ives, asked Mr. Speaker to inform him on this point. If the majority of the Commons went to the King with the minority of the Lords, might not the majority of the Lords go to the King with the minority of the Commons. A dilemma could not be more wittily expressed, but Pym had the Puritan's whole-hearted detestation of wit.

Moreover this remark contained an unpalatable truth. Godolphin was reprimanded and had to make submission.

Pym's attack on the House of Lords was followed by an attempt to strip the Crown of its highest prerogative. This was the famous proposal made on December 7th for settling the Militia.

This was introduced by the hare-brained Sir Arthur. Haselrig, Pym's "dove out of the Ark." Clarendon says it was drawn up by Mr. Solicitor St. John. It proposed to appoint a Lord General and a High Admiral, and to give to them large powers to raise forces. The Bill was received with anger by many in the House.[1] There were cries of " Away with it," " Cast it out," and Culpepper moved its rejection. Mallory thought the Bill was fit to be burned in Westminster Palace Yard; nevertheless the proposal to reject it was thrown out by 158 votes to 125, and on December 21st it was read for the first time, and three days later for the third.

It was at this time that Charles removed Sir William Balfour from the Lieutenancy of the Tower, and gave it to Colonel Lunsford, " a man given to drinking, swearing and quarrelling, much in debt and very desperate." It was a mistake, for the Commons saw in it a direct menace to themselves. The Lord Mayor assured Charles that unless Lunsford were removed the apprentices would try to storm the Tower. Charles yielded, and appointed Sir John Byron, a man of the highest character. That no act of violence was meditated when Lunsford was appointed, is perhaps sufficiently proved by the refusal of the Lords to join the Commons in a petition for his removal, but the appointment was, nevertheless, impolitic at such a moment.

Meantime Pym had been strengthening his position. On December 11th, a petition from the City was presented to the Commons. It besought the removal of Bishops and of Catholic Peers from the House of Lords, and purported to be signed by 20,000 persons. This was Pym's reply to the favourable reception which Charles had received in the City on his return from Scotland. But he was not content with this. On December 27th, as the Bishops proceeded to the House of Lords they were

[1] F. G. R. 385-387.

rabbled in the approved Scottish style of Pym's northern allies, by a mob of apprentices in Palace Yard. Williams, Archbishop of York, was especially attacked and his gown torn. " If he had not been seasonably rescued, it was believed they would have murdered him." The rascals then rushed into Westminster Hall, whence Lunsford and a party of officers drove them at the point of the sword. Next day they were back again, keen for some more Bishop baiting. But they were disappointed, only two prelates had the courage to attend. So they rushed off to Westminster Abbey, there to break down the altar and the organ. Here again they were baulked. Some gentlemen helped Williams's servant to throw them out.

This was too much for the Lords. They invited the Commons to join in a declaration against riotous assemblies, and in a petition to the King for a guard. Pym's reply is memorable. "God forbid," he said, "the House of Commons should proceed, in any way, to dishearten people to obtain their just desires in such a way." [1]

At this moment, when there was a prospect of a rally to Charles of all those who, within the House or without, hated mob violence and those who excited it to their profit, an act of incredible fatuity was committed by Williams. He brought to the King on December 29th a protest signed by himself and eleven of the Bishops. They declared that they went in fear of their lives, that no redress or protection had been given to them, and that therefore all laws, orders, notes, resolutions and determinations made in their enforced absence from Parliament were null and void. Charles sent the Protest to the Lords. They were furious, and at once notified the Commons that they had received something " deep

[1] Cl. IV. 114.

intrenching upon the fundamental privileges and being of Parliament." Pym must indeed have been delighted. Here, at last, " was *digitus Dei* to bring that to pass which they could not otherwise have compassed." [1] The wildest excess of his mobs could not have served him so well as this. He moved that the doors of the House be closed. Then he declared his profound conviction that some baleful design was to be attempted against the House that very day. He proposed that the City Fathers should be requested to send their trained bands for a guard. D'Ewes thus records the scene: " Then he moved that there being a design to be executed on this day upon the House of Commons, we might send instantly to the City of London. That there was a plot for the destroying of the House of Commons this day. That we should therefore desire them to come down with the Train Bands for our assistance. . . . Some few seconded Mr. Pym's motion but more opposed it ; and some wished that we might adjourn ourselves to the Guildhall." Pym was asked to state the precise grounds for his apprehensions, but did not reply. Even now the House was not frightened, possibly familiarity with Pym's bogies had robbed them of something of their terror. At any rate they preferred to appeal again to the Lords to join in a request for a guard. Foiled in this, Pym moved that the Bishops be impeached of high treason for endeavouring to subvert the fundamental laws of the Kingdom and the very being of Parliament. With this the House concurred, the Lords accepted the Impeachment, and ere nightfall all twelve were in confinement, and we read that Laud, himself a prisoner in the Tower, was much amused by the self-inflicted downfall of his old rival Williams. [2]

[1] Cl. IV. 142.   [2] F. 5 M. 103.

On January 1st, 1642, Charles took an extraordinary step. He sent for Pym and offered him the Chancellorship of the Exchequer. It is not known whether Pym refused to come, but the post was given to Culpepper. Falkland was made Secretary, and office was proposed to Hyde, but he preferred to do what he could for the King in a private capacity in the House of Commons. It seemed as if moderation were now to sway the counsels of Charles.

On January 1st, then, the King offered Pym a position under the Crown. On January 3rd he impeached him of High Treason.

What was the reason of this extraordinary change? There can be little doubt that it was Charles's love for his wife. It had come to his knowledge that Pym and Hampden had decided upon her impeachment. He knew that it would be only too easy to substantiate against her wild statements: crude schemes of help from abroad. At all costs she must be saved. "To save her from insult and ruin he had sacrificed his most faithful Minister. For her dear sake he was now ready to stake his throne." [1]

On January 3rd, Herbert, the Attorney-General, appeared before the Lords. With him he bore "Articles of High Treason and other high misdemeanours against the Lord Kimbolton, Mr. Denzil Holles, Sir Arthur Haselrig, Mr. John Pym, Mr. John Hampden, and Mr. William Strode." [2]

Edward Montague, Lord Kimbolton in his own right, was better known as Viscount Mandeville. In the civil war, as Earl of Manchester, he was the Parliamentary General whose openly expressed resolution "not to beat the King too much" at the second battle at Newbury,

[1] G. X. 103, 129. [2] R. III, i. 473.

brought upon him the tempestuous fury of Cromwell. The shelter which his house at Chelsea had afforded to Pym and his allies, and the fact that he was an Adventurer marked him of their company, and Digby offered to prove that when the rabble appeared at the doors of Parliament Mandeville had bidden them go to Whitehall.

The Articles of Impeachment ran as follows:—
1. That they have traitorously endeavoured to subvert the Fundamental Laws and Government of the Kingdom of England, to deprive the King of his Royal Power and to place in subjects an arbitrary and tyrannical power over the lives, liberties and estates of his Majesty's liege people.
2. That they have traitorously endeavoured, by many foul aspersions upon His Majesty and his government, to alienate the affections of his people, and to make His Majesty odious unto them.
3. That they have endeavoured to draw His Majesty's late army to disobedience to His Majesty's command, and to side with them in their traitorous designs.
4. That they have traitorously invited and encouraged a foreign Power to invade His Majesty's Kingdom of England.
5. That they have traitorously endeavoured to subvert the rights and the very being of Parliaments.
6. That for the completing of their traitorous designs they have endeavoured, so far as in them lay, by force and terror to compel the Parliament to join with them in their traitorous designs, and to that end have actually raised and countenanced tumults against the King and Parliament.
7. And that they have traitorously conspired to levy, and actually have levied war against the King.

Whether Charles should have proceeded by a Bill before a Grand Jury and not by way of Impeachment, is a matter which need not be discussed here. Whether all six members were equally guilty of all the charges contained in the Seven Articles my fairly be disputed, but this at least is certain, that on each and every count, John Pym was guilty. As the law stood, he was a traitor, and his life forfeit. He had done Strafford to death by his own interpretation of " fundamental laws " ; it was now for Charles to do the like for him. Strafford was a Revolutionary and Strafford had paid the penalty. What Ireland had been to Strafford, Scotland must be to Pym. At his door now stood the two-handed engine ready to smite. Charles had instructed Herbert that from the secret committee which he was to demand from the Lords to examine evidence, must be excluded Essex, Warwick, Holland, Saye, Mandeville, Wharton and Brook, for these he intended to call as witnesses.[1] It is to be noted that no fewer than six of these seven were Adventurers of Providence Island.

The Lords proceeded to inquire whether the action of the Attorney-General in thus impeaching on behalf of the Crown were legal. They had not raised any objection when Bristol was thus impeached in 1626.

Meanwhile in the House of Commons Pym was speaking on the well-worn topic of danger. D'Ewes preserved scraps of his sentences : " The Great Council of the Kingdom should sit as a Free Council—No force about them without consent—Not only a guard of soldiers but many officers in Whitehall—Divers desperate and loose persons are listed and combined together under pretext to do his Majesty's service . . . one Mr. Buckle had said the Earl of Strafford's death must be avenged, and the

[1] G. X. 103, 130.

House of Commons were a company of giddy-brained fellows."[1]

Fiennes spoke next, but was interrupted dramatically by the appearance of the servants of Pym and Holles. " Mr. Fiennes' relation was scarce made when the whole House, at least the most of us, were much amazed with Mr. Pym's information who showed that his trunks, study, and chamber, and also those of Mr. Denzil Holles, and Mr. Hampden were sealed up by some sent from His Majesty."[2]

This was at once declared to be a breach of privilege, and a committee of conference was nominated to proceed to the Lords. At this moment Mr. Francis, the King's Serjeant-at-Arms, appeared at the door of the Commons with a message from the King to Mr. Speaker.[3] At the bar of the House he demanded the five members by name. Four members of the House—Culpepper, Falkland, Hotham and Stapleton—were bidden to go to his Majesty, with the assurance that the House would take into instant consideration his message, which concerned the privilege of all the Commons of England, and that the five members accused would stand ready to answer any legal charge made against them. Mr. Speaker then admonished each member of the five, that he should attend in his place from day to day, until further order. The House also gave order to the members for London—Pennington and Venn—that they should bring up a Military Guard ifor the protection of the House, and this was done at once. The seals affixed to the studies of the five members were ordered to be broken, and warrants were issued for the arrest of the King's agents who had sealed them.

There was little rest for Charles that night. So far he

[1] F. 5 M. 119.   [2] Ibid. 120.   [3] R. III, i, 475.

THE GREAT ADVENTURE

had failed : instead of the persons of the six members, he had obtained only a dilatory answer. What was to be his next step ? Clarendon repudiates, alike for himself, for Culpepper and for Falkland, any participation in the decision at which Charles ultimately arrived—the forcible arrest of the five within the very walls of the House. " The three persons before named, without whose privity the King had promised that he would enter upon no new counsel, were so much displeased and dejected that they were inclined never more to take upon them the care of anything to be transacted in the House, finding already that they could not avoid being looked upon as the authors of those counsels, to which they were so absolute strangers and which they so perfectly detested." [1]

The responsibility for Charles's decision probably rests with the Queen. A story which has some claim to authenticity, represents her as upbraiding her husband fiercely, when in the early hours of morning he was describing to her the difficulties involved in proceedings so violent. " *Allez, poltron.* Go, pull these rogues out by the ears, *ou, ne me revoyez jamais !* " Whereupon, without reply, the King left the room.[2] Digby, it is probable, supported a design so consonant with his own impetuous nature, and there was in Charles's own temperament a gusty waywardness which made sudden spurts of opposition to his advisers positively agreeable to him. Be this as it may, the decision was come to, and at three o'clock in the afternoon the King set out. With him was his nephew, the young Elector Palatine, Charles Lewis, and some three hundred men-at-arms.

Thus Charles began the great adventure of his life— five hours too late. If such a deed were to be done, it should have been at the earliest moment of the House's

[1] Cl. IV. 158. [2] F. 5 M. 138.

sitting. The procrastination showed the man. If such a deed were to be done, it had been more fitly done fourteen months before. Not Charles Lewis, a crafty faithless lad, soon to cherish hopes of his uncle's ruined throne, but Strafford, the unflinching, the loyal, should have ridden at his side. No juggling with legal forms of trial, but Pym and his fellows blindfold, their backs against the walls of Westminster Hall, and a single roll of musketry. Thus Cromwell was to deal with his old friends the Levellers in Burford Churchyard, and thus a greater than Cromwell with his fellow-citizens. "It is false," said Napoleon of Vendémiaire 13th Year, "it is false that we fired first with blank charge: it had been a waste of life to do that." Speed and secrecy are two essentials of violence: the unfortunate King had ensured neither. He had set out too late, and his victims knew he was coming. Worst of all, he did not know that he was violent.

It may well be, as Clarendon has it, that Digby had spoken of the great design to his friend William Murray of the Bedchamber, it may have been the French Ambassador who had his watch well set, who betrayed the secret. It is certain that it was Charles's evil genius, the dearly-loved wife of his bosom. Scarcely had Charles left Whitehall ere she turned to Lady Carlisle; "Rejoice," she cried, "for I hope that the King is now Master in his States, and Pym his prisoner." Forthwith that false waiting woman sent a trusty messenger to the hero of her transferred affections, and within an hour Pym knew all. Bitterly indeed, in the grievous days that lay before her, did the widowed Queen lament her indiscretion. She told Charles all, and he did not reproach her. "Never did he treat me for a moment," she used to say, "with less kindness than before it happened, although I had ruined him." [1]

What meanwhile of the Commons?

Forster inserts here a long, and highly-ornate oration, which he attributes to the mouth of Pym on this morning of the 4th of January. He says of it: "The clearness, force and beauty of his speech will be felt by all," and describes it as "a masterly vindication." [2] Unfortunately Gardiner found it necessary to let the chill of criticism fall upon the masterly vindication. He points out not only that the speech cannot have been spoken by Pym on this day, but that it cannot have been spoken by him at all, unless he possessed the gift of prophecy. It is but one of those forgeries, which needy scholars from both Universities were producing in Grub Street at the very reasonable charge of half-a-crown apiece, and uncommouly well has the writer caught Pym's tricks of style. So soon as Fiennes had announced the fact of Charles's departure from Whitehall, the five members were urged to fly. Strode alone showed fight. He was, as he always had been, one of the fiercest "men of the party and of the party only for his fierceness." Eleven years imprisonment in the Tower had but made him keener for another round with the King. It is impossible not to admire him, but his friend Erle was undoubtedly right in seizing him, and forcibly compelling him to join the masterly retreat to the river which Pym and Hampden were conducting. Now came a message from the King announcing his arrival. The House sat silent, the Speaker in his chair, the Mace before him.

There was a crash of many feet outside, a clanging of arms, the voice of the King raised loud, "Come not in, your lives upon it!" Then a loud knock, and for the first

[1] F. 5 M. 139 and P. 237. [2] F. P. 237, G. X. 103, 135.

time in the history of the world a King of England stood in the House of Commons.

Every man in the House arose with head uncovered, and Charles came in, his nephew by his side. None else, but the Earl of Roxburgh leaned against the door so that it might not shut, beside him was Captain David Hyde, "one of the greatest scoundrels in England," behind him a vista of fierce faces, of pistols and of swords. The King's glance was turned in the direction of Pym's usual seat by the bar. "His Majesty not seeing him there (knowing him well) went up to the chair." He bowed to either side as he advanced, and the members returned his salutation. Lenthall stepped out, to meet him, and then for the first time Charles spoke.[1] "By your leave, Mr. Speaker, I must borrow your chair a little." He remained standing, and looked intently upon the men around him. Then he addressed them: "Gentlemen, I am sorry for this occasion of coming unto you. Yesterday I sent a Serjeant-at-Arms upon a very important occasion to apprehend some that by my command were accused of high treason, whereunto I did expect obedience, and not a message: and I must declare unto you here that, albeit no King that ever was in England shall be more careful of your privileges, to maintain them to the uttermost of his power, than I shall be, yet you must know that in cases of Treason no person hath a privilege: and therefore I am come to know if any of these persons that were accused are here."

Here he stopped, and again looked intently at the House.

"I do not see any of them," he said, "and I think I should know them."

Then he continued his address: "For I must tell you,

[1] R. III. i. 477-478.   F. 5 M. 186-193.

gentlemen, that so long as those persons that I have accused—for no slight crime but for treason—are here I cannot expect that this House can be in the right way that I do heartily wish it. Therefore I am come to tell you that I must have them wheresoever I find them."

He then put the direct question " Is Mr. Pym here ? " " Is Mr. Holles here ? " There was, of course, silence, and he turned to the Speaker. " Are any of these persons in the House ? Do you see any of them ? Where are they ? "

Lenthall fell on his knees.

" May it please your Majesty," he said, " I have neither eyes to see nor tongue to speak in this place but as this House is pleased to direct me, whose servant I am here : and I humbly beg your Majesty's pardon that I cannot give any other answer than this to what your Majesty is pleased to demand of me."

" Well," said Charles, " I think my eyes are as good as another's, I see all the birds are flown. I do expect from you that you shall send them unto me as soon as they return hither. If not I will seek them myself, for their treason is foul, and such a one as you will thank me to discover. But I assure you on the word of a King, I never did intend any force, but shall proceed against them in a legal and fair way, for I never meant any other. I see I cannot do what I came for. I think this is no unfit occasion to repeat what I have said formerly, that whatsoever I have done in favour and to the good of my subjects I do mean to maintain it."

He then left the House. Behind him rose a murmur, " Privilege, Privilege," before him mutterings of his escort, dissatisfied with failure.

That Charles meant no violence is certain, that his action might have precipitated violence is no less certain.

The " Eikon " presents his view if not his actual words : " My going to the House of Commons to demand justice upon the five members was an act which my enemies loaded with all the obloquies and exasperations they could. It filled indifferent men with great jealousies and fears, yea, and many of my friends resented it as a motion rising rather from passion than reason, and not guided with such discretion as the touchiness of those times required. . . . That I went attended with some gentlemen, as it was no unwonted thing for the Majesty and safety of a King to be so attended, especially in discontented times, so were my followers at that time short of my ordinary guard and no way proportionable to hazard a tumultuary conflict."[1]

Among the spectators of this great drama was Oliver Cromwell. Eleven years were to pass—not this time of unparliamentary but of unkingly government—years of bloodshed, of misery and of oppression, before he, the obscure member for Cambridge, should play the part that Charles had played that day, in that very House, to the remnants of that very assembly.

It is Wednesday, the twentieth day of April, 1653. Charles is lying in his bloody grave, Pym rests in the Abbey at Westminster among the tombs of Kings; Cromwell is standing where Charles had stood. Carlyle tells the story : [2] "*Call them in, adds he briefly to Harrison in word of command, and some twenty or thirty grim musketeers enter with bullets in their snaphances, grimly prompt for orders, and stand in some attitude of Carry arms there. Veteran men, men of might and men of war . . . not beautiful to honourable gentlemen at this moment. . . . ' Depart I say, and let us have done*

---
[1] Eikon Basilike III.   [2] Carlyle, "Cromwell's Letters and Speeches," after Letter 187.

with you. In the name of God, go!' My Lord General lifting the sacred Mace itself said, 'What shall we do with this bauble? Take it away!' and gave it to a musketeer. And now 'Fetch him down,' says he to Harrison flashing on the Speaker. Speaker Lenthall, more an ancient Roman than anything else, declares he will not come till forced. 'Sir,' said Harrison, 'I will lend you a hand.' On which Speaker Lenthall came down and gloomily vanished. They all vanished; flooding gloomily, clamourously out to their ulterior businesses and respective places of abode: the Long Parliament is dissolved."

There were no cries of " Privilege, Privilege " this time. *" We did not hear a dog bark at their going,"* said the tyrant grimly.

If responsibility is rightly to be assigned rather to those who make crimes possible than to those who commit them, that unparalleled scene of savage violence, that gradual degradation of the House of Commons which made its destruction even by a Cromwell acceptable, must be laid to the charge of John Pym, who from this moment of Charles's discomfiture and retreat became in fact a King.

CHAPTER XIII

" KING PYM "

THE five members were scarcely clear of the precincts before the King was in Palace Yard, and he was actually in the House before they were embarked on the river, but they reached the City safely and were installed in a house in Coleman Street.

Charles had no intention of abandoning the pursuit. He drove next day to the Guildhall and addressed the Common Council. His reception was not hostile, and he remained to dine with one of the Sheriffs. But he could not induce the Council to hand over to him the five members.

Meantime the Houses met at Westminster. The nerves of the Commons may well have been shaken by the events of the previous day; D'Ewes, indeed, had taken the precaution of making his will. We read in the *Journals* that after prayers, " Ordered That the Door be locked and the Key brought up : and the outward Doors cleared of all Persons but Servants to Members of the House : and that no Member do offer to go out without Leave : and also that some Members do send forth their Servants to see what Numbers of People are repairing towards Westminster, and to bring notice to this House." [1] The House then drew up a Vindication of Privileges and adjourned until the eleventh, appointing a Committee of the whole House to sit meantime in the Guildhall.

This committee on the following day voted the Impeachment to be illegal, still more so the attempted arrest, for in neither case had the subject any remedy against the

[1] C. J. II. 368, i.

King should the process be proved unjustified. Next day the Committee, meeting in Grocer's Hall, directed the five members to be in their seats on the 10th. On the 8th the Committee passed a resolution of very great importance. It declared that it was legal to order Sheriffs to bring their forces for the protection of Parliament, and further empowered the Mayor, Aldermen, and Common Council to raise troops. This they proceeded to do, appointing Philip Skippon to be commander of the City trained bands. In this the Lords acquiesced, and Charles's rebuff was complete. He determined to leave Westminster to his rival Monarch, and on this day, Monday, January 10, 1642, he set out from Whitehall with his wife and children. Seven years later to the very month, he saw it once again, when, defeated and dethroned, he was to make there, with unshaken faith and unflinching courage, his last full expiation for his betrayal of Strafford.

Next day the uncrowned King entered upon his Kingdom. The sun shone bright and the streets were gay with bunting from London Bridge to Westminster; Pym, Hampden and the others were rowed up the Thames while cannon pealed a welcome.

Curiously enough Pym had an opportune letter [1] to read to the House. It had been directed to Mr. Bridgeman, and ran as follows:—

"To the worshipful and my much honoured friend Orlando Bridgeman Esquire and a Burgess of the Parliament, at his chamber in the Inner Temple. These present.

"Sir,

"We are your friends: These are to advise you to look to yourself: and to advise others of my Lord of Strafford's friends to take heed lest they be involved in

[1] C. J. II. 369, ii. Cl. IV 204.

the common calamity. Our advice is to be gone, to pretend business till the great hubbub be passed : Withdraw lest you suffer among the Puritans. We entreat you to send away this inclosed letter to Mr. Anderton inclosed to some trusty friend, that it may be carried safely without suspicion, for it concerns the common safety : So desire your friends in Common[1] Garden January 4."

This was the letter enclosed :—

"To the worshipful and my much honoured friend Mr. Anderton : these present.

"Sir,

"Although many designs have been defeated, yet that of Ireland holds well, and now our last plot works as hopefully as that of Ireland. We must bear with something in the Man : his will is strong enough as long as he is fed with hopes. The Woman is true to us and real. Her counsel about her is very good. I doubt not but to send you by the next very joyful news : For the present our Arch-Enemies Pym, Hampden, Strode, Hollis and Haselrig, are blemished, challenged for no less than treason. Before I write next, we doubt not but to have them in the Tower ; or their heads from their shoulders.

"The Solicitor and Fynes and Erle we must serve with the same Sauce, and in the House of the Lords Mandeville is touched: But Essex, Warwick, Saye, Brooke and Pagett must follow, or else we shall not be quiet. Falkland and Culpepper are made friends ; to our side at leastwise they will do us no hurt. The Protestants and Puritans are so divided that we need not fear them. The Protestants in a great part will join with us or stand neuters, while the Puritan is suppressed : If we can bring them under, the Protestant will either fall in

[1] C. J. "Common." Cl. "Covent."

FORGED LETTERS

with us, or else if they do not, they are so indifferent that either by fair or foul means we shall be able to command them. The mischievous Londoners and the Apprentices may do us some hurt for [the] present. But we need not much fear them, they do nothing orderly but tumultuously: Therefore we doubt not but to have them under command after one brunt, for our party is strong in the City, especially Holborne, the New Buildings and Westminster. We are afraid of nothing but the Scotts appearing again, but we have made a party there at the King's last being there, which will hold their hands behind them while we act our parts at home. Let us acquit ourselves like men. For our Religion and Country now or never.

"The King's heart is Protestant, but our friends can persuade him and make him believe anything. He hates the Puritan Party, and is made irreconcilable to that side, so that the sun the moon and the seven stars are for us. There are no less than twenty thousand ministers in England, the greater half will, in their places, be our Friends to avenge the Bishops' dishonour. Let our friends be encouraged, the work is more than half done.

"Your Servant
"R. E."

The effect of such a letter as this at such a moment can scarcely be exaggerated. Its not obscure reference to Gunpowder Plot, the threat against the lives of the five members, the defiance of the London apprentices, and the adroit reference to a second appearance of the Scots, all make it difficult to believe that this letter was not written to order by one of the many forgers then busy in London. Clarendon asserts that it was so. "These letters were no sooner read (though the forgery was so gross that every discerning and sober person clearly discovered it) but many seemed much moved by them, and concluded that there was some desperate design against the Parliament which was not yet fully discovered.[1] Mr. Bridgeman had acquaintance with no such man." It is notable that it was sent up to the Lords by Sir John Hotham, and the same day Sir Philip Stapleton was sent to them with a request that they would join with the Commons in an order that some companies of trained bands of the parts next adjoining to Hull, forthwith be put into that town for the safeguard of that place and magazine there, and be under the command of Sir John Hotham. The House then offered their thanks to the mariners, the Sheriffs of London, Skippon, and representatives of a crowd of four thousand men from Buckingham—a gigantic exhibition of strength arranged by Hampden.

Next day, " one Mr. Cecil Cave, was reported to have said that within these few days blood would be sold as cheap as milk."[2] By such rumours judiciously circulated day by day the temper of the House was kept at fever heat, and any chance of an accommodation with Charles made impossible.

The House being thus tuned, Pym directed his course boldly. Herbert, Digby, Lunsford, Byron, Richmond were all attacked. Dering was expelled from the House and confined in the Tower for publishing a volume of his own speeches and attempting to explain why he had deserted the Root and Branch party. Smaller fry were not overlooked. "An information of words spoken by Allen Prickett, and avowed by Matthias Bennett against Mr. Pym . . . was this day read and ordered to be referred to the Committee for Informations."[3]

Hotham was sent to Hull, Goring to Portsmouth, with orders to permit no removal of ordnance or ammunition

[1] Cl. IV. 204, Macray from MS.   [2] C. J. II. 373, i.   [3] C. J. II. 377, i.

"without the King's authority signified by both Houses of Parliament." Similar instructions were given to the Lieutenant of the Tower. But on January 24th, the Lords refused to join the Commons in a petition that the fortresses and Militia might be placed in the hands of persons in whom Parliament had confidence. Pym followed his usual method; he had in hand petitions from London, Middlesex, Hertfordshire and Essex supporting him. These he laid before the Lords and rated them soundly: "We have received many more, but it would take up too much time and be too great a trouble to peruse all. . . . My Lords, in these four petitions you may hear the voice, or rather the cry, of all England." He went on to complain of "obstruction to the measures of the Commons in Religion, obstruction in trade, obstruction in the matter of Ireland, obstruction in the prosecution of delinquents, in the protection of privileges and in the defence of the Kingdom." Obstruction became a catch word of the mob, as no doubt he had intended that it should. Into each of these topics he entered at length. He then drew the conclusion: "The Commons will be glad to have your concurrence and help in saving the Kingdom, but if they fail of it, it shall not discourage them in doing their duty. And whether the Kingdom be lost or saved (I hope through God's blessing it will be saved) they shall be sorry that the story of this present Parliament should tell posterity that in so great a danger and extremity the House of Commons should be enforced to save the Kingdom alone, and that the Peers should have no part in the honour of the preservation of it."[1]

As the Lords showed irritation at this plain dictation, Pym brought pressure upon them in the shape of a petition from the "Artificers of London and Westminster,"

[1] F. P. 252.

declaring their miserable condition and lack of livelihood. Holles was sent with this to the Lords, who when they came to Palace Yard next day found a crowd of women there with children. They cried that they had brought them to the Lords' door rather than let them starve at home. This was too much for the Lords, and they agreed to join the Commons in the petition as to the fortresses and Militia. But Pym had not done with them even yet. Three days later a petition was actually carried to the very doors of the House by representatives of " the Gentlewomen, Tradesmen's wives, and many others of the Female Sex, all inhabitants of the City of London and the suburbs thereof." Mrs. Ann Stagg, the wife of a brewer, headed the deputation. " Notwithstanding that many worthy deeds have been done by you," said the petitioners, "great danger and fear do still attend us and will, as long as Popish Lords and superstitious Bishops are suffered to have their voice in the House of Peers, that accursed and abominable idol of the Mass suffered in the Kingdom, and that arch enemy of our Prosperity [Archbishop Laud] and reformation lieth in the Tower not yet receiving his deserved punishment." The horrors in Ireland terrified them also. " Have we not just cause to fear they will prove forerunners of *our* ruin, except Almighty God, by the wisdom and care of this Parliament be pleased to succour us, our husbands and children, which are as dear and tender to us as the lives and blood of our hearts ? To see them murdered and mangled and cut to pieces before our eyes : to see our children dashed against the stones, and the mothers' milk mingled with the infants' blood running down the streets; to see our houses on flaming fire over our heads !" They concluded—perhaps a little lamely—" Oh ! how dreadful this would be ! "

The apprentices and sailors of London were not behind the ladies in religious zeal; they too had their petition, and the street porters followed suit. The lords had had enough, and on February 5th passed the Bill "disabling all persons in holy orders to exercise any Temporal Jurisdiction or Authority." The nature of these petitions and the avocations of the petitioners afforded much mirth to the Royalists.

What it is more necessary to note here is the extraordinary skill with which Pym and Hampden used their material: unverified letters, unsubstantial rumours, petitions, mob tumult, everything that could intimidate, terrify, annoy. Could they have done it without the collusion and activity of the Adventurers who had so long worked together? The weapons they used, it is true, were not very clean, but Pym was not, nor Hampden, the man to be too nice so the wound were mortal. *Male posita est lex quae tumultuarie posita est*, remarked Hyde, sagaciously adding that the Civilian's opinion, *fieri non debuit, factum valet* prevailed with many who disliked it.

On February 14th, Charles gave his assent to the Bishops' Exclusion Bill. This is the solitary exception to his invariable obedience to his father's maxim, "No Bishop, no King," and here, as so often, the explanation is to be found in the Queen, to protect whom he was above all things anxious. She was now about to accompany her daughter Mary to her affianced husband, the Prince of Orange, and also to seek his assistance, if need should be, for Charles. On February 23rd, Charles saw her set sail from Dover and there was no longer a possibility of Pym intercepting her by a process of impeachment. The King, moreover, by yielding on the Bishop's votes, staved off the question of Militia. He now returned from

Dover to Greenwich, where his sons, Charles and James, joined him, though Pym vainly tried to stop them. Then he passed northward by Theobalds, Royston, Newmarket, Huntingdon, Newark and Doncaster. On March 19th, he was at York, now to be his capital till the war broke out five months later. At every stage of his journey he was bombarded by petitions, representations, and requests from the Commons. As he removed further and further from the Houses his refusals became firmer. So much so, that when at Newmarket the Earl of Pembroke suggested that he might grant the power of the Militia to Parliament for a limited period, he was able to answer, "No, by God, not for an hour!" There was hope that when Charles should reach the bracing and loyal air of York he would feel himself a King once more.

While still at Greenwich he had made a most politic agreement with Hyde, who had there sought an interview with him. Hyde was to remain at Westminster and thence send to the King information of all that went on, and with every message which the Houses sent to his Majesty, was to draft a reply, which the King would copy and return as his own. During the next few months, therefore, there was a voluminous war of words between Pym on the one hand and Hyde on the other. The piquancy of the situation was enhanced by the fact that until May 21st Hyde still sat in the House and assisted in the hammering of those bolts which he himself was to turn against the arch-forger. How much Pym knew of this game is uncertain, but Hyde says it was more than suspected, and the situation grew daily more dangerous for him. In this logomachy Pym was no match for Hyde, who had all the lawyer's skill in picking out the weak places of an opponent's position and also of diverting the enemies attack from his own less defensible redoubt.

He had a definite policy throughout, which was to show Pym as the revolutionist, and Charles as the defender of the Constitution, a policy which the House daily made easier. The fifth book of his *History* is entirely devoted to this controversy, and its services to the Monarchy would alone entitle Hyde to his future distinction of being the grandfather of two English monarchs. Before the keen point of his dialectic, Pym's ponderous commonplaces were riven to shreds. Events now moved rapidly towards war. On April 20th, Charles appeared before the gates of Hull and was personally refused admission by Hotham. Parliament at once ratified Hotham's action and removed the munitions of war to London by sea. On the other hand, Charles declared their Militia ordinance illegal. On May 14th the Lords passed a Bill to restrain any new Peers who might be created by the King at this crisis from taking their seats in the House. Charles now ordered the attendance at York of Essex, Holland, Salisbury and Savile, not as Peers, but as officers of State. All refused to come and were deprived of their positions. With Littleton, the Lord Keeper, the King was more successful. The Great Seal was forwarded to York and Littleton himself followed it. This was the signal for a general rally to the King, and a month later, of the effective strength of the House of Lords thirty peers were at York, forty-two at Westminster. There was a similar stampede from the Commons; Hyde dared no longer remain and fled with Littleton, his friends Falkland and Culpepper followed him. Then the rush began, and by the beginning of July the average attendance of the Commons was little more than one hundred out of an original five hundred.[1] By the beginning of June arms and ammunition had arrived from Holland,

[1] Masson, Milton II. 414-15. Firth, "H. of L. during Civil War," Ch. 3, p. 115.

purchased by the sale of Crown Jewels by the Queen; Nobles were drawing up lists of troops, and the Colleges of both Universities were sending in their plate.

On June 1st, the Houses, such as they were, despatched the Nineteen Propositions to the King.[1]

These famous Propositions were neither more nor less than Capitulations. They were terms which might have been offered to a captured King. By them it was proposed to abrogate entirely the power of the Crown and to place full sovereignty in the Houses of Parliament, or, more correctly, in the predominant Puritan party in the House of Commons. Henceforward, without the consent of Parliament the King might not appoint Privy Councillor, nor official of the Crown nor Judge, nor yet a governor or tutor for his own children; nor might any of these children marry without that consent. Jesuits, priests, and Popish recusants were to be harried without any tolerance whatever, and the children of Romanists were to be brought up as Protestants. The Church was to be reformed in government and in doctrine as Parliament should advise in consultation with Divines. Preaching ministers were to be maintained throughout the Kingdom, and innovations and superstitions were to cease out of the land. The Militia ordinance must be accepted by his Majesty, and he must withdraw his declarations and proclamations against it. Justice of Parliament was to pass upon all delinquents whether within the Kingdom or fugitives, and Parliament might except whom it chose from any general pardon. The King must abandon his forts, castles, and guards, and must make a strict alliance with the States of the United Provinces against the Pope and his adherents. He must also clear the Lord Kimbolton and the five members of the House of

[1] L. J. V. 97. R. III. i 722-4.

Commons of the charge of treason. Furthermore, he must consent that no Peer created hereafter might take his seat or vote in Parliament until both Houses of Parliament should have consented thereunto.

There could be but one answer to this document. On August 22nd Charles raised his standard at Nottingham.

Into the fortunes of war during the next sixteen months it is not necessary here to look, except so far as they affect the career of Pym. He did not live to see the end of the war which he had brought about, or to contribute his share to the magnificent installation, regal in all but name, of his friend the member for Cambridge, in 1653. He had not even the happiness of knowing that he had contributed to that momentous ceremony in Westminster Hall, for during those sixteen months of harassed life that still were left to him he witnessed only defeat and disappointment. Two days after the dispatch of the Nineteen Propositions to Charles, he was made one of a Committee of Safety of fifteen members. Parliament was badly served by the choice of Essex for Commander-in-Chief. He was now a man of some fifty years, soured alike by those early matrimonial infelicities which had made him the laughing-stock of James's Court, and by the deprivation of the acres which had been added to his estates by stealthy annexations, and reassumed by the inquiry into encroachments on the royal forests in 1633. But he was, as we have seen, one of the Adventurers and a good friend of Pym. Of military ability he was entirely destitute, but the Houses had formed a high opinion of his personal integrity.

Even at this last hour Charles hoped that the Houses would listen to him. He sent to them Southampton and Culpepper, who appeared before their respective colleagues on August 27th. " The Earl of Southampton went to the House of Peers where he was scarce sat down in his place, when with great passion he was called upon to withdraw," and presently " they sent him word that he should at his peril immediately depart the town, and that they would take care that their answer to the message should be sent to him." [1] Culpepper was not allowed to be heard. Strode moved to expel him, and when Pym rose to oppose his hot-headed follower he was howled down.[2] At last Culpepper was allowed to deliver his message at the bar in writing, after which he immediately withdrew. The Houses answered the King as might have been expected. Until he should have taken down his standard and withdrawn his declaration that their leaders were traitors, they could do nothing. On September 28th, Charles received a request from Essex that he would listen to a petition from Parliament asking him to return to Westminster, and to leave to their deserved punishment his evil counsellors. He replied that he would receive nothing from the hands of a traitor.

This answer roused Pym to fury. " With great vehemence and passion he bade the House observe what counsellors were about his Majesty, seeing that he had refused the petition of both Houses from a person of so great honour as the Earl of Essex was, and that therefore they should now resolve of some new way of linking themselves together in a more firm bond and union than formerly, and to that end he desired that a committee might be appointed to draw a new Covenant or association which all might enter into, and that a new oath might be framed for the observing of the said association, which all might take, and such as refused it . . . might be cast out of the House."[3] So the sheep should be separated from the goats : so completely was Pym

[1] Cl. VI. 12. [2] G. Civ. War. I. 1, 14. [3] Ibid. I. 2, 39.

THE FIRST BATTLES

under the domination of his Scottish accomplices. For the present the proposal came to nothing.

The course of events taught Pym the dangers that beset him who taketh the sword. On October 23rd, the first battle of the Civil War was fought at Edgehill. The ill-advised impetuosity of Rupert's cavalry charge robbed his uncle of a victory which might have decided the war, but, nevertheless, Essex was unable to stop the King from continuing his march upon London by way of Oxford.

This was not quite what the Commons had expected, and on November 10th, Pym went to the Guildhall to explain that new proposals of peace had been made to Charles. Any peace which would secure their religion and liberty would be pleasing to Parliament. But such liberty must be real. "To have printed liberties and not to have liberties in truth and realities is but to mock the Kingdom." On the 13th, Charles was at Brentford and took the town after a fine fight. Now was the moment for a dash on London. There would have been some bloodshed, for the trained bands had poured out of the City and ranged themselves on Turnham Green, much outnumbering Charles' forces. Skippon who commanded them was a sturdy fellow. None the less, Rupert's cavalry should have mowed them down like swathes before the scythe. But Charles made no movement. Like Henry VI after the second battle of St. Albans in 1461, he stayed his hand when the fruits of victory were within his grasp. Like Henry he had no other chance.

Pym now thought that both armies should be disbanded and the old traffic of representations resumed. But he still persisted in his demand for the punishment of " delinquents " by Parliamentary procedure. His vacillation may well be pardoned, for he was beginning to feel the difficulty Charles had known so well, of finding supplies for an unpopular war. The Houses had hitherto maintained their government by voluntary gifts or loans, but the voluntary nature was shown in the treatment of those who refused to contribute. Fountain, a lawyer, was one of these. He appealed to the Petition of Right, whereupon Martin told him that the Petition of Right was intended to restrain Kings and not Parliaments. Fountain was therefore committed to prison. The Houses now resolved to take upon themselves the power of direct taxation, and Pym announced this to the City on November 25th. The tyrant's plea, " necessity," which Pym had so eloquently denounced in the past, was driving him along. When it was asserted that the assessors of the new tax could not be given power to administer an oath, he brushed the objection aside. " The law is clear," he said, " No man may take or give an oath in settled time, but now we may give power to take an oath." [1] Events were teaching him the meaning of that phrase " sovereign power," which he had refused to recognise in opposition. The ordinance imposing the payment was voted on February 24th. Commissioners were appointed for every county in England who were to assess owners of property at their discretion. In January, 1643, he made another effort to bring about a national association with Scotland, but his proposal was negatived. He suffered a still severer rebuff in the rejection of his suggestion that an excise should be imposed on all goods bought and sold, or if not on all, then on luxuries. He was rebuked by one member soundly " that he who pretended to stand so much for the liberty of the subject, should propose such an unjust, scandalous and destructive project." [2] He met, in fact, the same fate which Walpole experienced in 1733.

[1] G. Civ. War I. 4, 74. [2] Ibid. 5, 102.

On May 1st he repeated his proposal for opening communication with the Scots and also with the Dutch, and this time the suggestion was accepted, but nothing was done immediately. On May 23rd, the Queen was impeached " and the impeachment carried up by Master Pym to the House of Peers, where it stuck for many months, but was afterwards passed there also." It was only three weeks before this that he had begun a secret correspondence with the Queen, attempting to induce her to persuade Charles to accept the terms offered by Parliament. On June 6th, he made a report on what is known as Waller's Plot. This was an attempt on the part of the chief Royalists in London to put into execution a Commission of Array, issued to them by Charles, and smuggled stealthily into London by the courageous Lady d'Aubigny, lately widowed at Edgehill. Edmund Waller, the poet, a member of Parliament still at Westminster, was implicated in the design, which aimed at seizing the Tower and other fortifications, and also the persons of the Lord Mayor and of the chief members of the Commons. May has an ingenuous comment: " The Plot was horrid and could not possibly have been put in execution without a great effusion of blood,"[1] as if effusion of blood were an unpardonable offence between belligerents. As a matter of fact the " Plot " was a perfectly legitimate operation of war, with little chance of success from its wide nature and the number of persons necessarily admitted to complicity. The Commons, on the other hand, made an equally legitimate exercise of their belligerency by hanging two of those implicated—Tomkins, brother-in-law of Waller, and Challoner. Why they did not hang Waller also, puzzled their contemporaries. " The only reason which I could

[1] May III. 2. 185.

ever hear given for it was that Master Waller had been so free in his Confessions at the first (without which the Plot could not have been clearly detected) that Master Pym and others of the examiners had engaged their promise to do whatever they could to preserve his life." [1]

A fortnight later a blow fell which must have afflicted Pym gravely. This was the death of Hampden at Chalgrove Field, where he had been defeated in a slight skirmish with some of Rupert's horse. As Adventurer, as intriguer, as mob organiser, he had been Pym's *alter ego*. What the Puritan d'Ewes called his "serpentine subtility" had enabled him to put a good face on many a bad business. " Mr. Hampden was a man of much greater cunning, and it may be of the most discerning spirit, and of the greatest address and insinuation to bring anything to pass which he desired of any man of that time, and who laid the design deepest." Such a man could ill be spared, for in the field fortune was setting strongly against the Houses.

In this, the second year of the war, operations were being carried on in four distinct areas: by the King and Essex between Oxford and London, in Yorkshire between Newcastle and the Fairfaxes, in the West between Hopton and William Waller, and in the Eastern Counties between Cromwell and Cavendish. In all these areas except the last victory lay with the Royalists. It seemed, indeed, as if Charles's plan of campaign would succeed. It was admirably devised. Newcastle was to advance from Yorkshire to a point on the North side of the Thames, Hopton similarly from Cornwall to a point on the South of the river, facing Newcastle. They would then throttle the river traffic, and hold up London, whereupon Charles, brushing aside the ineffective Essex, would hurl himself

[1] May III. 2, 186. Waller was cousin to Hampden and Cromwell.

on the capital. Oxford was the pivot of the nutcracker; Newcastle and Hopton the steel legs, Charles the clenched hand, Pym's head the nut. On June 30th at Atherton Moor, near Bradford, the Fairfaxes, father and son, were defeated by Newcastle. In the West, Hopton drove the rebels before him at Stratton, Lansdown, and Roundway Down, and in the main command the Parliamentary forces were paralysed by the defeat and death of Hampden at Chalgrove Field. Nathaniel Fiennes surrendered Bristol to Rupert. Only at Gainsborough was there a gleam of success, where Cromwell, on July 25th defeated and slew Cavendish. This he did with those Puritan forces of the associated Eastern Counties, of which he was the organiser and the inspirer. That victory was the ray of dawn which would struggle into the perfect day of Marston Moor and Naseby, but ere that day had dawned Pym the great protagonist had closed his tired eyes for ever.

But there were three flies in the Royal amber; these were Hull, Gloucester and Plymouth. The King's forces could not be thoroughly mobile until the Parliamentary garrisons in these strongholds had been demolished or masked. Newcastle, with a fatuity which ranks him the peer of Essex, sat down to besiege Hull, a town upon an arm of the sea across which no boom could be thrown sufficiently strong to resist the action of the tide, and with the power of the sea in the hands of his enemy. While Newcastle was thus amusing himself, like Crœsus outside the walls of ancient Miletus, Charles employed himself in the siege of Gloucester. The bellicose London mobs were in sad case; it was one thing to rabble a fat Archbishop, or to dance and sing because Strafford's head was off; it was quite another to have Rupert's cavalry hovering round London ready and anxious to split their weazands. It was an anxious time for Pym. But his friends the ministers stood by him staunchly; the shrill bell of St. Antholin in the City tinkled incessantly, and the shriller tongues of Puritan ministers within that famous church preached fiercely the sword of the Lord and of Gideon.

None the less the peace movement spread. On August 8th, Palace Yard was filled with a multitude of women. They had stuck white ribbons in their hats, and they shouted for peace. Next day they were back again, wilder than before, and many others had joined them; they presented a petition for peace, they forced their way to the door of the House and battered it; they yelled for Pym and Strode and Saye. " Give us that dog Pym." " Let us throw the dog Pym into the Thames," they cried. We do not know if the gentle Mistress Stagg, the wife of the brewer of London, were there. Pym's famous guard fired powder; still the women pressed on. They threw stones; then the soldiers shot bullets; two men behind the crowd were killed. The women were beside themselves; they yelled and rushed on. Just then a troop of Waller's Horse came up from the City. On the instant they were at them. " Waller's dogs! Waller's dogs!" they shouted, and tried to tear the ribbons from the soldier's hats. The men drew their swords; they laid about them first with the flat, then with the edge. The women fell bleeding, were trampled on; the scene was horrible! " God forbid " John Pym had said six months before, " God forbid the House of Commons should proceed in any way to dishearten people to obtain their desires in such a way." What he said now is not recorded, but D'Ewes wrote : "No man can excuse the indiscreet violence of these women, but the remedy used against them by the procurement of Pym and others . . . was most cruel and barbarous, for not content to have them supprest by the ordinary footguards which had been sufficient, there was divers horsemen called down who hunted the said women up and down the back Palace Yard and wounded them with their swords and pistols with no less inhumanity than if they had been brute beasts . . . many had just cause to wonder that when those great multitudes of mean and factious people, being men and not women, which came down and offered so much violence to divers of the Lords being Peers of the Realm . . . had no course at all taken against them, and yet that such severe cruelty was used against these women who were only misled by their wicked and unlawful example." [1]

It was clear that the time had come to swallow scruples. The King was winning. Better the Presbytery than Laud. The way was easy. In the alarm consequent of the discovery of Waller's Plot, the Lords had at last assented to an ordinance which they had long resisted. This was the authorisation of the meeting of an assembly of Divines to regulate the Church after the ideal set before them by the Puritans in the Commons. There were at this time sixteen Peers only in the House. They also followed the example of the Commons in signing a new covenant, whereby they undertook to supply the Parliamentary forces against those of the King. An assembly of Divines was to meet on July 1st at Westminster, and the Scots were asked to send a number of ministers to assist, when the news arrived of the Parliamentary defeats at Atherton Moor and Roundway Down. Pým was at last able to bring about his cherished scheme of a new offensive alliance with the Scots. On July 19th the Earl of

[1] From "Woman Petitioners and the Long Parliament," by Miss McArthur. "English Historical Review," Vol. XXIV. p. 698 (1909).

Rutland, the younger Vane, and three others, were sent to Edinburgh to ask for an army of eleven thousand men.

This proposal was distasteful to many even of the Commons. But the trend of events forced it upon them. On September 5th Essex raised the siege of Gloucester and the King threw his army between him and London. The first battle of Newbury was the result; it was indecisive, save that Falkland followed his former friend Hampden from the troubles of a world of which he was very weary. The prospect was indeed gloomy and might well have broken the courage even of Pym. It was not only the enemy who caused him anxiety. The incapacity of Essex was now patent to all, and on June 26th Pym had to convey to him the censure of the Commons upon his slackness. Some six weeks later his diplomacy had to adjust a rivalry, little creditable to either, between his two Adventurers, Essex and Sir Wilham Waller. Twice he had to stiffen the back of the commander of the Parliamentary forces against adopting proposals of peace, first of his own, then of the Lords' suggestion. "Mr. Pym," writes Clarendon, "always opposed all overtures of peace and accommodation, and when the Earl of Essex was disposed the last summer by those Lords to an inclination towards a treaty, as is before remembered, Mr. Pym's power and dexterity wholly changed him and wrought him to that temper which he afterwards swerved not from. He was wonderfully solicitous for the Scots coming to their assistance, though his indisposition of body was so great that it might well have made another impression on his mind." Everywhere his hand was to be seen, his voice heard. Not only in the House but in the Guildhall he was continually exhorting, warning, denouncing. He towered head and shoulders above the leaders of his party, and he was proportionately detested by the Royalists. He was persistently accused of being a taker of bribes, for which there is no sufficient evidence. It is true that the mansion of the Earl of Derby at Westminster was granted to him for a residence, and that after his death the Commons voted ten thousand pounds to pay his debts and to provide for his younger children. His moral character was assailed equally persistently, and the ephemeral press of the day abounds in scandalous allusions to his supposed amours. Such charges are as incapable of disproof as of proof, and there is probably as little foundation for them as for the allegations of his dishonesty.

Whatever may have been his life and the value of his work, both were now nearly done. In September the House reluctantly accepted his argument that though modified Episcopacy might be a better medicine than Presbyterianism, it was little use for a man, however sick, to betake himself to his medicine if a murderer were approaching him. He must take to his sword or be killed. On September 25th, one hundred and twelve members of the House of Commons subscribed the Solemn League and Covenant. A new sword was unsheathed upon England and her Church.

This is the last achievement of John Pym. Even while he signed the Covenant the hand of Death was upon him. An internal abscess had lately developed a malignancy more than Arminian. His enemies were waiting gleefully for what should soon befall "that good fat man, Master John Pym."

In the first days of December, 1643, Ormonde received a letter from Trevor. " From London we hear that Pym is crawling to his grave as fast as he can."

CHAPTER XIV

THE END

THE dim light of a winter afternoon in London had given place to the darkness of nightfall when, at Derby House, the soul of John Pym passed from its wrecked tabernacle.

It was the eight day of December, 1643.

To the last he had never a doubt of himself. Always in the depths of his terrible pain he had maintained that evenness of spirit which he had ever shown in the time of his health. Was he to live, so much the better for his work; was he to die, others would do that work and he would be with God.

There was joy in Oxford—a feast and bonfires. "The reason was because they heard that Master Pym was dead."

At Westminster grief as great. Forthwith a committee " to consider of the estate of Mr. Pym, deceased, and to offer what they think fit to be done in consideration to the House; likewise to take care to prepare a monument for him at the charge of the Commonwealth."

The burial, too, must be in the Abbey " without any charge for breaking open the ground there, and that the Speaker with the whole House do accompany his body to the interment."

Seven days later he was buried " with wonderful pomp and magnificence in that place where our English Kings and Princes are committed to their rest."

Seventeen years later his bones were tipped into a pit by the common hangman.

He was borne to his grave by Holles, Haselrig, the

younger Vane, St. John, Strode, Gerard, Clotworthy, Poole, Wray and Knightly. Behind his coffin walked his two sons, Charles and Alexander; before it two heralds of arms bearing his crest. Behind his sons came all that his handiwork had left of the two Houses.

Thus they came to the chapel of King Henry VII.

Stephen Marshall preached the funeral service from a verse of Micah : " Woe is me for the good man is perished out of the earth." He began with lamentation, " Our Parliament is weakened, our armies wasted, our treasure exhausted, our enemies increased . . . and now we are come to lament the fall of this choice and excellent man, in whose death the Almighty testifies against us...I am ready to call for such a mourning as that of Hadadrimon in the valley of Megiddon."

Then he rose to a more comfortable note : " I mean not that you should mourn for him. His work is done, his warfare is accomplished : he is delivered from sin and sorrow and from all the evils which we may fear are coming upon ourselves . . ." He ended with confidence and eloquence : " No ! No ! beloved, this cause must prosper, and although we were all dead, our armies overthrown, and even our Parliaments dissolved, this cause must prevail."

" Surely," cried Baxter, " Pym is now a member of a more knowing, unerring, well-ordered, right-aiming, self-denying, unanimous, honourable, triumphant Senate than that from whence he was taken."

Looking at the English Parliament as Pym's hands had left it, we are able to agree with the good writer of the " Saints' Everlasting Rest," that it is indeed possible that Pym might find himself in an assembly more worthy of these adjectives.

It is more profitable to consider here what place, if

any, Pym takes amongst Statesmen. Assuredly he is not in the highest flight of all: amongst those men of genius who have created or remodelled the framework of a State. He has no place beside the maker of modern France or Italy; to compare him with Peter the Great would be to mock him. Even by the side of Bismarck we should place Strafford and not Pym. But the greatest of his foreign critics says of him: " In Pym there is something both of Sieyes and of Mirabeau; he is one of the greatest revolutionary leaders known to history. Characters like his stand midway between the present which they shatter for ever, and the future, which however generally develops itself on principles different from those which they have laid down." [1] Von Ranke goes on to maintain that although Pym's Parliamentary and religious system failed, yet to him was due the separation of spiritual from political tendencies in royalty, which brought the Crown back into the path of Parliamentary government and laid the foundations for an ultimate fusion of the English and Scottish nationalities. Even in face of so great authority we would rather maintain that the fusion of those nationalities was begun by the Stuart and completed by the trader. Englishmen and Scots became British not in Church or conventicle but in a common court and a common shop. " He possessed talents created for times of revolution, capable at once of shaking and destroying existing institutions and of establishing new ones, as resolute in passing great measures as in devising small means: audacious in his projects but practical in executing them, at once active and unyielding, bold and prudent, systematic and pliant, full of thought for his friends, devoid of all consideration for those against whose rights he was battling."

[1] Von Ranke II. 394.

It is possible to estimate fairly a man's success or failure only if we know the object at which he was aiming. This is exactly what we lack in the case of Pym. Did he wish, with the younger Vane, for a Republic? Did he wish for the deposition of Charles and the substitution for him of the young Prince of Wales or even of the undoubted Protestant his nephew, Charles Lewis of the Palatinate? Against that stand his emphatic words in his *Declaration and Vindication*: " I neither directly or indirectly ever had a thought tending to the least disobedience or disloyalty to his Majesty, whom I acknowledge my lawful King and Sovereign and would expend my blood as soon in his service as any subject he hath." [1]

Yet it was Pym who twice brought in armed intervention from Scotland, who with Hampden so " poisoned the heart of the people " against Charles that every word and every act of the King, however plainly within his royal prerogative, became suspect. It was Pym, moreover, who on two occasions refused to be made Chancellor of the Exchequer, who preferred to exasperate from without when he might have modified from within. Were, then, his protestations of loyalty the merest lip service? Did he, indeed, believe all the absurdities concerning " evil counsellors " and " libertines " and " malignants " with which he filled his vast speeches and the exuberant sections of the Grand Remonstrance? Are we to see in the Nineteen Propositions the ideal of a patriotic King as it presented itself to Pym? That King was to be a monarch obedient to the behests of an assembly which could be dissolved only by its own consent and with powers limited only by its own pleasure.

History, as it sometimes will, made its own ironic comment. When in August, 1652, the discredited Rump

[1] Cf. Appendix IX.

of this famous Long Parliament brought in their Perpetuation Bill they were but carrying to its conclusion the principle of their late illustrious leader. Their new House of Commons was to consist of four hundred. All present members were to keep their seats and to enjoy a right of veto in the election of new members. We have already seen what Cromwell's answer was: he had learnt from Charles's mistakes. Moreover, Pym's popular King, thus circumscribed by his masters in the assembly, was still further lopped. He was to have no control whatever of the military forces, no choice of civil officials, no legislative veto, and, of course, no power of the purse.

Such was the purport of the Nineteen Propositions. But, it may be urged, such a position is not very far different from that assigned to the English monarch under the Revolutionary Settlement of 1688, and its immediate consequences. As a matter of fact it is entirely different, and for this reason: under the last Stuarts the assembly was subject to change, even to rapid change; under Pym's leadership it was not. Not England's Constitution as it was under William and Mary, or as it was under Anne, but England's Constitution as it was from the Hanoverian accession until George III made Bute Prime Minister is the parallel, if indeed there be a parallel at all. For in those years, as during the leadership of Pym, one party and one interest was dominant, and the monarchy was, in effect, put into commission by the Whig oligarchy.

Since, then, a man is to be taken to intend the necessary or probable consequences of his acts, Pym must be credited with the design of some such *Roi Fainéant* with an unreformable House of Commons for his *Maire du Palais*. The end was inevitable. "A House of Commons, in fact, that assumes to command the army, must always end in giving the army command over its own destinies. The day on which Pym first took from the senseless brain of Haselrig to his own scheming intellect the question of the Militia was the parent of that day when Cromwell's pikemen removed the ' bauble.' " [1]

It is not necessary to suppose that Pym understood this. There is nothing in his speeches that betrays any political imagination, nothing to indicate that he was the contemporary of Francis Bacon and of Thomas Hobbes, and but little the junior of that Jean Bodin, whom his legal colleagues so often quoted in the House of Commons. Like Cromwell, Pym never knew where he was going till he got there, though at each stage of his journey he knew precisely at which station he would find himself next. Such men are the most dangerous of revolutionaries. It is the man of imagination who will pause and doubt, and ask, " And after ? And after ? And after ? "

What, then, in the case of Pym was the next step which he always saw so clearly that he never saw beyond ? The answer is not difficult. Like the infamous Jeffreys he could smell a Presbyterian forty miles, but unlike Jeffreys he found the odour savoury. The four pre-eminent accomplishments of his life are the first Scottish intervention, the compilation of the Grand Remonstrance, the Nineteen Propositions and the Solemn League and Covenant with which he bought the second Scottish intervention. When he is remembered at all he is remembered for these. But he is most characteristically himself when he is hard on the trail of some Popish schoolmaster or expounding the doctrinal enormities of an Arminian Bishop. His first and main interest was what he called Religion. " The greatest liberty of our Kingdom is Religion," he had said. When he and

[1] " Quarterly Review " No. 216, 544, 1860.

Wentworth were reformers together, though their paths for long ran side by side, their goals were quite distinct. The muddled mismanagement of Buckingham, the great opportunities which Charles was flinging away with both hands roused Wentworth to opposition; it was superstition and idolatry and the rags of Antichrist against which Pym first and foremost directed his great gifts. Nor did religion mean to him that quiet culture of the soul which irradiated the life of George Herbert at Bemerton ; it was not the heartfelt devotion to the unseen God of his imagining which gave immortality to the pathetic and ludicrous visions of Bunyan. In the sublime heights where Milton soars free from his Puritan bonds and Puritan venom, Pym and his like would have yawned. He is of the house and lineage of Wilham Laud, whom of all men he most abhorred ; he is definitive, positive. But where the Archbishop must needs bow to the great cloud of witnesses, not always entirely harmonious, whom the Church has accepted for Fathers and teachers, the Puritan must rely upon himself and those few exponents of eternal verity to whom illumination had been granted in the sixteenth century of the Christian era. In the great corporation of faithful Churchmen there were saints like Andrewes, fighting men like Montague. In the ranks of the Puritans there were seers like Milton, there were truculent psalm singers like Cromwell, for ever hewing Agags to the greater glory of God in the very words and spirit of the sheiks of Palestine. Pym is none such, nor is Laud ; they stand midway, they are the embodiment of politics viewed in the light of a theory of religion. Hence they fail where either the fanatic or the politique would have succeeded.

The distortion runs through the times. No 'inquirer into the blunders, the crimes, and the heroism of our

RELIGION AND POLITICS BLENDED

Civil Wars has yet disentangled that skein wherein Religion and Politics were blended. And when at last the Revolution settlement finished the strife of which all were weary, it was the politiques and the Gallios who did it all. "Here and here we are safe, for these be the work of men's hands!" said they, "and, for the rest, guess as you please."

APPENDICES

APPENDIX I
(i) THE ADDLED PARLIAMENT OF 1614

IT is necessary to show cause for the statement that John Pym did not sit in the Addled Parliament of 1614.

Forster in his life of Pym [1] says: "In the Parliamentary returns of the year 1614 the name of John Pym is to be found as member for the borough of Calne." He gives no authority for this assertion and it is sufficiently refuted by the fact that there are no Parliamentary returns for 1614. [2] Only one list of its members is known to exist—that which was discovered in the muniment room of Kimbolton Castle. [3] In this list the name of Pym does not appear and the representatives of Calne are stated to be Sir Edward Carey and Richard Lowe.

Gardiner in his article on Pym in the *Encyclopædia Britannica* [4] says explicitly that the statement that Pym sat in the Addled Parliament is now known to be incorrect. In his History, [5] although he alludes to the chief leaders of the anti-court party, *e.g.*, Sir Thomas Wentworth and Sir John Eliot, he does not mention Pym, but he gives the reference to the Kimbolton list, pointing out that it is the only one in existence. Nevertheless, writing some years later his account of Pym in the *Dictionary of National Biography* [6] he states: ". . . we know nothing of his career till he entered the House of Commons as Member for Calne in 1614." He gives no reason for thus altering his opinion, and thereby implicitly denying the authority of the Kimbolton list.

It is at least significant that in the *Journals of the House of Commons* the name of Pym does not occur once either as speaker or as a Committee in 1614. It is true that the duration of this assembly was short, and that Pym was eminently cautious in feeling his way when confronted with new conditions. Nevertheless, it is difficult to believe that in such a stirring drama he would have been content to be *muta persona*.

[1] Forster Pym, c. 1, p. 2. [2] Parl. papers 1878, Return of Members of Parl., Part I. [3] Palatine Note Book, III, No. 30. [4] Encyclop. Brit. 9th and 10th Edd. sub. "Pym." [5] G. Hist. Vol. II, ch. XVII, pp. 230-1. [6] D. N. B. Vol, 47, sub. "Pym."

(2) PYM'S CONSTITUENCIES

THE PARLIAMENT OF 1621.—*Calne*, with colleague John Ducket.

THE PARLIAMENT OF 1623.—*Chippenham*, and also for Tavistock. Pym chose Tavistock. Colleague Sampson Hele. Calne was represented by Sir Edward Howard as colleague with John Ducket; Chippenham by John Maynard and Sir Francis Popham.

THE PARLIAMENT OF 1625.—*Tavistock*. Colleague Sir Francis Glanvill.

THE PARLIAMENT OF 1625-6.—*Tavistock*. Colleague Sir John Radcliffe.

THE PARLIAMENT OF 1628.—*Tavistock*. Colleague Sir Francis Glanvill.

THE PARLIAMENT OF 1640 (Short Parliament).—*Tavistock*. Colleague The Right Hon. William Lord Russell (son of Pym's friend and patron, and afterwards 5th Earl and 1st Duke of Bedford). The same county, Devon, returned Peard (Barnstaple), Strode (Beeralston), Oliver St. John and John Maynard (both Totnes).

THE PARLIAMENT OF 1640 (Long Parliament).—*Tavistock*.—On authority of Rushworth, but the only returns given for the borough are these: John Russell Vice Wm. Lord Russell now Earl of Bedford. Also Elisha Crimes and Edmund Fowell.

Accounts and Papers 1878, vol. 17, part I, Members of Parliament. See under respective years and constituencies.

APPENDIX II

PYM'S ACTIVITY IN THE PARLIAMENT OF 1621

Feb. 16.—Speaks in case of Sheppard. C.J. I., 524, i, P. & D. I. 51-2.

Feb. 27.—Speaks against Mompesson. C.J. I., 530, i. Com. to report on Mompesson. C.J. I. 530, ii. P. & D. I, 124.

March 6.—Com. to report on an Act for Restraint of Abuses in levying debts for common persons in the name and Prerogative of the King. C.J. I., 540, i. Sub.-committee on Mompesson "For Concealments." C.J. I., 540, i, 541, ii.

March 12.—Speaks on question of sending other Bills with Subsidy. C.J. I., 550, i.

March 22.—Com. on three private Bills, Ayton's, Douglas's and another matter. C.J. I., 570, i.

March 26.—Speaks on Petition of Borough of Ilchester within the County of Somerset for sending Burgesses. C.J. I., 572, ii.

April 18.—Speaks against Tobacco. C.J. I,. 581, ii.

April 20.—Speaks in matter of Sir John Bennett. C.J. I., 583, ii.

April 21.—Com. with eleven others added to previous Com. in Sir J. Bennett's case. C.J. I., 586, i.

April 24.—Com. to draw several Bills for regulating of Inns and Alehouses and the prices of horse meat, etc., and of the Clerk of the Market. C.J. I., 590, i.

April 25.—Moveth about the Fine [*i.e.* "end" legal] of Bowdler and Megges which ordered here are yet proceeded in contrary. C.J. I., 590, ii. Com. for regulating the Court of Chancery by Bill. C.J. I., 591, i.

April 26.—Com. to consider of the State of all the Business of the House, and to report to the House, to which also the Sub.-Com. of the Vacation may report their proceedings, and this Com. also to consider and report which businesses they think fittest to have priority. C.J. I., 592, ii.

April 27.—Mr. Pymme and three others to examine into the matter of putting the Great Seal to this Privy Seal and of the Enrollment without Warrant—others added later. C.J. I., 594, ii.

April 28.—Speaks in regard to last mentioned—that the Com. may have power to send for the Masters not attendant in the Upper House. C.J. I., 596, i.

May 1.—Speaks in Floyd's case—to whip him except within some reasonable time he pay £1,000 fine. C.J. I,, 602, i.

May 7.—Moves for a new writ for Minehead. C.J. I., 612, i. Com. to meet Lords (?) in Floyd's case. C.J. I., 612, i.

May 16.—Com. with very important members and chiefly lawyers,

APPENDIX

e.g., Coke, Hakewill, Sir Thomas Wentworth, Noy, St. John, Mr. Solicitor to reduce into writing the patents already damned or hereafter to be damned in this House : to be prepared to be offered to the King : and all other grievances fit to be tendered by Petition to him. C.J. I., 621, i. Speaks as Seconder to Mr. Solicitor's motion—we have not transferred the matter of Floyd only to the Lords. C.J. I., 623.

May 18.—Speaks in matter of Floyd's trunk which the Lords demand. C.J. I., 624, ii.

May 24.—Com. to represent Commons at Conference desired by Lords to consider Bill of the Sabbath and that of Certioraris. C.J. I., 626, i.

May 30.—Speaks on question of adjournment. C.J. I., 631, ii., 632, i. Speaks again on question of Adjournment. C.J. I., 632, ii.

November 24.—Speaks. M.S. defective in C.J. I., 643, ii. Com. on subject of Speech last mentioned. M.S. defective as above. Mentioned by Speaker as having a letter addressed to the House, and handed to him by Speaker. Pym Absent. C.J. I., 644, ii. Produces letter mentioned above. C.J. I., 647, i.

Nov. 27.—Speaks on subject of the Palatinate. C.J. I., 647, ii.

Nov. 29.—Com. on Bill for the better granting of Administrations. C.J. I., 650, ii. Com. to examine all matters concerning Sir H. Spiller. C.J. I., 652, ii.

Dec. 3.—Speaks for early sitting next day for reading of fair copy of the Remonstrance and Petition and the Instruction. C.J. I., 657.

Dec. 5.—Speaks on subject of King's letter from Newmarket. C.J. I., 659.

Dec. 7.—Speaks on question whether or not Speaker shall seek audience of King at Newmarket. Advises against. C.J. I., 661, ii.

Dec. 8.—Revises the Petition to King. C.J. I., 661, ii.

Dec 13.—Speaks advising the quick dispatch of Petition. C.J. I., 663, i.

Dec. 17.—Speaks advising that measures be taken for preserving Records of the House. C.J. 1., 667, ii.

Dec. 18.—Accordant to Sir George Moore moving for a penalty from those who came late after Prayers "and to renew the former orders in that behalf made." C.J. I., 668, i. Speaks advising first to satisfy the King, then to look to our Privileges. C.J. I., 668, i. Chosen with others on Mr. Alford's motion to view the Clerk's book. C.J. I., 669, ii.

END OF PARLIAMENT OF 1621.

APPENDIX III
PYM'S ACTIVITY IN THE PARLIAMENT OF 1624

Feb. 23.—Speaks to except Private Bills at fit Times from the operation of Sir T. Hobby's motion that no new Bills to be considered till old ones twice read and committed. C.J. I., 716, i. Com. for Privileges. C.J. I., 716, i. Speaks for Motion that Counsel be admitted to the Com. Agreed. C.J. I., 716, i.

Feb. 24.—Com. on Concealments. C.J. I., 673, i, 717, ii.

Feb. 25.—Speaks against admission of Sir Francis Popham into House and propounds question about his Election. C.J. I., 673, i, 717, ii. Com. to read Clerk's book every Saturday afternoon. C.J. I., 673, 718, i. Com. to peruse and compare with former copy a Bill for explaining a branch of a Statute 3rd Jac. intituled An Act for the Better Discovery and Repressing of Popish Recusants. C.J. I., 673, ii., 718, i.

Feb. 26.—Com. to examine the particular abuses in Fees or otherwise in the Exchequer. C.J. I., 674, ii, 719, i. Speaks and is Com. on an Act concerning Monopolies and Dispensations with Penal Laws and Forfeiture thereof. C.J. I., 674, ii, 719, ii.

March 1.—Speaks on question of Match and Palatinate against continuance of any Treaty. Prays for Conference with Lords after a Message to the King. C.J. I., 675, i, 722, ii.

March 2.—Speaks to give thanks to the Prince—revives Sir D. Digges' Motion. C.J. I., 725, i.

March 3.—Com. with 47 others to confer with Lords as to Reasons for an Advice to the King. C.J. I., 676, ii, 726, i.

March 9.—Com. on a private Act concerning lands of Magdalene College, Cambridge. C.J. I., 680, i, 731, i.

March 10.—Chooses to sit for Tavistock rather than for Chippenham, for which he had also been elected. C.J. I., 681, ii, 732, ii.

March 12.—Mentioned in account of the Chippenham Election and the Question of Sir Francis Popham. C.J. I., 684, i, 735, i.

March 13.—Com. on Continuance or Repeal of Divers Statutes. C.J. I., 736, ii.

March 19.—Speaks on Question of Subsidies for War. C.J. I., 741, ii.

March 22.—Com. on an Act for the further description of a Bankrupt. C.J. I., 744, ii. Com. on an Act to make Ministers capable of leases. C.J. I., 746, i.

March 23.—Presents a petition from the creditors of Cope.

APPENDIX

C.J. I., 747, i. Speaks to have the House (*sic*) that this afternoon a Com. of both Houses may meet to agree upon a Report to be made before the Recess. C.J. I., 747, ii.

March 24.—Com. on an Act against Abuses in levying of debts for common persons under the name and prerogative of the King. C.J. I., 748, ii.

April 1.—Speaks to have the Com. consider of all real Recusants as well as legal Recusants. C.J. I., 752, i.

April 3.—Com. one of 48 to confer with the Lords. C.J. I., 754, i.

April 7.—Com. on Lady Jermy's Bill. C.J. I., 757, i. Com. on an Act to make sale of lands of Aucher, James, and Wroth. C.J. I., 757, i. Com. one of 64 to confer with Lords about Bill of Monopolies. C.J. I., 757, ii.

April 8.—Wolferstone's Bill. Sir Henry Fane desires to be left out of the Com. Mr. Pymme . . . (entry incomplete). C.J. I., 758, i. Com. on Act for Restitution in Blood of Carew Rawleigh, son of Sir Walter Rawleigh, attainted of High Treason. C.J. I., 758, i.

April 9.—Mentioned in decision on contested Election at Chippenham. Sir Francis Popham elected. C.J. I., 759, i.

April 10.—Com. on Act for Establishing of three lectures in Divinity. C.J. I., 762, i–ii.

April 12.—Com. on Act to enable Vincent Lowe to sell certain lands. C.J. I., 762, i. Com. on Act to prevent Simony in Colleges and Halls. C.J. I., 762, ii.

April 13.—Com. to consider of the offence of Fowles, prisoner in the Fleet, and likewise of the manufacture of gold and silver thread. C.J. I., 765, ii.

April 14.—Com. on Act for Naturalising of James, Lord Marquis of Hamilton. C.J. I., 767, i.

April 15.—Com. on an Act for the relief of divers Artisan Clothworkers in London. C.J. I., 767, ii.

April 17.—Com. on Lead Ore and Lead Mine Tithes. C.J. I., 769, i.

April 19.—Com. to view the Petitions exhibited to the Committee for Courts of Justice and to agree upon some course to regulate the inconveniences they shall find. C.J. I., 770, ii.

April 21.—Com. on Act for settling and assuring of certain lands to Dame Mary Scudamore in nature of a Jointure. C.J. I., 772, i.

April 22.—Com. on several Patents and Provisions tendered to the Bill of Monopolies, and on the increase of Fees in the Subpœna Office. C.J. I., 773, i.

April 23.—Com. for Bonnington's Estate. C.J. I., 689, i, 773, i.

April 26.—Com. for Somervyle's Estate. C.J. I., 690, ii, 775, i.
April 28.—Com. (added) for Erith and Plumstead Marshes. C.J. I., 692, i, 777, i. Sub-Committee to consider a report from committee for Grievances past and present with the view of presenting them to the King. C.J. I., 692, i, 777, ii. Com. to consider of the Exactions of the Heralds, etc. C.J. I., 692, ii. Com. to consider Petition against Anyon, President of C.C.C. Oxford, Richardson, Master of Trin. Coll. Cambridge, and Dormer, a Popish Schoolmaster, and all other complaints of this nature concerning Religion or Learning . . . and have power to send for Parties, Witnesses, Records and Writings. C.J. I., 777, ii.
April 29.—Com. on Sea Coals. C.J. I., 693, ii. Com. (added to) on presentment of Recusants. C.J. I., 694, i. Also to take into consideration such persons as live in any place near the sea coast in dangerous places to let in any enemies, also those that are in office in any County or City though not living in the country. C.J. I., 779, i. Com. on Act for Sale of Manor of Little Munden in County of Hertford. C.J. I., 778, ii.
April 30.—Com. on Pointz Private Act for Sale of a Manor. C.J. I., 694, ii. Abbots Hill in County of Sussex. C.J. I., 779, ii, 780, i. Felt-Makers' Bill. C.J. I., 695, i, 780, i.
May 1.—Com. to peruse Sir Simon Harvey's books and the Patent granted to Sir. W Hewett. C.J. I., 696, i., 781, ii. Com. for speedy levying of Penalty of twelve pence a Sunday forfeited by married women for not repairing to the Church to hear Divine Service. C.J. I., 696, i, 781, ii. Added to Com. on Morgan's Bill "with all the lawyers of the House." C.J. I., 698, i, 783, i.
May 4.—Com. on Act for naturalising three persons named. C.J. I., 783, ii.
May 7.—Speaks (not reported) on a private Petition regarding Presentation to an advowson appendant to a manor. C.J. I., 699, ii.
May 8.—Reports Erith and Plumstead Marshes Bill, twice read. Ingrossetur. C.J. I., 700, ii, 785, ii.
May 13.—Reports from the Com. for Corruption in Religion and Learning, a Petition and Articles against a book printed and published by Richard Montague "full fraught with dangerous opinions of Arminius, quite contrary to the articles established in five several points." Resolved that Pym with four others shall, as from the House, acquaint the Lord Archbishop of Canterbury with the Petition against the book, and with the book itself. C.J. I., 704, i, 788, ii.
May 14.—Speaks in opposition to an Act to settle Josse Glover

APPENDIX

Clerk because the Bill gives Institution, Admission and Induction, "Three Episcopal Points of Jurisdiction which the Bishops above will oppose." C.J. I., 704, 789, i.

May 15.—Com. to consider heads of charge against Bishop of Norwich, C.J. I., 705, i, 789, ii.

May 22.—Com. to consider Bill for removing of Actions out of inferior Courts. C.J. I., 708, ii, 792, ii. Com. on Bill of Concealments, C.J. I., 793, i. Com. with Ravenscroft after motion of letter to examine a catalogue of some seven or eight score Popish books printed within these two years, and to report for some course against printing and selling of Popish books. C.J. I., 709, ii.

May 26.—Com. on the Patent of Survey of Sea Coals. C.J. I., 712, i, 795, ii.

May 27.—Com. to draw Petition to King for removal of Dr. Anyon from Presidency of C.C.C. Oxford, as a disgraceful person. C.J. I., 713, i, 796, ii.

May 28.—Com. of 30 to attend Mr. Solicitor to meet King at Whitehall and present Grievances. C.J. I., 714, i., 797, ii. Appointed to collect the Charge against Bishop of Norwich and to present it to the House. C.J. I., 714, i., 797, ii.

May 29.—"The Matters objected against the Lord Bishop of Norwich reduced into writing by Mr. Pymme, which read in the House by him and ordered to be kept here by the Clerk." C.J. I., 715, ii, 798, ii.

END OF JAMES 1ST'S FOURTH PARLIAMENT

APPENDIX IV

PYM'S ACTIVITY IN THE FIRST PARLIAMENT OF CHARLES I.—1625

June 21.—Supports Motion for a Fast Day for Members of the House—yet moveth to have it general, and to send to the Lords to join with us in a Petition to the King for his Direction in it—Com. to draw a Petition and then to send to the Lords to join in it. C.J. I., 799, i. Com. to draw Petition as above. *ibid.* Com. of Privileges. C.J. I., 799, ii.

June 22.—Com. on an Act for Punishing of Divers Abuses committed on the Lord's Day called Sunday. C.J. I., 800, ii.

July 4.—Moves for Authority to send for the Party or Witnesses concerning Montague's Book (*Apello Cæsarem*). C.J. I., 802, ii. Com. to make certain Alterations in Declaration. C.J. I., 803, i.

July 7.—Com. to set down in writing the Particulars against Montague. C.J. I., 806, i.

July 8.—Com. on Lord Dorset's Bill. C.J. I., 807, i.
July 11.—Com. on Act to enable Spiritual Persons to take Farms. C.J. I., 808, i–ii.

ADJOURNMENT TO OXFORD

August 2.—Com. on Bill against Simony. C.J. I., 809, ii.
August 8.—Com. for Conference with Lords. C.J. I., 812, i. Reporter of Conference with Lords. C.J. I., 812, ii.
August 9.—Relates the Lord Treasurer's Speech (No report given). C.J. I., 813, i.

END OF CHARLES' FIRST PARLIAMENT.

APPENDIX V

PYM'S ACTIVITY IN CHARLES 1ST.'S SECOND PARLIAMENT.—1626

Feb. 10.—"Motion for Mr. Pymme his Man to have Privilege to stay the Suit : *ib.* concerning Mr. Pymme—granted." C.J. I., 817, i. Moves that the Committee for Religion may also consider of certain other Articles set down last Parl. but not put into (the) Petition : or anything else concerning Religion. C.J. I., 817, ii. Com. for Religion. *ibid.* Com. with five others to peruse the Clerk's Entries every Saturday. C.J. I., 818, i.
Feb. 11.—Com. to examine abuses in Sutton's Hospital of the Charter House. C.J. I., 818, i. Com. on Act to minister an oath to accountants to make true accounts. C.J. I., 818, i. Added to Com. for Privileges. C.J. I., 818, ii.
Feb. 14.—Com. on Act to prevent Corruptions in Presentations and Collations to Benefices and in Elections to Headships, Fellowships and Scholars' Places in Colleges and Halls. C.J. I., 819, i. Com. on Bill of Concealments. C.J. I., 819, i. Com. on Act for restraining of Exportation of Ordnance. C.J. I., 819, ii. Com. on an Act for the Quiet of Ecclesiastical Persons and Preservation of Rights of Patrons. C.J. I., 819, ii.
Feb. 15.—Recusants' Children. "Mr. Pymme, Mr. Cage and Mr. Solicitor to desire a Bill from Mr. Attorney-General, concerning the same subject." C.J. I., 819, ii. Com. on Act against scandalous and unworthy Ministers. C.J. I., 819, ii.
Feb. 18.—Com. to prepare facts relating to grievances of traders against France. C.J. I., 821, ii. Com. on Act for annexing Feyford Prebend unto the Vicarage of St. Mary's Church near the market place of Lichfield and for making the said Church a Parish Church. C.J. I., 821, ii.

APPENDIX 325

Feb. 25.—Com. on question of Privilege in matter of Sir H. Martyn. C.J. I., 824, ii.
Feb. 28.—Com. Select to consider of the Questions to be asked the Council of War at their coming (and other matters connected therewith). C.J. I., 826, i.
March 1.—Com. on Bill for Recusants' Children. C.J. I., 826, ii.
March 2.—Reports from the Committee for Religion, the Presentment of Recusants. C.J. I., 828, i. Select Com. to consider how such Recusants as the Committee shall think dangerous Persons to the State shall be presented. C.J. I., 828, ii [aimed at Sir Toby Matthew, son of the Archbishop of York, a Romanist and Bacon's chief friend].
March 3.—Com. for Bill on Bribery. C.J. I., 829, ii. Com. on an Act for the Increase of Trade, *ibid*.
March 4.—Com. with four others to reform the Order concerning the Lord Admiral. C.J. I., 830, i. Com. of 64 to meet Lords in conference concerning the Commons' demand to Buckingham for account of his proceedings. C.J. I., 830, i. Appointed with Sir J. Finch to assist Sir Dug. Digges to make the report of this Conference. C.J. I., 830, i. An Act against Adultery and Fornication. C.J. I., 830, ii.
March 6.—Moves from the Committee of Religion concerning one Symon Dormer a Popish Schoolmaster in Suffolk, that he may be sent for. C.J. I., 831, i.
March 7.—Com. on King's Revenue. C.J. I., 831, ii. Com. to attend Conference with Lords. C.J. I., 832, i. Com. with five others to take notes of this Conference and to decide amongst themselves who shall report. C.J. I., 832, ii.
March 8.—Reports from Conference with Lords, Speech of Archbishop of Canterbury that the Lords have desired this meeting. C.J. I., 832, ii. Com. upon a Question to consider what Answer fit to be made to the Lords and presented to the House. C.J. I., 833, i.
March 9.—Com. to repair to Lord Brooke, Lord Conway and Sir Thomas Button to take their several answers in writing (Council of War under exam^n) to this Question only. C.J. I., 834, i.
March 13.—Com. to consider a Petition from Turkey Company. C.J. I., 836, ii.
March 14.—Com. on Sheriff's Accounts. C.J. I., 836, ii.
March 16.—Com. to consider Heads of Conference with Lords touching the French Merchants' Petition. C.J. I., 837, ii.
March 20.—Com. on Petition to his Majesty for Presenting of Recusants. C.J. I., 838, ii.
March 21.—Com. for Precedence for Dr. Turnor's case. C.J. I., 839, i.

APPENDIX

March 22.—Com. to examine Election of Sir Thomas Monke. C.J. I., 839, ii. Com. on unexpert Commanders, especially Heaman's Ship. C.J. I., 840, i.

March 23.—Reports from the Committee of Religion concerning a letter written to the Mayor of York concerning Recusants. C.J. I., 840, ii.

March 24.—Com. on an Act for the Restitution in Blood of Carew Raleigh, son of Sir Walter Raleigh, Knight, lately attainted of High Treason. C.J. I., 840, ii.

March 25.—Reports from the Committee of Religion concerning certain Popish Schoolmasters. C.J. I., 841, i.

March 30.—Com. to report in matter of King's Speech of yesterday. C.J. I., 843, i.

April 1.—Begins the Residue of the Report with Lords. C.J. I., 843, i.

April 3.—Reports from the Sub-committee for a remonstrance to his Majesty that they cannot be ready till 3 o'clock this afternoon. *ibid.*

April 17.—Reports concerning Montague's books. C.J. I., 845, i.

April 21.—Com. on Duke of Buckingham "the great Business now in hand." C.J. I., 847, i.

April 29.—Com. to set down Reasons to be used at Conference with Lords about a General Fast. C.J. I., 851, ii. Reports on Montague's books and is entrusted to deliver this to the Lords. *ibid.*

May 1.—Reports on suspected Papists, Claydon and Lewys. C.J. I., 852, i.

May 3.—Reports from the Committee about Recusants. C.J. I., 853, ii. Charges against Buckingham allotted to 8 persons with two assistants each, Pym to have Sir Nath. Rich and Mr. Browne. C.J. I., 854, i.

May 5.—Com. to prepare Preamble for Act of Subsidy. C.J. I., 856, i.

May 12.—"Mr. Vice-Chamberlain commendeth Mr. Pymme's Speech and Advice yesterday to do Things nicely and temperately and not tumultuarily." C.J. I., 859, ii.

May 16.—Upon question the House declares that Pym and the other Managers have not exceeded their Commission. C.J. I., 860, ii.

May 24.—Com. to perfect a Recusancy Petition against Warreyne a Minister of Suffolk. C.J. I., 863, i. Com. to draw against stopping any proceedings in the High Commission Court, Star Chamber, etc. *ibid.* Moves from the Com. of Religion that Tendering "one that hath taken great Pains in Discovery of

APPENDIX

Papists " may have £10 out of the Money given at the Communion, etc. C.J. I., 864, i.
June 1.—Com. to enable the Sale of the Manor and Lands of Richard Fust, deceased. C.J. I., 865, ii.
June 6.—Com. to consider Exceptions taken to the Letter to be sent to Cambridge. C.J. I., 867, i. Reports concerning Letter. Message from King that it be not sent. C.J. I., 867, i.
June 8.—Com. to frame Remonstrance to the King concerning Tunnage and Poundage. C.J. I., 868, i.
June 10.—Reports concerning Morgan Lewis, Schoolmaster of Aburgeny and suspected Recusant. C.J. I., 869, ii.
June 13.—Com. on Act concerning divers Privileges of Parliament. C.J. I., 870, ii.
June 14.—Com. on Act for the better Continuance of Peace and Unity in the Church and Commonwealth. C.J. I., 871, i. Com. to set down heads of Introduction to be made by Mr. Speaker with Reasons for enforcing Declaration to be presented to the King. C.J. I., 871, ii. Charles promises answer to-morrow.

END OF CHARLES 1ST'S SECOND PARLIAMENT

APPENDIX VI
PYM'S ACTIVITY IN CHARLES'S THIRD PARLIAMENT
MARCH, 1628—MARCH, 1629

1628.
March 20.—Com. on Privileges. C.J. I., 873, i. Com. concerning Cornwall Election. *ibid*. Com. to frame Petition to King about a general Fast. *ibid*.
March 21.—Com. to attend Conference with Lords on general Fast. C.J. I., 874, i.
March 28.—Com. to give reasons to Committée of Lords for alteration in Petition. C.J. I., 877, i.
March 31.—Com. to assist Mr. Secretary Coke to make the Report of Meeting of King and Committee of both Houses. C.J. I., 877, ii.
April 1.—Com. on Act for the further Reformation of Sunday Abuses committed on the Lord's Day, commonly called Sunday. C.J. I., 877, ii.
April 3.—Com. to consider concerning the Personal Liberty of the Subjects and the Propriety of their Goods. C.J. I., 879, i.
April 4.—Chosen with Sir B. Rudyerd to assist Sir D. Digges to

prepare Introduction on Liberty of Subject for Conference with Lords. C.J. I., 879, ii.

April 7.—Com. on Act for better Continuance of Peace and Unity in Church and Commonwealth. C.J. I., 879, ii.

April 8.—Com. on Act for Establishing and Confirming of the Foundation of the Hospital of King James, founded in Charterhouse in the County of Middlesex, at the humble Petition and at the only Costs and Charges of Thomas Sutton, Esq., and of the Possessions thereof. C.J. I., 880, i.

April 10.—Com. to agree upon Heads for an Introduction to be made by Mr. Speaker of Petition to be presented to King by whole House, concerning Billeting of Soldiers. C.J. I., 881, ii. Com. to consider the Question of a Recess at this time, whether advisable or not. *ibid*.

April 14.—Com. to consider an alleged Aspersion of Selden by Earl of Suffolk. C.J. I., 883, ii.

April 18.—Com. on Act for better Ordering of the Office of the Clerk of the Market and Reformation of false Weights and Measures. C.J. I., 885, ii.

April 19.—Com. on an Act against scandalous Ministers and Unworthy. *ibid*.

April 21.—Com. to consider what fit to be done upon Contempt to the House of Sir Reginald Mohun, Sir Richard Greenevyle, and Sir William Wray in their Petition. C.J. I., 886, i. Com. on an Act concerning the Inheritance, Freehold and Possessions of William, Earl of Devonshire. *ibid*.

April 23.—Com. to be Member of Conference with Lords. C.J. I., 887, ii. Com. on an Act against the Procuring Judicial Places for Money or other Reward and against giving and taking of Bribes. C.J. I., 888, i.

April 24.—Com. to take names of Recusants presented by the Knights of Shires. C.J. I., 888, ii.

April 25.—Com. to consider Decay of Shipping and of Timber fit for building Ships. C.J. I., 889, i.

April 26.—Com. to examine Contempt of Pemberton both in the first arrest and Words since [he had refused to come over with the Serjeant, for he said he hoped the Parliament would be dissolved within three days]. C.J. I., 889, i.

April 28.—Reports from the Committee for Religion concerning Montague and Burgess, Vicar of Witney, and Com. to go to Archbishop of Canterbury to ask him about Popish Schoolmaster. C.J. I., 889, ii. [The others were Digges, Rich and Rudyerd.] Com. to frame a Bill expressing the Substance of the Statutes of Magna Charta, and the other Statutes, and of the Resolutions made in this House concerning the Liberty of

APPENDIX 329

the Subjects in their Persons and Estates appointed upon Question without one negative. C.J. I., 890, i.

May 2.—Com. to draw a Petition to the King for Release of Clegate. C.J. I., 891, ii.

May 5.—Com. to set down and bring to the House the King's Answer in Writing. C.J. I., 892, i.

May 8.—Com. with three others to examine the Petition of Right when fair written. C.J. I., 894, i.

May 9.—Reports from the Com. for Religion, that Burgess, Vicar of Witney, refuses to answer; he committed to Tower. C.J.I., 894, ii.

May 10.—Com. to consider Petition against Sir Simeon Stewart by the inhabitants of the Isle of Ely. C.J. I., 895, i.

May 12.—Com. on an Act for making the River Medway navigable for Barges, Boats and Lighters from Maidstone to Penshurst. C.J. I., 895, ii. Com. to draw the Complaints and Accusations against Burgess, Vicar of Witney, into the Form of a Parliamentary Charge. C.J. I., 896, ii,

May 13.—Com. to have power to maintain by Reasons our Petition otherwise than according to said opinion of the Grand Com. as formerly sent up to the Lords, and to report any Reasons used by the Lords to the contrary. C.J. I., 897, i.

May 14.—Reports from the Grand Com. for Religion on Manwaring's Sermons and is added to Sub-Com. to draw up the Charge against him. C.J. I., 897, ii. In the margin is written by the Clerk " Quaere this Report at large from Mr. Pymme."

May 15.—Com. to consider and report the best Course to compel those not now of the House to pay the Arrearage of Contribution last Parl. C.J. I., 898, ii.

May 16.—Com. on Sewster's Estate. C.J. I., 898, ii.

May 19.—Com. to examine Mr. Burgess. C.J. I., 901, i.

May 20.—Com. on Petition from Michael Sparke. C.J. I., 901, ii.

May 21.—Com. to search for Records and Precedents in the Matter of Billeting Soldiers. C.J. I., 902, i.

May 23.—Com. to assist Sir H. Martin with Sir N. Rich to argue with Lords certain objections of latter in Matter of Petition of Right. C.J. I., 903, i. Com. on Act for Confirmation of Letters Patent made by the late King's Majesty with John, Earl of Bristol, by the name of John Digby Knight. C.J. I., 903. Reporter, with four others, of Conference with Lords. C.J. I., *Ibid.*

May 24.—Reports from Com. for Religion, the Case of Elizabeth Milbourne, and made Com. to pen a Petition to King in matter of Brooke (deportation of Papists' children abroad). C.J. I., 904, i. In the margin is written by the Clerk " Quaere the

APPENDIX

Report at large of Mr. Pymme." Appointed with Sir D. Digges and Sir V. Rich to give certain Reasons of the House to the Lords in matter of Petition of Right. C.J. I., 904, ii.

May 26.—Com. to report at Conference with Lords on Petition of Right. C.J. I., 905, i.

May 27.—Com. to consider the way for presenting the Petition of Right. C.J. I., 905, ii. Appointed to deliver the Charge against Dr. Manwaring and to strengthen it. C.J. I., 906, i.

May 31.—Reports from the Com. for Manwaring's Charge two Sermons late made by him. C.J. I., 907, ii.

June 3.—Burgesses Petition, Pym to be present with his Notes at Com. on this matter. C.J. I., 908, i. Com. on a Petition from the Planters of the Summer Islands. C.J. I., 908, ii.

June 4.—Com. to examine into Scarcity, Dearness and other Abuses about Powder. C.J. I., 908, ii.

June 7.—To be a Reporter of Conferences of both Houses to consider the King's Answer to the Petition of Right. C.J. I., 910, i. Com. to draw up the Preamble of the Subsidy. C.J. I., 910, i.

June 11.—Reports the business against Dr. Montague. . . . He is appointed to present them to the Lords, C.J. I., 911. Com. to frame a Remonstrance upon these nine things. C.J. I., 911, ii.

June 12.—Com. to frame a Petition to his Majesty concerning Coat and Conduct Money and Money for billeting of Soldiers. C.J. I., 912, i.

June 13.—Six others appointed to assist Pym concerning Montague. C.J. I., 912, ii.

June 16.—Reports from the Com. for the Summer Islands . . . and with three others is to draw up a Petition to his Majesty concerning this imposition. C.J. I., 914, i.

June 18.—Com. on Bowdler's Petition (Administration). C.J. I., 914, ii.

June 20.—Com. on Petition from Mr. Serjeant concerning his Fees of the Cornish men. C.J. I., 915, ii. Com. to view and dispose the Businesses of this House and to take Consideration of the Commission about Knights. C.J. I., 916, i.

April 21.—Com. to agree upon a Message to be sent to His Majesty. C.J. I., 916, ii.

June 23.—Com. to Report on a letter sealed up and found under the Door. C.J. I., 917, i, and with others to take this Letter of "Some Jesuitical Spirit" to the King. *ibid.* ii. Com. to peruse the Pardon compare it with that of 21 Jac., and report to House. C.J. I., 918, ii.

June 25.—Pym to bring in and leave with the Clerk To-morrow

morning, all the Writings he has concerning Religion. C.J. I., 919, ii.
JUNE 26.—PARLIAMENT PROROGUED, MEETS AGAIN JAN. 20, 1629.
Jan. 21.—Com. to take consideration of the matter so entered. [King's Speech at the prorog. on June 26, on the Journal] and to view and search for any Precedents they shall think fit and to present their opinions thereof to the House. C.J.I., 920, ii.
Jan. 22.—Select com. on Rolles' Complaint "to take into Consideration the particulars of the Relation made by Mr. Rolles wherein the Subjects' Liberty in general hath been invaded." C.J. I., 921, i.
Jan. 23.—Com. on an Act for enlarging the Liberty of hearing the Word of God preached. C.J. I., 921, ii. Com. on Act against the Procuring of judicial Places for Money or other Reward and against Giving and Taking of Bribes. C.J. I., 922, i.
Jan. 26.—Com. to frame a Petition to his Majesty for a General Fast. C.J. I., 922, ii.
Jan. 27.—Reports from the Com. of Religion concerning the King's obtaining of the Remonstrance. C.J.I., 922, ii. Com. to start a Com, of both Houses to meet the King with the Petition. C.J. I., 923, i.
Jan. 29.—Com. to draw and present to the House Bill concerning Appropriations and Vicarages. C.J. I., 924, i. Moves for Leave for Sir John Eppesley a Member of it to answer a Petition preferred against him in the Lords' House. Refused. C.J. I., 924, i. Reports to the House a Frame of a Declaration agreed upon by the Com. of Religion. C.J. I., 924, i–ii.
Jan. 30.—Com. to view the Entries in the Clerk's Book every Saturday in the afternoon. C.J. I., 924, ii. Com. to examine into matter of Aleyne accused by one John Pregion concerning his petition to his Majesty against the Lord Bishop of Lincoln. C.J. I., 925.
Feb. 5.—Com. to take Consideration of the Differences in the several Impressions of the 39 Articles established by Act of Parl. 13 Eliz. and of all Incidents thereunto. C.J. I., 926, ii. Reports from Grand Com. for Religion, a Petition by Ogle against Whittington and Cosens. *ibid.*
Feb. 10.—Com. on Act for Confirmation of the King's Letters Patents made by our late Sovereign Lord [in margin "Summer Islands"]. C.J. I., 928, i.
Feb. 11.—Com. on Act for Increase of Trade. C.J. I., 928, ii. Reports from the Grand com. for Religion. Further information given against the Bishop of Winchester. C.J. I., 921, i.
Feb. 12.—Com. on Hammond's Estate. C.J. I., 929, i.

APPENDIX

Feb. 13.—Com. to consider of, and pen, the Letters to be sent to the Universities. C.J. I., 930, i.

Feb. 14.—Com. to consider a question of Privilege (Sir John Eppesley). *ibid*. Com. concerning Injunctions and other proceedings in Exchequer regarding Goods of Merchants detained for not payment of certain Duties. *ibid*.

END OF CHARLES'S THIRD PARLIAMENT

APPENDIX VII

PYM'S ACTIVITY IN THE SHORT PARLIAMENT.—1640
APRIL 13—MAY 5

April 15.—Com. to prepare a Conference with Lords concerning a Fast day for both Houses. C.J. II., 4, i. Com. for Privileges, *ibid*.

April 17.—Com. to peruse Journals and Records and consider their state. C.J. II., 4, ii.

April 18.—Com. to report concerning the Violation of the Privilege of Parl. the last day of last Parl. C.J. II., 6, ii. Mr. Pymme excuses himself for the word "Defend." *ibid*.

April 20.—Com. to re-collect material points of Grievances mentioned in Petitions from Counties. C.J. II., 7, ii.

April 21.—Com. to consider Petition from Treasuries of three Subsidies and three fifteens. C.J. II., 8 i. Com. to take view of Commission now lately granted to Convocation. *ibid*. Com. to consider records of Baite's Case and Vassall's Case and consider procedure. C.J. II., 8, ii.

April 22.—Asks leave for Sir Thomas Cheeke for ten days' absence. C.J. II., 8, ii. Com. to consider Petition from Peter Smart. C.J. II., 8, ii. Mr. Dell takes exception to words of Mr. Pymme. Mr. Pymme cleared. Mr. Dell apologises. C.J. II., 9, i. Com. to take view of the Commission to Convocation. C.J. II., 9, ii.

April 23.—Pym to give notice [concerning Fast Day, and Sacrament at St. Margaret's]. C.J. II., 9, ii. Com. to set out Reasons for Conference with Lords on Religion, Goods, Liberties, Privileges, Supply. C.J. II., 10, i.

April 24.—Com. to prepare and direct the managing of Business of the Conference with Lords. C.J. II., 12, i.

April 25.—Pym appointed Reporter of Conference with Lords with four others. C.J. II., 12, ii.

April 27.—Com. to prepare in writing an Address to the Lords for Righting Privileges concerning Supply introduced by Lords. C.J. II., 14, i.

April 28.—Mr. Pymme to go up to the Lords with the Address

APPENDIX

just read. C.J. II., 15, i. Delivered by Mr. Pym who returns and informs the House that Lords say they will return Answer. Ordered "Thanks should be returned Mr. Pymme from this House for the good service he did them in his exact and faithful Delivery of this Address." His Report ordered to be entered in the Journal of this House. *ibid.*

April 29.—Appointed to take charge of the first Head of Grievances *i.e.*, Innovations in Matter of Religion and to make Introduction into the whole business. C.J. II., 16, i.

May 1.—Pym a Reporter of Conference with Lords. C.J. II., 18, i. An Extract of Sermon of Dr. Beale, Master of St. John's Coll., Cambridge, delivered to Pym, to be reported on by Com. *ibid.*

May 2.—Com. to consider Petitions upon second Elections especially that of Sir Edward Bishop. C.J. II., 18, ii.

END OF SHORT PARLIAMENT

[Pym's activity in the Long Parliament is sufficiently indicated in the text.]

APPENDIX VIII
(a) THE COMMONS' PROTESTATION IN 1621

"The Commons now assembled in Parliament being justly occasioned thereunto, concerning sundry liberties, franchises, and privileges of Parliament, amongst others not herein mentioned do make this protestation following : That the liberties, franchises, privileges and jurisdictions of Parliament are the ancient and undoubted birthright and inheritance of the subjects of England; and that the arduous and urgent affairs concerning the King, State, and defence of the realm and of the Church of England, and the making and maintenance of laws, and redress of grievances, which daily happen within this realm, are proper subjects and matter of counsel and debate in Parliament; and that in the handling and proceeding of those businesses every member of the House hath, and of right ought to have, freedom of speech, to propound, treat, reason and bring to conclusion the same :—

"That the Commons in Parliament have like liberty and freedom to treat of those matters, in such order as in their judgments shall seem fittest, and that every such member of the said House hath like freedom from all impeachment, imprisonment and molestation other than by the censure of the House itself, for or concerning any Bill, speaking, reasoning, or declaring of any matter or matters touching the Parliament or Parliament business ; and that, if any of the said members be complained of and questioned for anything said or done in Parliament the same is to be showed to the King by the advice and assent of all the Commons assembled in Parliament before the King give credence to any private information." [1]

(b) THE COMMONS' PROTESTATION IN 1641

" I, A. B., in the presence of Almighty God, promise, vow and protest to maintain and defend, as far as lawfully I may, with my life, power, and estate, the true Reformed Protestant Religion, expressed in the doctrine of the Church of England, against all Popery and Popish innovations within this realm contrary to the same doctrine, and, according to the duty of my allegiance, his Majesty's Royal person, honour, and estate, as also the power and privileges of Parliament, the lawful rights and liberties of the subjects, and every person that maketh the protestation, in whatsoever he shall do in the lawful pursuance of the same ; and to my power and as far as lawfully I may, I will oppose and by all good ways and means endeavour to bring to condign punishment, all such as shall either by force, practice, counsels, plots, conspiracies, or otherwise do anything to the contrary of anything in this present protestation contained ; and further that I shall in all just and honourable ways, endeavour to preserve the union and peace between the three kingdoms of England, Scotland, and Ireland ; and neither for hope fear nor other respect shall relinquish this promise, vow and protestation." [2]

APPENDIX IX

A DECLARATION AND VINDICATION OF JOHN PYM, ESQ.

[Published in 1643]

It is not unknown to all the world (especially to the inhabitants in and about London), with what desperate and fame-wounding aspersions my reputation, and the integrity of my intentions to God, my King, and my country, hath been invaded by the malice and fury of malignants, and ill-affected persons to the good of the commonwealth ; some charging me to have been the promoter and patroniser of all the innovations which have been obtruded upon the ecclesiastical government of the Church of England ; others, of more spiteful and exorbitant spirits, alleging, that I have been the man who have begot and fostered all the so-lamented distractions which are now rife in this kingdom. And though such calumnies are ever more harmful to the authors than to those whom they strive to wound with them, when they arrive only to the censure of judicious persons, who can distinguish

[1] P. and D. ii, 359. [2] L. J. IV. 234.

forms, and see the difference betwixt truth and falsehood; yet, because the scandals inflicted upon my innocence have been obvious to people of all conditions, many of which may entertain a belief of those reproachful reports, though in my own soul I am far above those ignominies, and so was once resolved to have waved them, as unworthy my notice, yet at last, for the assertion of my integrity, I concluded to declare myself in this matter, that all the world, but such as will not be convinced, either by reason or truth, may bear testimony of my innocency. To pass by therefore the Earl of Strafford's business, in which some have been so impudent as to charge me of too much partiality and malice, I shall declare myself fully concerning the rest of their aspersions; namely, that I have promoted and fomented the differences now abounding in the English Church.

How unlikely that is, and improbable shall to every indifferent man be quickly rendered perspicuous. For that I am, and ever was, and so will die, a faithful son of the Protestant religion, without having the least relation in my belief to those gross errors of Anabaptism, Brownism and the like, every man that hath any acquaintance with my conversation can bear me righteous witness. These being but aspersions cast upon me by some of the discontented clergy, and their factors and abettors; because they might perhaps conceive that I had been a main instrument in extenuating the haughty power and ambitious pride of the bishops and prelates. As I only delivered my opinion as a member of the House of Commons, that attempt or action of mine had been justifiable both to God and a good conscience; and had no way concluded me guilty of a revolt from the orthodox doctrine of the Church of England, because I sought a reformation of some gross abuses crept into the government by the cunning and perverseness of the bishops and their substitutes; for was it not high time to seek to regulate their power when, instead of looking to the cure of men's souls (which is their genuine office) they inflicted punishment on men's bodies, banishing them to remote and desolate places, after stigmatising their faces, only for the testimony of a good conscience; when, not contented with those insufferable insolencies, they sought to bring in unheard of canons into the Church—Arminian or Papistical ceremonies (whether you please to term them—there is not much difference)—imposing burdens upon men's consciences, which they were not able to bear, and introducing the old, abolished superstition of bowing to the altar? If it savoured either of Brownism or Anabaptism to endeavour to suppress the growth of those Romish errors, I appeal to any equal-minded Protestant, either for my judge or witness. Nay, had the attempts of the bishops desisted here, tolerable they had been, and their power not so much questioned as since it hath: for when they saw the honourable the high court of Parliament begun to look into their enormities and abuses; beholding how they wrested religion like a waxen nose, to the furtherance of their ambitious purposes; then Troy was taken in—then they began to despair of holding any longer their usurped authority! and therefore, as much as in them lay, both by public declarations and private councils they laboured to foment the civil differences between his Majesty and his Parliament, abetting the proceedings of the malignants with large supplies of men and money, and stirring up the people to tumults by their seditious sermons.

Surely, then, no man can account me an ill son of the Commonwealth, if I delivered my opinion and passed my vote freely for their abolishment; which may by the same equity be put in practice by this Parliament, as the dissolution of monasteries and their lazy inhabitants, monks and friars, were in Henry the Eighth's time. For without dispute these carried as much reputation in the kingdom then as bishops have done in it since; and yet a Parliament then had power to put them down. Why then should not a Parliament have power to do the like to these, every way guilty of as many offences against the State as the former? For my own part I attest God Almighty, the Knower of all hearts, that neither envy or any private grudge to all or any of the bishops hath made me averse to their function; but merely my zeal to religion and God's cause, which I perceived to be trampled under foot by the too-extended authority of the prelates, who according to the purity of their institution should have been men of upright hearts and humble minds, shearing their flocks and not flaying them, when it is evident that they were the quite contrary.

And whereas some will allege, it is no good argument to dissolve the function of bishops, because some bishops are vicious; to that I answer, since the vice of these bishops was derivative from the authority of their function, it is very fitting the function, which is the cause thereof, be corrected, and its authority divested of its borrowed feathers; otherwise it is impossible but the same power which made these present bishops (should the episcopal and prelatical dignity continue in its ancient height and vigour) so proud and arrogant would infuse the same vices into their successors.

But this is but a mole-hill to that mountain of scandalous reports that have been inflicted on my integrity to his Sacred Majesty: some boldly averring me for the author of the present distractions between his Majesty and his Parliament; when I take God and all that know my proceedings to be my vouchers, that I neither directly nor indirectly ever had a thought tending to the least disobedience or disloyalty to his Majesty, whom I acknowledge my lawful King and Sovereign, and would expend my blood as soon in his service as any subject he hath. 'Tis true when I perceived my life aimed at, and heard myself proscribed a traitor merely for my intireness of heart to the service of my country; was informed that I, with some other honourable and worthy members of the Parliament were, against the privileges thereof demanded, even in the Parliament House by his Majesty, attended by a multitude of men at arms and malignants, who, I verily believe had, for some ill ends of their own, persuaded his Majesty to that excess of rigour against us; when for my own part (my conscience is to me a thousand witnesses in that behalf) I never harboured a thought which tendered to any disservice to his Majesty, nor ever had an intention prejudicial to the State; when, I say, notwithstanding my own innocence, I saw myself in such apparent danger, no man will think me blameworthy, in that I took a care of my own safety, and fled for refuge to the protection of the Parliament: which, making my case their own, not only purged me and the rest of the guilt of high treason, but also secured our lives from the storm that was ready to burst out upon us.

And if this hath been the occasion that hath withdrawn his Majesty from the Parliament, surely the fault can no way be imputed to me, or any proceeding of mine, which never went further, either since his Majesty's departure, nor before then, so far as they were warranted by the known laws of the land, and authorised by the indisputable and undeniable power of the Parliament: And so long as I am secure in my own conscience that this is truth, I account myself above all their calumnies and falsehoods, which shall return upon themselves and not wound my reputation in good and impartial men's opinions.

But in that devilish conspiracy of Cataline against the State and Senate of Rome, none among the senators was so obnoxious to the envy of the conspirators, or liable to their traducements, as that orator and patriot of his country, Cicero, because by his council and zeal to the commonwealth, their plot for the ruin thereof was discovered and prevented. Though I will not be so arrogant to parallel myself with that worthy, yet my case (if we may compare lesser things with great) hath to his a very near resemblance. The cause that I am so much maligned and reproached by ill-affected persons being, because I have been forward in advancing the affairs of the kingdom, and have been taken notice of for that forwardness: they, out of their malice converting that to a vice, which, without boast be it spoken, I esteem as my principal virtue, my care to the public utility. And since it is for that cause that I suffer these scandals, I shall endure them with patience ; hoping that God in His great mercy will at last reconcile his Majesty to his high court of Parliament ; and then I doubt not, but to give his royal self (though he be much incensed against me) a sufficient account of my integrity. In the interim, I hope the world will believe that I am not the first innocent man that hath been injured, and so will suspend their further censures of me.[1]

APPENDIX X

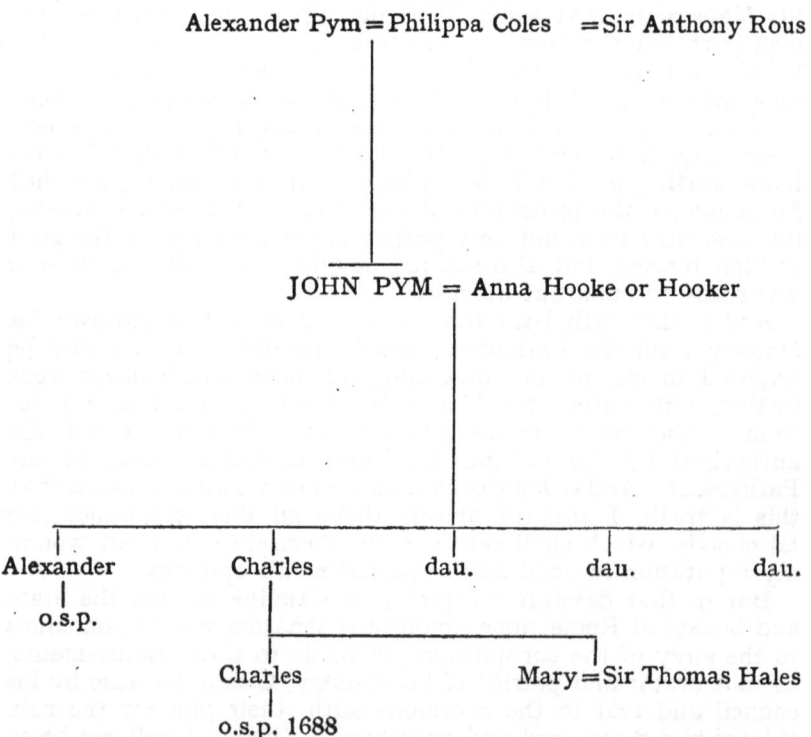

Alexander Pym = Philippa Coles = Sir Anthony Rous

JOHN PYM = Anna Hooke or Hooker

Alexander — o.s.p.

Charles

dau.　dau.　dau.

Charles — o.s.p. 1688

Mary = Sir Thomas Hales

The following letter from Pym to his elder son was printed by J. L. Sanford in his *Studies and Illustrations of the Great Rebellion* :—

To my Son Alexander Pym, one of the Gentlemen of Colonel Herbert's Company in the States' Army. Deliver these with speed.

[1] R. III. ii, 376-378.

APPENDIX 339

LONDON, *23rd Nov.*, 1634.

Alexander,—I lately writ to you by a messenger sent by Allen the post, and delivered him £10 to be paid unto you by the same messenger. In that letter I gave you leave to go from the army if you would, and to live in what part you thought good, till you should receive further direction from me. Since that time I have spoken with Mr. Darley, and he hath given me a good report of you ; whereupon I have conceived some hope that I shall find you a changed man. Wherefore I am very willing to call you home. But, because I have not yet compounded with your creditors, though I have set one awork to treaty with two of the greatest of them which I can find—that is Wroth and Robins ; Peek I know not where to inquire for ; the rest I know none but Mr. Darley and Mr. Knightley—that I may have the most time to compound with them, I would not have you here till the end of January ; and when you shall land, I would not have you come to me till you hear from me, for if they ever take notice you are reconciled to me, I shall bring them to no reason. Therefore keep yourself private, and send to me before you come. I will then give you directions what to do. I have delivered Allen £5 more, which he hath promised that you shall receive with this letter, which I hope will be sufficient to bring you home. Yet, lest you might have some extraordinary occasion, I have promised him to pay £5 more, if you take up so much of his servant, which he saith shall furnish you, if there be need. Now let me see by your thrifty and discreet carriage in this small matter how I may trust you in greater, and assure yourself, as I am very apt to receive you, if you be truly a reformed man, so you will easily fall back into my displeasure, if you bring home your old faults and follies with you. Thus I pray God direct you in his fear, and commend you to his blessing. Resting your loving Father.

JO. PYM.

(Across the back). I have appointed Allen to pay all charges for this and the former money. If you can send me a private note of your other debts, and where I may find Mr. Peek, to whom you owe £500, I shall see better. Make all ready for your return, how soon I permit you to come, in a private manner, and to be here by the end of January.

"It is satisfactory to know that Alexander Pym became a reformed character, a respectable member of society, and a Colonel in the Puritan Army." [1]

[1] Sanford, 143-144.

Some Works of Reference.

Contemporary.

Journals of the House of Lords. Vols. III-VI (L.J.).

Journals of the House of Commons. Vols. I-III (C.J.).

Rushworth's Historical Collections. Vols. I, II 1, II 2, III; III ii (R).

,, Trial of the Earl of Strafford. (R. Straff.)

Clarendon's History of the Great Rebellion, ed. Macray. 1888. (Cl.)

Parliamentary History (Cobbett's). Vols. I-III. 1806.

The Earl of Strafford's Letters and Despatches, ed. Knowler, 2 vols. 1739. (Straff. L. and D.)

Laud's Diary and History of his Troubles and Trial. 1695 (L.).

Proceedings and Debates of the Parliament of 1621. 2 Vols. (P. and D.)

May's History of the Long Parliament, ed. Maseres. 1812. (May.)

Verney's Notes of Proceedings in the Long Parliament (Camden, 1845).

Baillie's Letters and Journals. 3 vols., ed. D. Laing. 1841. (B.)

Eikon Basilike. The Pourtraicture of His Sacred Majesty. 1648.

Wood Anthony. Athenæ Oxonienses, ed. Bliss. 4 vols. 1813-20.

Later. Firth C. H. The House of Lords during the Civil War. 1910.

Forster J. John Pym. 1837 and 1840. (F. P.)

,, John Eliot, 2 Vols. 1864. (F. E.)

Debates on the Grand Remonstrance, 1860. (F. G.R.)

,, Arrest of the Five Members. 1860. (F. 5 M.)

Gardiner S. R. History of England. Vols. 4-10. (G.).

,, ,, ,, the Great Civil War. Vol. I. (G. Civ. W.)

,, Constitutional Documents of the Puritan Revolution, 1889.

SOME WORKS OF REFERENCE

Gardiner S. R. England and Germany, 1618-1619. Camden, 1865.
,,   The Thirty Years' War. 1874.
Hallam H. Constitutional History.
Hutton W. H. The English Church (Charles I to Anne). 1903.
,,   William Laud (Leaders of Religion). 1895.
Green M. A. E. Life of Elizabeth, Queen of Bohemia, ed. Lomax. 1909.
Masson D. Life of John Milton. Vols. I and II, 1881.
Sanford J. L. Studies and Illustrations of the Great Rebellion. 1858.
Von Ranke L. A History of England principally in the XVII Century. Engl. Trsl. Vols. I and II, 1875.
Calendar of State Papers, Colonial. Vol. I, ed. Sainsbury (Cal. S. P. Col. I). 1860.
Cambridge Modern History. Vol. 4. 1906.
Dictionary of National Biography (D. N. B.).

The letters in brackets indicate the work as cited in the notes; if none, the work is not cited or is named in full.

INDEX

ABBOT, GEORGE, ARCHBISHOP OF CANTERBURY urges Frederick's acceptance of Bohemian Crown, 13; accidental homicide by, 58; sometime Master of University College, Oxford, 58; Clarendon's opinion of, 58; prejudices James against Laud, 59; has interview with Montague, 105; reports to Commons on Montague, 105.

ACUÑA, DIEGO SARMIENTO DE, COUNT OF GONDOMAR, Ambassador from Spain to and friend of James I, 2; his influence over James aimed at by Pym, 64; writes impudent letter to James, 68; delighted when James tears Protestation, 79.

ANDREWES, LANCELOT, BISHOP OF WINCHESTER, preaches before James I, 20; unable to attend James' death-bed, 95.

ANHALT, CHRISTIAN OF, real leader of Protestant Union, 7; his policy, 7; designs for Frederick V, 9; urges his acceptance of Bohemian Crown, 12; suggests Duke of Savoy for Emperor, 12; defeated at White Hill, 13.

ANNE OF DENMARK, Queen Consort of James I, her death, 1.

AUGSBURG, PEACE OF, 1555. Ecclesiastical Reservation made by, 6.

BACON, SIR FRANCIS, Lord Verulam, Viscount St. Alban, quoted, 3; addresses Parliament of 1621 as Lord Chancellor, 23; downfall of, 47; comment of, on his successor, 58.

BAVARIA, MAXIMILIAN OF, leader of the Catholic League, 7; obtains Frederick's Electorate, 80.

BALFOUR, SIR WILLIAM, Lieutenant of the Tower of London, refuses to admit Captain Billingsley, 212; refuses Strafford's request to see Laud, 218; advises him to take coach to execution, 219; removed, 272.

BEDFORD, FRANCIS RUSSELL, FOURTH EARL OF, patron of Pym, 17 and 19; proposal that he shall be Treasurer, 223; death of, 224.

BENNETT, SIR JOHN, reported for bribery as Referee and fined by Star Chamber, 48.

BERKELEY, SIR ROBERT, Justice of the King's Bench, removed therefrom by Commons, 223.

BERWICK, TREATY OF, concludes First Bishop's War, 174.

BISHOP'S PROTEST, THE, 273.

BOHEMIA, storm centre in 1618, 7; its position and character, Hercynian Forest; Slavonic Czech and Celtic population, Hus, Jerome, Young Czech movement, Utraquists, Council of Basel, 8; throne elective, 8; Diet elects Ferdinand of Styria, 9; he guarantees Letter of Majesty, 9; affair of Braunau and of Klostergrab, 10; action of Defensores under Thurn, 10; meeting at Prague and defenestration of Slawata, Martinitz and Fabricius, 10.

344 INDEX

BROOKE, ROBERT GREVILLE, SECOND LORD, Adventurer for Providence Island, 151-2; resolves to go to Plantation, 162; his papers seized, 164; refuses oath, 174; his house searched, 180.

BUCKINGHAM, GEORGE VILLIERS, DUKE OF, at opening of Parliament of 1621, 20; James praises his economies, 22; procures release of Sandys and the others, 61; Spanish journey of, 82-3; demands war with Spain, 84; his early friendship with Eliot, 89; hostile to Cranfield, 92; his supreme position in 1624, 96; has full confidence of Charles, 99; why hostile to Williams, 100; in Paris, 101; makes agreement with French Government, 109; addresses the Houses at Oxford, 111; attacked by Seymour and Phelips, 112; absentee Generalissimo of fleet against Cadiz, 113; obtains nothing on security of Crown jewels in Amsterdam, 115; his device of making Sheriffs of opponents, 115; Charles defends, 120; Eliot attacks, 121; explains his policy, 122; is impeached, 123; Pym's speech against, 123-4; compared by Eliot with Sejanus, 125; is elected Chancellor of the University of Cambridge, 127; leads Expedition to La Rochelle, 132; his pacific speech at the Council Table, 137; attacked in the Remonstrance of the Commons, 142 murdered at Portsmouth, 147.

CADIZ. Expedition to, decided upon, 113; failure of, 114.

CALVERT, SIR GEORGE, LORD BALTIMORE, Knight of Shire of York with Sir Thomas Wentworth, 21; as Secretary of State addresses Commons for King, 50; financial statement of, 51; soothes the House of Commons, 56; explains imprisonment of Sandys and the others, 61; answers Phelips, 61; deprecates anger of Commons at James' "slip," 77; urges Wentworth to pay forced loan, 132.

CATHOLIC UNION of German Princes under Duke of Bavaria, 7.

CECIL, SIR EDWARD, VISCOUNT WIMBLEDON, leads Cadiz Expedition, 113.

CHARLES, PRINCE OF WALES, decides to go to Madrid, 82; the journey, 83; the return, 84; is proclaimed King Charles I, 99.

CHARLES I leaves Theobalds for London, 99; his dependence on Buckingham, 99; attends his father's funeral, 101; is married by proxy in Paris, 101; meets his wife at Dover, 101; addresses his first Parliament, 101; financial difficulties of, 108; liberates imprisoned Romish priests, 110; addresses Commons, 110; dissolves his first Parliament, 112; pricks as Sheriffs opponents of Buckingham, 115; asks for immediate supply, 119; anger of, at words of Clement Coke and of Dr. Turner, 120; addresses Commons and warns them, 120; again urges need of supply, 120; threatens Commons, 122; receives Remonstrance from them, 122; " I must be Tiberius," 126; addresses Lords in favour of Buckingham, 126; dissolves his Second Parliament to save Buckingham, 128; dismisses Queen's French attendants, 129; addresses his Third Parliament, 133; controversy with Commons on Petition of Right, 138; warns Commons, 141; gives assent to Petition of Right, 142; receives Remonstrance, 142; prorogues Parliament, 143; makes peace with France and Spain, 165; devices for revenue, 166;

INDEX 345

goes to Scotland, 173; summons Wentworth from Ireland, 174; his views on Parliaments, 176; will, for twelve subsidies, abandon Ship Money, 180; dissolves Short Parliament, 180; receives petition from twelve Peers, 182; summons a Great Council, 183; makes provisional terms with Scots, 183; summons Strafford to London, 188; assents to Triennial Bill and comments thereupon, 194; refuses to disband Irish Army, 210; writes to Strafford in the Tower, 210; addresses the Houses in his favour, 211; is put to his election, 217; seeks counsel, yields, 217; receives Pym twice, 224; sets out for Scotland, 241; his disappointing visit and return, 242; entertained by the City, 254; receives Grand Remonstrance and deprecates publication, 271; sends Bishops' Protest to Lords, 273; offers to make Pym Chancellor of the Exchequer: impeaches him and five others, 275; having heard of proposed impeachment of Queen, 275; excludes seven Lords by name from committee on impeachment, 277; decides upon arrest of the Five Members, 279; enters House and addresses Speaker and Commons, 282; asks for Pym and the rest, 283; his justification in Eikon Basilike, 284; goes to the Guildhall, 286; leaves London, 287; assents to Bishops' Exclusion Bill, 293; joined by his sons, 294; refuses to grant control of Militia to Parliament, 294; his agreement with Hyde, 294; is refused admission to Hull, 295; declares Militia ordinance illegal, 295; summons Royal officers to York, 295; raises Standard at Nottingham, 297; sends messages to the Houses, 297; describes Essex as traitor, 298; at Edghill, Brentford and Turnham Green, 299.

CHARLES, LEWIS, ELECTOR PALATINE, assumes title on death of his father, Frederick V, 165; accompanies Charles to House of Commons, 279.

CHRISTIAN IV, OF DENMARK, brother-in-law of James I, makes military alliance with him, 16.

CLOTWORTHY, SIR JOHN, put up by Pym against Strafford, 189; Clarendon's opinion of, 189; charges against Strafford, 192; informs Pym of Suckling's plot, 212; member of Commission on Army Plot, 250; his servant O'Conolly discloses Irish danger to Lords Justices, 250.

COKE, SIR EDWARD, his views on Spanish marriage treaty, 11-12; M.P. for Liskeard in 1621, 21; speeches on Sheppard, 28-29; on Floyd, 31; on constitutional question concerning Floyd's punishment, 34; hairsplitting, 35; on monopolies, 38; on Michell, 42; motion regarding Michell, 42-43; reports on punishing of Mompesson, 44; reminiscences of Gunpowder Plot, 51; financial report, 52; is for refusing supply, 61; questions King's gracious intent, 78; sent to Tower, 80; pricked as Sheriff, 115; Committee to draw up Bill on Liberty of Subject, 137; on Petition of Right, 139.

COKE, SIR JOHN, Secretary of State, reports to House of Commons, 136; demurs from Pym's view, 138; gives King's message to House, 147.

COKE, CLEMENT, senseless remark of, deprecates seditious intent, 120.

CONVOCATION, grant of six subsidies by, 180.

INDEX

COTTINGTON, SIR FRANCIS, to go to Madrid with Prince Charles, his reluctance, 82; Chancellor of the Exchequer, 223; Master of the Wards, 224.
COVENTRY, LORD KEEPER, SIR THOMAS, addresses Charles I's Second Parliament, 1626, 116; reminds Commons of difference between counsel and control, 122.
CRANFIELD, LIONEL, EARL OF MIDDLESEX, 59; career of, 91-93; impeachment and sentence, 93; silence of Pym concerning, 94; comparison of the two, 94.
CREW, RANULPH, Speaker of Addled Parliament of 1614, 24; Chief Justice, dismissed on matter of Forced Loan, 133.
CREW, THOMAS, speaks in favour of Petition, 67; Speaker of James I's Fourth Parliament, 85; Speaker of Charles I's First Parliament, 102.
CROMWELL, OLIVER, moves second reading of Bill for ensuring regular assembly of Parliaments, 194; with younger Vane brings in Root and Branch Bill, 235; Clarendon's anecdote of, 263 and 266; and the Levellers, 280; dismissal of Long Parliament by, 285; victory of, at Gainsborough, 303.
CULPEPPER, SIR JOHN, on monopolies, 166; says Ireland must be defended, 253; against Grand Remonstrance, 263; protests against printing it, 266; is made Chancellor of the Exchequer, 275; joins King in York, 295; sent to Commons by Charles, 297; his violent reception in House, 298.

DEFENSORES, under Letter of Majesty of Bohemia, 10.
DELFT, murder of William the Silent by Balthazar Gerard, in 1584.
DERING, SIR EDWARD, persuaded to introduce Root and Branch Bill, 235; against Grand Remonstrance, 263; expelled from the House, 290.
D'EWES, SIR SIMON, rebukes Pym, 231; advises procedure by ordinance, 241; opposes Pym, 253; reports Pym's speech on Danger, 277; makes his will, 286; and Pym's treatment of the Women Petitioners, 305.
DIGBY, JOHN, EARL OF BRISTOL, treats about Palatinate, 14; his knowledge of European affairs, 60; speech after adjournment, 60; returns to Madrid, 80; recalled, 84.
DIGBY, GEORGE (son of John Digby), speaks against Attainder of Strafford, 205-209; his speech denounced, 209; riot in the House arising from another speech of his, 209; is made a Peer by Charles, 209; declared a delinquent by the Commons, 210; ridicules London petitioners, 229; his charge against Mandeville, 276.
DIKE, JOHN, London Merchant of Billiter Street, Deputy Governor of Providence Island, 151; bondsman for, 152.
DONCASTER, JOHN HAY, VISCOUNT DONCASTER, EARL OF CARLISLE, treats about Palatinate, 14; at Charles' wedding, 101.

ELIOT, SIR JOHN, his works and character, 87-8; May's view of, 88; youthful irregularity, 88; obtains patronage of Buckingham, 89; speaks on the proposed war, 89; monstrous proposal, 90; rhetorical attack on Spain, 91; speech on Religion, 102; foolish attack on

INDEX

Wentworth, 108; Wentworth's opinion of, 109; demands enquiry into Cadiz expedition, 116; attacks Buckingham, 121; advises a Remonstrance, 122; a manager of Buckingham's impeachment, 123; his epilogue, 124-5; his qualities, 126; imprisoned in the Tower, 126; released, 127; in Third Parliament of Charles I, 135; makebate, 137; Committee to draw up Bill on Liberty of the Subject, 137; enumerates grievances, 140; on Tunnage and Poundage, 148; burns his declaration, 149; imprisoned and dies in Tower, 150.

ELIZABETH, QUEEN OF ENGLAND, a Politique, 3; contrast between her position and that of her successor, 3.

ELIZABETH, PRINCESS PALATINE, QUEEN OF BOHEMIA, marriage of, 4-5; strong Protestant convictions of, 5.

ERLE, SIR WALTER, speaks on plots, 216; compels Strode to fly, 281.

ESSEX, ROBERT DEVEREUX, Third Earl of, second in command of Cadiz Expedition, 113; misbehaviour during, 114; serves in First Bishops' war, 174; brutal speech of, concerning Strafford, 204; commands Parliament's Guard, 248; made Commander-in-Chief of Parliamentary forces, 297; in second year of the war, 302; censured by Houses, 306; his quarrel with Waller, 306.

FABRICIUS, Secretary to Regents at Prague, defenestration of, 10.

FALKLAND, LUCIUS CAREY, VISCOUNT, questions propriety of Pym's action against Strafford, 191; Pym's reply to, 191; opposes Root and Branch Bill, 235; severe reply of, to Hampden, 248; protests against phrase *Bellum Episcopale*, 263; is made Secretary, 275; joins King in York, 295; death of, 306

FERDINAND OF STYRIA, Carinthia and Carniola, 7-8; character, 9; elected King of Bohemia, 9; guarantees Letter of Majesty, 9; deposed from throne of Bohemia, elected Emperor, 12; denounces election of Frederick to Kingdom of Bohemia, 13; routs Frederick at White Hill, 14; overawes Bohemia, 14; puts Frederick to ban of the Empire, 14.

FINCH, SIR JOHN, Speaker of Charles I's Third Parliament, forbids Eliot to proceed, 141; seeks audience of Charles, 142; held in chair by force, 149; Lord Keeper, impeached, 193; flies, 223.

FINCH, SIR HENEAGE, Recorder of London, Speaker of Charles I's Second Parliament, 1626, 116.

FLOYD, EDWARD, Barrister-at-Law, prisoner in Fleet, Roman Catholic, 30; his alleged scurrility, 31-2; punishments suggested, 32-3; sentence on, 33; his sentence revised by Lords, 35.

FREDERICK V, ELECTORAL PRINCE PALATINE, KING OF BOHEMIA, marriage to Elizabeth, daughter of James I, 5; character, 9; succeeds his father, 1610, 9; falls under influence of Anhalt, 9; votes as Elector for Ferdinand, 12; accepts throne of Bohemia, 12; is crowned, 13; called upon to retire, 13; defeated at White Hill, 13; flies, and is put to ban of the Empire, 14; death of, 165.

GLYN, JOHN, speech of against Strafford, 202.

GODOLPHIN, SIDNEY, twits Pym and has to apologise, 271.

348 INDEX

GOLDEN BULL of Emperor Charles IV, 1356, remodels Empire in interest of great feudatories, 6.
GONDOMAR, *v.* sub. ACUÑA.
GUNPOWDER PLOT spoils James' foreign policy and provokes Puritan intolerance, 4.
GORING, SIR GEORGE, afterwards Lord, suggests punishment for Floyd, 33; and Portsmouth, 217.

HAKEWILL, WILLIAM, distinguished lawyer, allusion to Pym, 16 and 45; in matter of Floyd, 34; in matter of Mompesson, 44.
HAMPDEN, JOHN, Adventurer for Providence Island, 126; his papers seized, 164; refuses to pay Ship Money, 168; case of, decided, 168; treasonable dealings with Scottish Commissioners, 177; canvasses counties, 178; supports Root and Branch Bill, 236; sent as spy on King in Scotland, 241; sends letters from Scotland, 247; returns, his surprise, 248; on Grand Remonstrance, 265; prevents riot in House, 266; impeached, 275; arranges great deputation from Bucks, 290; death of, 302.
HARLEY, SIR ROBERT, comments on Floyd's case, 33; presents petition for reform of Episcopacy, 228.
HASELRIG, SIR ARTHUR, introduces the Bill of Attainder against Strafford, 201; and presses Root and Branch Bill upon Dering, 235; one of Commons to present Grand Remonstrance, 270; introduces Militia Bill, 271; impeached, 275.
HEATH, MR., SOLICITOR-GENERAL, advises explanatory clause in Petition, 67; defends the Government, 111; speaks concerning the *St. Peter,* 119.
HENDERSON, ALEXANDER, a Scottish Commissioner in England, desires abolition of Episcopacy in England, 232; indignation thereat, 232 and 236.
HENRIETTA MARIA, QUEEN, marriage and arrival in England, 101; her French attendants make mischief and are dismissed by Charles, 130; denounced by mobs, 217; attacked in the Ten Propositions, 238; persecuted by Commons, 240; is not allowed to go to Spa, 240; persuades Charles to seize the Five Members, 280; lets this be known, 280; sails for United Provinces, 293; sells Crown Jewels and buys munitions of war, 296.
HENRY, PRINCE OF WALES, eldest son of James I, suggested marriage for, aggressive Protestant, death, 1612, 5.
HOBBY, SIR THOMAS POSTHUMOUS, M.P. for Ripon, 1621, hurt by Sheppard's reference to Justices of the Peace, 28.
HOLLAND, HENRY RICH, EARL OF, at Charles' marriage in Paris, 101; Governor of Company of Adventurers for Providence Island, 151-2; serves in First Bishops' War, 174; ordered by Commons to secure Hull, 241.
HOLLES, DENZIL, with Valentine, holds Speaker Finch down in chair, recites Eliot's protestation from memory, 149; imprisoned, submits, 150; proposal to make him Secretary of State, 224; on Grand Remonstrance, 265; impeached, 275.
HORSEY, SIR JEREMY, M.P. for Eastlow, 1621, tells a terrible tale, 29; wishes to slit Floyd's tongue, 32.

INDEX 349

HOTHAM, SIR JOHN, takes the forged letter to Lords, 290 ; is appointed to charge of Magazine at Hull, 290 ; refuses to admit Charles into Hull, 295.

IRELAND, James sends three members to, 81 ; Wentworth in, 175-176 ; Rebellion breaks out in, 249.

JAMES I, KING, lover of peace, 3 ; his position contrasted with that of Elizabeth, 3 ; his objects at accession, 11 ; marriage treaty with Spain, 11 and 14 ; attitude towards Bohemian Revolution and Frederick, 13 and 14 ; makes military alliance with Denmark, 15 ; summons his Third Parliament, 15 ; opens it, 20 ; addresses it, 21-23 ; raises constitutional question regarding Floyd, 34 ; refers sentence to Lords, 35 ; reference to the thief at Newark, 43 ; underestimates his necessities, 51 ; desires further subsidies, 53 ; resolves on adjournment, 54 ; is displeased with Pym, 64 ; refuses audience to, and demands explanation from Pym, 65 ; his angry letter to Speaker Richardson from Newmarket, 69-70 ; receives Petition jovially, 73 ; his answer to Commons Petition, 74-6 ; his second letter to Commons, 77 ; his third letter, 78 ; dissolves his Third Parliament, 79 ; tears Protestation out of Commons Journals, 79 ; his grief at Charles' and Buckingham's proposed journey to Madrid, 82 ; desire for their return, 83 ; orders writs for his Fourth Parliament, 84 ; addresses it, 84-5 ; receives joint committee at Theobalds, 85 ; his offer, 86 ; and impeachment of Cranfield, 93 ; death of, 98 ; his interview with Montague and opinion of his book, *The New Gag*: he sanctions his "*Appello Caesarem*," 105.

JESSOP, WILLIAM, Secretary to the Company of Adventurers for Providence Island, 151.

JUXON, WILLIAM, President of St. John's College, Oxford, Bishop of London, Treasurer, 170 ; repudiates Vane's stolen document, 200 ; advises Charles not to abandon Strafford, 217.

LAUD, WILLIAM, Dean of Gloucester, Bishop of St. David's, 58 ; refuses consecration by Abbot, 58 ; sometime President of St. John's College, Oxford, 59 ; his dream concerning Williams, 99-100 ; on unity, 103 ; Primate, 170 ; metropolitical visitation by, 171 ; activity against Puritans, is Head of Commission to control English Colonies, 171 ; accompanies Charles to Scotland, 173 ; introduces new Liturgy and Canons there, 173 ; induces Convocation to grant six subsidies, 180 ; his impeachment moved by Pym, 194 ; his farewell to Strafford, 219 ; Articles of Impeachment against, 232 ; Pym's speech upon, 233 ; his last years, 234 ; amused at downfall of Williams, 274.

LA ROCHELLE, Huguenots besieged in, 129 ; Buckingham fails before, 132 ; surrenders to King of France, 147.

LECTURERS. Clerks in Holy Orders without any cure of souls, 171.

LENTHALL, WILLIAM, Speaker of Long Parliament, 186 ; receives Charles in House, 282 ; replies to his questions, 283.

INDEX

LESLIE, ALEXANDER, in command of Scottish rebels, 174 ; crosses Tweed at Coldstream, 182 ; is made Earl of Leven, 242.
LETTER OF MAJESTY, guarantee of Protestants in Bohemia, 9.
LOAN, THE FORCED, of 1626, opposition to, 131 ; Chief Justice Crew, dismissed, 133 ; The Five Knights refused Habeas Corpus, 133.
LONDONERS' PETITION, 194.
LUNSFORD, COLONEL, appointed Lieutenant of Tower : removed, 272 ; drives mob out of Westminster Hall, 273.
LYTTELTON, LORD KEEPER, refuses to use Great Seal without King's express instructions, 241 ; joins King at York, 295.

MANDEVILLE, LORD, Earl Kimbolton, Duke of Manchester, admitted Adventurer for Providence Island, 161 ; resides at Chelsea, 255 ; impeached, 275-6.
MANWARING, DR. ROGER, two sermons of, 143 ; *Religion and Allegiance* of, 144 ; Commons' declaration concerning, 144 ; Pym's report upon, 144-146 ; sentenced by Lords, 146 ; pardoned and promoted by Charles, 146.
MARTIN, HENRY, curious report on disappearance of the younger Vane's stolen document, 200 ; says Petition of Right binds Kings not Parliaments, 300.
MARTINITZ, Regent at Prague, defenestration of, 10 ; his cry, 10.
MATTHIAS, EMPEROR, succeeded Rudolph II in 1612, 7 ; failed to suppress Bohemian Reformers, 8 ; died March 20, 1618.
MAXIMILIAN OF BAVARIA. (See Bavaria.)
MAYNARD, JOHN, his jibe at Edmund Waller, 204.
MILITIA BILL, THE, introduced, 271-2.
MICHELL, SIR FRANCIS, Monopolist, as Justice of the Peace, 42 ; sentence on, 42 ; constitutional question thereby raised, 42.
MOMPESSON, SIR GILES, Monopolist, constitutional issue raised in case of, 34 ; M.P. for Great Bedwin, 40 ; character connections and system, 41 ; escapes, 43.
MONOPOLIES considered by Commons in 1621, 38; nature of, 39-40; abolished by Elizabeth, 40 ; abolished in 1624, 94-5 ; Pym's contribution to debate upon, 95 ; revival of in new form, 166 ; Culpepper on, 166-7.
MONTAGUE, RICHARD, his cures, 103 ; his *New Gag for an Old Goose*, 104 ; his ecclesiastical position, 104 ; interview with Abbot and with James, 105; his second book, *Appello Caesarem*, 105; Pym's report on, 105-6 ; Charles makes him Chaplain in Ordinary and sends message to Commons, 106 ; further proceedings of Commons regarding, 107 ; political questions raised in case of, 107 ; two decisions of Bishops concerning, 117 ; Pym's report upon, 117-118 ; Commons pray for his punishment ; Charles makes him Bishop of Chichester, 118; special pardon granted him and *Appello Caesarem* called in, 118.

NEWPORT, MONTJOY BLOUNT, EARL OF, Constable of the Tower, undertakes murder of Strafford, ordered to reside in Tower, 241.
NOY, WILLIAM, in matter of Floyd, 34 ; made chairman of committee on King's letter, 71 ; revives Ship Money, 167.

INDEX

ORDINANCE of two kinds, 241.
OXFORD, Parliament of, 1625, adjourned to, 109; meets in Christ Church Hall, 109; dissolved, 112.

PARIS, Murder of Henri IV by Ravaillac, 1572, 4.
PARKER, MATTHEW, Archbishop of Canterbury, his *via media*, 2.
PHELIPS, SIR ROBERT, suggests punishment for Floyd, 32; on Referees, 47; fears another Gunpowder Plot, 50; bold speech against King's proposed adjournment, 55; is for refusing Supply, 61; encourages Commons to discuss Spanish Treaties, 66; motion on reception of angry King's letter, 70; speaks on " this soul-killing letter," 71; approves King's answer to their Petition, 76; sent to the Tower, 80; speech on Supply in Parliament of 1625, 108; attacks the Government, 111; attacks Buckingham personally, 112.
PENNINGTON, ISAAC, Alderman of London presents petition against Bishops, 225; brings Guard for Houses, 278.
PENNINGTON, SIR JOHN, in command of the eight ships lent to France, 109; his fleet returns, 112.
PERROT, SIR JAMES, his detective Communion, 25; his father, 25; his wife a Recusant, 26; moves to make a declaration concerning Palatinate, 57; moves for a committee on Religion and Privileges, 76; sent to Ireland, 80.
PROPOSITIONS, THE TEN, 238-240.
PROPOSITIONS, THE NINETEEN, 296-7.
PROTESTANT UNION of German Princes under Elector Palatine, 7.
PROTESTATION OF THE COMMONS in 1621, on their Privileges suggested by Brooke, 76; passed, 78; text of in Appendix VIII, gist of, 78.
PROVIDENCE AND HENRIETTA ISLANDS of the Bahamas group in West Indies, first voyage of Adventure to, 151; Patent of Incorporation to Company of Adventurers for, 152; powers of Company 152; new patent for trading with mainland desired by, 159.
PRYNNE, WILLIAM, punishment of, 170; works diligently for destruction of Laud, 223.
PYM, JOHN (1584-1643), spokesman of Puritan rancour, 4; birth and education, 15; occupation, marriage, 16; no lawyer, 16-17; not in Addled Parliament of 1614, 17 and Appendix I; three documents relating to his work as Receiver of Wiltshire, 18; his wife and children, 19 and Appendix IX; befriended by Earl of Bedford, 19; M.P. for Calne in 1621, 21; reports on Sheppard's speech, 28-29; speaks on Floyd's case, 37-38; appointed to view Clerk's book, 45; and case of Mompesson, 45-6; speaks on Bennett's case, 48; on Subsidy Bill, 52; speaks on proposed adjournment, 55-6; again speaks on same, 56; speaks on Supply and moves for an association, 61-62; again in committee, would have Papists treated as madmen, 63; incurs James' displeasure, 64; asks audience of James, is refused, 64; summarises his two speeches for James, 65; his faculty of interpretating ordinary opinion and of organising such opinion effectively, 66; chiefly responsible for

352 INDEX

draft of Petition, 67; moves for engrossing the Petition, 68; pacifies House, 71; speaks in committee on King's letter, wishes to know who those fiery turbulent spirits are, 71-2; does not wish Speaker to go to King, 72; does not go himself, 72; reads over the Petition, 73; advises as to Privileges, 78; imprisoned, 81; speak on proposed war, 90; recalls House to business, 91; and abolition of monopolies, 95; his work in Parliament of 1624, 96-8 and Appendix III, and charges against the Bishop of Norwich, 97; and charges against Montague, 98; supports Strode's motion for a fast and would have it general, 103; reports on Montague's *New Gag for an old Goose*, 104; Reports for committee on Montague, 105-6.; servant may stay suit, 116; moves for wider reference for committee on Religion and is empowered to view Clerk's book weekly, 116; reports on Montague, 117-18; one of managers of impeachment of Buckingham, 118 and 123; his share therein, 123-4; wise advice to House, 126; pays forced loan, 132; committee on privileges, 134; speaks on Grievances, 135; again, 136; committee to draw up Bill on Liberty of Subject, 137; speech on Charles' answer, 138; speaks on phrase "sovereign power," 139-140; and Manwaring's sermons and book, 144-6; on grievances in "Religion," 147-8; takes wider view than Eliot of Privilege, 148-9; out of politics, 150; Treasurer of Company of Adventurers for Providence Island, 151-163; Deputy Governor, 163-164; his papers seized, 164; influence over Henry Vane the younger, 173; story of his decision to go to New England, 173; great speech at opening of Short Parliament, 177-9; plans made at his lodgings in Gray's Inn Lane, 178; charges Lords with breach of privilege, 180; plot with Scottish Commissioners, 180; plottings with Scots about the time of the Short Parliament, 181; views for Long Parliament and his policy therein, 184; alleged threat to Wentworth, 186; Committee on Strafford, 189; puts up Clotworthy against Strafford, 189; speech against Strafford, 189-90; replies to Falkland's objection, 191; obtains committal of Strafford from Lords, 191; carries to Lords nine charges against Strafford, 192; his sinister answer to Jermyn, 193; moves impeachment of Laud, 194; Committee to consider Bill for regular assembly of Parliament, 194; presents detailed charges against Strafford, 195; his speech against Strafford, 196-7; the younger Vane's stolen document disappears from his lodging, 201; question of his responsibility for attainder of Strafford, 201; answers Strafford's defence, 202-3; breaks down, 203; Digby's charge against, 207; on the attainder of Strafford, 213; speaks on plots, 216; proposal that he should be Chancellor of the Exchequer, 223; received twice by Charles, his views on "Root and Branch," 229-30; suggests that Londoners be compelled to lend, 229; is rebuked, 231; similar proposal previously, 231; speech for Laud's impeachment, 233; supports Root and Branch Bill, 236; carries the Ten Propositions to the Lords, 238; discloses reports of the "Incident," 244; reports for Committee sitting during recess, and from conference with Lords, 247; attempt on life of, 248-9; proposes to refuse help against rebels in Ireland, 251; Edmund Waller attacks him and is made to apologise, 251; his motion rejected, 252; another threat to King by, 252; carries motion, 253; presents the Grand Remonstrance to the King, 255; resides at Chelsea, 255; the Grand Remonstrance his work, 261; speaks again on Army Plot, 262; defends Grand Remonstrance, 264; obtains removal of Dorset's guard, 269; indignant, 270; obtains new guard, 270; threatens Lords, 271; supports rioters, 273; speaks of Plots and moves impeachment of the twelve Bishops, 274; offered Chancellorship of Exchequer; impeached, 275; his guilt, 277; speaks on public danger, 277; news arrives of sealing of his trunks and study, 278; learns of Charles' plans from Lady Carlisle, 280; takes refuge in city, 286; returns to Westminster, 287; attacks Lords, 291; his agents and methods, 293; one of the Committee of Safety, 297; howled down, 298; wrath against Charles, 298; desires an Association, 298; speech at the Guildhall, 299; vacillation of, 299; announces to City that the Houses have assumed power of direct taxation, 300; claims for Houses power to administer an oath, 300; fails to bring about national association with Scotland and to introduce an Excise, 300; carries proposal for foreign negotiations, 301; carries up to Lords impeachment of Queen, 301; his secret correspondence with her, 301; attacked by women, 304; makes new offensive alliance with Scots, 305; conveys censure on Essex, 306; adjusts quarrel of Essex and Waller, 306; opposes peace overtures, 306; receives mansion of Earl of Derby, 307; persuades House to accept Presbyterianism and sign the solemn League and Covenant, 307; dies, 308; funeral, 308-9; estimate of, 310-314.

RALEIGH, SIR WALTER, execution of, 1; and its meaning, 2.
RAVENSCROFT, WILLIAM, would spare Floyd flogging, 32; with Pym examines Popish books, 97.
REFEREES, Law officers who inspected proposed patents, 46.
REFORMATION, temporal issue raised by, 6.
REMONSTRANCE, THE GRAND, presented to Charles, 255; its contents, 256-61; carried, 265; motion that it be printed, 266.
RICH, SIR NATHANIEL, on Mompesson's case, 46; moves that Petition be presented to His Majesty, 68; sent to Ireland, 81; makes five propositions, 111; Pym selects him for his assistant in the impeachment of Buckingham, 123; asks Lords for restraint of Buckingham, 126; Committee to draw up Bill on Liberty of Subject, 137; plain speaking about King's answer, 138; another bold speech, 141; Adventurer for Providence Island, 151; Deputy Governor, 160; deceased, 162.
RICHARDSON, SIR THOMAS, Speaker of Parliament of 1621, receives angry letter from James, 69; himself moves for a committee, 71; question whether he shall be sent to the King, 72.
RUDOLPH II, EMPEROR, fails to suppress Bohemian Reformers, 8.
RUDYERD, SIR BENJAMIN, deprecates opposition to King's wish for adjournment, 54; summarises wishes of Commons, 87; Adventurer for Providence Island, 152; suggests diocesan councils of clergy, 229; against Grand Remonstrance, 263.
RUDYERD, WILLIAM, officer of Providence Island, 151; commander

of *Seaflower*, 153 ; accusations against and procedure thereupon, 154.
RUSHWORTH, JOHN, Clerk of the House of Commons, present on scaffold with Strafford, 218 ; reads plague letter, 249.
ROUS, SIR ANTHONY, step-father of Pym, 19, 152.
ROUS, ARTHUR, Minister to Providence Island, 154 ; painful details concerning, 158 ; " since deceased," 158.
ROUS, LIEUTENANT, officer of Providence Island, 151 ; at Pym's request pardoned for striking Forman, 159.

ST. PETER, case of the, 119.
ST. JOHN, OLIVER, Adventurer for Providence Island, 151-2 ; Counsel for Hampden in Ship Money case, 168 ; his views for Long Parliament, 184 ; draws up detailed charges against Strafford with Pym, 195 ; his brutal speech against Strafford, 204 ; made Solicitor-General, 224 ; probably author of Militia Bill, 272.
SANDYS, SIR EDWARD, wise counsel of, concerning Floyd, 33 ; regrets King's proposed adjournment of House, 54 ; arrested during adjournment, 59.
SAVOY, DUKE OF, has a plan for marriage of James' elder children, 5 ; is Anhalt's candidate for Empire, 12.
SAYE AND SELE, WILLIAM FIENNES, VISCOUNT, Adventurer for Providence Island, 152 ; his papers seized, 164 ; refuses to pay Ship Money, 168 ; refuses oath to fight, 174 ; proposed as Master of the Wards, 224.
SCOTLAND. Introduction of new Liturgy at Edinburgh : riots, 173 ; Charles in, 173 ; National League and Covenant signed, 174 ; Rebellion of, and First Bishops' War, 174 ; Scottish Commissioners in London and Adventurers' treasonable dealings with them, 177 and 181 ; Scottish Army under Leslie invades England, 182 ; Scots petition for an English Parliament, 183.
STRAFFORD, THOMAS WENTWORTH, EARL OF (see Wentworth), advises Charles to summon Parliament, 176 ; incurs hatred of Sir Henry Vane, 177 ; created Lord Lieutenant of Ireland, 177 ; his efforts there for the war against the Scots, 177 ; in command against Scots, 182 ; Pym's alleged threat to, 186 ; circle of his enemies, 188 ; summoned to London, 188 ; advises King to attack the plotters, 188 ; speech of Clotworthy against, 189 ; speech of Pym against, 189-90 ; enters House of Lords, 191 ; is committed by Lords on request of Pym, 191 ; his letter to his wife, 193 ; another, 195 ; presents his answer to charges, 195 ; his trial begins in Westminster Hall, 196 ; Pym's speech against, 196-7 ; he replies, 197 ; charges against him relating to England, 198 ; turn of feeling in favour of, 200 ; Bill of Attainder introduced, 201 ; defends himself, 202 ; receives in Tower letter from Charles, 211 ; advises Charles not to address the Houses, 211 ; writes to Charles offering his life, 214-16 ; asks to see Laud, 218 ; Rushworth's account of him, 218 ; his last meeting with Laud, 219 ; his reply to the Lieutenant, 219 ; speaks to the people, 220 ; to his brother, 220 ; is beheaded, 221.

INDEX 355

SELDEN, JOHN, arrested during adjournment, 59; a manager of Buckingham's impeachment, 123; produces the Petition of Right, 139; opposes Root and Branch Bill, 235; introduces three Bills limiting Prerogative, 236.

SEYMOUR, SIR FRANCIS, suggests punishment for Floyd, 32; holds that King has been misled, 71; would have House wary of its Privileges, 76; speech on Religion, 102; has no confidence in the Government, 111; attacks Buckingham by name, 112.

SHEPPARD, THOMAS, flippant speech of, 27-8; Pym's report thereupon, 28; removed from the House, 30.

SHIP MONEY revived, 167; Clarendon on, 167-8; Judges' sanction, 168.

SIBTHORPE, DR. ROBERT, sermon of, 143.

SKIPPON, PHILIP, appointed Commander of City trained bands, 287; at Turnham Green, 299.

SLAWATA, Regent at Prague, thrown out of window, 10.

STAR CHAMBER and other extra-ordinary Courts, 169; Clarendon thereupon, 169.

SOVEREIGN POWER, discussion on the phrase, 139-40; *Absolute Power*, Adventurers dislike to, 146.

STRODE, WILLIAM, his long imprisonment in Tower, 151; introduces Bill for regular assembly of Parliament, 194; his motion respecting Grand Remonstrance, 262; impeached, 275; refuses to fly, 281; moves to expel Culpepper, 298.

SUCKLING, SIR JOHN, poet, makes absurd proposals for a plot, 212.

THIRTY YEARS' WAR (1618-1648), 1; hampers James' foreign policy, 4; begins at Prague, 1618, May 25, 10; Battle of White Hill, 13; flight of Frederick, 14; failure of Mansfeld, 108; death of Mansfeld, 129; victories of Wallenstein, 129; Gustavus Adolphus in Pomerania, death of at Lützen, 165.

THURN, COUNT MATTHIAS, leader of Defensores at Prague, 10; hurls Slawata from window, 10.

TUNNAGE AND POUNDAGE, 148.

TURNER, DR., says Buckingham is cause of all their evils, 120; deprecates seditious intent, 120.

USSHER, JAMES, Bishop of Meath and Archbishop of Armagh, preaches before Commons, 26-27; advises King not to abandon Strafford, 217; conveys Strafford's message to Laud, 218; is on scaffold with Strafford, 221.

UTRAQUISTS, 8.

VANE, SIR HENRY, Secretary of State, his hatred of Strafford, 177; announces Charles' conditional willingness to abandon Ship Money, 180; and his son and the stolen document, 200; George Digby's reference to, 207.

VANE, SIR HENRY, (THE YOUNGER), 172; Pym's influence over, 173; a Republican, 185; and the stolen document, 200; brings in with Cromwell the Root and Branch Bill, 235; proposes to have Diocesan Commissioners instead of Bishops, 235.

INDEX

VERE, SIR HORACE, afterwards Lord, takes out English Volunteers to defend Lower Palatinate, 14.

WALLER, EDMUND, the poet, desires to know what are fundamental laws, 204; attacks Pym and is made to apologise, 251; his plot, 301; why he was not hanged, 301.

WALLER, SIR WILLIAM, Adventurer for Providence Island, 161; commands in West in second year of war, 302; quarrels with Essex, 306.

WARWICK, ROBERT RICH, EARL OF, Adventurer for Providence and Henrietta Islands, 151-2; resolves to go to Plantation, 162; his papers seized, 164.

WENTWORTH, SIR THOMAS, Knight of Shire of York, 21; views on Floyd's case, 37; deprecates violent opposition to King's proposed adjournment, 55; desires a committee of whole House on King's angry letter, 71; for postponement of session until Michaelmas, 102; contested election of, and Eliot's foolish speech on, 108; complains of depredations of pirates, 112; pricked as Sheriff, 115; his letter thereupon, 115; Earl of Clare to him, 116; refuses to pay forced loan, 130; letter concerning, 131; Baltimore advises, 131; committed by Privy Council and imprisoned, 132; Holles' letter to, about failure at La Rochelle, 132; takes lead against illegal acts of Government, 134; his view thereupon, 135; Committee to draw up Bill on Liberty of Subject, 137; suggests modification, 138; on common lawyers, 168; called to England by Charles, 174; his great work as Lord Deputy for Ireland, 175-6; created Earl of Strafford, 176. (See Strafford.)

WESTON, RICHARD, EARL OF PORTLAND, Chancellor of the Exchequer, warns Commons against dealing with high matters of State, 66; asks for immediate supply for Charles, 119; death of, 170.

WESTMINSTER ASSEMBLY of Divines, 305.

WILLIAMS, JOHN, Archbishop of York, Dean of Westminster, 26; opposes Commons wish that Ussher be preacher, silenced by James, 27; Bishop of Lincoln and Lord Chancellor, 58; refuses consecration by Abbot, 58; his speech after adjournment as Chancellor, 59; advises release of Sandys and the others, 61; replies to Speaker at opening of James I's Fourth Parliament, 85; at James' deathbed, 95; preaches his funeral sermon, 99; falls from favour, 99; reasons for this, 100; ceases to be Lord Keeper, 100; addresses Charles' First Parliament, 102; advises Charles to sacrifice Strafford, 217; proposes diocesan committees, 236; rabbled by mob, 273; and Bishop's Protest, 273; committed to Tower, 274.

Printed by Sir Isaac Pitman & Sons, Ltd., Bath.
(2217)

[Catalogue O]

A CATALOGUE

OF

GENERAL LITERATURE

PUBLISHED BY

SIR ISAAC PITMAN & SONS, LTD.

(*Incorporating Isbister & Co.*)

ANTHOLOGY, AUTOBIOGRAPHY, ART, BIOGRAPHY, ECCLESIOLOGY, FICTION, HISTORY, METALLURGY, NATURAL HISTORY, POETRY, CRITICISM AND LITERARY HISTORY, SCIENCE, SOCIOLOGY, TRAVEL, TOPOGRAPHY, ETC., ETC., ETC.

Other Catalogues may be obtained by applying to SIR ISAAC PITMAN & SONS, Ltd., 1 Amen Corner, London, E.C. (See abridged List at end of this Catalogue.)

SIR ISAAC PITMAN AND SONS, LTD.
LONDON, BATH, AND NEW YORK

CONTENTS

	PAGE
ANTHOLOGY	3
ANGLO-SAXON LIBRARY	3 & 4
ART	4 & 5
AUTOBIOGRAPHY	5
BIOGRAPHY	6-8
CATALOGUES	24
COLLECTIVE BIOGRAPHIES	8 & 9
DAINTY VOLUME LIBRARY	9
ECCLESIOLOGY	10
FICTION	10 & 11
HISTORY	11, 12 & 13
METALLURGY	13
MISCELLANEOUS	14-18
NATURAL HISTORY	14
PERIODICALS	24
POETRY, CRITICISM, AND LITERARY HISTORY	18
POLITICS	19
SCIENCE	20
SOCIOLOGY	20 & 21
TRAVEL, TOPOGRAPHY, AND SPORT	21-23

ANTHOLOGY, ETC.

ANTHOLOGY

THE SUNLIT ROAD: Readings in Verse and Prose for Every Day in the Year. By the Rev. W. GARRETT HORDER. In demy 16mo, cloth gilt, gilt corners, 3s. net; leather gilt, gilt corners, 4s. net.

"A dainty and delightful little 'day book' for quiet moments. It is the most charming book of its kind we have seen for a very long time, for Mr. Horder has given no day without a thought to crown it, a thought pure and sweet and true, to brighten the hours of workaday life."— *Lady*.

A BOOK OF THE LOVE OF JESUS. By ROBERT [HUGH BENSON. In foolscap 8vo, leather gilt, gilt top, 3s. 6d. net; cloth 2s. net.

"An anthology of some old Catholic devotions, slightly modernized, which will appeal to many by reason of its simplicity and beauty."—*To-Day*.

ANGLO-SAXON LIBRARY

THE ANGLO-SAXON LIBRARY OF ENGLISH AND AMERICAN CLASSICS. In fcap. 8vo, limp lambskin gilt, gilt top. With frontispieces. 2s. 6d. net each volume. Also in cloth 1s. 6d. per volume net.

> **THE REVERIES OF A BACHELOR:** Or, A Book of the Heart. By the late IK MARVEL. With an Introduction by ARLO BATES. (In limp lambskin only, 2s. 6d. net.)
>
> **ESSAYS BY RALPH WALDO EMERSON.** First Series. (In cloth only, 1s. 6d. net.)
>
> **ESSAYS BY RALPH WALDO EMERSON.** Second Series.
>
> **NATURE AND OTHER ADDRESSES AND LECTURES.** By RALPH WALDO EMERSON.
>
> **THE CONDUCT OF LIFE.** By RALPH WALDO EMERSON. With an introduction by ANDREW J. GEORGE, M.A.
>
> **THE AUTOCRAT OF THE BREAKFAST TABLE.** By OLIVER WENDELL HOLMES. With an Introduction by RICHARD BURTON.
>
> **THE PROFESSOR AT THE BREAKFAST TABLE.** By OLIVER WENDELL HOLMES. With an Introduction by RICHARD BURTON.
>
> **SOME LITERARY ESSAYS OF THOMAS BABINGTON MACAULAY.** Selected and edited by GEORGE A. WATROUS.

PITMAN'S CATALOGUE OF GENERAL LITERATURE

ANGLO-SAXON LIBRARY (contd.)

SOME HISTORICAL ESSAYS OF THOMAS BABINGTON MACAULAY. Selected and edited by GEORGE A. WATROUS.
NO CROSS NO CROWN. By WILLIAM PENN. With an Introduction by J. DEANE HILTON. (In cloth only, 1s. 6d. net.)

ART

OXFORD AND CAMBRIDGE. Delineated by HANSLIP FLETCHER. With an Introductory Chapter by the late J. WILLIS CLARK, M.A., Registrary of the University of Cambridge, and described by various writers, including : The Provost of King's, The Warden of Keble, W. H. Hutton, Edward Bell, Desmond Coke, Eric Parker, F. D. How, Athelstan Riley, T. A. Lacey, John Murray, John Buchan, The Warden of Wadham, Arthur Waugh, Arthur Reynolds, H. P. Stokes, Arthur Gray, E. B. Chancellor. In demy 4to, cloth gilt, gilt top, with about 60 illustrations. 21s. net.

" An excellent idea enabling us to compare in comfort the different styles followed by the architects of the two Universities."—*Evening Standard.*

GREAT PAINTERS OF THE 19th CENTURY AND THEIR PAINTINGS. By LÉONCE BÉNÉDITE, Keeper of the Musée National de Luxembourg. With over 400 illustrations and 13 coloured plates. In large demy 4to, cloth gilt, gilt top, 10s. 6d. net.

" It is a splendid survey of the progress of painting in Europe and America during the nineteenth century, and combines art criticism with biography in a scholarly and instructive manner.—*Western Mail.*

THE HISTORY OF MUSIC : A Handbook and Guide. By WALDO SELDEN PRATT. With 130 illustrations and three maps. In demy 8vo, cloth gilt. 7s. 6d. net.

" A most convenient and valuable work of reference . . . the book may be said to cover the whole extensive field to which it is devoted, in a remarkably thorough and comprehensive fashion."—*Westminster Gazette.* " Indispensable in the music-lover's library."—*Pall Mall Gazette.* " A book which for terseness and inclusiveness has never been equalled in music literature."—*Sheffield Telegraph.*

SEVEN ANGELS OF THE RENASCENCE : The Story of Art from Cimabue to Claude. By the late Sir WYKE BAYLISS, F.S.A. (*sometime President of the Royal Society of British Artists*), author of *The Likeness of Christ Rex Regum*, etc., with 40 plate illustrations. In demy 8vo, buckram gilt, gilt top, bevelled boards, 10s. 6d. net.

ART AND AUTOBIOGRAPHY.

ART (*contd.*)

COLOUR PRINTING AND COLOUR PRINTERS. By R. M. BURCH. With a chapter on Modern Processes by W. GAMBLE. With 23 colour prints and 8 half-tone illustrations. In super royal 8vo, cloth gilt. 12s. 6d. net.

"An important contribution to the history of colour printing, and should take its place as the best and most authoritative work on the interesting subject."—*British and Colonial Printer.*

"Though it is the first devoted to the subject, it has been done with a thoroughness and completeness which call for the heartiest recognition. . . . The thanks of everyone interested in the subject are due to Mr. Burch for the painstaking labour he must have devoted to the production of his book. It will certainly become a classic."—*British Journal of Photography.*

"In his excellent work recently published on this subject—a work which is to be heartily commended for the thorough knowledge it displays of colour printing in all its phases as well as for the clear and pleasant style in which this knowledge is communicated—Mr. Burch has traced the history of the colour print from the first doubtful experiments of the Fifteenth Century down to the present day."—*Morning Post.*

AUTOBIOGRAPHY

THE RECOLLECTIONS OF A HUMOURIST. Grave and Gay. By the late ARTHUR À BECKET (*late Assistant Editor of "Punch."*) With Photogravure Portrait. In demy 8vo, cloth gilt, gilt top, 12s. 6d. net.

NEW ZEALAND REVISITED. Recollections of the Days of My Youth. By the Right Hon. Sir JOHN ELDON GORST. With 16 illustrations. In demy 8vo, cloth gilt, gilt top, 12s. 6d. net.

"Mature and mellow with the judgment of a wise and far-reaching career. . . . Full of the fruits of keen observation and mature judgment. . . . The author's descriptions are bright and stimulating to the fancy."—*Daily Telegraph.*

REMINISCENCES OF MY LIFE. By Sir CHARLES SANTLEY. In demy 8vo, cloth gilt, gilt top, with 15 illustrations, 16s. net.

"Not a trace of the weary veteran is discernible in this entertaining volume, to the intrinsic interest of which its author's perennial youthfulness of spirit and almost boyish love of fun add a peculiar and an irresistible charm."—*The World.*

MY WORK IN LONDON. By ARTHUR W. JEPHSON, M.A., *Hon. Canon of Southwark, Rector of Ecton; Sometime Curate of Croydon, Vicar of St. John's, Waterloo Road, Vicar of St. John's, Walworth.* In crown 8vo, cloth gilt, with portrait, 3s. 6d. net.

"It is a work full of practical hints for social work among the very poor, it is written with admirable directness and vigour, and is full of lessons for town workers. Here is a rousing book touching every aspect of Church work, and it deserves to be read far and wide."—*Contemporary Review.*

PITMAN'S CATALOGUE OF GENERAL LITERATURE

BIOGRAPHY

BOSWELL'S JOHNSON. (*See* " Life of Samuel Johnson.")

JOHN BUNYAN : His Life, Times and Work. By the Rev. JOHN BROWN, B.A., D.D. With portrait and illustrations by WHYMPER. Cheap edition. In demy 8vo, cloth gilt, 7s. 6d.

" The best life of John Bunyan."—*Literary World.*

(*See also* Dainty Volume Library, page 9.)

THE CAMBRIDGE APOSTLES. By Mrs. CHARLES BROOKFIELD. With twelve full-page illustrations. In demy 8vo, cloth gilt, gilt top, 21s. net.

" This book—not one for the casual reader but one to be loved and remembered by serious men—conveys without effort a wonderful impression of the commanding ability, the sincere and noble ideals, the loftiness of purpose of the Apostles."—*Morning Leader.*

MRS. GASKELL. Haunts, Homes, and Stories. By Mrs. ELLIS H. CHADWICK. In royal 8vo, cloth gilt, gilt top, photogravure frontispiece, and 38 other illustrations. 16s. net.

" The volume is certain of an enduring place among those which deal with the literary history of this country, and it is certainly indispensable to any who wish to understand the woman of whose life it tells, or the value of her work and influence . . . indeed, a sympathetic and faithful picture not only of Mrs. Gaskell, but also of the days in which she lived."—*Manchester Daily Despatch.*

THE COUNTESS OF HUNTINGDON AND HER CIRCLE. By SARAH TYTLER. With photogravure portrait and eight other illustrations. In demy 8vo, cloth gilt, gilt top, 12s. 6d. net.

THE LIFE OF DANTE. By the late E. H. PLUMPTRE, D.D., Dean of Wells. Edited by ARTHUR JOHN BUTLER. In fcap. 8vo, lambskin gilt, 2s. 6d. net. Also in cloth, 1s. 6d. net, and paper, 1s. net.

GEORGE FOX'S JOURNAL. (*See* Dainty Volume Library, page 10.)

BIOGRAPHY

BISHOP WALSHAM HOW. A Memoir. By his Son, FREDERICK DOUGLAS HOW. Cheap Edition. In crown 8vo, cloth gilt, 6s.

"Extremely well done . . . altogether a book which cannot be read without profit and encouragement."—*Guardian.*

THE LIFE OF SAMUEL JOHNSON, LL.D. By JAMES BOSWELL. Newly edited with notes by ROGER INGPEN. With 568 illustrations, including 12 photogravure plates, fully indexed. In two vols., crown 4to, half morocco, 21s. net. (Also in two vols., handsome cloth gilt, 18s. net.)

"A singularly complete and attractive edition. The greatest judgment has been shown in selecting pictures which should illustrate Johnson's period, and bring before the reader's eye the actual features of the men and women among whom he moved. Altogether the New 'Boswell' is one which will be certain to secure a fresh band of admirers for a work which will ever remain one of the treasures of our literature."—*Westminster Gazette.*

GEORGE MACDONALD. A Biographical and Critical Appreciation. By JOSEPH JOHNSON. In crown 8vo, cloth gilt, 2s. 6d. net.

FRIDTJOF NANSEN. By JACOB B. BULL. A book for the young. Translated from the Norwegian by the Rev. MORDAUNT R. BERNARD, one of the translators of *Farthest North*. Illustrated. In crown 8vo, 2s. 6d.

THE LIFE OF NELSON. By ROBERT SOUTHEY. In fcap. 8vo, leather gilt, gilt top, 2s. 6d. net.

DANIEL O'CONNELL : HIS EARLY LIFE AND JOURNAL, 1795-1802. Edited with an introduction and explanatory notes by ARTHUR HOUSTON, LL.D., K.C. With three full-page plate illustrations. In demy 8vo, cloth gilt, gilt top, 12s. 6d. net.

THE LIFE OF SIR ISAAC PITMAN (Inventor of Phonography). By ALFRED BAKER. In demy 8vo, cloth gilt, gilt top, with about 50 illustrations, including photogravure and steel plates, 7s. 6d.

"The book is very well done. It gives a life-like picture of a strenuous reformer, an original personality, an inventor to whom every newspaper, every public body, and every great business house owes an incalculable debt."—*Christian World.*

PITMAN'S CATALOGUE OF GENERAL LITERATURE

LIFE OF REGINALD POLE. By MARTIN HAILE. Second, Revised, and Cheaper edition. In demy 8vo, cloth gilt, gilt top, with eight illustrations, 7s. 6d. net.

" An excellent book, based on a first-hand acquaintance with documents, some of which are here utilised for the first time. It gives a vivid and most faithful picture of the last Archbishop of Canterbury who acknowledged the See of Rome."—*Daily Chronicle.*

THE LETTERS OF PERCY BYSSHE SHELLEY. Containing about 480 letters. Collected and edited by ROGER INGPEN. With 42 illustrations and two photogravures. New and cheaper edition, with corrections and additional matter. In two volumes, large crown 8vo, cloth gilt, gilt top, 12s. 6d. net. Hand-made paper *edition de luxe*, half leather, large demy 8vo, 21s. net.

" Mr. Ingpen has done all that can be done to provide us with a perfect edition of one of the most interesting series of letters in English literature. The edition is worthy of the magnificent material with which it deals."—*Daily News.*

THE LIFE AND WORK OF BISHOP THOROLD. Rochester, 1877-91 ; Winchester, 1891-95. Prelate of the most noble Order of the Garter. New and cheap edition. By C. H. SIMPKINSON, M.A. In crown 8vo, cloth gilt, gilt top, 6s.

MRS. E. M. WARD'S REMINISCENCES. Edited by ELLIOTT O'DONNELL. In royal 8vo, cloth gilt, gilt top, with six photogravure plates, 12s. 6d. net.

" Mrs. E. M. Ward throughout all these pages displays a wide sympathy, a charming personality, and an interesting acquaintance with men and things which make her book a sweet, wholesome, and delightful volume . . . . will win an established place among the records of the Victorian Era."—*Daily Telegraph.*

COLLECTIVE BIOGRAPHIES

GREAT ASTRONOMERS. By Sir ROBERT BALL. Illustrated. In demy 8vo, cloth gilt, gilt top, 3s. 6d. net.

THE HEROIC IN MISSIONS. Pioneers in six fields. By the Rev. A. R. Buckland, M.A. In crown 8vo, cloth gilt, 1s. 6d.

MODERN PAINTERS AND THEIR PAINTINGS. By SARAH TYTLER. For the use of Schools and Learners in Art. In crown 8vo, quarter cloth gilt, 4s. 6d.

MUSICAL COMPOSERS AND THEIR WORKS. By the same Author. For the use of Schools and Students in Music. Revised. In crown 8vo, quarter cloth gilt, 4s. 6d.

COLLECTIVE BIOGRAPHIES, ETC.

COLLECTIVE BIOGRAPHIES (*contd.*)

THE OLD MASTERS AND THEIR PICTURES. By the same Author. For the use of Schools and Learners in Art. New and enlarged edition. In crown 8vo, quarter cloth gilt, 4s. 6d.

THE ORGAN AND ITS MASTERS. A short account of the most celebrated organists of former days, and of the present time, together with a brief sketch of the development of organ construction, organ music, and organ playing. By HENRY C. LAHEE. In large crown 8vo, cloth richly gilt, gilt top, with 14 full-page plate illustrations. 6s. net.

MODERN COMPOSERS OF EUROPE. Being an account of the most recent musical progress in the various European nations with some notes on their history, and critical and biographical sketches of the contemporary musical leaders in each country. By ARTHUR ELSON. In large crown 8vo, cloth gilt, gilt top, with 24 full-page plate illustrations. 6s. net.

PITMAN'S
DAINTY VOLUME LIBRARY

Each in fcap. 8vo, limp lambskin gilt, gilt top, with Photogravure Frontispiece, 2s. 6d. per volume net.

DANTE. THE DIVINA COMMEDIA AND CANZONIERE. Translated by the late DEAN PLUMPTRE. With Notes, Studies, Estimates, and Life. In five volumes.

THE LIFE OF DANTE. By the same Author. In one volume.

THE TRAGEDIES OF ÆSCHYLOS. Translated by DEAN PLUMPTRE. In two volumes.

THE TRAGEDIES OF SOPHOCLES. Translated by DEAN PLUMPTRE. In two volumes.

BOSWELL'S LIFE OF JOHNSON. (Abridged.) With an Introduction by G. K. CHESTERTON. In two volumes.

THE POETRY OF ROBERT BROWNING. By STOPFORD A. BROOKE, M.A., LL.D. In two volumes.

TENNYSON: HIS ART AND RELATION TO MODERN LIFE. By STOPFORD A. BROOKE, M.A., LL.D. In two volumes.

JOHN BUNYAN: HIS LIFE, TIMES AND WORK. By JOHN BROWN, D.D. In two volumes.

JOHN WESLEY'S JOURNAL. (Abridged.) With Appreciation by the Rt. Hon. AUGUSTINE BIRRELL, M.P. In two volumes.

GEORGE FOX'S JOURNAL. (Abridged.) With Introduction by Sir W. ROBERTSON NICOLL, M.A., LL.D. In two volumes.

NO CROSS, NO CROWN. By WILLIAM PENN. With an Introduction by J. DEANE HILTON. In one vol.

CLOUGH, ARNOLD, ROSSETTI, AND MORRIS: A Study. By STOPFORD A. BROOKE, M.A., LL.D. In one volume, with four illustrations, 306 pp., 3s. 6d. net.

PITMAN'S CATALOGUE OF GENERAL LITERATURE

ECCLESIOLOGY

ROODSCREENS AND ROODLOFTS. By F. BLIGH BOND, F.R.I.B.A., and The Rev. DOM BEDE CAMM, O.S.B. With over 88 full-page collotype reproductions, and upwards of 300 other beautiful illustrations. In demy 4to, two vols., handsome cloth gilt, gilt top, 32s. net.
"A magnificent work."—*Evening Standard.*

FICTION

THE SEPARATIST. By ANON. 6s.

BY WHAT AUTHORITY? By ROBERT HUGH BENSON. 6s.

THE LIGHT INVISIBLE. By ROBERT HUGH BENSON. 3s. 6d.

RICHARD RAYNAL, SOLITARY. By ROBERT HUGH BENSON. 3s. 6d.

THE KING'S ACHIEVEMENT. By ROBERT HUGH BENSON. 6s.

THE QUEEN'S TRAGEDY. By ROBERT HUGH BENSON. 6s.

THE SENTIMENTALISTS. By ROBERT HUGH BENSON. 6s.

A MIRROR OF SHALOTT. By ROBERT HUGH BENSON. 6s.

LORD OF THE WORLD. By ROBERT HUGH BENSON. 6s.

MY LORD OF ESSEX. The romantic episode of Cadiz. By FRANCES M. BROOKFIELD. With photogravure frontispiece. 6s.

MY LADY OF AROS. A Tale of Mull and the Macleans. By JOHN BRANDANE. With coloured frontispiece. 6s.

MEN OF THE MOSS-HAGS. By S. R. CROCKETT. Illustrated. 6s.

WOLFVILLE. By ALFRED HENRY LEWIS. Illustrated. 6s.

THE GOD OF HIS FATHERS. By JACK LONDON. Tales of the Klondyke. 6s.

THE SON OF THE WOLF. By JACK LONDON. Tales of the Far North. 6s.

ANNE OF GREEN GABLES. By L. M. MONTGOMERY. 6s.

ANNE OF AVONLEA. By the same author. Coloured frontispiece. 6s.

KILMENY OF THE ORCHARD. By the same Author. With four coloured illustrations. 6s.

THE STORY GIRL. By the same Author. With coloured frontispiece. 6s.

FICTION

FICTION (*contd.*)

PRINCESS JOYCE. By KEIGHLEY SNOWDEN. 6s.

THE GLORY OF THE CONQUERED. The Story of a Great Love. By SUSAN GLASPELL. 6s.

MY HEART AND STEPHANIE. By R. W. KAUFFMAN. With coloured frontispiece. 6s.

THE LEAD OF HONOUR. By NORVAL RICHARDSON. Coloured frontispiece. 6s.

GEORGE THORNE. By the same Author. With coloured frontispiece. 6s.

HISTORY

THE ENGLISH IN CHINA. Being an account of the Intercourse and Relations between England and China. From the year 1600 to the year 1843 and a summary of Later Developments. By J. BROMLEY EAMES, M.A., B.C.L. In demy 8vo, cloth gilt, gilt top, with maps and illustrations. 20s. net.

OUTLINES OF THE ECONOMIC HISTORY OF ENGLAND. A Study in Social Development. By H. O. MEREDITH, M.A., M.Com. In demy 8vo, cloth gilt, 5s. net.

THE CORONATION BOOK ; or, The Hallowing of the Sovereigns of England. By the Rev. JOCELYN PERKINS, M.A., *Sacrist and Minor Canon of Westminster Abbey*. In demy 8vo, cloth gilt, gilt top, with many illustrations by Mrs. Temple Perkins. 7s. 6d. net.

*****THE BRITISH MUSEUM : ITS HISTORY AND TREASURES.** A view of the origins of that great Institution, sketches of its Early Benefactors and Principal Officers, and a survey of the priceless objects preserved within its walls. By HENRY C. SHELLEY. *Author of " Inns and Taverns of Old London."* With fifty illustrations. Size 6½ in. by 9⅝ in., elaborate cloth gilt, gilt top, 12s. 6d. net.

THE ROMANTIC STORY OF THE MAYFLOWER PILGRIMS AND ITS PLACE IN THE LIFE OF TO-DAY. By A. C. ADDISON. With numerous original illustrations. Size 6½ by 9⅝ in., cloth gilt, gilt top, 7s. 6d. net.

A beautifully illustrated book, in which the Pilgrims are followed into the New World, their individual fortunes are traced out, and details are given of recent efforts to perpetuate their memory.

* *Ready shortly.*

PITMAN'S CATALOGUE OF GENERAL LITERATURE

HISTORY (contd.)

INNS AND TAVERNS OF OLD LONDON. Setting forth the historical and literary associations of those ancient hostelries, together with an account of the most notable coffee-houses, clubs, and pleasure gardens of the British metropolis. By HENRY C. SHELLEY. In large crown 8vo, cloth gilt, gilt top, with coloured frontispiece and 48 other illustrations. 7s. 6d. net.

OLD COUNTRY INNS. By HENRY P. MASKELL and EDWARD W. GREGORY. With 50 illustrations by the authors. In large crown 8vo, cloth gilt, gilt top, 7s. 6d. net.

"Messrs. Maskell and Gregory have written this history of theirs very well indeed. They classify the inns of England according to their origin, rating them as manorial, monastic, Church inns, and so on. They discourse in a pleasant gossipy strain on coaching inns, wayside inns, haunted inns, the inns of literature and art, historical and fanciful signs and curious signboards; of inn furniture, etc.—*Bookman.*

THE BEGINNINGS OF THE AMERICAN REVOLUTION. Based on Contemporary Letters, Diaries, and other Documents. By ELLEN CHASE. In royal 8vo, cloth gilt, gilt top, 1,500 pp. with 75 full-page plates. Three Vols. 25s. net.

"A serviceable contribution to historical literature, because it gives, with a minuteness and wealth of colour unapproached by any other work of the kind known to us, a panoramic view of the life of Massachusetts in the early stages of the Civil War. It is a social, political, military picture on a great scale. The scenes, the people, and their doings, their thoughts, the motives of their acts, are depicted with meticulous accuracy, often in the actual words of the actors in the drama."—*Birmingham Daily Post.*

A HUNDRED YEARS OF IRISH HISTORY. By R. BARRY O'BRIEN. With Introductions by JOHN E. REDMOND, M.P. New Edition. In crown 8vo, cloth, 184 pp., 1s. 6d. net.

"This book, so clear, so telling, so convincing, should be given a wide circulation. The author has conferred a boon upon all fair-minded men who, anxious to know the facts of Ireland's later history, will be delighted to read them in these pages instinct with interest and instruction. The book will do untold good."—*Catholic Times.*

MAKERS OF NATIONAL HISTORY. Edited by THE VEN. W. H. HUTTON, B.D. Each volume in this series—the aim of which is to do fuller justice to men whose lives have not hitherto been adequately dealt with—is in crown 8vo, cloth gilt, with a frontispiece, 3s. 6d. net.

HISTORY, JEUX D'ESPRIT, METALLURGY, ETC.

MAKERS OF NATIONAL HISTORY (*contd.*)

CARDINAL BEAUFORT. By the Rev. L. B. RADFORD, D.D.
"Studiously impartial . . . carefully written."—*Glasgow Herald.*

VISCOUNT CASTLEREAGH. By ARTHUR HASSALL, M.A.
"It is brilliantly written . . . exceptionally clear and vivid . . . a book which was needed."—*The Morning Leader.*

ARCHBISHOP PARKER. By W. M. KENNEDY, B.A.
"Exceedingly well conceived, clearly expressed, and compiled with great care."—*The Guardian.*

GENERAL WOLFE. By EDWARD SALMON.
"A picture and an estimate of Wolfe which could not be more complete."—*Canada.*

FRANCIS ATTERBURY, Bishop of Rochester (1662-1732). By the Very Rev. H. C. BEECHING, M.A., Litt.D., Dean of Norwich.
"A most delightful as well as a most valuable book."—*Guardian.*

EDWARD THE FOURTH. By LAURENCE STRATFORD, B.A.

THOMAS BECKET, Archbishop of Canterbury. By The Ven. W. H. HUTTON, B.D., Canon of Peterborough, and Archdeacon of Northampton.

THE DISSOLUTION OF THE MONASTERIES. As illustrated by the Suppression of the Religious Houses of Staffordshire. By FRANCIS AIDAN HIBBERT, M.A., *of St. John's College, Cambridge, Headmaster of Denstone.* In crown 8vo, cloth gilt, 5s. net.
"An erudite and scholarly contribution to local history which also throws some light on the larger problems connected with the Dissolution."—*Manchester Guardian.*

KNIGHTSBRIDGE AND BELGRAVIA. Their history, topography, and famous inhabitants. By E. BERESFORD CHANCELLOR. In super royal 8vo, cloth gilt, gilt top, with 20 illustrations, 20s. net.

METALLURGY, ETC.

AUSTRALIAN MINING AND METALLURGY. By DONALD CLARK, B.C.E., M.M.E. A detailed description of the Metallurgic Methods employed in the process of Ore Treatment and Gold Recovery. With numerous illustrations and diagrams. Royal 8vo, cloth gilt, 21s. net.

REFINING OF GOLD. By DONALD CLARK, B.C.E. In demy 8vo, cloth gilt, with illustrations, 12s. 6d. net.

THE METALLURGY OF TIN. By P. J. THIBAULT, F.C.S. (Lond.). With numerous illustrations. In demy 8vo, cloth gilt, 12s. 6d. net.

THE DREDGING OF GOLD PLACERS. By J. E. HODGSON, F.R.G.S. With 17 illustrations. In demy 8vo, cloth gilt, gilt top, 5s. net. Principally intended for Company Directors, Property Managers, Prospectors, and the investing public.

PITMAN'S CATALOGUE OF GENERAL LITERATURE

NATURAL HISTORY, ETC.

MY BACKYARD ZOO. A Course of Natural History. By the late Rev. J. C. WOOD. In crown 8vo, cloth gilt, 2s.
"Really a complete course of natural history."—*Times*.

THE A B C OF POULTRY. By E. B. JOHNSTONE. In crown 8vo, cloth, cheap edition, 1s. net.
"A capital addition to the many books devoted to the outdoor life."—*World*.

CATS FOR PLEASURE AND PROFIT. By Miss FRANCES SIMPSON. Third Edition. In crown 8vo, with 25 beautifully reproduced photographs of famous prize-winning cats. 2s. net.
"The author explains that her object has been 'to help those who desire to combine pleasure with profit.' This aim is very successfully achieved."—*Pall Mall Gazette*.

REPTILES OF THE WORLD. Tortoises and Turtles, Crocodilians, Lizards and Snakes of the Eastern and Western Hemispheres. By Professor RAYMOND L. DITMARS. With frontispiece in colour, and nearly 200 illustrations from photographs taken by the author. In royal 8vo, cloth gilt, gilt top. 20s. net.

BRITISH FERNS. A pocket help for the Student and Collector (comprising all the native species and showing where found). By FRANCIS G. HEATH. Size 6¼ in. by 3½ in., cloth, with 50 illustrations. 2s. net.

PEEPS INTO NATURE'S WAYS. By JOHN J. WARD. Being chapters on insect, plant and minute life. Illustrated from photographs and photo-micrographs taken by the Author. Cheaper Edition. In demy 8vo, cloth gilt, gilt top, 3s. 6d. net.

MISCELLANEOUS

BODY AND SOUL. By PERCY DEARMER, M.A. An Enquiry into the effects of Religion upon health with a description of Christian works of healing from the New Testament to the present day. Eighth Impression. In crown 8vo, cloth gilt, 6s. net.

COMMON COMMODITIES OF COMMERCE. Each handbook is dealt with by an expert writer. Beginning with the life history of the plant, or other natural product, he follows its development until it becomes a commercial commodity, and so on through the various phases of its sale on the market and its purchase by the consumer. Each is in crown 8vo, cloth, about 120 pp., with map, coloured frontispiece, chart and illustrations, 1s. 6d. net. Tea, from Grower to Consumer, by ALEXANDER IBBETSON. Coffee, from Grower to Consumer, by B. B. KEABLE. Cotton. From the Raw Material to the Finished Product. By R. J. PEAKE. Oil; Animal, Vegetable, Essential and Mineral. By C. AINSWORTH MITCHELL. Sugar—Cane and Beet. By GEO. MARTINEAU, C.B., and Rubber, Production and utilisation of the raw material. By C. BEADLE and H. P. STEVENS, M.A., Ph.D. Iron and Steel. Their production and manufacture. By C. HOOD. Silk. Its production and manufacture. By LUTHER HOOPER.
Other Volumes in preparation.

MISCELLANEOUS

CLERICAL HUMOUR OF OLDEN TIME. By F. D. How. Being Sketches of some clerical humorists between the Twelfth and the Eighteenth Centuries. In large crown 8vo, cloth gilt, gilt top, with frontispiece. 6s. net.

EDUCATION AND SOCIAL LIFE. By the Rev. J. WILSON HARPER, D.D. In crown 8vo, cloth, 4s. 6d. net. An attempt to show that the goal of education is social service.

FOR HOME SERVICE AND OTHER STORIES. By LYDE HOWARD. With coloured frontispiece and black and white illustrations. In f'cap 4to, cloth, decorated, coloured top, and end papers, 2s. 6d. net.

"This is one of the sweetest of this year's books. The tone is far above the average, and every touch is that of a master hand. The children's feelings and expressions are perfectly natural. We recommend this book with genuine pleasure."—*British Weekly.*

HOME GYMNASTICS FOR OLD AND YOUNG. By T. J. HARTELIUS, M.D. Translated and adapted from the Swedish by C. LÖFVING. With 31 illustrations. Fifth Edition, revised. With a prefatory note by ARTHUR A. BEALE, M.B. In stiff boards, 1s. 6d.

HOW TO CHOOSE A HOUSE. How to Take and Keep it. By CHARLES EMANUEL, M.A., and E. M. JOSEPH, A.R.I.B.A. In crown 8vo, cloth, with illustrations. Cheap edition, 1s. net.

"This book seems to us to contain well nigh all the information that a person desiring to acquire a property could desire."—*Record.*

HYPNOTISM AND SUGGESTION. In Daily Life, Education, and Medical Practice. By BERNARD HOLLANDER, M.D. In crown 8vo, cloth gilt, 6s. net.

"We specially welcome the book before us. It is the work of a man of established reputation, who has devoted himself for years to the subject, and whose aim is to tell the English-speaking world what Hypnotism really is, what it can do, and to what conclusions it seems to point. It is written in a thoroughly scientific spirit, No fact is shirked, and no evidence is either suppressed or rated above its real value."—*Globe.*

IN WIND AND WILD. By ERIC PARKER. In crown 8vo, cloth gilt, gilt top, silk register, 5s. net.

"A collection of 'Nature' Essays which have a singularly varied charm, and an almost invariable distinction."—*Evening Standard.*

LAY SERMONS FROM "THE SPECTATOR." By M. C. E. With an Introduction by J. ST. LOE STRACHEY. In crown 8vo, cloth gilt, gilt top, silk register, 5s. net.

LIGHTER MOMENTS. From the note-book of BISHOP WALSHAM HOW. Edited by his son, FREDERICK DOUGLAS HOW. In small crown 8vo, cloth gilt, gilt top, 2s. 6d.

PITMAN'S CATALOGUE OF GENERAL LITERATURE

LIGHTER STUDIES OF A COUNTRY RECTOR. By the Rev. JOHN VAUGHAN, M.A., Canon of Winchester. In crown 8vo, cloth gilt, gilt top, silk register, 5s. net.

"Studies of men, birds, flowers, and places, ... thoughtful and descriptive, informing and pleasant."—*Bookman.*

MODERNISM. A Record and Review. By the Rev. A. LESLIE LILLEY, M.A. In demy 8vo, cloth gilt, 6s. net.

"Mr. Lilley is admirably suited, both by knowledge and sympathy, to be the medium through which the modernist position may be made known to the English public."—*Church Times.*

THE NEW ART OF FLYING. By WALDEMAR KAEMPFFERT. In crown 8vo, cloth gilt, gilt top, with 86 illustrations, 7s. 6d. net.

"One of the most lucid popular explanations of the principles of flight that we have yet read."—*Yorkshire Post.*

ON LIFE'S THRESHOLD : Talks to Young People on Character and Conduct. By Pastor CHARLES WAGNER. Translated by EDNA ST. JOHN. In crown 8vo, cloth gilt, gilt top, 3s. 6d.

ON THE QUEEN'S ERRANDS. By Captain PHILIP WYNTER. In demy 8vo, cloth gilt, gilt top, 10s. 6d. net.

"His varied experiences as a Queen's messenger on foreign service are recounted with an unfailing vivacity, and with a liberal infusion of good stories."—*World.*

OVERHEARD AT THE ZOO. By GLADYS DAVIDSON. With 2 coloured plates and 26 black and white illustrations. Cloth, 2s. 6d. net.

The author has catered for all children who love animals. Her aim has been to present the animals' own point of view, so far as it may be divined by sympathetic study.

PUBLIC SCHOOL LIFE. Each in f'cap 8vo, cloth, with 32 full page plate illustrations. 2s. net.

    WESTMINSTER. By W. TEIGNMOUTH SHORE.

    ETON. By AN OLD ETONIAN.

    HARROW. By ARCHIBALD FOX.

    RUGBY. By H. H. HARDY.

PITMAN'S PUBLIC MAN'S GUIDE. A Handbook for all who take an interest in questions of the day. Edited by J. A. SLATER, B.A., LL.B. (Lond.). In crown 8vo, cloth gilt, 442 pp., 3s. 6d. net.

SELECTIONS FROM THE WORKS OF BISHOP THOROLD. With a Portrait. Preface by the Most Hon. and Most Rev. RANDALL DAVIDSON, Lord Archbishop of Canterbury. In crown 8vo, cloth gilt, gilt top, 5s.

THE BOOK OF THE CHILD. An Attempt to Set Down what is in the Mind of Children. By FREDERICK DOUGLAS HOW. In foolscap 8vo, leather, with dainty cover design, gilt corners, 3s. 6d. net ; cloth 2s. net.

MISCELLANEOUS

THE INNER LIFE OF THE NAVY. Being an Account of the Social Life of the Navy as seen below deck. By LIONEL YEXLEY (Editor of *The Fleet*). With 16 illustrations. In demy 8vo, cloth gilt, gilt top, 10s. 6d. net.

THE PERSIAN PROBLEM. By H. J. WHIGHAM. With maps and illustrations. In demy 8vo, cloth gilt, 12s. 6d.

THE SPRING OF THE DAY. Spiritual Analogies from the Things of Nature. By the late HUGH MACMILLAN, D.D., LL.D. In crown 8vo, cloth gilt, 3s. 6d. net.

THE CLOCK OF NATURE. By the late HUGH MACMILLAN, D.D., LL.D. In crown 8vo, cloth gilt, 3s. 6d. net.

THE POETRY OF PLANTS. By the late HUGH MACMILLAN, D.D., LL.D. In crown 8vo, cloth gilt, 3s. 6d. net.

A collection of popular studies, showing the many points of beauty and interest about some of the commonest of our trees and wild flowers.

SCIENCE AND THE CRIMINAL. By C. AINSWORTH MITCHELL. In crown 8vo, cloth gilt, 250 pp., with 28 illustrations. Price 6s. net.

"The systems of personal identification are discussed, and the uses of photography, anthropometry, and finger prints are indicated. The selection of the cases and the manner in which the whole book is written show good judgment."—*Lancet*.

THE SOCIAL RESULTS OF EARLY CHRISTIANITY. By C. SCHMIDT. Translated by Mrs. THORPE. With Preliminary Essay by R. W. DALE, LL.D. In crown 8vo, cloth gilt, 3s. 6d. net.

"An easy book to read, and the educated layman will find it full of vital interest."—*Nottingham Daily Express*.

THE SOCIAL WORKERS' GUIDE. A Handbook of Information and Counsel for all who are interested in Public Welfare. Edited by the REV. J. B. HALDANE, *Secretary of the Southwark Diocesan Social Service Committee*, with assistance from **Fifty** Experts. Cloth, 500 pp., with over 500 articles. 3s. 6d. net.

"A book of reference of more than average value. The need of such a book is patent, and we do not know of any other publication which attempts to supply it. The notes are arranged in alphabetical order, and, generally speaking, they are wonderfully exhaustive."—*The Guardian*.

PITMAN'S STUDIES IN ELOCUTION. A guide to the theory and practice of the art of public speaking and reciting, with over 100 selections for Reciters and Readers. By E. M. CORBOULD (Mrs. Mark Robinson). In crown 8vo, cloth gilt, gilt top, silk register, 2s. 6d. net.

"This treasury of prose and verse will appeal to all who cultivate the art of elocution or appreciate a choice store of literary gems. —*Educational News*.

PITMAN'S CATALOGUE OF GENERAL LITERATURE

THE SIMPLE LIFE. By Pastor CHARLES WAGNER. Translated from the French by MARY LOUISE HENDEE. With an Introduction and Biographical sketch by GRACE KING. In foolscap 8vo, cloth gilt, 1s. net. Cheaper Edition.

THE WORLD'S COMMERCIAL PRODUCTS. A Descriptive Account of the Economic Plants of the World and of their Commercial Uses. By W. G. FREEMAN, B.Sc., F.L.S., and S. E. CHANDLER, D.Sc., F.L.S. With contributions by T. A. HENRY, D.Sc., F.C.S., C. E. JONES, B.Sc., F.L.S., and E. H. WILSON. With 420 illustrations from photographs and 12 coloured plates and 10 maps. In demy 4to, cloth gilt, gilt top, 10s. 6d. net.

THE BEGINNINGS OF THE TEACHING OF MODERN SUBJECTS IN ENGLAND. By FOSTER WATSON, M.A. (Professor of Education in the University College of Wales; Aberystwyth). In crown 8vo, cloth, 7s. 6d. net.

IF, A Nightmare in the Conditional Mood. By the authors of *Wisdom While You Wait*. 1s. net.

FARTHEST FROM THE TRUTH. A Series of Dashes. By the same Authors. 1s. net.
  " It rocks with merriment from start to finish."—*Daily Telegraph*.

POETRY, CRITICISM, & LITERARY HISTORY

THE POETRY OF ROBERT BROWNING. By STOPFORD A. BROOKE. Original issue. In demy 8vo, cloth gilt, 10s. 6d.
  " The most satisfactory and stimulating criticism of the poet yet published."—*Times*.

  (*See also* **Dainty** Volume Library, page 9.)

TENNYSON: HIS ART AND RELATION TO MODERN LIFE. By the same Author. Original issue. In demy 8vo, cloth gilt, 7s. 6d.
  " Will make a strong appeal to all lovers of our great Laureate."—*Quarterly Review*.

  (*See also* **Dainty** Volume Library, page 9.)

A STUDY OF CLOUGH, ARNOLD, ROSSETTI, AND MORRIS. With an Introduction on the Course of Poetry from 1822 to 1852. By the same Author. In demy 8vo, cloth gilt, 6s. net.
  " The book is a brilliant and remarkable study."—*Standard*.

  (*See also* **Dainty** Volume Library, page 9.)

EXPERIMENTS IN PLAY WRITING. Six plays in Verse and Prose with an Introductory Essay. By JOHN LAWRENCE LAMBE. In demy 8vo, cloth gilt 5s. net.

POETRY, CRITICISM, ETC.

THE POEMS OF JAMES HOGG. The Ettrick Shepherd. Selected and edited, with an introduction, by WILLIAM WALLACE, LL.D. With photogravure portrait frontispiece. In crown 8vo, cloth gilt, gilt top, 5s.

WITH THE WILD GEESE. Songs of Irish Exile and Lament. By EMILY LAWLESS. With an Introduction by STOPFORD A. BROOKE. In square 8vo, cloth gilt, 4s. 6d. net.

MODERN FRENCH LITERATURE. By B. W. WELLS, Ph.D. In crown 8vo, cloth gilt, 520 pp. 6s. net.

MODERN ITALIAN LITERATURE. By LACY COLLISON-MORLEY, Author of *Guiseppe Baretti and his Friends*. In crown 8vo, cloth gilt, 360 pp. 6s. net.

A SHORT HISTORY OF GREEK LITERATURE. From Homer to Julian. By WILMER CAVE WRIGHT, Ph.D., late of Girton College, Cambridge. In crown 8vo, cloth gilt, 544 pp. 6s. net.

GREEK INFLUENCE ON ENGLISH POETRY. By the late Professor JOHN CHURTON COLLINS. Edited with Introduction, by Professor M. MACMILLAN. In crown 8vo, cloth gilt, with portrait. 3s. 6d. net.

POLITICS, ETC.

ALIEN IMMIGRATION: Should Restrictions be Imposed? By FREDERICK BRADSHAW, M.A., and CHARLES EMANUEL, M.A. In crown 8vo, cloth, 2s. 6d. net.

RELIGIOUS LIBERTY IN ENGLAND: A Scheme for Providing and Securing Religious Liberty in England and Wales. By J. FOVARGUE BRADLEY. With Introductions by the Rev. DUGALD MACFADYEN, M.A., and the Rev. T. A. LACEY. In demy 8vo, 1s. net.

THE CASE AGAINST WELSH DISENDOWMENT. By the same author. In demy 8vo, 1s. net.

NONCONFORMITY AND POLITICS. By a NONCONFORMIST MINISTER. Cheap Edition. In crown 8vo, 1s. net.

"It is in every way a serious and notable work."—*Daily News.*

FAMOUS SPEECHES. From Cromwell to Gladstone. Selected and Edited with Introductory Notes by HERBERT PAUL. Demy 8vo, cloth, 470 pp. 7s. 6d. net.

"A book of selections such as this is delightful reading. Mr. Herbert Paul has chosen discreetly in the wide field from Cromwell to Gladstone, and has prefaced each orator with a judicious criticism."—*Spectator.*

PITMAN'S CATALOGUE OF GENERAL LITERATURE

SCIENCE

GREAT ASTRONOMERS. By Sir ROBERT BALL, D.Sc., LL.D., F.R.S. With numerous full-page and other illustrations. In demy 8vo, cloth gilt, gilt top, 3s. 6d. net.

" Sir Robert Ball's gifts as a narrator are very great. He is, of course, a master of his subject. . . . The most earth-bound mortal who opens this book must go on with it."—*Daily Chronicle*.

IN STARRY REALMS. By the same Author. The Wonders of the Heavens. With numerous full-page and other illustrations. In demy 8vo, cloth gilt, gilt top, 3s. 6d. net.

" The style of popular exposition adopted throughout is indeed admirable, the illustrations are excellent, the binding is tasteful, and the print good."—*Saturday Review*.

IN THE HIGH HEAVENS. By the same Author. A popular account of recent interesting astronomical events and phenomena, with numerous full-page and other illustrations. In demy 8vo, cloth gilt, gilt top, 3s. 6d. net.

" It has," says *The Scotsman*, " the freshest knowledge and the best scientific thought."

ASTRONOMY FOR EVERYBODY. By Professor SIMON NEWCOMBE, LL.D. With an Introduction by Sir ROBERT BALL. Illustrated. A popular exposition of the wonders of the Heavens. In demy 8vo, cloth gilt, gilt top. 3s. 6d. net.

BY LAND AND SKY. By the Rev. JOHN M. BACON, M.A., F.R.A.S. The Record of a Balloonist. With four illustrations. In demy 8vo, cloth gilt, gilt top, 3s. 6d. net.

SOCIOLOGY

SOCIALISM. By Professor ROBERT FLINT, LL.D. New, Revised and Cheaper Edition. In demy 8vo, cloth gilt, 6s. net.

" A new, revised and cheaper edition of Professor Flint's masterly study will be generally welcomed. The revision has been carefully carried out, but the original text has been as far as possible preserved. References show that the additional notes are well up to date."—*Daily Mail*.

THE PEOPLE OF THE ABYSS. By JACK LONDON. A study of the social and economic conditions of life in the East End of London. By the author of *The Call of the Wild*. With 24 illustrations from actual photographs. In crown 8vo, cloth gilt, 6s.

" . . . Mr. Jack London, who is already known to the British public as a fine descriptive writer, has done for the East End of London what he did for the Klondyke—has described it fully and faithfully, looking at it as intimately as dispassionately."—*Daily Chronicle*.

SOCIOLOGY, TRAVEL, TOPOGRAPHY, ETC.

WHAT IS SOCIALISM? By "Scotsburn." An attempt to examine the principles and policy propounded by the advocates of Socialism. In demy 8vo, cloth gilt, 7s. 6d.

TRAVEL, TOPOGRAPHY, AND SPORT

THE ADVENTURER IN SPAIN. By S. R. Crockett. With 162 illustrations by Gordon Browne and from photographs taken by the Author. In large crown 8vo, cloth gilt, 6s.

AROUND AFGHANISTAN. By Major de Bouillane de Lacoste. Translated from the French by J. G. Anderson. With five maps and 113 illustrations. In super royal 8vo, cloth gilt, gilt top, 10s. 6d. net.

"This beautifully illustrated book of travels takes the reader through Persia, to Yarkand, and other famous cities of Turkestan, including Samarkand, with its majestic tomb of Tamerlane. A valuable photographic record of little-trodden regions."—*Evening Standard.*

CASTLES AND CHATEAUX OF OLD TOURAINE and the Loire Country. By Francis Miltoun and Blanche McManus. With seventy illustrations reproduced from paintings made on the spot, and maps, plans, etc. In large crown 8vo, cloth richly gilt, gilt top, 7s. 6d. net.

"One of the most delightful travel books that we have come across for some time."—*Country Life.*

CASTLES AND CHATEAUX OF OLD NAVARRE and the Basque Provinces. By the same Authors. With 63 illustrations (some in colour), maps, plans, etc. In large crown 8vo, cloth richly gilt, gilt top, 7s. 6d. net.

"The book is well worth reading, not merely as a travel handbook, but for its sympathetic, social and historical review of a very interesting section of the French people."—*Irish Times.*

CASTLES AND CHATEAUX OF OLD BURGUNDY and the Border Provinces. By the same Authors. With 59 illustrations (some in colour), maps, plans, etc. In large crown 8vo, cloth richly gilt, gilt top, 7s. 6d. net.

"Their new volume strikes the reader as the most readable and most instructive they have yet given us."—*Nottingham Guardian.*

IN THE LAND OF MOSQUES AND MINARETS. By the same Authors. With 75 illustrations, in colour and black and white, maps, plans, etc. In large crown 8vo, cloth gilt, gilt top, with cover of charming design, 7s. 6d. net.

"A comprehensive account of Morocco, Algiers, and Tunis, and of Mussulman government, religion, art, culture, and French influence. Picturesquely illustrated."—*Times.*

PITMAN'S CATALOGUE OF GENERAL LITERATURE

Countries and Peoples Series

Each in imperial 16mo, cloth gilt, gilt top, with about 30 full-page plate illustrations, 6s. net.

ITALY OF THE ITALIANS. By HELEN ZIMMERN.

" The knowledge and judgment displayed in the volume are truly astounding, and the labour the author has expended on it has made it as indispensable as Baedeker to the traveller, as well as invaluable to the student of modern times."—*Daily Telegraph*.

FRANCE OF THE FRENCH. By E. HARRISON BARKER.

" A book of general information concerning the life and genius of the French people, with especial reference to contemporary France. Covers every phase of French intellectual life—architecture, players, science, and invention, etc.—*Times*.

SPAIN OF THE SPANISH. By Mrs. VILLIERS-WARDELL.

" Within little more than 250 pages she has collected a mass of ordered information which must be simply invaluable to any one who wants to know the facts of Spanish life at the present day. Nowhere else, so far as we are aware, can a more complete and yet compendious account of modern Spain be found."—*Pall Mall Gazette*.

SWITZERLAND OF THE SWISS. By FRANK WEBB.

" Mr. Webb's account of that unknown country is intimate faithful, and interesting. It is an attempt to convey a real know ledge of a striking people—an admirably successful attempt."— *Morning Leader*.

GERMANY OF THE GERMANS. By ROBERT M. BERRY.

" Mr. Berry abundantly proves his ability to write of ' Germany of the Germans ' in an able and informing fashion. What he does is to state so far as can be done within the scope of a single handy volume, particulars of all aspects of life as lived in Germany to-day." —*Daily Telegraph*.

TURKEY OF THE OTTOMANS. By LUCY M. J GARNETT.

" There could hardly be a better handbook for the newspaper reader who wants to understand all the conditions of the ' danger zone.' "—*Spectator*.

BELGIUM OF THE BELGIANS. By DEMETRIUS C. BOULGER.

" A very complete handbook to the country."—*World*.

SERVIA OF THE SERVIANS. By CHEDO MIJATOVICH.

** *Volumes on Japan, Russia, Austria, etc., are in preparation.*

TRAVEL, TOPOGRAPHY, AND SPORT

TRAVEL, TOPOGRAPHY, AND SPORT (*contd.*)

The " All Red " Series.

Each volume is in demy 8vo, cloth gilt, red edges, with 16 full-page plate illustrations, maps, etc., 7s. 6d. net.

THE COMMONWEALTH OF AUSTRALIA. By the Hon. BERNHARD RINGROSE WISE (formerly Attorney-General of New South Wales)

" The 'All Red' Series should become known as the Well-Read Series within a short space of time. Nobody is better qualified to write of Australia than the late Attorney-General of New South Wales, who knows the country intimately and writes of it with enthusiasm. It is one of the best accounts of the Island Continent that has yet been published. We desire to give a hearty welcome to this series."—*Globe.*

THE DOMINION OF NEW ZEALAND. By Sir ARTHUR P. DOUGLAS, Bt., formerly Under-Secretary for Defence, New Zealand, and previously a Lieutenant, R.N.

" Those who have failed to find romance in the history of the British Empire should read *The Dominion of New Zealand.* Sir Arthur Douglas contrives to present in the 444 pages of his book an admirable account of life in New Zealand and an impartial summary of her development up to the present time. It is a most alluring picture that one conjures up after reading it."—*Standard.*

THE DOMINION OF CANADA. By W. L. GRIFFITH, *Secretary to the Office of the High Commissioner for Canada.*

" The publishers could hardly have found an author better qualified than Mr. Griffith to represent the premier British Dominion . . . an excellent plain account of Canada, one of the best and most comprehensive yet published . . . trustworthy."—*Athenæum.*

Other volumes in preparation.

THREE YEARS' SPORT IN MOZAMBIQUE. By W. VASSE. Translated from the French by R. LYDEKKER, F.R.S., and H. M. LYDEKKER. With 80 illustrations. In super royal 8vo, cloth gilt, 8s. 6d. net.

NATIVE LIFE IN EAST AFRICA. By Professor KARL WEULE. Translated from the German with Introduction and Notes by ALICE WERNER. With four maps and 196 illustrations. In royal 8vo, cloth gilt, 12s. 6d. net.

PITMAN'S CATALOGUE OF GENERAL LITERATURE

CATALOGUES, ETC.

Sir Isaac Pitman & Sons, Ltd., have pleasure in calling attention to the following Catalogues of Books published by them. They will be pleased to send on application any of these Catalogues, all of which have been brought up to date.

[B] PITMAN'S COMMERCIAL SERIES. A list of Books suitable for use in Evening Schools and Classes and for Reference in Business Houses. 40 pp.

[D] PITMAN'S EDUCATIONAL BOOKS (Primary). 48 pp.

[F] SOME TEXT-BOOKS specially adapted for Evening and Commercial Schools. Illustrated. 64 pp.

[G] PITMAN'S BUSINESS HANDBOOKS. 16 pp.

[H] PITMAN'S SHORTHAND, TYPEWRITING, STATIONERY AND COMMERCIAL LANGUAGES CATALOGUE. 32 pp.

[N] A CATALOGUE OF THEOLOGICAL AND RELIGIOUS LITERATURE. 16 pp.

PERIODICALS

PITMAN'S JOURNAL; PITMAN'S SHORTHAND WEEKLY; THE POSTAGE STAMP; UNITED EMPIRE; PITMAN'S COMMERCIAL TEACHER'S MAGAZINE; ETC., ETC.

Specimens on Application (except "United Empire.")

Any who may happen to be in the neighbourhood of St. Paul's Cathedral are cordially invited to visit Sir Isaac Pitman & Sons' Show Room, at 14 Warwick Lane, where their publications may be examined at leisure.

Sir Isaac Pitman & Sons, Ltd., London, Bath, and New York.

WS - #0049 - 050225 - C0 - 229/152/21 - PB - 9781331261209 - Gloss Lamination